EUROPEA

SAGE Modern Politics Series
sponsored by the European Consortium
for Political Research/ECPR

EUROPEAN FOREIGN POLICY

The EC and Changing Perspectives in Europe

edited by

Walter Carlsnaes and Steve Smith

SAGE Modern Politics Series Volume 34
Sponsored by the European Consortium for
Political Research/ECPR

SAGE Publications
London • Thousand Oaks • New Delhi

Editorial arrangement © Walter Carlsnaes and Steve Smith
Chapter 1 © Steve Smith 1994
Chapter 2 © Michael Smith 1994
Chapter 3 © Thomas Risse-Kappen 1994
Chapter 4 © Roger Tooze 1994
Chapter 5 © Gerd Junne 1994
Chapter 6 © Ben Soetendorp 1994
Chapter 7 © Frank Pfetsch 1994
Chapter 8 © Alfred van Staden 1994
Chapter 9 © Hans Mouritzen 1994
Chapter 10 © Bengt Sundelius 1994
Chapter 11 © Olav F. Knudsen 1994
Chapter 12 © Marysia Zalewski 1994
Chapter 13 © Ole Wæver 1994
Chapter 14 © Walter Carlsnaes 1994

First published 1994
Reprinted 1995

SAGE Publications Ltd
6 Bonhill Street
London EC2A 4PU

SAGE Publications Inc
2455 Teller Road
Thousand Oaks, California 91320

SAGE Publications India Pvt Ltd
32, M-Block Market
Greater Kailash – I
New Delhi 110 048

British Library Cataloguing in Publication Data

European Foreign Policy: EC and Changing Perspectives in Europe. –
(Sage Modern Politics Series; Vol. 34)
  I. Carlsnaes, Walter   II. Smith, Steve   III. Series
  327.094

  ISBN 0–8039–8816–8
  ISBN 0–8039–8817–6 (pbk)

Library of Congress catalog card number 93–087486

Typeset by Mayhew Typesetting, Rhayader, Powys
Printed and bound in Great Britain by
Biddles Ltd, Guildford and King's Lynn

Contents

Contributors

Walter Carlsnaes is Associate Professor of Political Science at Uppsala University, research coordinator of its Centre for European Studies and editor of the newly established *European Journal of International Relations*.

Gerd Junne is Professor in International Relations at the Department of International Relations and Public International Law, University of Amsterdam.

Olav F. Knudsen is Director of the Norwegian Institute of International Affairs in Oslo.

Hans Mouritzen is a Project Director at the Centre for Peace and Conflict Research, Copenhagen, and Associate Professor of Political Science at the University of Copenhagen.

Frank Pfetsch is Professor of Political Science at the University of Heidelberg.

Thomas Risse-Kappen is Professor of International Politics, Faculty of Administrative Sciences, University of Konstanz.

Michael Smith is Professor of European Politics, Loughborough University.

Steve Smith is Professor of International Politics, University of Wales, Aberystwyth.

Ben Soetendorp is Associate Professor in International Relations at Leiden University.

Bengt Sundelius is a Senior Fellow in European Political Studies with the Swedish Research Council for the Humanities and Social Sciences, posted at the University of Stockholm.

Roger Tooze is Professor of International Relations, Nottingham Trent University.

Alfred van Staden is Professor of International Relations at the Department of Political Science, Leiden University, as well as

Chairman of the Netherlands Government Advisory Council on Peace and Security.

Ole Wæver is a Senior Research Fellow at the Centre for Peace and Conflict Research, Copenhagen, and a part-time Lecturer at the Institute of Political Science at the University of Copenhagen.

Marysia Zalewski is Lecturer in Gender and International Politics at the University of Wales, Aberystwyth.

PART I   INTRODUCTION

1

Foreign Policy Theory and the New Europe

Steve Smith

This book is concerned primarily with foreign policy theory, and is especially interested in the extent to which that theory applies to developments in Europe since the late 1980s. The aim of the book is to examine the extent to which the main theories of foreign policy can explain two sets of developments: the end of the Cold War in Europe and the increasing integration of West European states. We are not pretending that the chapters that follow can be anything more than a contribution to an analysis of the utility of the main theories of foreign policy behaviour, but we do insist that events in Europe since the mid 1980s constitute a fascinating case-study for theoretically inclined foreign policy specialists. In short, our concern is to take stock and see how useful have been our dominant theories. It is only through such a stock-taking that we can move forward in theory construction.

However, we also want this book to be more than that, as the reader will see from the second half of this introductory chapter and from the final three chapters. In this sense, we want to contribute to the development of foreign policy theory by using our findings to provide something of a self-reflective critique of the theoretical bases of foreign policy theory. We also want to link foreign policy theory to wider debates in the social sciences, and this will be reflected in the final three chapters.

This book is the product of a research project which emerged from a meeting of foreign policy scholars held in Rimini, in September 1990, under the auspices of the European Consortium for Political Research (ECPR). This group was brought together by Walter Carlsnaes in order to look at the issue of the 'new' Europe. As foreign policy specialists, we naturally had considerable interest in what was going on in Europe at that time. The revolutions of 1989 and the probable ending of the Cold War were fresh in our memories, and the year of 1992 held out the promise of a new stage in European integration. We came together to see what these developments meant for the assumptions and theory of the subject of foreign policy analysis. During our discussions it became clear that there were two issues that we needed to discuss at greater length, and this volume is the result of the two-year research project that resulted from the Rimini meeting.

The best way to set the scene is to outline the two issues that dominated our Rimini discussions. The first issue was empirical and was concerned with the nature of the new Europe. There are two aspects of the new Europe. The first refers to the changing nature of Europe following the end of the Cold War; the second is to do with the developments from the Single European Act to the implementation of the Maastricht agreement, scheduled to come into force at the end of 1992. Of course, we did not know when we started this research project that the Danish people would reject the Maastricht agreement, nor that by the end of 1992 the exchange rate mechanism would be in tatters. In essence these developments do not fundamentally alter the analysis undertaken in this book, since the final drafts of chapters were not submitted until the end of 1992. Our concern when we started the project was to look at the two issues in terms of their impact on the main theories rather than try to predict the outcome of developments. We were not interested in crystal ball gazing. But, as foreign policy scholars, it is not surprising that we have been particularly interested in the effects of the twin 'revolutions' of the end of the Cold War and the further integration of the European Community (EC). The events of 1989 shatter many of the common-sense assumptions that political scientists have made about the political processes in Eastern Europe, whilst for international relations scholars they provide a unique opportunity to examine the utility of the main theories of system stability. At the very least the evaporation of the Soviet threat, and the transformation of the European security system, means that we are now in a very different international environment from before. Maastricht and 1992 represent an evolution or maybe a revolution of a very different type. It is not yet at all clear what kind of actor will emerge after 1992, whether intergovernmental, supranational or even national. What is clear is that the EC is in the process of transformation, and that developments since the mid 1980s represent unprecedented change.

The end of the Cold War and the increasing pace of European

integration each have important and fundamental foreign policy consequences. The end of the Cold War affects foreign policy because it involves such phenomenal changes in the post-war order that the foreign policy orientations of all European states have had to undergo fundamental adjustment. Not only is there the issue of how the events of 1989 could have happened, but there is also the question of how to explain the resulting international structure. More concretely, there is the question of how to conceptualize the foreign policies of the newly independent powers of Eastern Europe. European integration poses rather different types of question, mainly concerned with how to explain the foreign policy of the new EC, how to portray the role of the EC as a foreign policy actor, and how to conceptualize the foreign policy processes of the individual member states.

But this empirical focus is only a small part of what lies behind this project. As international relations scholars, it was obvious that we would be interested in the radical developments of the end of the Cold War and increasing European integration, but the fact that we are foreign policy specialists gives the project its theoretical purpose. This is because there is a major debate under way in the theoretical literature of foreign policy analysis (FPA) which the empirical developments mentioned above allow us to examine in particularly stark form. The theoretical debate we have in mind is that concerning the utility of the various approaches to explaining foreign policy behaviour. In its simplest form, the new Europe gives us a chance to test the theoretical utility of the major models and theories in the foreign policy analysis literature. This is important because these theories are rarely subjected to any form of comparative testing. This was the second issue discussed at Rimini.

At the most general level, there are a number of rival theories in the subject of international relations. This is not the place to rehearse the development of the subject, or to run through the main approaches; suffice it to say that there exist three main competing paradigms in the discipline (see Banks, 1984; Little and Smith, 1991; McGrew and Lewis, 1992; Viotti and Kauppi, 1987). These are realism (or, as its most recent variant is called, neo-realism), pluralism and structuralism. Of these, realism has dominated the subject of international relations, with pluralism being particularly influential during the 1970s. Each of these three approaches has a different world view, and each sees a different set of issues and processes at work in international relations. More graphically, the three perspectives may be characterized as the billiard-ball, cobweb and layer-cake models of international relations.

For realists, such as Morgenthau (1973) and Waltz (1979), the key actors are states, and the main processes at work involve a search for security, which is usually defined in military terms, although one of the key contributions of neo-realism has been to offer a powerful account of international political economy. States are treated, in good Weberian fashion, as monoliths with interests, dominant of which is the maximization of power. This combination of actors and processes leads to a world most notable for a struggle for dominance. War is therefore an ever-present possibility, and this is only held at bay by a mixture of skilful diplomacy, emerging international law, and, above all, the systemic mechanism of the balance of power. Indeed, one may discern two distinct strands in realism. The first is a structural strand, stressing the impact of the system on its units, and this has a heritage that runs from Thucydides through to Waltz. The second strand is more practical in orientation, stressing the role of individuals in dealing with the dangers of anarchy through the use of diplomacy. This practical strand is most clearly exemplified by Machiavelli. Unfortunately, the 'father' of contemporary realism, Hans Morgenthau, can be read in both ways; I say 'unfortunately' because there is an obvious tension in these two accounts, which I will return to at the end of this chapter.

Pluralists (see Keohane and Nye, 1972; Mansbach et al., 1976; Morse, 1976) accept the importance of the state, but argue that it increasingly has to operate in a world in which other types of actors are important. These non-state actors, such as revolutionary groups and, most notably, multinational corporations, reduce the autonomy of states and increase the costs for states to get their own way. An array of subnational, transnational and supranational actors challenge the dominance of the state across a wide range of issues. This results in a very different view of the world from that of the realists. Gone is the realist notion of a monolithic state pursuing national interests; gone is the idea, central to realists, of a clear analytic division between domestic and international politics; and gone is the conception of a hierarchy of values with military issues being most important. In their place is a world where national actors comprise many competing bureaucracies, with foreign policy being at best a compromise between these various organizations' views of the national interest and at worst the unintended outcome of the pulling and hauling between national bureaucracies. The notion of separate domestic and international environments disappears to be replaced with a crosscutting view of world politics, with the question of where domestic politics begins and ends being essentially problematic. Finally, this is a world where a range of issues competes for decision-makers' attention, with there being no clear hierarchy of issues. In this mixed-actor system, the focus is on the twin forces of trans-nationalism and interdependence. The first of these removes the state from centre stage; the second forces us to look at the linkages between societies and to stress the importance of economic matters in foreign policy. Together, they refocus analysis away from national control and the balance of power towards the management of the structural situation of complex interdependence. This situation is one in which national actors struggle to control a fluid external environment, and where the analytic focus is on management and bargaining within and between national actors.

Structuralists (see Brewer, 1990) examine international relations from a very different perspective altogether. For them, the state is dominant but only in the sense that it represents a set of economic interests. Inspired by Marx's writings on international economics and politics, this perspective sees states not as separate actors in themselves, but rather as the tools of the dominant economic class. International relations is, therefore, a struggle for power, but in a very different sense from that portrayed by the realists. The struggle is for economic dominance, and the key basic actors are classes. The state is important for its role in promoting class interests, which leads to the analysis of international relations in terms of core–periphery relations. International politics is the result of the fundamental developments at work in these core–periphery economic relations. International relations is therefore concerned with exploitation, imperialism and underdevelopment, and the main outcome is one of the continued exploitation of the poor periphery by the rich core. For structuralists, the pluralists' concern with management and changing hierarchies of values is nothing more than another form of core dominance. The long historical domination by capitalism indicates its ability to alter its form to continue domination. The so-called victory of capitalism over communism makes capitalism *the* global model, thereby increasing the importance of the core–periphery cleavage as the dominant one in international relations.

These three perspectives are usually discussed in terms of an inter-paradigm debate, and most of the literature presents them as three competing world views. I shall say more about that later when I discuss whether the approaches are compatible, but for now it is important to note that this move is somewhat problematic, since it serves to prevent real debate between the rival perspectives. The so-called inter-paradigm debate stifles discussion by employing a kind of academic division of labour, whereby realists deal with the problems they can explain best, and pluralists and structuralists keep to their territory. The three paradigms do not so much debate, or stand in opposition to one another, as offer accounts of parts of the subject whilst not treading on one another's territory. In this light the debate is very conservative since it defends each paradigm against competition; it is defensive as well, ending up with a version of 'we speak different languages' or 'we see the world differently', as if this is not an ideological or privileged perspective. The question of whether the approaches can in fact be combined will be discussed later on, but the point to be stressed at this stage is that the way that the inter-paradigm debate has tended to work has been particularly anaesthetizing to debate between the paradigms.

In the 1980s and early 1990s this point has been made via the emergence of what Yosef Lapid (1989) has termed the 'post-positivist' revolution, which has involved a number of simultaneous challenges to these three research paradigms, and to the notion of the inter-paradigm debate. Broadly speaking we can identify four main components of the post-positivist revolution. The first is the rise of a critical theory of international relations, most clearly illustrated in the work of Robert Cox (1981), Mark Hoffman (1987) and Andrew Linklater (1990). The second is the post-modern intervention into international relations, typified by the works of James Der Derian, Richard Ashley and Rob Walker (see their essays in Der Derian and Shapiro, 1989). Third there is the feminist literature, represented clearly in the work of Cynthia Enloe (1989), Christine Sylvester and Ann Tickner (these writers are discussed in Zalewski, 1992; see also Grant and Newland, 1991). Finally, there is the contribution of historical sociology, as developed in the writings of Michael Mann, John Hall and Charles Tilly (this literature is summarized in Halliday, 1987 and Jarvis, 1989). There is no space to summarize these vibrant and insightful literatures, but it is important to note that they pose fundamental challenges to the dominant orthodoxies of international relations, whether realist, pluralist of structuralist. But, to beg a question that applies to all the theories dealt with in this volume, are the four components of the post-positivist revolution compatible, or are they mutually exclusive? Again this point will be returned to at the end of this chapter.

These comments on the theoretical problematique that frames this project will hopefully provide links to the three critical chapters that end this volume. Before turning to make some comments about the current state of foreign policy theory, I need to say how the volume will proceed.

The combination of an empirical concern with the nature of developments in the new Europe and a theoretical concern over the state of FPA provides the basis for our research project. Surely, as FPA scholars, we should be able to say something about the new Europe, since the twin developments of the end of the Cold War and the further integration of the EC alter the European foreign policy setting in a fundamental way. Theoretically, the two developments offer us a unique opportunity to examine the utility and explanatory reach of the main theories in FPA.

Our way of approaching these issues was to ask a group of the leading European FPA scholars to look at specific empirical aspects of the new Europe and to answer the simple question: do you find any of the main theories of international relations and FPA particularly helpful in explaining the empirical changes you are examining? Our concern is not to require each specialist to test a common set of theories and approaches, since this would be practically impossible within the time and space constraints. Such a rigid requirement would also lead our choice of theories and frameworks to foreclose the views of the individual writers. Rather, we approached FPA scholars who specialize in a specific empirical area, and asked them to write about that area in terms of how FPA theories and frameworks helped explain events.

In order to focus attention, we outlined a set of major approaches for the participants to think about in the context of the new Europe. We did not expect individual authors to go through the main approaches one by one, commenting on the relative utility of each in turn. Instead, we suggested that each writer should feel free to select the approaches that he or she thought were best in explaining the empirical area under consideration.

Approaching the topic in this way has one obvious potential disadvantage, which is that the writers will look at very different sets of approaches. Some approaches might get ignored altogether, whilst others will get dealt with in each chapter. Our view on this is that there is no practical alternative to this way of proceeding, since the only way of avoiding this would be for one author to look at one issue in detail using all the approaches in a form of comparative testing. Such a way forward would not, however, achieve what we want to achieve in this research project. Our primary concern is not empirical, it is theoretical; that is to say, we want to use the empirical problematique to say something about the current state of FPA theory. What motivates us is an interest in seeing how far the theories and approaches we use in our daily professional lives can shed light on the major changes we are living through. To answer that sort of question we need to bring together more specialisms than any one scholar can possibly muster.

Thus, the question that we asked our contributors was: which of the main theories in foreign policy analysis and international relations do you find of most use in explaining the empirical developments in your empirical area? We suggested in draft introductions a list or menu of the main approaches, most of them being the central theoretical perspectives in foreign policy analysis, with a few others being the general paradigms mentioned previously.

Of course, this was a grab-bag of a list, and contributors were invited to suggest additions to it. But the central message was clear enough: given that there are a number of major approaches in FPA, or to explaining foreign policy behaviour, then are they of use in explaining the parts of the new Europe that you deal with? We did not ask contributors to test each account against the evidence; rather we simply asked them to reflect on the theoretical utility of the main approaches. We did not ask contributors to say which approach they preferred, and some clearly found that no approach did very well.

We asked each contributor to follow a four-step procedure in writing his or her chapter. *First*, the chapter would outline the empirical domain to be addressed. *Second*, it would outline the dominant theories in the literature which purport to explain the events in this empirical domain. *Third*, it would evaluate the ability of the dominant theories to explain or account for the empirical domain. *Finally*, the chapter would conclude with the author either offering his or her own version of events, suggesting some further theoretical development, or outlining a research agenda for the further analysis of the topic.

There are two other initial comments to make about our way of proceeding. First, note that we are not saying anything about methodology and epistemology. Although each approach has its own specific methods, it is also clear that each can be analysed in a number of different ways. We leave it to each contributor to comment on the utility of specific methodologies. Second, we ought to say that we decided on the empirical areas to look at in the meeting in Rimini. That is to say we discussed at length the nature of the changing European foreign policy context, and in the light of this discussion we listed the main empirical dimensions to be examined. We then listed who we considered to be the most qualified people working within the broad arena of FPA to write on each empirical area. This does not mean that we have necessarily identified all of the main issues worthy of examination, but it is important to note at this stage that we thought of the empirical areas first, and only then approached the people to write about them. Our aim, of course, was to avoid the trap of selecting FPA scholars and then letting that list determine the empirical menu. We met in Stockholm in September 1991 to discuss the first draft of this chapter and to outline how each contributor would write his or her chapter. The first drafts of these chapters were presented at a meeting in Oslo in May 1992. These meetings gave us the opportunity to discuss interpretations, and they certainly indicated that there was no agreed party line over the issues discussed in this introduction.

But there were dangers with proceeding in this way, primarily that we constituted too much of an identifiable group, all conversant with the same set of theories and approaches and myopic with regard to the wider international relations setting. For this reason we also approached two scholars from outside FPA to write critical chapters after having read all the other contributions. Because our primary aim is to evaluate the state of FPA rather than describe the developments in the new Europe, we wanted to have some critical analysis of our work, and therefore of course of FPA, from scholars writing in intellectual positions very different from the FPA mainstream. The two most potentially exciting areas of criticism, from what was previously termed the post-positivist perspective, were critical theory/post-modernism, and feminist theory. Accordingly, we have asked people from these two specialisms to comment on the portrayal of the new Europe found in our study. Please note that we do not simply add these chapters because it would be nice to have some gentle critical comments at the end of the book. Rather we see the importance of these areas as substantive intellectual traditions, each of which is powerfully examining the assumptions of the subject of international relations. The two chapters are there to examine the accounts offered by FPA and to subject our common, and often unstated, assumptions to rigorous criticism. In this sense we wanted each of these two contributors to look at our empirical and theoretical problematiques, including the introductory and concluding chapters, from outside the tradition within which the bulk of the contributors work. In this sense, the three concluding chapters can be read, in conjunction with this introduction, as a theoretical evaluation of the state of FPA theory.

I now want to make three comments about the current state of FPA specifically and international relations theory generally. These three comments will hopefully frame the discussion in the three concluding chapters, most explicitly by providing a link with the concluding chapter written by Walter Carlsnaes.

The first comment is simply to pose the question of whether the theories that dominate FPA and international relations theory are comparable. Earlier I noted that the subject had, during the 1980s, adopted a conservative position of saying that each approach captured part of reality. But this implies that there may be a way of combining them. This is what I want to question now. Can we ever test the three rival paradigms, or are they, in the Kuhnian sense of the word, incommensurable? Quite a lot hangs on the answer one gives to this question, and it is a theme that will be returned to both later in this chapter and in the conclusion to this volume. The central problem is that the three perspectives or paradigms seem superficially to offer a kind of pick-and-mix option to theorists; that is to say, one may seem better suited to explaining this issue whereas another seems better suited to explaining that issue. Note that whilst this may be an accurate reflection of the explanatory power of each theory, it is doubly problematic. First, it may not be possible to find a neutral set of data from which to test the approaches. That is to say that the world views of the three theories are so different that agreement between them as to what constitutes the facts of the situation may be impossible. Proponents of each approach simply see different worlds. The second problem is that the pick-and-mix approach leads all too easily to the assumption that the three approaches can be combined to produce an overall account. This is a flawed view because the three perspectives involve very different assumptions about the key structures and processes of international relations. I will return to this later when I look at the structure–agency issue.

My second comment relates to the sociology of knowledge and concerns the fact that the main theories of FPA and international relations theory have been developed in the US academic community. It is vital to make it clear that this comment does not reflect some simple notion that European theories or approaches would be 'better' or more appropriate, only that the national setting in which theories are developed may make a difference to their explanatory power in other settings.

Nonetheless, it is important to reflect on the fact that the US academic community does dominate international relations theory, and this must cause any group of European scholars to reflect on the applicability of the dominant theory in its area of concern. Perhaps the best way to put things is to say that those of us involved in the research project were concerned with the explanatory power of the dominant theories in our area, and had as a *secondary* concern to enquire whether it matters that they have been developed mainly in the US. I therefore leave it as an open question as to whether the fact that international relations is a subject dominated by the US academic community is important in explaining the utility of the dominant theories for understanding the empirical problematique. Our contributors are asked to comment on the explanatory power of the dominant theories, rather than reflect on the countries in which these theories originated.

However, it clearly is an important question for the sociology of knowledge to enquire whether the social setting in which ideas develop affects the empirical domain that these theories can explain. My own view is that this is an important issue and I want to proceed by outlining the reasons why I think that it matters that the subfield of FPA has been mainly developed in the US.

FPA is overwhelmingly an American subject, despite the presence of a robust and healthy European research community. But the Europeans tend to follow the theoretical lead of the US research community, mainly because US approaches dominate the literature to such an extent that being part of the subject axiomatically means addressing US concepts and, more problematically, US policy concerns. It is in this sense that international relations is, to quote Stanley Hoffmann, an American social science. The impact of this simple fact on the development of FPA in Europe has been profound. Rare is the European foreign policy specialist who has not started his or her career by looking at a US theory. FPA has therefore become an international research community precisely because it has been based on common approaches, a common literature, and a common world view.

This is not to say that there have not been dissenting voices muttering off-stage. Indeed, to many US FPA scholars the Europeans seem to spend their time criticizing the work of US colleagues rather than developing frameworks and theory of their own. Yet the problem remains that, for European FPA specialists, their work will only be accepted as relevant if it addresses the concerns and approaches of the US research community. The obvious danger is that US FPA may not be relevant to the European setting.

There are three main dimensions of this problem. First there is the question of the utility of US *theories* for the European setting. This is problematic because the US political system is very clearly different from those found in Europe. The pluralist nature of the political system and the role of bureaucracies in the making and implementation of foreign policy in the US are fundamentally different from the situation in Europe. This has certainly led to very US-based theories, such as bureaucratic politics. This dimension of the problem is probably the least problematic, however, because the literature on foreign policy theory tends to be based on a notion of states as states, rather than on a specific version of the state. In other words, theories which identify key causal relationships in the foreign policy process are likely to travel well to other countries which have similar foreign policy processes. This is not tautological because there have been several theories developed in the US that focus on very specifically US features; but, in the main, FPA is based on approaches that are overtly general and not country specific.

The second dimension is *epistemological*. Here there are much deeper problems, because the bulk of the work emanating from the US FPA community is positivistic in a stark form. US FPA scholars do not, on the whole, accept this charge, seeing themselves as far more sophisticated than that. The self-image is one of having rejected behaviouralism in the 1960s, or, at the latest, in the 1970s, so to be accused of positivism in the 1990s seems to them to be both simplistic and outdated. This is certainly the response that European critics have received when making this charge. However, my own view is that positivism still rules US FPA in the sense that the research community works on a set of assumptions that requires a notion of truth or an approximation to the truth that can be approached, if not entirely apprehended. To be clear, by positivism I simply mean the notion that there is one truth, one world which can be more and more accurately portrayed or represented, especially via the gathering of quantitative data. This position, which I believe is at the heart of the core approaches in US FPA, stands in marked contrast to the kind of critical theory that I prefer. Specifically, US FPA's epistemology does not provide the grounds for exploring the linkage between its theories and concepts and the evidence it examines.

As just noted, FPA is still overwhelmingly quantitative in approach, with data manipulation a central skill and research focus. General theory may not still be the name of the game, but it remains the goal. If Rosenauian excesses have been abandoned, progress within identifiable and distinct research communities is the preferred method of working. Kuhn has had a significant impact on the approach, but in an importantly misleading way: whilst Kuhn was never convinced of the applicability of his work on paradigms for the social sciences, his message, or more accurately a simplified version of it, has been grafted on to the work of FPA scholars. They now see themselves as working within Lakatosian research frameworks, without taking on board the implications of Lakatos for their epistemological foundations. Moreover, inductivism still rules, which muddies the water still further. In simple terms, the epistemological assumptions of FPA seem very confused and problematic; yet it is this epistemology that European scholars address and use. My concern is whether European scholars, raised in rather different epistemological traditions, can take US theory without having to take US epistemology. The problem is that in adapting or testing US theories it is simply not easy, or even possible, to alter or dispose of the epistemology that accompanies them. And, if European FPA is to be taken seriously in the international FPA community, then this means referring to US approaches. Can we in Europe, in other words, develop an FPA which does not require us to buy into the positivism of US FPA? What are the consequences of trying to develop a distinctly European approach? The realities of power within the international relations community mean that the few dozen European foreign policy analysts face an uphill task in trying to influence the 500 or so US FPA scholars. I suppose that I am here calling for the creation of a more critical (in its critical theory sense) FPA. Can we do this and still be part of the identifiable FPA research community? Alternatively, maybe the US community is not as positivistic as here portrayed. The problem, though, for European FPA analysts is acute when it comes to the epistemology of US FPA, and there seems no easy way out of the difficulty.

Finally, there is the question of the *policy agenda* dealt with by US FPA. This is also surmountable, although the sheer size of the US academic community means that it is difficult to swim against the tide, and to hold out for an alternative policy agenda as the focus. The history of international relations has seen US policy concerns sweeping through the discipline, with scant regard being paid to the extent that these are primarily only US concerns. Interdependence is a classic example, especially since it had been present in the European arena long before it became fashionable to write about it in the US literature. There are dozens of other examples, but within FPA it is interesting to note the timing of the second (Allison) wave of bureaucratic politics, and the publication of Janis's seminal study of groupthink. More generally, think of why behaviouralism took root in the US when it did, and why the post-behavioural revolution occurred when it did. Why did Rosenau pronounce on the death of comparative foreign policy (CFP) analysis when he did, that is in 1975? In each case the real world events facing US leaders lie powerfully in the background. In short, the rise and fall of various FPA approaches have more to do with the changing agenda facing the US than with any theoretical deficiencies. Moreover, do the silences of FPA theories tell us something about the subject? Perhaps what is most important is not what the theories include but what they exclude.

Of course, it is the combination of these three dimensions of US FPA hegemony that forces European scholars into the choice of being either peripheral to the discipline or accepting the specific mental baggage of the US literature. In essence, it is this combination that has resulted in the absence of a specifically European FPA. Maybe such an ethnocentric European response is unnecessary, since there is a universal foreign policy theory waiting to be developed. But the trend in FPA has so clearly been in the opposite direction that this conclusion seems unwarranted. The history of FPA as an academic subfield of international relations is one of the rise and fall of general theory. This is the case both generally and specifically: generally, in the sense that the approach has been characterized by a search for a general theory in the 1950s, 1960s and early 1970s, a search that most involved saw as fruitless by the late 1970s; specifically, in that each main approach to come out of the US community has started off with claims of universal application, claims which are then progressively watered down as the approach undergoes critical examination and application. This picture may not be entirely accurate, but the general and specific propositions surely hold. In the 1990s, then, US FPA is an interesting mixture of a set of research frameworks all attempting to capture as accurately as possible the empirical dimensions of foreign policy behaviour, coexisting along with very diverse middle-range theories, each of which can offer powerful explanations of aspects of foreign policy behaviour. European scholars tend to be more at home with the latter than with the former, which makes even more problematic the fact that these middle-range theories may well be incompatible. Furthermore, a European FPA would also reflect precisely the sociology of knowledge problems raised earlier in connection with the US literature; the problem would simply be reversed, not avoided. In short, if the positivistic route towards general theory is a route only to a dead-end, and if the middle-range theories are epistemologically or more likely ontologically incompatible, then the outlook for European FPA is bleak. This is the theoretical concern that underlies this research project: which way should European FPA go now?

Having said which, I now need to add a health warning. The warning is that the above discussion of the development of FPA is open to the charge of oversimplification. Certainly, it would not be accepted by many European FPA specialists. Some contributors to this volume are themselves major contributors to the development of FPA, and they may well reject the notion that they have carelessly accepted US positivism or that they have been blind adherents to the US view of the policy agenda. They would point out that they have contributed to the subject despite having a very different epistemological background and despite seeing a very different policy agenda. They may say that they have created exactly the kind of generally applicable, or even Europe-relevant, FPA that I am claiming does not exist. In short they have contributed to the development of FPA as theory and not as US-based theory.

It could also be pointed out that there is nothing like the coherence in the US FPA community that is suggested by my caricature. The differences in the US community are profound and therefore it is simply misleading for me to paint that community with the broad brush of positivism. Many US scholars, they would argue, would be more European than US on this score.

Finally, many would object to the stark dichotomization on which my discussion is based. The two academic communities are not separable in the way I suggest, with the result that there is a much more international community with cross-cutting academic cleavages than I depict. My characterization is too all-embracing and simplistic. FPA has divisions over methodology and epistemology, but these are more likely to occur within academic communities than between them. In essence the community is not so simply marked by *a* US and *a* European approach as implied above. Despite these objections, I hold to the general view outlined above.

My final comment on the state of FPA returns us to the question of compatibility. In other words, to what extent is it possible to use the different approaches to provide an overall explanation of the foreign policy context of the new Europe? This seems a superficial question at first glance, since the approaches obviously deal with different causal relationships in the foreign policy process. Accordingly, if neo-realism can say something about the changing structure of the international system represented by the events of 1989, integration theory something about the effects on the European foreign policy context after 1992, and bureaucratic politics something about the difficulties in creating *a* European foreign policy, then isn't this simply because all three approaches work at different levels of analysis? This, as noted above, is the standard pick-and-mix assumption in the FPA and international relations literature.

The problem with this answer is that it hides a fundamental problem, one that FPA has not yet dealt with in any depth. This is the possibility that the various approaches may not be compatible at all, because they have hidden epistemological and ontological assumptions that cannot be combined. If the twin developments of the end of the Cold War and the further integration of the EC are our empirical focus, and if our theoretical concern is with the utility of FPA for examining that empirical focus, then our guiding philosophy of social science concern is whether the attempt to apply the approaches to the empirical material tells us anything at all about the compatibility of FPA approaches.

The attempt to see which approaches are of most use in explaining the foreign policy context of the new Europe will pave the way for a concluding chapter which will look at this question of the compatibility of the main approaches in FPA. This chapter will be informed by the findings contained in the individual chapters, but it will also do rather more than this. My coeditor and I feel that we disagree so fundamentally on the issue of compatibility in foreign policy theory that we have agreed to use the conclusion for him to respond to the arguments that follow. In an important sense, these differences became more apparent as we steered this research project through to fruition. Walter Carlsnaes's conclusion will, therefore, take up where this chapter ends. This chapter and the conclusion can, of course, be read as a pair in which we debate what we both agree is the central philosophical problem at issue in FPA.

This problem is that there is, in my view, a deep flaw in the common-sense logic of FPA that approach X will explain best the foreign policy situations of type A, whereas approach Y deals best with situations of type B. The deep flaw is that even if there is a regular pattern of the explanatory potential of theories, combining them may not be possible for the simple reason that they take very different stances on the age-old agency–structure debate (see Wendt, 1987; 1991; 1992b; Dessler, 1989; Hollis and Smith, 1991; 1992; Carlsnaes, 1992).

At its simplest, the agency–structure debate is about whether accounts of human social behaviour are to be grounded in terms of the actors' intentions and definitions of the situation, or whether they are to be based on a model of the natural sciences, in which no conscious agency is required. This dispute is very much alive in the social sciences, but has been virtually ignored in international relations generally and FPA specifically. However, the rise of neo-realism as an account of international relations, especially in its Waltzian form, has brought the issue of system–unit linkages to the fore. Yet, this problem is usually portrayed as one to do with the amount of explanatory power accruing to each level of the system–unit debate. That is to say, the issue is framed as if the two levels are different maps of the same world. This is exactly the metaphor used by Singer in his early and very influential discussion of the problem. Yet as Singer suggested, and although this was largely forgotten by those who referred to Singer's work, there are grounds for treating the two levels of analysis as incompatible in some fundamental way. This is because the social world is not like the natural world, and therefore any two views of it may be *qualitatively* more difficult to combine than is the case with the natural world. While there is no great mystery about two views of a mountain or a vase of flowers, the same cannot be said about social action. Whereas two maps of the world distort the shape of territories at the poles and the equator, this distortion is purely mathematical, and capable of resolution; hence Singer's injunction to use whichever map was most accurate for the area you were concerned with. This is not at all like the social world, where action can be seen in different ways without any such hope of resolving differences.

The implication of the agency–structure debate is that there may always be two accounts, and that there is no way of combining these accounts. Many argue that such a combination is possible, the most well-known example being Giddens, with his concept of structuration. Yet, the chance to test FPA theories against the evidence of the new Europe allows us to assess the claim that the agency–structure debate is resolvable. If we find that combining the various approaches is not easy then this could well be because they, probably implicitly, take different positions on the agency–structure debate. The claim that this debate is unresolvable would then preclude compatibility or absorption into one overarching theoretical framework.

It is necessary to say a few words about why the debate might be unresolvable, especially since the philosophical assumptions of FPA, by implying that different approaches explain different aspects of foreign policy behaviour, tend to suggest that it is resolvable after all. There are three main lines of argument. The first is methodological: to believe that there is a way of combining accounts that stress agency with accounts that stress structure implies that there is some way of knowing when which account is to the fore. Yet there is no position external to each account that gives the observer a secure place from which to assess the relative potencies of the accounts. It is simply not possible to say that empirical behaviour is in this instance 75 per cent agency and 25 per cent structure. To reiterate a point made above, there may be always two stories to tell, and each contains its own criteria for selecting evidence. Now, given that FPA is broadly positivistic, it is not surprising that this problem has not been widely discussed. But, once the core assumption of positivism, concerning the role of data and their neutrality, is called into question by seeing data as ineluctably theory-laden, then the secure vantage point disappears, and the possibility of devising a methodological procedure to combine the accounts vanishes.

A second line of argument is epistemological: there exists no common epistemology between the two accounts. Agency accounts have to proceed by treating the actor as a choosing individual, and therefore work from the intentions and definitions of the situation to behaviour. Above all the aim is to find out what behaviour meant for the actor, and what counts as knowledge is the rational reconceptualization of the actor's intentions. FPA is replete with examples of this form of assumption at work: think only of the founding FPA work, the Snyder, Bruck and Sapin framework. Structure accounts, on the other hand, work from the model of knowledge found in the hard sciences, in which behaviour is analysed without dealing with the intentions of actors. Again, FPA provides excellent examples: Rosenau's pre-theory and the whole US CFP approach to this day are located in this epistemological tradition. Yet, how do you combine accounts stressing such mutually exclusive epistemologies? When Allison (1971) tried to do this in a famous footnote in *Essence of Decision*, the result was a logical contradiction. If bureaucratic position is really to explain behaviour, then it must determine policy preferences. Rational calculators cannot simply be grafted on to robots or puppets. A common confusion is to equate the structure–agency debate with the level of analysis problem. They are, in fact, two very different debates. Compromises between holists and individualists are much easier to contemplate than are compromises between structural and agency accounts, or, to put it more precisely, between explaining and understanding accounts.

The third line of argument is ontological: agency accounts see individuals as ontologically prior, and systems or societies as the unintended or consequential by-products of interactions between individuals. Structure accounts start with ontologically prior structures and see individuals in terms of the roles they occupy within these structures. FPA has clear examples of each of these ontological positions, with the belief systems literature a good example of the former and the bureaucratic politics literature a paradigm example of the latter. Yet clearly both agents and structure cannot be ontologically prior, and attempts to treat them as coexisting merely reduce the problem to a further level of analysis, in this case to a debate about psychology. I do not need to offer straw-person forms of either type of account, since in our view the problem occurs at whatever level of sophistication applies. In other words the argument against transcending the debate holds that there are always two stories to tell, and that these two stories can apply at any level at which international relations is analysed. Be it a debate about relations between system and the unit (state), between the state (as system) and bureaucracies, or between bureaucracies (as system) and the individual, the debate is the same. And, as just noted, reducing it to the individual does not remove the problem: the two accounts, at whatever level, simply see a different individual in social life. Again, note that there are two dimensions to this debate, and they must not be confused. The first is the ontological issue of individual or structural primacy, and compromise on this issue is less problematic than it is on the second dimension, which concerns the question of whether the social world is to be understood or explained.

This problem does not, of course, apply only to FPA. As noted above, it runs throughout international relations theory. Morgenthau was discussed earlier in terms of an unfortunate tendency to represent two distinct versions of realism at different points in his work. These two versions, labelled structural and practical realism, differ most fundamentally because each takes a very different stance on the agency–structure debate. Similarly, if the four strands of the post-positivist debate are incompatible, this will reflect different positions over agency and structure.

I will leave the agency–structure issue here. We will return to it in the concluding chapter, but for now it is sufficient to note that this debate is of critical importance in the philosophy of social science, and that there are many possible positions to take on it. My view is that it offers a potentially path-breaking explanation of the lack of cumulative progress in FPA. This will be one central theme in the concluding chapter.

As will by now hopefully be clear, this project is ambitious, and we do not pretend for a minute that we will solve all the puzzles we have set for ourselves. Nor do we imply that the participants will necessarily agree with the theoretical arguments of this chapter. We are clear, in fact, that the editors disagree on the agency–structure debate. However, our main concern is to use the case-study of the vast changes sweeping Europe to inform our analysis of the state of FPA. If, along the way, we can say something about the nature of those changes, that will be a bonus.

But this introduction should have set up the project for contributors and readers alike. We will return in the conclusion to the findings of our individual chapters. Having asked the contributors which approaches they find to be most useful in accounting for the changes represented by the twin developments of the end of the Cold War and the further integration of the European Community, we will discuss what their findings tell us about the current state of FPA. Our primary theoretical concern will be whether the dominant theories can explain the empirical domain, and, as this chapter has argued, we think that the answer to this question will say something about the agency–structure debate in FPA. Our secondary concern is whether FPA is truly international, or is too US-based in its theoretical concerns, its epistemology and its policy focus to be of any help in analysing the current European situation. In the concluding chapter we will return to these theoretical concerns and use the answers provided by the chapters to discuss whether or not FPA approaches can be combined within an overall theory or analytical framework. This will give us the opportunity to return to the agency–structure debate, and to see if that debate can shed any light on our findings. In our discussion of the agency–structure debate we believe we are dealing with the underlying reason why the current state of FPA is one of no overall theory, and why there is little prospect of integrating the middle-range theories. It is in this sense that our project may contribute in a new way to the development of FPA.

PART II THE CHANGING FOREIGN POLICY CONTEXT OF THE NEW EUROPE

2

Beyond the Stable State? Foreign Policy Challenges and Opportunities in the New Europe

Michael Smith

The starting point of this chapter is an empirical and theoretical puzzle, which can be simply stated. During the 1990s, the state as an organization and as a focus of political aspiration has achieved a new salience in Europe. At the same time the state has been subjected to fundamental challenges which have undermined its stability both as a form of human organization and as a value for those active in the international arena. From the point of view of foreign policy analysis, which has the centrality of the state and of state powers as a *point d'appui*, this is both a major source of problems and a significant opportunity for new development. The chapter proposes to explore the empirical domain of state forms and actions in the international order of the 'new Europe', and to use this as the base for an appraisal of existing and potential theories in the domain of foreign policy analysis.

Before commencing this analysis and development, let us look a little more closely at the nature of the puzzle as it appears in the mid 1990s. In effect, it is a cluster of puzzles, in which the common factor is the state – its operation, its status as a value for political activity, and the challenges to it in all of these areas. The onset of radical political and social change in Europe since the mid 1980s has meant that the state has become a focus for intense political action and the centrepiece of new political thinking. In a broad sense, the political changes of the late 1980s and early 1990s in Eastern Europe have created new momentum behind a vision of the state which would have been recognized by the unifiers of Italy and the followers of Woodrow Wilson, with a focus on national autonomy and self-determination within an international 'society of states'. But it is clear that in this case, the new states of Eastern Europe and the former Soviet Union have come to a sometimes painful birth in a very different world from that of the 1860s, the 1890s or the 1920s. Within the new world, there are major questions about the ability of the new states to provide state services and to establish their legitimacy both internally and at the international level.

The crisis of statehood is not simply a phenomenon of Eastern Europe and the former Soviet Union. In the case of Western Europe, the crisis may take different forms but it is in many ways no less pressing. The development of interconnectedness and interdependence, and the practical and symbolic effects of the development of the European Community, mean that state forms and functions in Western Europe are unstable, and that their continuing legitimacy is in question. In this context, it is no longer clear what the state is *for* and what it can *do* in an increasingly transnational world; the responses both of political elites and of broader populations to the Maastricht agreements of 1991 demonstrated this in an often disturbing way. Although it would be tempting – and is, for many political leaders – to put the problems of state stability in East and West in separate boxes, the reality is that they are intensely interconnected, and that the nature of state legitimacy in the East and the West is a common problem with different manifestations in different political and social contexts.

The problem, of course, is not merely one of practical action and day-to-day dealings between European societies. It is also one which challenges established thinking about the state and statehood. The conventional notion of the nation-state, of sovereignty and of legitimacy derived from domestic and international recognition, can be defined in this context as an ideological construct, not merely an ideal type. Given that status, it is clear that developments of the kind we have witnessed in Europe form an attack at the level of ideology and value systems as well as at the level of political action. For foreign policy analysis, this is crucial: after all, the central conceptual building block of the field is the notion of state and governmental power, and the unity of focus which this provides gives analytical clarity to what could be a very disorderly enterprise. The credentials of the state are at issue in the political and social arena, but so are those of the field. If the solidity and the stability of state forms and functions come under attack in Europe, the position is not unlike that faced by international relations theory in the 1950s and 1960s, when John Herz and others identified the challenges emerging from the impact of nuclear weapons and the creation of the Third World (Herz, 1976). Given the question marks hanging over the empirical and ideological condition of statehood, how can the field adapt and survive?

The question is posed in an extreme fashion, but it is nonetheless central to the enterprise on which we are engaged. If statehood is defined not as a condition of international action and interaction but as an experimental process with an ideological dimension and no determinate boundaries, then the activity of foreign policy analysis must come under scrutiny. If the state in Europe no longer reflects the archetype of sovereign statehood which was largely a function of the historical development of European international relations, then how should we start to think of those international relations and the structures to which they give rise or within which they are conducted? If the state no longer effectively represents the society to which it lays claim, or if it can no longer intervene effectively in relations between citizens of Europe, what can we then say about the credentials both of state action and of the analysis which focuses upon it?

Although the issues are posed here in terms of FPA, they actually have much wider referents in the social science study of the state. Stuart Hall (1984) has noted that the key concepts of power, sovereignty, autonomy and representation derive as much from domestic as from international existence, and that the relation of the state to civil society on the one hand and international society on the other is a key element in studies of statehood from Machiavelli and Hobbes to the present. The notion of rule, and its association with the right or the power to enforce the state's will, is central not only to the state as domestic actor but also to the notion of foreign policy. The concept of public power, distinct from the power of individual rulers or regimes, is essential to analysis not only of the domestic state but also of the state in the international arena. The challenge of change in contemporary Europe is not only to the credentials of rulers (and their ability to define the context for actions by their citizens) at home but also to the effects and the effectiveness of their international actions.

This chapter thus represents an attempt both to place the current problems of FPA within the context of change in Europe and its implications for what we might call the 'European state', and to remind us of the linkages between FPA and state theory, which are often left unquestioned by actually existing FPA. The chapter proceeds in the following stages. First, it attempts to expose the central features of change in contemporary Europe and the contemporary European order. This, as already noted, constitutes the empirical domain on which the chapter is centred. Second, it examines a range of available theoretical approaches and evaluates the extent to which they can account for or explain the changing order and the role of states. In conducting this evaluation, the chapter brings together the second and third elements of the framework around which this book is constructed (see Chapter 1). The chapter addresses the fourth element of the overall framework by pursuing two strands of theoretical development – on the one hand the notion of state adjustment strategies as proposed by John Ikenberry, and on the other the ideas of Robert Cox on states, social forces and world orders – in order to explore their relevance to the European situation and their contrasting assumptions. On this basis, the final part of the chapter assesses the possibility of bringing together state theories from the state and the structural levels to give a richer understanding of the ways in which FPA might develop during the 1990s. It argues that the 'neo-liberal institutionalism' of Robert Keohane provides a potentially fruitful form of synthesis, permitting the analysis of state behaviours and forms within the context of international structures of rules and conventions. These are not necessarily new questions or ideas, but they are explored here in a new context, which demands a new and critical appraisal of existing state theories.

The changing European order

The first task is to identify the nature of the order in Europe, along with the implications of change for the order itself and for states within it. There are effectively four components to the problem. First, there is the notion of an order; second, there is the concept of change; third, there is the question of responses to change; finally, there is the issue of impact, and the ways in which changes in the order and in the actions of major participants feed into further processes of change. These will be stated in general form with relation to the new Europe, whilst the following parts of the chapter will relate them to the development of theory and the issue of the state.

In empirical terms, the changing order in Europe can be linked to a number of major trends (Smith and Woolcock, 1993, Chapter 1). In the first place, there has been a process of radical structural change entailing a restructuring of relationships both between European states and within the broader context of US/Soviet relations and the global economy. Inseparable from this process has been the rise of new states in Europe and the search for the building blocks for a new European state system. At the same time, changes in the economic and security order outside Europe have raised questions about the boundaries of the system and the interests of European state authorities. Often, there have been new and sometimes unexpected linkages between political, security and economic concerns, which have challenged the capacity of state authorities both to recognize and to respond to new needs for action. Finally, there has been an institutional challenge relating to the adequacy of existing institutions for international action, and to the potential for coordination between state and other authorities.

What does this mean for analysis of the European order in more general and conceptual terms? The notion of an international order implies a formal or informal set of relationships which produce regularities and expected patterns of behaviour, and in which there are shared assumptions about such issues as precedence, legitimacy and regulation (Cox, 1986; Smith, 1991). The basis for such an order may be the power of a specific state or states, the power of supranational or transnational authorities, the power of norms of behaviour and of the perceived boundaries of acceptable behaviour. If all of these are in congruence, then the order may be exceptionally robust. Commonly, they are not, and the limitations of international orders are what give rise to some of the more interesting questions about conflict and cooperation, change and stability in the global arena. In particular, these limitations can give rise to important questions about the 'ownership' of the international order, and about the relationship between the demands of the order and the needs or aspirations of individual actors within it. For our purposes here, the most significant of these actors are states.

From this general base, specific international orders can be explored in terms of their geographical and functional scope, their degree of institutionalization, and their strength or fragility. An important feature of this form of analysis is that in order to get beyond the crudely positivist it must include not only the observable and empirical, but also the ideological and normative components of any given order. These components are also central when it comes to analysis of change in any given order. At the centre of the problem is the pervasiveness of what might be termed 'potentially relevant crude change' in the international arena, taking place at a number of interconnected levels or layers from the local to the global. Only some of these changes will be significant or relevant either to the future of the order or to the policy concerns of individual actors, but it is important to attempt an estimate.

Change in the international arena, in particular as it affects foreign policy, can be analysed in a number of ways (Smith, 1981; 1991). First, it can be explored in terms of the mode of change. The problem for policy-makers and state or other authorities is that different modes and paces of change can coexist, posing problems of attention and recognition. In similar fashion, the potential costs and benefits of change can be assessed. Often, however, the confusion of the long and the short term, and the mingling of tangible and intangible elements, can lead to uncertainty and potential confusion. A third element is that of centrality: which changes are central to the persistence or transformation of the established order, and which are essentially marginal? Here, an important datum is the inevitable differences of perception between different participants in a given order, which can be exacerbated by the pace and pervasiveness of change. Finally, the spillover effects of change are important to the establishment, preservation or transformation of a given order. Often, the initial impact of changes can be magnified or contained by the ways in which they relate to the surrounding order, and the ways in which linkages may or may not be made.

A further element of the analysis of international orders relates to the impact of changes in the order on the participants in it. There is clearly in all international orders a tension between the whole and the parts, and this is vital to an understanding of the ways in which national authorities are affected by change. There are problems of 'learning capacity', posed by the rate and pervasiveness of change and by the adaptive capacity of state authorities. In addition, there are problems of 'carrying capacity', reflecting the differential ability of participants to bear the burden of change and their capacity to act within what may be a confused and confusing context. Where change is pervasive and central to the concerns of different authorities, this can pose problems of attention, of 'requisite variety' in the instruments for taking action, and of the ability to control actions. As a rule, these problems can be suppressed by a set of standard operating procedures and by the relative predictability of the international order, but where these props are knocked away there can be intense problems of conceptualization and action.

The tension between the parts and the whole is again evident when it comes to the analysis of responses to a changing international order. Where responses of national and other authorities are appropriate and consistent, then the order can be sustained even in turbulent conditions. Where they are non-existent or inconsistent, the overall problem of stability can be magnified and the order itself can be jeopardized. Inappropriate or destabilizing policy responses can arise from a number of sources. Policy-makers can find themselves, or feel themselves, without alternatives, leading to under- or over-reaction. They may simply be unable to mobilize appropriate instruments or capabilities, either because they do not possess them or because they cannot agree on their use. In any case, the problem of policy consistency is exacerbated by intense change. Where this change not only is within the established order, but implies change of the order itself at either the tangible or the intangible level, then the result may be crisis both within the order and within the major participants. The implications of such a situation for policy legitimacy and for regime stability are an important issue for exploration (Smith, 1981; George, 1980).

Given this general and conceptual analysis, what can be said about the nature of change in the European order during the late 1980s and 1990s? In the first place, it can be argued that the old European order was on the surface extraordinarily robust (DePorte, 1986; Clark and Serfaty, 1991; Buzan et al., 1990). The combined effect of Soviet–American hostility, a specific distribution of state power, the building of institutions in both East and West, and the ideological commitment of state and other forces to the established way of doing things created a situation of polarization and rigidity between the blocs. Although the Western alliance did permit of a degree of pluralism, the net effect of the continuing Soviet challenge and the tacit acceptance of a geographically and functionally divided continent was to give a high degree of practical conformity in the behaviour of Europeans everywhere. There is an important argument to be had about the extent to which conformity extended beyond international behaviour to domestic structures, but this cannot be explored in detail here.

The transformation of the 1990s, though, has exposed the limitations of what appeared at times to be a permanent order in Europe. Both the formal and the informal, the tangible and the intangible components of the order have been thrown into question. In terms of the discussion earlier, it can be seen that change has been pervasive and convulsive, rather than contained and deliberative. Politically, it has raised questions about the persistence of nationalism and ancient conflicts which were for long suppressed by the dominant structure of Soviet–American rivalry.

Militarily, it has largely removed the security blanket provided by the Americans and the Soviets. Economically, it has uncovered instabilities and distortions which have proved worse than most commentators' imaginings, with immense potential costs and needs for transfers of resources. At the same time, these changes have taken place within and been affected by a changing global arena, in which the appeal to a 'new world order' by the Americans and others appears to be in many respects either self-serving or self-defeating (Smith and Woolcock, 1993, Chapters 1 and 2).

Two vital sets of implications for the argument here flow from this discussion. In the first place, the European order is essentially fluid and transitional during the 1990s. As Buzan and others have argued, the possible future orders for European security fall into a spectrum between 'Cold War III', 'the triumph of integration' and 'the triumph of anarchy' (Buzan et al., 1990; see also Rosecrance, 1991; Hoffmann, 1992). Whilst the first of these may now effectively have been ruled out, the other two form widely separated poles between which violent local and regional fluctuations are possible. A focus on military aspects of security, though, tends to play down the role of economic and social contacts in either moderating or magnifying the movements towards one pole or the other. Finally, at the level of the order in general, the role of ideology and the capacity to build a consensus about the future of the European order – an essential part of any analysis – is widely contested.

The second major implication for the argument here is the tension between the characteristics of the order as a whole and the nature and needs of the participants within it. We have noted that this tension can take a number of forms, but whatever the forms it is an essential driving force of both the establishment of order and their breakdown. The changes described here form the basis for perhaps the most spectacular and fundamental challenge in this area since the Napoleonic period. The collapse of the USSR, the rise of the new Germany, the proliferation of new and fragile states, the problems of defining the European boundary, the linkages between issues, the redundancy or new vigour of international institutions: all of these pose challenges in two dimensions to states and other authorities. On the one hand, they challenge state structures, strategies and potential for adaptation. On the other, they challenge normative structures and the consensus on the relations between European states and the European order which was so painfully and arguably profitlessly formed during the 1945–89 period (Treverton 1992; Clark and Serfaty, 1991).

Theory, change and the state in the new Europe

The newly questionable nature of the state in the new Europe forms the central focus in this chapter, but the role and position of the state are central to much existing international theory. As already argued, the state is one of the governing assumptions of FPA, and is frequently an unquestioned or unrecognized assumption. It is clear that such a silence about the state is impossible in the changed European context, but what theory is there which might provide the starting point for a critical analysis? In this part of the chapter, four sets of ideas are reviewed, in order to set the scene for the later development of specific lines of argument.

The first set of arguments is that of the realists. As many other contributors to this volume have pointed out, the realist position on the role and position of the state is based on a number of central features. The state is assumed to be monolithic, to be relatively autonomous and formally sovereign, and to be capable of controlling its territory and its citizens. Although the reality of statehood can and does diverge from this ideal type, and the state is a variable concept even for realists, the assumptions reflect powerful perceptions about the pervasive strength of states and their historical domination of the global arena. Most importantly for the argument here, the realist conception of the state has quintessentially European roots: the early establishment of state power and legitimacy in the European arena can be seen as the source of much later thinking about the state as an international phenomenon (Bull, 1977; 1979; Mastanduno et al., 1989).

Realist thought, again as many have pointed out, is not reducible to power politics and a crude form of international social Darwinism. More sophisticated realist approaches emphasize not the drive for power and naked competition between states but rather the development of responsible state government and the development of international governance by a form of continuous negotiation between state authorities (Miller, 1981). The state is a form of 'continuous public power' (Vincent, 1987), and this is a source of a great deal of international predictability and stability. It is therefore not surprising that Hedley Bull (1979) can point to the state's positive role in world affairs not only as expressed in the balance of power but also as expressed in the maintenance of domestic tranquillity. Likewise, Northedge (1978) can point to the underlying purpose of international life as being the maintenance of the maximum level of order in the parts with the minimum of disorder in the whole.

Can realists, though, deal with the realities of life in the Europe of the 1990s? Two important areas of deficiency can be identified. On the one hand, the ideology of state dominance in the international system comes into question when the state itself is a fluctuating phenomenon. We are faced not with a system of autonomous, monolithic and in-control states, but with a host of state forms ranging from the very strong to the very weak. The system itself appears to contain actors which call themselves states but which do not possess the required attributes, as in the former Soviet Union and Yugoslavia. In many cases, the requirement of responsible state government is not present, and thus the parallel requirement of responsible international governance cannot be met, as in the case of arms control efforts or nuclear non-proliferation policies. Importantly, the position of foreign policy itself, which the realists see as privileged, is no longer unquestioned, and is frequently supplanted by action emanating from intense domestic fluctuations and conflicts. The dual derivation of state legitimacy from national authority and international recognition thus cannot be taken for granted; beyond this formal level, the ability of states to earn legitimacy through the performance of state services is also often in question, both in the East and in the West of the continent. Nonetheless, the forms of statehood remain a prime focus of political strivings and ambitions throughout the continent. The inability to re-create classical statehood is thus a potent source of frictions and instability.

It appears therefore that the essence of classical realist thought can no longer be applied in many areas of the new Europe, particularly as it reflects the quasi-ideology of state dominance. What, though, of neo-realism? The promise of Waltz (1979) and his followers is to fill the gap created by the questioning of state forms and to focus instead on the structures within which states and other actors function. State competition is not naked; it is constrained and can be channelled into forms of relatively permanent stability given the rational responses of state actors to the emergence of a new set of structural imperatives. As Thomas Risse-Kappen points out in Chapter 3, though, the structural realists face problems with the new Europe, particularly since it appears impossible for state authorities to re-create in the mid 1990s the comparative predictability of bipolarity and the Soviet–American standoff. The fact of the matter is that state authorities in the European arena are now more various than at any time since the mid nineteenth century, and thus that the possibility of their being able to form a tacit consensus and to contain the variations between them are quite small if those possibilities are seen to rest on a *conventional* notion of statehood. Not only this, but the cultural variations between states with increasingly diverse roots and modes of operation mean that Europe in the 1990s bears some resemblance to the global system of the 1960s and 1970s, without the comforting clarity of the division into First, Second and Third Worlds but with much of the diversity that such a stratification entailed.

Liberal-pluralist thought represents almost a direct response in many ways to the limitations of classical realism: but is it any more effective as a means of capturing and accounting for the changing nature of European order and foreign policies? According to the liberal pluralists, the state must be seen very much as an emanation of society and social groupings, rather than as a dominant force shaping society. Whereas the realists would stress the ways in which processes of modernization have given the state more power to intervene in society and to define state interests for domestic and foreign purposes, the pluralists have countered this by proposing a view of the state as penetrated, acting more as an umpire or the channel for group interests than as the dominant policing and coercive force. Among the powerful interests given prominence by the pluralists are those of transnational groupings and institutions, which have arisen not as a means of reflecting state interests but rather as a means of performing tasks beyond the ambit of states acting individually or collectively (Smith, 1992).

There is no doubt that liberal-pluralist interpretation helps in an understanding of certain features in the new Europe, particularly in relation to the growth of transnational and even supranational groupings. The problem is that the basis of liberal pluralism is exactly that: the assumption of a strong social consensus which operates to constrain and to channel the actions of non-state groupings. In a way, the assumption means that a strong state is not necessary: there is almost a tautological relationship between strength of society and social groupings and lack of centralized or coercive state power, both in the national and in the international context. In the Europe of the 1990s, there is undoubtedly great pluralism, but it is often not liberal or (implicitly) constitutional in its direction. Indeed, it is the kind of pluralism which can degenerate into anarchy and random violence, or alternatively into strong and undemocratic state rule. The implications for foreign policy are significant, since it is apparent that the assumed containment of subversive forces and the role of the state as an umpire or international representative can be maintained only with great difficulty in such circumstances. The state as foreign policy actor is constrained not only by the lack of international order but also by the lack of domestic consensus. Whilst at one level the subversion of the state by factional forces may be an outcome, at another the inadequacy of the state as an expression for societal welfare needs can lead to the desire for more international administration, and to a parallel weakening of the liberal-pluralist ideal. Examples are not difficult to find: on the one hand there is the social disintegration characteristic of many areas in the former Soviet bloc, whilst on the other there is the profound ambivalence of attitudes towards the development of European union through the Maastricht agreements.

A final state theory available for application to the contemporary European arena is that of world-systems analysis. In this perspective, the state as a phenomenon is seen as an expression of global forces, and particularly those of the capitalist world system. States are the agents of groups which wish to intervene in the world economy and the world system and to bias its operation in their favour. In many ways, states are epiphenomena of the world system, without autonomy and without the capacity to act independently. Change at the state level does not in principle affect the operation of the world system, since states are constrained by their positions in the system. At the level of the domestic state, it is apparent that the world system penetrates national societies and structures them in accordance with its priorities, rather than those of national elites or subnational groupings. Although it may be felt by elites and other groups that they are running 'their' state, this is an illusion: their state is being run for them along the relatively narrow lines provided by the global process of accumulation (Wallerstein, 1991).

The relevance of this perspective to the emergence of a large number of new states in the European arena is plain; no less can it give an insight into the supplanting of state functions at the national level in Western Europe by the expansion of the European Community. It might appear that the capitalist world economy has simply brought to a head the logic of Soviet state incapacity and the incorporation of Eastern Europe into the liberal capitalist nexus. Although many of the new states are still dependent and peripheral, there is already the makings of a semi-periphery with the Hungarians, the Czechs and the Poles as its first denizens. But is this enough to prove the credentials of the approach? It appears that there are forces of resistance to the world capitalist order, and that there is a stubborn reluctance to admit that the new states lack autonomy; in fact, the drive for autonomy and self-determination is one of the most disruptive forces in the current situation, and demonstrates the potency of values and local action as well as the logic of the global capitalist order. Statehood is seen as having a lot to offer, and the logic of national self-abnegation is lost on many of the peoples both East and West in the 'new continent'. Whilst there is much power to the notion that 'new statehood' is the means for extension of the global capitalist order, there are distinct limitations to its power at the level of foreign policy and national action.

This discussion makes it clear that states and statehood are central to the evolution of the new Europe. Equally, it demonstrates that the linkage between state theory and the nature of foreign policy is a vital part of the political process emerging in the old continent. It is important here to note the connection between these conclusions and the previous discussion of the changing European order. If one assumes that the changing European order throws up questions not only of a pragmatic kind about the appropriate state structures and policy responses to the new Europe but also of a normative kind about the appropriateness of concepts and the critical appreciation of the bases of order in both national and international contexts, then the discussion of available theories gains an additional dimension. Those theories are not simply available to describe and/or explain the changing European order: they are themselves changed by it, and given a new critical significance in the operation of state authorities. In the next section of the chapter, two lines of critical and theoretical enquiry will be pursued in the hope of demonstrating the force of this observation and developing an agenda for further conceptual clarification.

States, stability and order in a changing Europe

The argument so far has focused on the questions raised about the role of states and their foreign policies in a changing European order. In this part of the chapter, the aim is to develop a view of the state which emphasizes not the limitations of state authorities and the increasing challenge to state legitimacy, but rather the possibilities of creative adjustment in state policies and the potential for creation of a new normative consensus focused by international organizations. In this exercise, the primary sources are those provided by John Ikenberry and Robert Cox (Ikenberry, 1986; Mastanduno et al., 1989; Cox, 1986; 1992). The chapter will explore the ways in which the differing assumptions and approaches of Ikenberry and Cox can illuminate the problems of foreign policy in the new Europe, and then go on to assess the ways in which they might be reconciled to produce a usable synthesis focusing on the interaction of states and international organizations in both the material and the value domains.

The active state and changing orders

One way forward in the analysis of states and a changing European order is to focus on the strategies of adjustment available to and used by state authorities. In this conception, the state and its ruling authorities exist in a complex bargaining relationship with both domestic and international forces, and the legitimacy and effectiveness of state authorities are a function of their ability to balance the costs and benefits of appealing to the different constituencies with which they are surrounded. A major exponent of this view is Ikenberry (1986; Mastanduno et al., 1989), although other theorists have drawn attention to the multilevel bargaining processes which arise between states and societies in conditions of complex interdependence (for example Hanrieder, 1978; Putnam, 1988). Here, the state is not seen as a passive entity subject to the claims either of interdependence or of international change; rather, it is active and creative in its attempts to recognize, adjust to and profit from the conditions which surround it. As Hanrieder (1978) suggests, the state is capable of extension and of effectively 'dissolving' international politics through the deepening of its involvement in both domestic and international arenas.

A central assumption of the approach under examination here is that 'the legitimacy of the state is always conditional' (Ikenberry, 1986, p. 55), whilst the central imperative of state authorities is survival and the maintenance of positions of power. It can be seen that this is by no means a simple-minded social Darwinist approach of the kind accepted by the cruder forms of realism: it posits a complex set of bargaining relationships and tradeoffs between national state authorities and their domestic and international audiences. Tellingly, Ikenberry also notes that this bargaining relationship can be most clearly identified at the moment of state creation, when the newly installed authorities face the most pressing calls to gather resources and recognition. It could also be argued by extension that this clarity can be identified at moments when states are faced with urgent demands to define and restructure their international organizational context: here also, the implicit bargains between state, society and international context are likely to be brought to the surface and made the focus of critical examination.

Ikenberry goes on to argue (following Gilpin) that the dynamic equilibrium characteristic of all international systems produces the most obvious test of the adjustment capacities of national authorities:

> Of the many domestic and international forces that set states in motion, none is more important than the constant pressure for national adjustment to international change produced by constant differential change between national and international systems. . . . This differential change may involve system-wide economic upheavals such as the Depression of the 1930s or the oil price revolution of the 1970s. It may be more gradual – as in the changing competitive position of particular industrial sectors in advanced industrial countries. It will either generate new opportunities for aggressive domestic response to international change, or it will generate pressure for defensive action to preserve existing domestic arrangements. (1986, p. 56)

From this base, Ikenberry goes on to discuss specific patterns of adjustment strategies, differentiating between offensive and defensive, domestic and international responses. Later development of the ideas by Mastanduno et al. (1989) focused especially on the ways in which resources (both tangible and intangible) are extracted and mobilized by state authorities in pursuit of international goals, from both the domestic and the international arena.

The importance of this approach to the earlier analysis of change in the European order is plain. Ikenberry's argument that the central value of state activity is the preservation of legitimacy and thus the conduct of bargaining between domestic and international constituencies is a potentially major contribution to an understanding of the ways in which states from the strongest to the weakest, in the East and the West, can be seen in the changing European context. As conceptualized in its original (1986) form, the linkage in the approach between political economy and national security could be seen as weak: the desirable focus on the tangible costs and benefits inherent in the economic domain raised questions about the extension to the less easily defined realm of political and security perceptions. In the Europe of the 1990s, it is very difficult to isolate such domains, given the intimate connection between national survival and consolidation and the domains of security and ideology. The later (1989) development of the framework provided a more explicit and substantial linkage, although it still did not dispose of the issue. Another ambiguity, although not so immediately obvious, is the implicit assumption that statehood is recognizable for all state authorities, and that the analyst can identify the state apparatus and its personnel in a definitive way. The experimental forms of statehood visible in the Eastern European and former Soviet territories stretch this assumption to the limit if not beyond, whilst the arrogation of state functions to the developing European Community provides another challenge to the parsimony of the framework. The focus in the 1989 article on 'hard' and 'soft' forms of statehood again provides a partial response, although the dichotomy begs questions in the light of contemporary European trends.

With these qualifications, though, the Ikenberry framework provides us with a way of conceptualizing the responses of states to changing international constraints and domestic demands. Ikenberry (1986, pp. 56–67) follows Lukes in suggesting that constraints on adjustment strategies can be separated into 'rational' and 'structural' constraints; whilst the latter may simply mean that state authorities are unable to prevail over the contextual demands or obstacles they face, the interesting issues in terms of adjustment strategies arise when rational constraints are explored. It is within the structural constraints constituted by power and position in the international and domestic arenas that state authorities can be creative and can attempt to control the costs of various policy options.

Clearly, one of the imperatives of life in the European order of the 1990s is creative adjustment and the recognition and/or allocation of costs and resources. But the states of Europe find themselves in markedly differing positions in terms of their legitimacy, their solidity and their capacities for creative adjustment. Thus, following Ikenberry, the logical outcome of this situation will be a complex set of bargaining relationships and strategies in which state authorities will seek to maximize the benefits and limit the costs of the turbulence with which they are faced at home and abroad. The difficulty is that the normative and even institutional consensus within which this set of processes might take place is notably lacking. Not only this, but the intimate linkages between issues of political economy and the politics of security and survival undermine the neatly costed options which are essential to the parsimony of the Ikenberry model.

Empirically, this line of argument can be pursued by examining on the one side the move towards European union and on the other the breakup of the Soviet Union and the emergence of the CIS. In the former case, many of the preconditions for application of the Ikenberry model are met: the state authorities are discernible, they are structured into a highly institutionalized environment, and their mutual relations take the form of continuous and highly complex negotiations. In principle, therefore, the model can effectively be applied, and the strategies of the various state authorities identified (including those of the European Commission in areas where it has state-like capacities). When it comes to the affairs of the CIS, there is much less certainty. Many of the state authorities concerned are literally inventing themselves; they are interacting within a context where there is little consensus on the bargaining process or on the measurement of outcomes, and they are centrally concerned with symbolic and by definition immeasurable outcomes.

This is not to deny the value of the Ikenberry framework; rather, it is simply to argue that the context and the structure are vital to the operation of adjustment strategies. Ikenberry himself argues that structures provide '*limits on and possibilities for* state action' (1986, p. 66: italics in original), and that within a given structure the creativeness of state authorities can significantly influence outcomes: compare, for example, the activities and the changing status of the Baltic states in the 1989–91 period, or the relative success of the proto-states in former Yugoslavia. Ikenberry, though, does at times imply that structures are neutral and relatively slow to change, just as he takes as a basic assumption that state authorities are composed of officials with a severely limited set of value preferences. This is neither true in the West, where the EC challenges policy-makers to shift preferences within a complex framework, nor in the East, where the sheer uncertainty of the context means that policy-makers have to adapt to situations in which the stakes and the risks are essentially unknown and unknowable.

Given this situation, a final element of Ikenberry's argument becomes potentially very important. State authorities, in their quest to achieve legitimacy and to limit the costs of governance, actively seek a favourable allocation of the costs. The best governance is cheap governance, and especially if the costs are paid by somebody else. In this quest, the role of international organizations is crucial: as Ikenberry notes, 'International redress of adjustment problems shifts the burden of change or at least distributes it more broadly' (1986, p. 62). The relevance to Europe East and West should be clear, although it is profoundly different in the different subregional contexts. This means that in the new Europe, the changing role of international organizations and their relationships with national state authorities are among the most important questions for the 1990s. At this stage, it is sufficient to signal the issue; it will be taken up explicitly in the final section of the chapter.

Social forces, states and the changing European order

As noted already, the state adjustment approach defined by Ikenberry necessarily down-plays the role of values and of ideology; to this extent, it falls within the prevailing neo-realist paradigm by focusing only on what is tangible, measurable and observable, although later development emphasized the classical realist focus on values of autonomy and international legitimacy (Mastanduno et al., 1989). Legitimacy and international structures in this perspective can be seen as effective commodities or assets to be deployed or purchased at specific if variable costs. The changing European order, though, implies that the nature of values such as legitimacy and the roles of international structures are strongly ideological and normative in their connotations. The second strand of argumentation to be assessed here gives these aspects a very high profile, and thus contrasts markedly with the Ikenberry approach.

Robert Cox (1986) takes as variables precisely some of the central fixed elements in the Ikenberry approach. He argues that the application of critical theory to problems of world order reveals the essentially ideological basis of assumptions about the nature of the international system, posing a strong contrast between 'problem-solving theory' which is designed to deal with the existing world order and 'critical theory' which is designed to expose the value underpinnings of the apparently unquestionable way of the world. In a later article, Cox (1992) argues that both world-systems approaches and classical realism can be seen as critical theories, since both are sensitive to the ways in which historical evolution and dynamics can shape the actions of states and other groupings. Ikenberry's assumptions about the nature of the international structure, and his view of the bargaining relationship between state authorities and domestic and international constituencies, at first glance fall pretty squarely into the realm of problem-solving theory within the definitions offered by Cox, and it is this contrast which can profitably be explored here.

A major implication of Cox's approach is that where the established order is self-evidently not fixed or supported with a consensus among the relevant elites, there is little role for problem-solving theory. In the context of contemporary Europe, the discussion in the early part of this chapter implies, the fluctuation of the existing order and the lack of relevant consensus destroy the basis for problem-solving theories; quite simply, the rate and scope of change is off the scale where such theories might be appropriate. A logical consequence is that attempts in the positivist vein to build a new European order are likely to be futile or self-defeating, since they are unlikely to overcome the deep structures of dissension which were long suppressed by the Cold War and the Soviet–American standoff. This is a major difficulty both at the level of domestic structures, where state authorities as we have seen are subject to internal and external challenges, and at the level of international procedures, where the variable interpretation and the contested nature of apparently neutral rules can prove a central obstacle to attempts at stabilization. Not only this, but the notion of a new order in itself is an ideological construct, reflecting the preferences and structural power of specific forces. It could thus form a weapon against those very liberated forces which appear to be destabilizing or destructive.

This line of argument reveals – or confirms – that the notion of order can become a tool in the hands of dominant or conservative forces. In addition, the weight of history can mean that the purported basis for the construction of a new order is backward-looking; in the European theatre, for example, this might mean that the supposed roles of the EC or of states and statehood themselves are cast in historical terms not appropriate to the new forces unleashed in the 1990s. A particular manifestation of the problem is the search in the 1990s for a new role for NATO and the United States' presence: without making any judgements on the abstract desirability of the Americans' continued engagement, it is clear that the debate could draw in many respects only on historical analogies with the 1940s or the Cold War period. In the circumstances, these analogies could be a diversion or an obstacle to fresh thinking on the part of European state authorities. Arguably, this could produce a paradoxical situation in which the search for stability and a new order creates greater instability by sharpening the contradictions between the new reality and the nostalgic or rhetorical call for different uses of existing structures.

For Cox, the stability or instability of world orders can be explored most effectively by taking as problematical precisely what many analysts take as given: the bases for the establishment and the functioning of orders themselves. Thus, he proposes the equation of stability with

> a concept of hegemony that is based on a coherent conjunction or fit between a configuration of material power, the prevalent collective image of world order (including certain norms) and a set of institutions which administer the order with a certain degree of universality (that is, not just as the overt instruments of a particular state's dominance). In this formulation, state power ceases to be the sole explanatory factor and becomes part of what is to be explained. (1986, pp. 222–3)

If approached in this light, there is no doubt that the European order of the 1990s reflects a profound lack of congruence or fit between the three elements of Cox's model. There is a lack of a recognized configuration of material power, given the collapse of the Soviet Union, the rise of new states and the move towards deeper forms of European union. In this context, the development of the EC itself is to be seen as destabilizing, since it strips away from states some of the recognized attributes of material power. Such a conclusion is if anything given greater weight by the turbulence which came to attend the ratification of the Maastricht agreements during 1992–93. At the same time, there is no collective image of world order (or of the regional order which might be established or recognized in Europe); the disappearance of the Cold War structures has removed one of the major constraints on state policies and the actions of social forces, not only in the security sphere but also in the economic domain. Finally, there is a lack of settled institutions: states are in question, both in their domestic and in their international existence, whilst there are no universally accepted institutions operating to express the norms of life in the new Europe.

This does not mean, though, that the European arena expresses nothing but anarchy. As Stanley Hoffmann (1992) has noted, the emerging order does not fit neatly into any of the existing categories, but that does not mean there is no order at all. What is going on is to a large extent experimental, both at the national level and at the level of international norms and institutions. For states and their foreign policies, the message is that order is transitional and partial, and thus that strategies need to be complex and flexible rather than stuck into one historically determined mode of action and expectation. That is in itself very difficult, since states are surrounded with the debris of a former historical order and may themselves be subject to questioning about their national and international credentials. Thus the governing authorities in France or Germany have had to respond to calls for an active role in constructing the new European order at the same time as they have been wrestling with domestic challenges and disorder of a more or less violent kind. There is an important potential linkage here in conceptual terms between the limits of state activism and autonomy (as questioned in the evaluation of Ikenberry's ideas) and the capacity or inclination to contribute to international restructuring. The costs of each may prove to be one of the greatest obstacles to the generation of a new fit between the major components of European order during the 1990s.

What Cox does for the theorist is to uncover the ideological assumptions behind calls for a new order based on the continuity of the old and the pouring of new wine into old bottles. Europe is in fact replete with institutions and the values they express; what may also be true is that the values are inappropriate to the 1990s or to the emerging new order. Take for example the Conference on Security and Cooperation in Europe (CSCE), which has played a major role in reflecting a value consensus based on non-intervention, human rights and responsible government. It expresses nothing so much as the idea of the liberal state in a world of states, which was a powerful ideological modifier as the Cold War was eroded. Does this mean that its values form a reliable basis for thought and action in the 1990s? This is a particularly germane question in the light of the arguments which see the CSCE as a civilizing influence for the new Europe, and as a prop for the foreign policies of new states. Somewhat similar arguments might be made about the values and ideology underpinning that well-known Cold War institution, the European Community: here, there is an implicit adherence to the functional supremacy of the state authorities and to their ability to satisfy the demands of markets and populations, whether through the Community or otherwise. Is this a practical basis for a new value consensus both within and outside the Community?

Another important implication of Cox's arguments is that the nature of state adjustment strategies – and the very capacity of state authorities to conceive of adjustment strategies – is likely to reflect the prevailing conditions of world order. We have noted already that this is one of the areas in which the active state approach relies upon unstated assumptions about the neutrality or the stability of broader structures, and these points need not be repeated here. What needs to be emphasized, though, is a related argument: state authorities' conceptions of the range and feasibility of adjustment strategies will reflect an implicit judgement about the boundaries of practical and legitimate behaviour which in turn will be derived however indirectly from the prevailing normative climate and constraints. It is at this point that one can begin to see the outlines of a possible reconciliation between the revised realism of Ikenberry and others and the critical approaches of Cox and his followers.

Conclusions: towards a synthesis?

This chapter has set out to provide not only a critique of existing theories about the relationship between the changing European order and European foreign policies, but also some ideas about the ways in which analytical progress might be made. In doing so, it has focused particularly on the notion of the active state as implied by Ikenberry's approach, and on the apparently conflicting approach through critical theory as espoused by Cox. As already noted, parts of the Ikenberry approach fall into the realm of problem-solving theory, emphasizing state strategies in response to shifts in domestic and international bargaining conditions. According to Cox, this form of analysis can contribute little to understanding in conditions where the foundations of order are in question and where there is little in the way of consensus about what foreign policy, or for that matter the state itself, is *for*. According to Ikenberry, it is important to explore and evaluate state strategies even where the broader order is at issue, since this will uncover the limits within which state authorities can mobilize support and undertake purposive action. The condition of Europe in the 1990s, as outlined in the earlier parts of the chapter, clearly raises questions about the relationship between stability and change, between the parts and the whole of the European order, and the capacity of state authorities to respond. These effectively span the divide between the Ikenberry and the Cox approaches, since it is one of the prime contentions of the chapter in general that the most interesting problems for FPA arise at the intersection of the parts and the whole.

From this starting point, it is possible to see that the contrasting perspectives symbolized by Ikenberry and Cox are more like different cuts from the same cake. Although there will no doubt be those who would argue that they are incommensurable on grounds of values and the role given to the reflexive as opposed to the rational mode of analysis, this is not the position taken here. Indeed, the argument espoused by Cox, that both classical realism and structuralist theories are effectively critical given their focus on and sensitivity to the forces of history, seems to provide the basis for a fruitful synthesis of the perspectives. More directly, they seem to intersect with the neo-liberal institutionalist approach adopted by Keohane and others (Keohane, 1988). It is here that one can begin to ask relevant questions about the ways in which foreign policy actions interact with the broader structures of values and institutions which are central to the developing European order.

How precisely might this be followed through? It appears that there are a number of intersecting propositions to which attention should be paid, and which have been central to the argument in this chapter:

1   The European order of the 1990s is complex, fluid and multi-layered. It thus raises important questions about the ownership of the order, about the relationships between the parts and the

whole, and about the capacity of state authorities to respond to change.

2   One approach to this problem is to emphasize the strategies adopted by state authorities in attempting to respond to changes in the order, and to balance the demands of the domestic audience and international (European or global) forces. Here, it is helpful to focus on the search for legitimacy and survival, and to explore the range of actions available to state authorities, which may or may not be adequate to the demands of the changing order.

3   At the same time, it is important to maintain a clear view of the ways in which the European order is changing, and the strength of its normative and institutional foundations. Given the focus of state strategies on the costs of adjustment (which are not simply material, but also relate to legitimacy and factors such as reputation), it is apparent that the absence of consensus about the rules of the order, and the uncertainty of recourse to international institutions, is a factor in the foreign policy actions and strategies to which reference has already been made.

4   Because of this intersection between state strategies and the international order, there is a crucial role to be played by international institutions. These institutions for Cox embody the elements of a normative consensus and set the limits of legitimate behaviour by states and other actors. For Ikenberry, they are essential to the defraying of costs (both material and non-material) incurred in the pursuit of state strategies.

5   This line of argument leads clearly to a neo-liberal institutional analysis. Such an analysis focuses on the functions performed by international institutions not only in national strategies (for example by providing information and spreading the costs of action) but also in the world order (by expressing a normative consensus and establishing rules by which to judge legitimacy). As set out by Keohane (1988, Chapter 1), the approach not only entails instrumental judgements about the regulation of international transactions or the costs to state authorities of participation; it also permits a focus on prevailing expectations and normative considerations affecting the validity and solidity of international agreements.

What, though, does such an analysis tell us about the state of Europe in the 1990s, actually and prospectively? As already noted, part of the problem with the changing European order is the lack of consensus and the incidence of change which threatens to burst the limits both of state adjustment capacities and of international institutions. The crowded institutional stage, and the existence of many state authorities whose legitimacy and capacity to act are in question, does not invalidate the neo-liberal institutional approach, since it is part of the essence of that approach that institutions both reflect and affect the changing order. The incapacities of international conventions, regimes or authorities are thus not a reason for jettisoning the approach; they are rather a reason for exploring its applicability to admittedly extreme conditions, in both the East and the West of Europe. By drawing attention to the intersection of national strategy, international norms and frameworks of rules, the approach does not solve the problem, either analytically or empirically. It does, however, throw it into sharper relief and render it capable of further research.

3

The Long-Term Future of European Security: Perpetual Anarchy or Community of Democracies?

Thomas Risse-Kappen

There seems to be no end to the revolutionary transformation of world politics which we have been experiencing since 1985. First came the Gorbachev revolution with *perestroika* and *glasnost*, resulting in a fundamental reorientation of Soviet foreign policy towards common security and international institution-building. When the West had just begun to grasp the significance of these changes, Soviet foreign policy revoked the Brezhnev doctrine, thereby enabling the emerging civil societies in central Eastern Europe to overthrow the communist regime through peaceful revolutions. The Warsaw Pact collapsed together with the Berlin Wall. Germany became united, before West and East Germans had time to think about the political, economic, cultural and psychological consequences. When Europe was just starting to adapt to the new situation, the coup attempt in Moscow occurred. Its failure showed that the forces of *perestroika* which Gorbachev had unleashed six years previously, and over which he had long lost control, finally saved him. The events in Moscow demonstrated the presence of a civil society and of emerging democratic institutions in the former Soviet Union. It is only understandable that the republics then rushed to deconstruct the central authoritarian state and that the Soviet Union ceased to exist. What will be the result? Will the new Commonwealth of Independent States (CIS) further disintegrate, leading to increasing conflicts and ultimately wars within and between the various former Soviet republics? In other words, will the successor states of the Soviet Union follow the Yugoslav script? Or will a democratic confederation of interdependent republics emerge out of the ashes of the Soviet state? And what are the implications of these developments for the future of European security?

International relations theory cannot answer these questions.

Rather than predict the future, I will outline in this chapter several possible pathways based on the assumptions of various theories. I will discuss four theoretical approaches and their predictions about European security: structural realism, realism-cum-cooperation, liberal republicanism and institutionalism. The first concept – based on peculiar notions about the peacekeeping forces of both bipolarity and nuclear weapons – forecasts that the post-Cold-War order will be nasty and brutish. The other three approaches, however, lead to surprisingly similar conclusions concerning a transition period to the institutionalization of a European peace order.

But they predict entirely different long-term futures. The 'cooperation under anarchy' perspective foresees the continued presence of the security dilemma which has to be constantly mitigated through security regimes and international institutions. Republicanism and institutionalism – two variants of liberal theory in international relations – predict the extension of the peaceful OECD world towards central Eastern Europe and the successor states of the Soviet Union. In other words, a community of democratic nations will emerge from Tokyo to San Francisco to Berlin and – hopefully – to Vladivostok.

The jury is, of course, out as to which prediction will prevail. However, I will argue that we can draw on insights from the past, particularly from interaction patterns in the transatlantic relationship as well as the European Community. Empirical analyses of these processes seem to suggest that liberal theories of international relations offer a better and richer understanding of cooperation among liberal democracies than traditional realist approaches. As a result, one can conclude that stable peace among liberal democracies is indeed possible.[1]

International relations theories and the future of European security

Structural realism: the nasty and brutish post-Cold-War world

Realist approaches to international politics share the assumptions that states

1   are the most important actors in world politics;
2   can be conceptualized as unitary, rational actors;
3   calculate their interests in terms of the relative distribution of power in the international system; and
4   have to look after themselves in a self-help system (anarchy).

Structural realism from Thomas Hobbes to Kenneth Waltz (1979) offers a straightforward explanation of the 'long peace' (Gaddis, 1987) after World War II and a gloomy prediction of European post-Cold-War disorder. In this view, a bipolar international order tends to be more peaceful than a multipolar one, since it ensures the predictability of behaviour of states. There are only two great powers in the system which by necessity are locked into a hegemonic rivalry. Smaller states, when forced to choose sides, will flock to the weaker power. In the end, a stable balance-of-power system emerges. Moreover, nuclear weapons make hegemonic wars irrational – and the long peace emerges.

John Lewis Gaddis (1991), John Mearsheimer (1990) and Kenneth Waltz (1993) have spelled out the consequences of this argument for the future of European security. After the breakdown of bipolarity as a consequence of the changes in the Soviet Union and in central Eastern Europe, the continent is returning to multipolarity with its ever-shifting coalitions. As a result, the new Europe will be fairly unpredictable and unstable. Nationalist and ethnic conflicts will spill over to the international level since they are no longer frozen under the bipolar order. The end of the Soviet central state will result in civil wars involving potentially nuclear armed states compared with which the Yugoslav civil war has been rather benign. The only hope would be 'managed nuclear proliferation', i.e. giving nuclear weapons to a united Germany.

There are various theoretical and empirical problems with this argument. First, the theory does not specify how the systemic condition of bipolarity and the unit-level power resource of nuclear weapons relate to each other in producing the long peace (Lebow, 1994). The thrust of Waltz's original theory focusing on structural conditions in the international system would suggest that bipolarity is the overriding stabilizer. Various attempts, however, to test the assumption that bipolar orders tend to be more peaceful than multipolar systems have been unsuccessful, suggesting that the number of poles in the system is underdetermining with respect to its war-proneness (Christensen and Snyder, 1990; Hopf, 1991; Levy, 1985; Van Evera, 1990/91, pp. 33–40). The proposition that bipolarity tends to be more stable and/or peaceful than multipolarity cannot be substantiated empirically.

Second, if the presence of nuclear weapons is considered the primary cause for the long peace, as the policy prescription in favour of managed nuclear proliferation suggests, structural realism has problems explaining *why* this should be the case. It is almost tautological to argue that mutual annihilation in an all-out nuclear war is irrational. But this does not lead to the logical conclusion that, therefore, nuclear weapons should not be used under any circumstances, even on a small-scale tactical level, or that both sides should avoid crises, confrontations or conventional skirmishes.[2] The norm of no (first) use of nuclear weapons took years to emerge, and both sides had to go through serious confrontations culminating in the Cuban missile crisis until they learned to restrain their conflict behaviour (Blair and Gottfried, 1988; Lebow, 1987; Lebow and Stein, 1994). Moreover, throughout nuclear history, a huge gap has existed between the self-deterring effects of nuclear weapons to induce caution and restraint on the one hand, and declaratory strategies and targeting doctrines emphasizing escalation control and even the ability to win nuclear wars on the other. In sum, the practices of the states – 'nuclear learning' – established the war-preventing and crisis-restraining function of nuclear weapons (Nye, 1987). Structural realism, which does not appreciate the principal openness of historical processes, cannot account for this.

Third, Mearsheimer's 'solution' – German acquisition of nuclear weapons – may actually make things worse. To begin with, German nuclear power does nothing to contain potential ethnic and nationalist conflicts such as those experienced in former Yugoslavia. At best, therefore, the proliferation of nuclear weapons to other European states is irrelevant with regard to the new conflict scenarios. At worst, it would add a new conflict dimension to what is already a difficult situation, given the breakup of the Soviet Union. Just imagine what might have happened in former Yugoslavia if Serbia, Croatia or Bosnia had been nuclear powers. This, however, is the scenario which Europe would have to face if violent conflicts broke out among the successor states of the Soviet Union. One has to be a very strong believer in nuclear deterrence to conclude that these potential conflicts would be restrained rather than exacerbated through nuclear proliferation.[3]

Even if one shares the prediction about a gloomy European future, one does not have to agree with the structural realist explanation for it. Nationalist and ethnic conflicts as experienced in former Yugoslavia and Armenia which might escalate on a much larger scale in other parts of the former Soviet Union do not result from the end of the bipolar order. These issues are first and foremost the consequence of more than 40 years of oppressive regimes which suppressed nationalist tendencies without regulating them in a peaceful way. Ethnic rivalries as such, however, do not necessarily lead to violent conflicts. Only combined with other economic and political conflicts do they threaten to result in internal violence, civil or even inter-state wars. In a similar way, the migration problems which the richer European countries are facing from both the East and the South are not simply *caused* by the breakdown of the bipolar Cold War order. They result from the welfare gap between the European Community countries and the poorer regions in Eastern Europe, the Middle East and Africa. Moreover, they are only likely to escalate if this welfare gap widens and/or the economic recovery in Eastern Europe and in the CIS stalls.

In sum, it is one thing to be concerned about the future problems of European security. It is quite different to accept the structural realist explanation and thus to conclude that practically nothing can be done about these potential conflicts short of a re-creation of some sort of Cold War order.

Cooperation under anarchy: fragile peace
Structural realism argues that states are doomed to take care of their own security in an essentially hostile world and that only an international quasi-Leviathan such as a hegemonic power or a tight bipolar structure might provide temporary relief from the repercussions of international anarchy. In contrast, John Locke's argument about rational individuals entering into a social contract, thereby ending the pre-social condition of nature and creating the state, can also be transferred into the realm of international relations. In fact, the cooperation under anarchy approach to international regimes shares the core realist assumptions about anarchy and states as rational, unitary actors, but disagrees with the structural realists that cooperation should, therefore, be rather impossible. Rational state actors might embark on cooperative behaviour to solve 'dilemmas of common interests and common aversion' (Stein, 1983; 1990; cf. also Keohane 1983; 1989; Oye, 1986). In the security area, this modified version of the realist argument is frequently linked to the notion of the security dilemma which allows for cooperative solutions under certain, specified conditions, particularly in long-term relationships (Herz, 1951; Jervis, 1978).

This perspective agrees with structural realism that the end of the Cold War has terminated the hegemonic rivalry between the US and the Soviet Union. Hegemonic conflicts, which are extremely sensitive to relative gains, do not easily lead to cooperative solutions: hence the difficulties of developing effective arms control regimes during the past decades (Rittberger, 1990; Rittberger and Zürn, 1991). However, while the hegemonic rivalry has gone, the security dilemma remains, but can be mitigated through international institutions and regime-building (see Kupchan and Kupchan, 1991; Snyder, 1990). The new Europe is better suited for such cooperative endeavours since the overall game changed from a mixed deadlock/prisoner's-dilemma (PD) structure to pure PD.[4] Moreover, international regimes in Europe do not have to be invented; they already exist – from the EC to the Conference on Security and Cooperation in Europe (CSCE) – and only need to be adjusted to the new tasks.

The cooperation under anarchy perspective shares the realist assumption that the new Europe will be a conflict-loaded place because of the ever-present security dilemma. Internal economic and political conflicts, ethnic and nationalistic rivalries are always threatening to spill over into the international system. In other words, a stable and perpetual European peace order is impossible and cooperative arrangements can always be terminated if states as the dominant actors in world politics change their interests and conclude that regimes no longer suit them. Modified realists nevertheless argue in contrast to structural realists that temporary cooperation among states is possible to pursue mutual gains and, thus, to prevent crises from escalating into armed conflicts and to build regimes enhancing cooperation.

Republicanism: perpetual peace among liberal democracies

Liberal views of world politics disagree with realism on at least two counts (Czempiel, 1986; Doyle, 1986; Keohane, 1990a):

1   States are not treated as unitary actors. Domestic political processes and structures account for variances in state behaviour.
2   Anarchy is not the predominant feature of the international system. As a pure self-help system, it only forms one end of a spectrum of more or less regulated behaviour rather than the norm (integration being the other end).

It follows that liberal approaches to world politics regard international cooperation not as exceptional but as far more common than realists would concede. To begin with, liberal republicanism holds that democracies behave more cooperatively in their relations with each other than authoritarian states do. This assertion has been empirically supported with regard to the use of military force. Democracies rarely fight each other (cf. *Journal of Conflict Resolution*, 1991; Maoz and Russett, 1991; Russett, 1993). However, this proposition only applies for relations among democratic systems. Republicanism does not suggest that democracies should behave cooperatively when dealing with authoritarian regimes.

It follows that the theory does not claim to explain East–West relations in the past, but offers an analysis of the underlying conflict structure which differs from realism. Liberalism holds that the East–West conflict was first and foremost an ideological dispute about human rights and the organization of political and economic life (Czempiel, 1984; Link, 1988; Schlesinger, 1967). This would account for the viciousness with which it has been fought and the difficulties in reaching even partial cooperative agreements. Now the Cold War is over not just because of Soviet hegemonic decline, but primarily because liberal values have won the competition over the more attractive political and economic system (cf. Deudney and Ikenberry, 1991a).

Republicanism holds that the security dilemma will be substantially reduced once Europe has become 'whole and free' (George Bush). The European states will move towards 'complex interdependence' (Keohane and Nye, 1977) as is already the case in the OECD world. There will be (trade) conflicts in the new Europe, but they will not result in militarized disputes or the use of force. After all, the members of the European Community do not maintain armed forces to provide for security against each other (at least, French suspicions about German intentions do not provide enough legitimacy to preserve large-scale armed forces). In other words, republicanism posits that the danger of armed conflict in the new Europe will be close to zero and that, therefore, the forces can be reduced to extremely low levels of armament except, maybe, for out-of-area threats. Liberals would then predict that the EC and the CSCE can be transformed into a 'pacific federation' – a stable peace order among liberal republics (Kant, 1795).

However, it should be noted that the assumptions of the theory apply only to *stable democracies* in which strong political institutions guarantee human rights and the rule of law. Republicanism has less to say for the current phase in which the central Eastern European states are still in transition towards democratic systems and market economies and in which the future of Russia remains in flux. This situation is simply beyond the scope of the argument. Since the transition phase might last for quite some time, republicanism is less relevant for what used to be called East–West relations in Europe, at least in the near term. But the theory offers at least the long-term perspective of stable peace in the northern hemisphere.

As it stands, the theory currently applies only to relations within the OECD world. Here, liberalism predicts that, despite current and frequent trade conflicts between North America, South East Asia and the EC, their relations are unlikely to degenerate into three competing trading blocs. The successful conclusion of the Uruguay Round and the strengthening of the GATT regime confirms liberal expectations.

Institutionalism: peace through international community-building

In contrast to the cooperation under anarchy perspective, which sees stable cooperation as possible but rather fragile in international relations because of the ever-present security dilemma, liberal institutionalism views world politics as essentially rule-governed. International society is regulated by practices, conventions, regimes, and international organizations on various levels of institutionalization. State interests are not taken as exogenously given, but are shaped and transformed by the interaction of international norms and domestic processes. Notions such as 'power' and 'anarchy' are themselves socially and historically constructed and represent shared understandings among the actors in international society (see, for example, Bull, 1977; Kratochwil, 1989; Wendt, 1992a; Young, 1989).

Liberal institutionalism interprets the Cold War system as essentially composed of two worlds governed by different norms and understandings among the actors. On the one hand, there has been the highly institutionalized OECD world characterized by complex interdependence and a sense of community among the states. More than 30 years ago, Karl W. Deutsch called this world a 'pluralistic security community' based upon shared values about political decision-making, mutual responsiveness towards each other's needs, international institutions favouring communication and consultation, and the mutual predictability of behaviour (Deutsch et al., 1957). In other words, traditional notions of economic and military power are incapable of explaining the interaction patterns inside a pluralistic security community. The notion comes close to and elaborates on what Immanuel Kant called the pacific federation among liberal republics.

On the other hand, there has been the world of the East–West conflict governed by rules of 'restrained confrontation' and 'antagonistic cooperation', by a strange mix of deterrence and *détente* practices which frequently contradicted each other and thus led to new frictions (Garthoff, 1985; Link, 1988; Zellentin, 1976). The Cold War was over and the sea-change occurred when the Soviet leadership under Gorbachev embraced the notion of common security which, while not creating a community of purpose in the strict sense, nevertheless transcended the traditional understanding of security as unilaterally achievable (Koslowski and Kratochwil, 1994). Common security was essentially a concept developed by the Western arms control and peace research community. It apparently found its way to the new thinkers in the former Soviet Union through transnational East–West contacts including, for example, the Palme Commission (1982) and the Pugwash movement, as well as social democratic and labour party exchanges with the former communist parties in East Europe and the Soviet Union (Risse-Kappen, 1994b).

Of course, if common security defines the rules of the interaction, institution-building should not be difficult. Given the revolutionary transformation processes in central Eastern Europe and Russia, institutionalists would therefore argue that the new Europe is in far better shape today than ever in its history to build the kind of international institutions which would help to stabilize the transition period towards a Europe of democratic welfare states (Senghaas, 1990; Van Evera, 1990/91). The EC project towards a single market and monetary as well as political union would be quoted by liberal institutionalists as supporting evidence.

In sum, those who argue from the cooperation under anarchy perspective, and liberal institutionalists, agree in their predictions and prescriptions concerning the current transition period in the new Europe, albeit for different reasons. They both emphasize the necessity of international institutions and regimes to deal with the conflicts which might occur in the immediate future. They part company, however, when it comes to the long-term perspective. While even modified realists cannot imagine a world without a security dilemma, liberal republicanists and institutionalists visualize a pluralistic security community in the northern hemisphere in which the use of force is excluded and disputes are resolved by peaceful means. Thus the two liberal approaches – republicanism and institutionalism – are easily reconcilable and complement each other.[5]

Enduring security dilemma or democratic community of nations? Lessons from the past

It is, of course, impossible to predict which of the four visions of the future European security will ultimately carry the day. However, past experience might offer some insights with regard to the main dividing lines between realism, 'cooperation under anarchy', and the two liberal approaches. The various theories offer distinct propositions concerning cooperation among states which can be tested by looking at the interactions in the OECD world over the last 40 years, in particular the transatlantic relationship, NATO and the EC. If it turns out that some approaches offer better explanations of past behaviour among democratic states than others, we could infer that they might also provide better guidelines for the future.

Stable cooperation among states poses, of course, an anomaly for structural realism which has to resort to auxiliary hypotheses to account for the transatlantic as well as the inter-European cooperation. Two approaches in the realist tradition might be looked at for answers: alliance theory and hegemonic stability theory.

To begin with, *alliance theory* would argue that cooperation among the Western states was a function of the perceived Soviet threat (Mearsheimer, 1990; Walt, 1987; Waltz, 1979). Cooperation resulted from the necessity to pool resources in order to globally contain Soviet power during the Cold War. While this account seems to offer a plausible explanation for the transatlantic security relationship, one has to make additional assumptions concerning the EC process. John Mearsheimer (1990), for example, has argued that, since security concerns override economic issues in the realist world, the economic cooperation in Western Europe was necessitated by alliance considerations in the light of the Soviet threat.

If this account is true, alliance cohesion during the Cold War should have been a function of the perceived level of threat: the more the allies were scared, the more they should have stuck together. In other words, intra-Western cooperation should have been greatest in times of East–West crises, while cracks in the relationship should have occurred during periods of *détente*. This assumption can be refuted. There is almost no correlation between the degree of alliance cohesion in the transatlantic relationship and the degree of East–West tensions (cf. Chernoff, 1992; Risse-Kappen 1994a). On the one hand, alliance cohesion was comparatively high during the Berlin crises of the 1950s and the Cuban missile crisis in 1962. On the other hand, Europeans strongly disagreed with US foreign policy both during the Korean War of 1950–3 and in the aftermath of the Soviet intervention in Afghanistan of 1980–1. The same holds true for the periods of US–Soviet *détente* during the Cold War. Britain strongly supported superpower arms control during the late 1950s and 1960s, while France and Germany were originally opposed to it. From the 1970s on, the Federal Republic became the staunchest supporter of East–West *détente* and arms control. While all

European allies came out in favour of the SALT negotiations, there was intra-allied friction over intermediate-range nuclear forces (INF) and arms control during the 1970s. Later on, however, all West European governments strongly opposed the attempts of the Reagan administration to terminate US–Soviet arms control efforts. Finally, the evolution of the European integration process seems equally unrelated to the overall state of East–West tensions. At least, one should have expected growing difficulties in the EC 1992 project when the Cold War faded. The opposite was the case, at least initially. In sum, the degree of intra-Western cooperation and conflict during the Cold War seems to be unrelated to the level of East–West tensions, as alliance theory would suggest.

A second approach in the realist tradition, *hegemonic stability theory*, argues that cooperation among states occurs if there is a hegemonic enforcer keeping order in the system (Gilpin, 1981; Kindleberger, 1973; for critical accounts see Grunberg, 1990; Keohane, 1984; Snidal, 1985). Cooperation among the weaker states would result from the presence of a hegemonic power which guarantees and enforces the rules. Hegemonic stability theory then predicts that such cooperative arrangements break down as a result of hegemonic decline. While there is an ongoing debate about the extent to which the US economic status in the world has actually declined over the past decades (cf. Kennedy, 1987; Nye, 1990; Russett, 1985), it is probably safe to argue that the US position *vis-à-vis* Europe has markedly changed from the 1950s as compared with, say, the 1980s. If the theory holds true, intra-Western cooperation should have become markedly more difficult during these recent years as compared with the early post-war period when US military and economic superiority was undisputed.

However, while the post-war global economic order is usually explained in terms of US hegemony, it is hard to see how this might account for the European integration process except, maybe, for its very beginning (cf. Hoffmann and Keohane, 1991; Wallace, 1990). The Marshall Aid Plan was indeed coupled with an American insistence on European economic cooperation. However, how can the continuing regional cooperation in Europe be explained in terms of hegemonic stability theory? Even if one argues that, for example, the European monetary system was a response to the breakdown of the Bretton Woods system resulting from American decline, this response is outside the realm of the theory. Once the hegemonic enforcer is gone, cooperation among the lesser powers should also decline rather than increase, as was the case with the EC.

With regard to NATO and the transatlantic security relationship, hegemonic stability theory suggests that intra-alliance cooperation should have been greater during the 1950s than, say, during the 1980s. The examples quoted above challenge this assumption. There does not seem to be any marked increase in NATO conflicts over time. Out-of-area issues, for example, have been constantly on the agenda of the Western alliance, from the Korean War and the Suez crisis to the Gulf War; so too have been conflicts about military strategy, from graduated deterrence to flexible response to the disputes over INF (cf. Risse-Kappen, 1988; Schwartz, 1983; Sherwood, 1990; Stuart and Tow, 1990). At the same time, intra-alliance conflicts have been solved cooperatively more often than not, with again no easily observable variation over time.

In sum, one would have to stretch structural realism to its limits in order to provide an explanation for the stable pattern of cooperation among the Western democracies throughout the Cold War. At the same time, the cooperation under anarchy perspective as well as republicanism or institutionalism should have no trouble in accounting for the security and economic cooperation in both the transatlantic and the intra-European relationships. Thus the three approaches agree over the cooperative *outcomes* of intra-Western relations. They part company, however, when it comes to the *processes* of interaction among states. Those who agree with the realist model of the state as a unitary, rational actor, describe cooperation essentially in terms of inter-state relations in which state interests are exogenously given (cf. Wendt, 1992a). Norms of international cooperation emerge only if they are in the interests of the respective states. At best, norms change state behaviour; they are not conceptualized as affecting the underlying preferences and interests.

Liberal theorists, on the other hand, emphasize the rule-governed character of international relations. International norms influence not only behaviour but also the way in which state actors perceive and define their interests. Regime norms become deeply embedded in the domestic discourses of the states, not only in determining outcomes but in framing the debates with regard to what is considered permissible behaviour (cf. Müller, 1993). As a result, norms contribute to change in the identity of actors. Moreover, liberal republicanists would argue that democracies tend to externalize their internal decision-making norms when dealing with other democracies to the extent that the distribution of economic and military power becomes almost irrelevant to explain interaction patterns among them. Finally, the liberal theory of international relations emphasizes *transnational relations* involving non-state actors as well as *transgovernmental coalition-building* which refers to instances when subunits of national governments ally with other subunits to pursue their goals in the absence of formal state decisions (Kaiser, 1969; Keohane and Nye, 1972; 1974; 1977).

There is growing evidence[6] that the liberal perspective indeed offers a richer and more adequate understanding of the interaction processes among the Western democracies than the interest-based and state-centred cooperation under anarchy account. As regards *NATO decisions* on military strategy and force deployments, accounts which predict outcomes on the basis of the distribution of power in the alliance do not offer good explanations for those decisions. The conventional wisdom, for example, that the US as the alliance leader got its way most of the time, is contradicted by the available evidence (Chernoff, 1992). NATO decisions on nuclear strategy and US nuclear deployments in Europe resembled much more alliance compromises than simply US preferences. For example, the flexible response doctrine (MC 14/3) adopted by the NATO Council in 1967 was very different from the original US plans put forward by the Kennedy administration (Buteux, 1983; Daalder, 1991; Stromseth, 1988). The same holds true for the most divisive nuclear issue NATO faced in the late 1970s and early 1980s: INF modernization and arms control. The alliance decisions pertaining both to the buildup and to arms control came closer to European initial preferences than to the original US plans (Daalder, 1991; Risse-Kappen, 1988).

Moreover, NATO decisions frequently resulted from transgovernmental coalitions. Even the alliance formation itself was the product of such coalition-building processes when US, British and French senior officials in the late 1940s first achieved consensus among themselves and only then gathered the necessary support in their respective capitals (Cook, 1989; Henderson, 1982; Riste, 1985). Similar transgovernmental alliances between mainly German Foreign Office and US State Department officials account for much of the INF story (Daalder, 1991; Risse-Kappen, 1988).

However, one can always argue with regard to NATO decisions involving European security affairs that cooperative bargaining and not simply US dominance should be expected, given the supreme West European interests at stake in such cases. I therefore studied whether and how European allies influenced American foreign policy in out-of-area and strategic arms control cases (Risse-Kappen 1994a). The evidence by and large confirmed the liberal assumptions about interaction processes among democracies. First, it can be shown that the US defined its national interests and thus its own identity in terms of being part of a community of democratic nations. Second, consultation norms secured European impact on decisions in vital cases such as, for example, the (non-)use of nuclear weapons during the Korean War. The interaction process was found to be heavily regulated by such norms which, even if they were violated in some cases, led to peculiar patterns of behaviour. Moreover, such norms became embedded in the domestic decision-making processes as predicted by liberal institutionalism. Finally, as was the case with many NATO decisions, transgovernmental coalition-building frequently guaranteed European influence on US decisions by tipping the internal bureaucratic balance in favour of the allied demands.

Analyses of decision-making processes within the European Community seem to confirm the argument (cf. Hoffmann and Keohane, 1991; Nugent, 1988; H. Wallace et al., 1983; W. Wallace 1990). The ongoing debate whether the EC 1992 process is driven by traditional inter-state bargains (Moravcsik, 1991) or by supranational integration (Sandholtz and Zysman, 1989) could be solved if republicanist and institutionalist arguments are brought in. Rather than engaging in fruitless debates between neo-functionalist integration theories emphasizing spillover processes and cooperation under anarchy viewpoints focusing on inter-state regime-building, analysts might look at normative integration as well as transnational and transgovernmental coalition-building. There is evidence that European institution-building has led to a redefinition of the identities of the various member states towards cooperative federalism. Decision-making in the European Community seems to resemble institutional rather than distributive bargaining (Young, 1989), that is to be framed by and embedded in the norms of the institution. As a result, national decision-making processes of the EC member countries would be influenced by the norms of European integration which change the nature of the domestic debates, as well as by transnational and trans-governmental coalition-building across state borders. Focusing on inter-state bargains in the European Council and the Council of Ministers obscures the view on the origins of the national decisions which are themselves heavily influenced by the institution.

Conclusions

This chapter has proceeded in two steps. First, I have laid out various theoretical approaches and their predictions about the future of European security in a post-Cold-War environment. It is, of course, impossible to predict which of the various paradigms will carry the day. Second, however, I have argued that a careful analysis of the cooperation among the Western democracies during the past 40 years might provide at least a glimpse of what to expect in the future. I have, therefore, sketched out how the four approaches would account for both the transatlantic and the intra-European relationships in the past. I have then tried to provide evidence that seems to suggest that liberal republican and institutionalist explanations offer a better and richer understanding of why and how democratic states are likely to build strong cooperative ties and institutions across issue areas.

This historical argument has two limitations, though. First, it is subject to historical contingency which one might have missed by looking at only a few variables to explain state behaviour. Second and more important, the argument pertains only to *stable* democratic systems. To infer from this that a peaceful community of democratic states is likely to emerge from Tokyo to San Francisco to Vladivostok implies that the current transition process in Eastern Europe and Russia can be managed and that backlashes can be avoided. It should be noted that this is a very big 'if' and that the transition process might take quite some time, as the war in former Yugoslavia and the internal turmoil in Russia and in other successor states of the former Soviet Union suggest.

However, fleshing out various futures of European security resulting from different theoretical approaches is not just an academic exercise. The paradigm in which policy-makers believe might determine which type of action they choose. In other words, gloomy or optimistic predictions of the future in an environment characterized by the uncertainties of the post-Cold-War world might become self-fulfilling prophecies. Thus, if it can be shown that a pacific federation of democratic states is indeed a possibility for the northern hemisphere and that the nasty and brutish world of realism can be overcome, this implies a moral obligation for policy-makers and social actors alike to work in this direction. To let slip the opportunity of building a stable peace order would also prevent Europe from being able to cope with the challenges of poverty in the South and of looming ecological catastrophes facing our planet.

Notes

1 The following analysis is rather sketchy and therefore simplistic because of space constraints and for the sake of making the argument clearer. Each of the four approaches discussed below are, of course, much richer and more complex than

presented here. For more detailed discussions see Risse-Kappen (1991) and Grunberg and Risse-Kappen (1992).

2 In fact, the strategic literature which shares all rational deterrence assumptions is almost equally split on precisely this point. Part of the deterrence debate has always maintained that nuclear weapons should be treated like any other weapon. See, for example, Gray (1979) and Wohlstetter (1985). For overviews and discussions see Jervis (1989) and Kull (1988).

3 Note, however, that John Mearsheimer (1990) does not support unconditional nuclear proliferation. Rather, he advocates nuclear weapons in the hands of 'reasonable' powers such as Germany. The question is then whether such proliferation can be contained once it has been started and, even if it can, whether it would do any good to deal with the likely conflict scenarios in the new Europe.

4 The preference order of 'deadlock' is $DC > DD > CC > CD$, where D stands for defection/non-cooperation and C stands for cooperation. Thus, mutual confrontation is generally preferred to mutual cooperation. In contrast, the preference order of a 'prisoner's dilemma' is $DC > CC > DD > CD$. Thus, there is at least the possibility for cooperative solutions under specific conditions (Downs et al., 1986; Downs and Rocke, 1987).

5 It should be noted that my interpretation of these theoretical traditions differs from the British institutionalists such as Hedley Bull and Martin Wight who, in my view, overemphasize the differences between the Kantian and the institutionalist traditions in international relations. Their interpretation seems to be based on a misunderstanding of Kant's 'perpetual peace' as an argument in favour of world government when, in fact, he claims that liberal republics are likely to form a 'pacific federation' which is not that far from concepts of international society as heavily institutionalized and rule-governed (cf. Bull, 1977; Kant, 1795).

6 The problem is, though, that the majority of studies on NATO and the transatlantic relationship are implicitly written from a state-centred, realist point of view. As a result, many authors do not even look at norms, transnational relations, and transgovernmental coalitions to explain outcomes.

4

Foreign Economic Policy in the New Europe: a Theoretical Audit of a Questionable Category

Roger Tooze

This chapter will focus on the problems of understanding 'foreign' economic policy and the arena of that policy, the global political economy, in the changing European foreign policy context.[1] The very inclusion of such a focus in a volume concerned with theory and foreign policy is itself noteworthy and, indeed, rather rare. The fact that this is so relates directly to the nature and purpose of the volume as a whole.

The study of foreign economic policy (FEP) has a long historical pedigree, particularly in its early links with mercantilism. The creation of an international and later a global economy naturally focuses the attention of governments on the policies necessary to achieve domestic and foreign economic goals. Examples of the problems of FEP are prominent in the history of most national political economies, but the modern study of FEP has been principally developed by American academics. This reflects both the supremacy of the United States in the post-1945 global political economy and the dominance of US scholars in the academic realm of international relations (IR). In this context FEP was developed as part of the increased attention given to the politics of international economic relations and then international political economy, taking its lead from the *economic* sphere rather than developing as an extension of (political) foreign policy analysis (FPA). The link between academic and intellectual production and the global political economy has been explained thus:

> The foreign economic actions taken by American officials . . . continue to have profound consequences for other states in the international system, as well as for American domestic politics and economics. Thus it is not surprising that the study of American foreign economic policy attracts considerable scholarly attention, and presently constitutes a major portion of the subfield of international political economy. (Ikenberry et al., 1988b, p. 1)

The genealogy of the discourses of international relations suggested

Figure 4.1   *Genealogy of IR discourses*

by this (admittedly ethnocentric) characterization is interesting, and can be represented by Figure 4.1. In this figure, any consideration of 'foreign economic policy' in Europe is presented with the prospect of using not the literature of foreign policy analysis as may have been expected, but the literature of international political economy. The separation and distinctiveness of these two approaches to international relations is remarked upon by James Rosenau as 'the puzzle of why the rapidly growing emphasis on international political economy (IPE) as an organizing focus for political scientists has had virtually no impact on the systematic or comparative study of foreign policy (CFP) and, indeed, why the latter has apparently been so irrelevant to the former' (Rosenau, 1988, p. 17). Rosenau's answer to this question is interesting, not least because it tells us about the condition of theory in contemporary FPA. He concludes that 'the gulf between the subfields is sustained by the nature of the outcomes that follow from the action that each regards as central' (1988, p. 22), and the differences in outcomes relate primarily to the distinction between the macro focus of IPE and the micro focus of FPA.

However, whatever the reasons for the 'formulation and conduct of foreign economic policy stand[ing] apart as a separate form of activity' (Rosenau, 1988, p. 20), the implication is that the theoretical resources (that is the empirical content of metatheoretical discourse) that this discussion is concerned with are not necessarily the same resources that most of the other chapters use. This changes not only the range of theories that are relevant but also the kind of questions that need to be asked about these theories.

Hence, the study of foreign economic policy sits uneasily beside the practice of foreign policy analysis: not a part of FPA, but nominally sharing the same broad empirical referents. FEP is appropriately linked to the development of international political economy, and is therefore reflective of the assumptions and values of what has become the orthodoxy of IPE, with all the benefits and costs that this entails (Murphy and Tooze, 1991). Consequently, this chapter has to deal with an additional set of questions because of its focus on a category of action/events/meaning that although nominally part of foreign policy does not share many of the characteristics of that field as presently defined.

Foreign economic policy in Europe

Facts are constituted theoretically. There can be no empirical domain without a pre-existing theory. Hence, the simple description of the complex empirical domain of FEP in Europe against which to evaluate existing FEP theory is not possible. Any such description can only be done on the basis of other theories. So what follows is the articulation of *a* description of the empirical domain that identifies certain features and problems for the purposes of this discussion. One key feature of this description of the empirical domain of Europe in this context is the multiplicity of levels and the complexity of structures, processes and organizations, which change the nature of the state as structure as well as the capacity of the state as agent. But this empirical feature, among a range of others, forces us to consider theoretical problems of explanation in terms of complex agent–structure relationships and could (should) serve to move us towards alternative ontologies, which in turn would pose different questions and produce different descriptions.

The empirical domain of foreign economic policy

'Foreign economic policy' as a term contains within itself a particular ontology which constitutes a clear but problematic empirical domain. The questions arising from this ontology need to be addressed before we can construct a relevant minimal description of the European domain.

The category of foreign policy conceived as foreign economic policy has been defined by one of its earliest analysts as including 'government actions with important impact on U.S. relations with other governments and on the production and distribution of goods and services at home and abroad' (Destler, 1980, p. 7). This at first sight seems to be a fairly straightforward conception. However, the identification and analysis of the empirical basis of this domain is highly problematic. Destler is very sensitive to this problem and, when considering the definition of the term, is forced to conclude that since it is difficult to find policy actions without some impact beyond (US) borders, and even harder to find 'actions without significant economic content', one is forced to 'retreat to the unsatisfying ground of relativity' (1980, p. 7). He decides that this definition is sufficient and also decides to analyse foreign economic policy as a separate sphere of activity; both of these decisions have implications for the analysis presented here. Because the key to the above definition is a judgement as to what constitutes 'important', and because this judgement is necessarily related to theory, let us initially consider the implied domain of FEP through a brief review of the genealogy of the term.

The category of FEP is a contemporary development and derives from the rediscovery of economics by (American) political science and international relations, largely as a result of the events of the late 1960s and early 1970s. Although foreign economic policy in the form of economic diplomacy had existed as long as the state system, and had been particularly important in the post-1945 context, it was rarely conceptualized or theorized within an explicit framework of *political* economy, except by the mercantilists and economic nationalists (who by and large had lost legitimacy through association with the economic policies of the Third Reich). The economization of political economy was a direct product of the institutionalized legitimacy of liberal economic ideology, and has a number of important consequences for our ability to understand (or not!) the contemporary global political economy.

Among the factors that prompted this rediscovery was the combination of the globalization of economic activity and the almost universal acceptance by governments of the responsibility for the macro management of national political economies. These two long-term structural changes were brought into sharp focus by the contemporaneous failure of the United States government to be able, or more properly to want, to maintain the hegemonic international economic system that had been constructed after 1945. One of the many consequences of this failure was the demonstration 'to scholars and practitioners alike that the world was no longer understandable in terms of the enforced separation of economics from politics' (Murphy and Tooze, 1991, p. 3).

Clearly this demonstration would apply to the state level as well as to the systemic, and could be expected to have an important impact upon foreign policy. Yet, the response from those aware of this so-called politicization of international economics was the development of the analysis of foreign economic policy apart from the mainstream of FPA, as already noted, and on the basis of a model of IPE whose principal assumptions were already in the process of being discredited by events.

Put simply, the term 'foreign economic policy' implies an empirical domain constituted by economic activity between and among states where the identities of these entities/processes are secure and the boundaries of the processes are discernible – between economics and politics and between the international and domestic. It also implies a model of international political economy and the way national economies fit into this IPE in order for policy to have the desired outcome. In this sense FEP is the direct foreign policy equivalent of the conventional IR response to the events of the 1970s, namely that problems are defined as both international (that is, intergovernmental) and primarily economic (that is, the national economy) to produce a systemic focus on the politics of international economic relations (Murphy and Tooze, 1991).

Equally simply, the world, and more particularly Europe, does not conform to the implicit assumptions of FEP. Economic activity takes place in an integrated system which combines both the 'traditional' form of exchange relations between states (or national economies) and newer forms of global production and services. Michalet has identified this as the coexistence of two forms of economy, the traditional international economy and the integrated world economy, together creating a more complex and different global structure in which national economies fit differently according to the extent of the integration of their key sectors of activity into the world economy and their range of activity in the traditional international economy (Michalet, 1982). The impact of this structural change in the nature of political economy is further to blur the boundaries between foreign and domestic and to change the ability of the state to achieve its policy goals.

At the present time and for most of the advanced industrial states it is extraordinarily difficult to identify what processes and policies are actually 'foreign' in the conventional sense of the term. The linkages through various forms of interdependence are so many and so complex that a practical distinction between foreign and domestic is not always possible. Indeed, the complexity of the empirical domain has led to some analysts preferring to focus upon international economic policy (Cohen, 1981). But, following Michalet, this is as restrictive an identification as 'foreign' and imposes an interpretation upon the problem which, although it makes some policy analysis possible, hinders the understanding and explanation of the actual domain of that policy and hence the efficacy of the policy itself in terms of implementation and outcomes.

The second aspect of the implied empirical domain of FEP is the relationship between economics and politics and the identification of economic issues. Because the literature (IPE as well as FPA and FEP) embodies a particular historical interpretation of that relationship it is necessary briefly to explore the dominant conception. Much of the literature on foreign economic policy was produced in the historical context of the post-1945 international political economy. The ideological and analytical frame for this FEP is American liberalism and this is linked but not necessarily derived from the material conditions, namely the hegemony of US capital in a system whose boundaries and political dynamics were dominated by the emergence of a bipolar security/military structure. The Bretton Woods system embodied the separation of politics and economics within its institutions and as the basis of orthodox thinking about the structure and operation of the international economic order. The institutionalized legitimacy of this separation came about partly as a reflection of the dominant ideology of liberalism in US policy, and partly because the resultant depoliticization of economics enabled difficult political problems to be categorized (and resolved) as *technical* issues, subject to rational economic analysis and abstract technical solutions. Nevertheless, the separation of politics and economics was real and effective – to such an extent that the late Fred Hirsch characterized the prevailing values of the system as 'Economics is when I have it, politics is when you want it.'

It is not surprising, then, that when the power structures supporting the separation of politics and economics underwent significant change, from about 1967 onwards, the FEP and IPE literature interpreted the ensuing political clashes as the politicization of the international economic order, and this has been the core assumption since: the pure field of economic relations has been corrupted by politics. The politicization thesis is important because it underpins so much of the FEP (and IR) literature and because it is so mistaken. To explore this statement would take a long discussion on the production of the discourse of political economy, but the key is in the assumption of the normality or common sense of the distinction: that is, that there exists in a real sense a pure economy, prior to and above politics, often represented by a market, that can be explained and under-stood in strictly conventional economic terms, with politics as an external or exogenous variable. Polanyi (1944), among others, clearly demonstrates that the separation of politics from economics in theory/doctrine as well as in practice was created to serve political purposes: in this case to serve the purpose of the emergent merchant class in their struggle for political legitimacy and power in the face of the totalizing ideology of a mercantilism which itself legitimated the power of the state (for classical mercantilism, power equals wealth, and politics equals economics).

In empirical terms, the problem is simple: can *any* economic activity have political import? If the answer to this question is 'maybe', rather than a definite 'no', the problems of policy (as well as explanation) multiply. It is not difficult to identify the contemporary core empirical concerns: the political management by national governments of the international economy to achieve growth and stability (and a redistribution of wealth?), the achievement of some form of social, political and economic security through interdependence (and dependence), and the necessity for cooperation, coordination and (even) harmonization of policies in order to achieve these goals. Empirically we need to know how the processes of interdependence work, how and to what extent each national economy/state is embedded in the European and global structure, what policies bring about the changes we desire, what are the appropriate political, economic and social structures that will facilitate our aims, how we can maintain a democratic control in Europe, and so on. Yet, for all the apparent simplicity of the articulation of the empirical, we do have real difficulty in explaining and understanding, in creating policies and structures, and in achieving the change we want. Some of this difficulty, I suggest, stems directly from the acceptance of the historically specified constitution of the content and nature of politics and economics as ahistorical, objective definitions.

The European domain

An empirical description of Europe will necessarily be complex and it is clear from the above that there are a number of dimensions and characteristics of contemporary Europe that do not conform to the expected contours of the existing study of FEP. Moreover, these characteristics are central to the evolving/contradictory structure of Europe in the 1990s. In what follows these characteristics are not considered in any hierarchy of significance.

The creation of formal political processes that are supranational and that have been institutionalized within the formal structures of the European Community (EC) has in turn both created and made possible new processes and structures. The complexity of the EC policy process is legendary, but a key feature is the extent to which transnational and transgovernmental relations form an integral part of the network of policy (Wallace et al., 1983). The cumulative impact of the development of the EC has changed the nature of the structure of the state. On a policy level it is clear that one has to analyse, say, the trade policy process of a member of the EC in a different way from non-members: formal framework, political dynamics, nature of output, constitution of interests, and so on. Related to policy but expressed on a broader social and political level are the interests that cut across or diverge from defined national priorities, which often tend to bypass national authorities, linking subnational interests to EC authority directly. Even though it is possible to track and chart the multilevelled, complex policy process in the EC, the characterization of the contemporary structure of authority and power is difficult. What is clear is that for the members of the EC the nature of the state as both structure and agent has changed (Wallace, 1990).

At the same time, and partly as a consequence of the political imperatives of the EC, the nature of the economic structure of the EC members and prospective members has changed, in tandem with the changes in the global political economy (see Chapter 5 by Gerd Junne in this volume; see also Michalet, 1982). The principal changes are in the level of intra-EC trade and in the structure of international production. The increases in the level of intra-EC trade amongst members is important, but should not be allowed to overshadow the changes in the pattern of direct investment and the integration of EC money markets. The countries of the EC now generate over 40 per cent of world exports and nearly 20 per cent of world manufacturing value added (MVA) (Dicken, 1992, p. 45), and the EC is currently the largest bloc in the triad of regions that constitute a multipolar global political economy. However, the nature of this trade and the structure of production (and services) in Europe and the world have changed drastically and are continuing to change. The most significant empirical feature is that 'an increasing proportion of world trade in manufactures is *intra-firm*, rather than inter-national trade.' This is 'trade which takes place between parts of the same firm but across national boundaries' (Dicken, 1992, p. 48). It is difficult to estimate the magnitude of this, primarily because government trade statistics are not configured in a way that enables the identification of intra-firm trade, but there is much evidence to suggest that this constitutes a fundamental shift in the structure of production on both a global and an EC level. What is clear is that a large slice of the empirical reality of Europe is lost if the changed nature of international production is ignored. Moreover, this is not just a question of identifying transnational corporations as important actors; it is a change in the structure of political economy that alters the nature of politics.

A third empirical characteristic in this description of Europe is the resurgence of nationalism(s), principally resulting from the breakup of the Soviet empire, including that entailed in the making possible of German unification, but also the nationalism generated by the combination of world economic recession and anti-EC bureaucracy sentiment. This has generated both centripetal and centrifugal forces of creation and destruction. The dismantling of the Soviet bloc was always going to result in the resumption of nationalist rivalries frozen by the Soviet hegemony. However, few expected the speed or the violence of the process. The creation of a host of new, generally capitalist, states in Europe (and Asia) alongside the explicit adoption of capitalism by the former centrally planned economies raises many questions, not the least being their prospects of economic and social survival and the direct threat to military stability if the economic/social processes of change do not work as expected. The demands of these economies for capital and trade are great and could have a significant effect on the stability of the EC economies, as the current situation in Germany demonstrates. Moreover their potential impact upon the political economy of Europe and the EC is such that questions concerning their integration into the global economy become highly salient, as do the longer-term political-economic consequences of present conflicts.

The conflation of these characteristics (and many more) enables us to make a number of comments on the characteristics of European order at this historical juncture. What is not in dispute is the presence of structural shifts at a number of levels in the global political economy. At the level of the global economy, changes in the structure of production, which includes changes in the international division of labour, signify changes in the nature and location of power. At the level of the EC, undoubted increases in economic interdependence have taken place within the context of complex and evolving political frameworks and a policy goal of a single market. What is interesting here is the overlay of these two orders (see Chapter 2 by Michael Smith in this volume): to what extent do they match, and what are the consequences if they are in conflict? There is at present seemingly a mismatch between the depth and extent of market interdependence, brought about by the impact of structural shifts at all levels, and the policy interdependence necessary to manage this situation.

On the level of the state in Europe, the distinction between domestic and international has waning relevance for policy, as does the distinction between economics and politics. This statement probably applies to any of the advanced industrial states, but the phenomenon is heightened by the stage of development of the EC and the depth of the incorporation of EC rules or governance into the practices of national political economies. However, for EC governments it may not be such a practical problem because for most members of the EC the distinctions may have lost policy relevance for most issues some time ago. The pragmatic necessity to deal with the reality of coordinated policies in an interdependent Europe often triumphs over the reluctance of national bureaucracies to change. As a result many national agencies that previously were domestic now have numbers of staff dealing with European and international issues. Consequently, much foreign economic policy is carried out by domestic or subnational actors, both private and public. With the deepening of the integration process within the EC and in Europe generally, this feature of interdependence has been institutionalized through the multilevel policy structures and networks that have been created. This has happened to such an extent that it is probably now meaningless for EC member states to class intra-EC economic relationships as the subject of foreign economic policy. They are neither foreign nor economic, and all too often are not confined to or by policy.

Theory of foreign economic policy

The theory of foreign economic policy derives from the theoretical literature of international political economy and, as previously indicated, forms a distinct and separate theoretical resource from that provided by foreign policy analysis. It is almost completely American and has recently been reviewed, evaluated and progressed by a number of practitioners of FEP in two interesting publications: the special edition of *International Organization* on *The State and American Foreign Economic Policy*, edited by G. John Ikenberry, David Lake and Michael Mastanduno (Ikenberry et al., 1988a); and a wide-ranging and important review article by John Odell, 'Understanding International Trade Policies: An Emerging Synthesis', in *World Politics* (Odell, 1990). The brief outline of the theory of FEP presented here draws heavily from these sources, and both provide excellent and extensive bibliographies.

The volume edited by Ikenberry et al. identifies three analytical and theoretical approaches to foreign economic policy as having major significance: system-centred, society-centred, and state-centred. 'International, or system-centered, approaches explain American policy as a function of the attributes or capabilities of the United States relative to other nation-states . . . Society-centered approaches view American policy either as reflecting the preferences of the dominant group or class in society, or as resulting from the struggle for influence that takes place among various interest groups or political parties', that is FEP is essentially a 'function of domestic politics'. State-centred approaches view FEP as 'highly constrained by domestic institutional relationships that have persisted over time, and also by the ability of state officials to realize their objectives in light of both international and domestic constraints' (Ikenberry et al., 1988b, pp. 1–2). John Odell categorizes analyses of international trade policy (the principal field of FEP theorizing) in a slightly different way – 'four prominent and distinct theoretical themes'. 'The four perspectives emphasize market conditions, leaders' values and beliefs, national political institutions, and global political-economic structures' (Odell, 1990, p. 140). These are fairly self-explanatory, with each identified factor being given causal status for trade policies and politics. Odell's last two perspectives are similar to Ikenberry et al.'s state- and system-centred approaches, and his market perspective seems to overlap with part of the society-centred approach. Odell's cognitive perspective could be part of each of the other unit analyses but, more often, is used to support state- or institutional-level explanations. The inclusion of the cognitive work is both interesting and significant and Odell himself has provided one of the best studies to use this perspective, although Judith Goldstein has successfully incorporated the analysis of belief into her innovative work on trade policy and institutions (Odell, 1982; Goldstein, 1989).

Both works emphasize that no single approach/theme dominates the field (currently), but while the Ikenberry et al. volume argues for (and demonstrates very well) a necessary focus on the American state and makes a strong case for an institutional approach, Odell's reading is of an emerging and welcome synthesis which is 'blending valuable insights from multiple perspectives' (Odell, 1990, p. 140). It is important to note that almost all of the theoretical work done in FEP is in the realm of what Rosenau would call 'pre-theory' – the configuring of perspectives and approaches which present questions, puzzles and problems rather than sets of propositions which can be empirically tested. And, with few exceptions, most FEP seems to be based on the view 'that an understanding of American foreign economic policy is best pursued by theoretically based historical inquiry' (Ikenberry, 1988, p. 241). So far, most of FEP's theoretically based historical inquiry has been concerned with the US itself, for as Odell points out, there is a paucity of studies of the EC that are comparable to the work done on American trade and foreign economic policy (Odell, 1990, p. 162).

At the metatheoretical level, then, FEP seems to be slowly moving beyond the confines of the contesting ideologies of IPE (Murphy and Tooze, 1991, p. 22), that is 'the classification of thought in political economy as either liberal, mercantilist, or Marxist is becoming less and less useful' (Odell, 1990, p. 160). However, this is happening within an FEP orthodoxy which is (still) bounded by the confines of positivism, or what Odell calls 'neo-positivism': 'At the level of epistemology, this community [of scholars writing trade policy] is neopositivist without apology; no poststructuralist or postmodernist dissent is evident here. Marxist thinking is also absent' (Odell, 1990, p. 161). This is a clear statement of the epistemological basis of FEP, yet at the same time is a statement of the limits of FEP orthodoxy, as will be discussed in the next part of the chapter.[2]

FEP theory and Europe: a questionable category?

Evaluating theory calls for much more than a consideration of the concepts and models incorporated in that theory (or range of theories) and the testing of general laws. It calls for more than an examination of the underlying assumptions of theory. In essence, evaluating theory demands inquiry into the nature and status of knowledge and knowledge production itself. Any evaluation of theory which does not consider the epistemological and ontological bases of that theory, whatever the conclusion concerning other aspects might be, merely reproduces the assumptions built into the metatheoretical bases of that theory. And these metatheoretical assumptions are not neutral, objective or scientific; they are socially produced and have political consequences (Lapid, 1989).

The implications of this view of knowledge are important. From this it can be argued that the social production of IR/FPA/IPE academic theory is an integral part of an international political economy of knowledge production and can be best understood and explained as such. In this sense the dominant or orthodox theories in FPA can themselves be seen as elements of the structure of power of international relations. The logical conclusion of this argument is succinctly stated by Pierre Bourdieu:

> The theory of knowledge is a dimension of political theory because the specifically symbolic power to impose the principles of the construction of reality – in particular social reality – *is a major dimension of political power*. (1977, p. 165: emphasis added)

In this section of the chapter I will consider the ability of FEP theory to capture the richness of the (described) empirical reality of Europe on a number of dimensions: the empirical content, including issues and concepts, the explanations and models used and the nature of the metatheoretical assumptions.[3] There is in the existing corpus of (American) FEP literature much that is useful and relevant for European foreign policy. The range of work now completed – issues, policies, processes and outcomes – is both wide and impressive. Much of this work is increasingly sensitive of the need to incorporate a broad institutional perspective, and with this comes a reappraisal of the role of history in analysing FEP. None of the arguments that follow are intended to claim that FEP is fatally flawed; they merely suggest that FEP is questionable in its application and relevance to Europe. In essence this is to question, and to doubt, 'the possibility, so eagerly grasped by those searching for empirically testable models, of transferring assumptions, metaphors, research strategies and accounts of rational action from one context to the other' (Walker, 1989, p. 166). The intention then is to suggest a critical frame of reception for FEP, to raise some points of contention – empirically and theoretically – and to indicate possible pathways for the development of theory.

Issues

FEP theory is dominated by the issue of trade: five out of the seven chapters of the Ikenberry et al. (1988a) volume are devoted to this topic, and trade has formed the subject of much of the literature of FEP. In this FEP has followed the practice of orthodox international political economy (Murphy and Tooze, 1991, pp. 25–7). There is no question that trade is important, but the privileging of trade has significant (theoretical) consequences for policy. These can be summarized as the assumption of three conditions: trade is regarded as the most important issue, and other issues are marginalized; all other issues/problems are only important in relation to their impact on trade; and trade is the key process of foreign economic policy and the international political economy. This produces a specific and limited model of FEP and one that may be challenged by other developments in the world economy. There is ample evidence to suggest that (particularly within Europe) these conditions are not empirically supported (Michalet, 1982; Tsoukalis, 1991; Dicken, 1992).

The explanation for the dominance of trade in FEP theory is not difficult: US liberal ideology has been institutionalized within the state (Goldstein, 1988) as well as in certain social groups, and that ideology produces a view of the international economy driven by trade; the domestic political economy of the US since 1945 has supported the dominance of trade and this view of the reality of the international economy; trade lends itself to political action in a pluralist system such as the US; and, critical for politics, because trade can be linked to specific group interests, trade conflicts can be 'won'. These 'real' and material interests condition the academic production of knowledge. Yet, this dominance, this privileging of trade runs the real risk that changes in other structures of the global political economy will not be accorded their real significance and the ensuing explanations and policy will not reflect the actuality of the world economy, with the result that more problems are created than resolved. Indeed, Susan Strange has argued for some time that trade is a secondary and derived activity of a world economy driven by other structures and forces, particularly finance, credit, technology and production (Strange, 1986; 1988), and her argument is convincing. The globalization of finance coupled with the growth of international production has changed the structures of global political economy, and this change has increased the problems of policy precisely because it alters the nature of the relationships between the structures of substate/state and national/global economy (*Economist*, 1992).

An FEP dominated by trade is not appropriate for Europe in the 1990s. FEP must incorporate finance, money and investment if it is to be relevant as theory. Some studies have begun to do this (Odell, 1982; Destler and Odell, 1987), but the European experience demands the theoretical integration of finance, money, production *and* trade for policy analysis as a matter of some urgency. Changes at the global level (the accelerating rate of technological change, the creation of a global system for creating and allocating credit, and the fall in the costs of transport and communication: Stopford and Strange, 1991) have underpinned developments consequent on the opening of the former Eastern bloc economies to create new and potentially very strong structures of production. The volume and direction of transborder acquisitions since 1989 indicate a redrawing of the production map of Europe, with the (longer-term) integration of the new capitalist economies extending the European market. In this process the creation of an extended European Economic Area (EEA) and the accession of more national economies to the EC, on the basis of a prior commitment to the creation of a single market and a unified monetary system, will create a unique structure of political economy (whatever the outcome of the current uncertainty). This will be unique not just in its historical and geographical dimensions, but also in the complex web of formal and informal structures constituting its political economy. As is already the case, the European state, and hence European governments, will occupy a very different position in this structure from that which the US state and government presently occupy in the global political economy.

Concepts and models

Just as the privileging of trade issues in current FEP derives from the experience and interests of the US political economy, many of the concepts and models utilized are similarly derived. The universe of IPE within which the FEP focus on trade is privileged has been constructed to reflect 'the policy concerns of the government of the United States throughout the era of US global supremacy and, especially, contemporary concerns about various challenges to that supremacy' (Murphy and Tooze, 1991, p. 24). The current US political and public reaction to inward investment (particularly from Japan) is a case in point. For me it would be surprising if FEP did not reflect these concerns, but what is problematic is the presentation of the FEP/IPE knowledge constructed on this basis as neo-positivist scientific knowledge embodying at least the implicit claim to be universally applicable in space and time.[4]

FEP shares many of its general concepts with orthodox IPE, that is, it presents a Western, male, privileged and largely materialist view of the totality of the universe of FEP. These characteristics are also shared with FPA in general and clearly need exposing to critical evaluation and reconstruction. FEP also, and almost by definition, presents a statist view of the world. What is meant by this is that the state or government by definition is the core actor and structure; other actors and structures are significant only to the extent that they impinge upon the realm of state concern. This, of course, is appropriate when we are posing the question 'how do we explain/understand foreign policy?', but only if we assume that the state is the only significant entity to have a foreign policy. The experience of Europe, indeed the experience of the US, indicates that this is not always the case. For example, it would be very difficult to explain both the nature and timing of the move to create a single market in the EC without considering the foreign policy of the large European transnational corporations.

Part of this statism is a particular conception of the state itself. This is logically necessary for the generation of empirical studies, but the state envisaged by American FEP is not necessarily the same as the state for members of the EC. Studies of FEP are able to assume the American state in an almost classical sense, certainly the state as sovereign. The myth of the American state as weak and politics as a process of pluralism was part of this assumption, but this has been firmly rejected by much of the FEP work of the past few years (Ikenberry, 1988; Goldstein, 1988; 1989). Simple application of FEP to the EC context immediately has to confront the supranationality of the EC and the fact that there is a crucial difference between foreign economic policy between and among members of the EC, and foreign economic policy external to the EC. One of the key empirical dimensions of the EC already identified is the clear mismatch between the levels of market interdependence created within and by the existing political economy of the EC, and the level of policy interdependence currently possible to meet the policy demands of that market interdependence.

Some of the lacunae in FEP theory have already been addressed by the latest work in this field. In particular, the retheorizing of the state within the context of what Ikenberry calls 'an institutional approach' makes the application of FEP easier in the European context (Ikenberry, 1988). Yet, a number of problems remain. One is the model of political economy that is embedded in FEP: we have already briefly considered this question in relation to the privileging of trade, but it is worth expanding. A model of the interactions of the world political economy that focuses primarily on trade is likely to be based on a conception of an international, as opposed to a world or global, economy: that is, the model assumes exchange relations between national economies as the dominant framework. This model is unlikely to capture the totality of FEP because we can identify another core structure, and this is international production. At the very least FEP analysis must be modified to take account of this phenomenon, as is beginning to happen (Milner, 1988; Destler and Odell, 1987), but the existence of two systems of economy demands a re-evaluation of the nature, measurement and impact of trade itself.

A second problem for FEP is the continued reproduction of the orthodox distinction between what is considered economics and what is politics. Because it is derived from the historical definition of economics ideologically separated from political economy, it continues to serve the purposes of that separation: namely, economics is 'the science investigating wealth production and distribution under scarcity, where wealth is somehow separate from "politics", and "politics" takes place where the realm of "economics" stops' (Murphy and Tooze, 1991, p. 24). The result for FEP is that a severe analytical disjunction is created whereby a value-based political economy accepts and utilizes in an instrumental sense a closed set of economic models and techniques. The core features of this set of economic models are rarely questioned by FEP writings, but include a particularly significant construction of rationality as the basis for human behaviour, a severely gendered construction of economic life, and a model of economics that currently ignores the problem of long-term global sustainability (each of these characteristics being interrelated). These features of neo-classical economics have major theoretical and political implications for FEP and should lead to a questioning of the basis of the model of economics that is accepted. Part of this problem is what is considered as rational economic behaviour and what are the appropriate empirical referents for a sustainable international political economy. In other words, the question of the empirical *economic* domain of foreign or international economic policy is not necessarily one with a clear and obvious answer, and we clearly need to rethink the empirical basis of economic activity. Susan George has argued that this rethink should be a return to political economy:

> If human beings are to deal with the urgent problems of the late twentieth century and make their global house fit to live in, the (social) science they need to apply is less neoclassical economics as practised in the late twentieth century than 'political economy' as understood in the eighteenth or nineteenth century. (George, 1992, p. 111)

Metatheory

The previous two sections indicate a number of theoretical reservations and problems concerning the transfer of FEP theory to Europe. However, these questions are overshadowed by the problems of FEP that derive from its metaphysical base. In his review of trade policies, John Odell devotes just four lines to the philosophical underpinnings of the analyses in question: a lost opportunity for his analysis, but not a surprise given that any form of positivism tends to marginalize considerations of these questions. Odell is quite clear, as already indicated, that 'at the level of epistemology, this community [of scholars writing trade policy] is neopositivist without apology; no poststructuralist or postmodernist dissent is evident here' (Odell, 1990, p. 161). That 'this community' is 'neopositivist without apology' is under-standable given their social context, but this fact is also one of the major impediments to their production of knowledge and one of the major limitations to the utility of FEP theory.

I am unsure as to the precise contours of neo-positivism in IPE, but it must necessarily incorporate the fundamental separation of subject and object to be included under the rubric of positivism. And it is this separation that is meaningful for theory. The key here is that positivistic knowledge 'although claiming a legitimacy derived from following a "scientific" process, denies the possibility that any form of (nonmaterial) intersubjective meaning may be part of the international political economy. It denies the possibility that beliefs and values are themselves just as real as the material structures and powers of the global political economy' (Murphy and Tooze, 1991, p. 18). Here, the nature of the positivist epistemology of FEP constitutes and confirms a specific ontology which excludes the reality of intersubjective meaning in the structure of policy-making at state and global levels.

That FEP scholars are content with their ontology is surprising given the direction in which the field is moving. A number of studies have sought to integrate ideas, values and belief systems into the study of FEP (see for example Odell, 1982; Goldstein, 1988; 1989), and Odell considers this perspective in his review of the field (Odell, 1990). However, the cognitive perspective in FEP has developed within its positivist context, and this has not only denied the reality of intersubjective meaning in the structure of political economy, but also led to the paradox that the role of ideas and values is accepted as an influence on policy and policy-makers, but not as an influence on those who would attempt to analyse this process. This point is borne out by John Odell's footnote: 'Cognitive interpretations might seem to introduce some interpretive or phenomenological elements, but in many cases they are offered as primitive social-scientific hypotheses to be sharpened and tested in principle in the same manner as other hypotheses' (Odell, 1990, p. 161, fn. 26). Here the academic/analyst is clearly considered a non-social participant in the process. It is the burden of my argument that precisely *because* cognitive interpretations are offered as 'primitive social-scientific hypotheses', they are extracted from the nexus of intersubjective meaning and lose what force they may have in explaining or understanding (see also Tooze, 1988).

In another sense, too, the direction of FEP seems to demand the incorporation of historical intersubjective meaning. In his concluding theoretical essay of the volume on *The State and American Foreign Policy*, John Ikenberry develops the outlines of an institutional approach to FEP (Ikenberry, 1988). This is an interesting and well-argued piece, which goes some way to balance some of the weaknesses of existing FEP theory that derive from the focus on American policy and the consequent predominance to date of system- and society-level explanations of FEP. Ikenberry locates his analysis within a discussion of history and historical structures and bases his argument on the assumption that 'the relative importance of specific variables is time-bound, and theories of foreign economic policy must therefore be placed within a larger historical and institutional framework' (1988, p. 223). This is all to the good, particularly as ideas and institutions are linked, in phrases suggestive of an element of structuration, but this line of argument is unfortunately not developed. Moreover, the historical specificity that Ikenberry allows for ideas and institutions is not extended to concepts and theories. Concepts such as 'institution' are assumed to be fixed rather than themselves constituted by historically specific structures. It would seem more helpful here to understand the content of a concept as being built up through 'contact with a particular situation which it helps to explain – a contact which also develops the meaning of the concept' (Cox, 1983, pp. 162–3). Such an understanding of concept formation is a necessary basis for the analysis of historical structures that Ikenberry is proposing.

Foreign economic policy, foreign policy and Europe

If, as Rosenau (1988) contends, part of the reason for the 'mutual boredom' shown by FPA and IPE is that IPE is macro and FPA is micro, then some of the recent developments of FEP confound this distinction, particularly the articulation of the 'institutional approach'. However, it is striking that even given this development the literature of FEP seems to be as distant from FPA as ever: the field-defining special issue of *International Organization* edited by Ikenberry et al. (1988a) contains comparatively few references to the classical FPA literature, even when that literature would have been useful. To my mind this phenomenon is easier to account for by looking at the academic divisions between politics and economics and the intellectual hegemony of economics, than by comparing the macro/micro orientations of each. However, the continuing division of labour raises fundamental questions concerning the theorization of both international political economy and foreign policy.

It is plainly nonsense that the theoretical apparatus of foreign policy does not include foreign economic policy, and it continues to be disturbing that theorizing of foreign economic policy does not properly include security. This is indeed an anomaly, particularly in the European context, and demands a retheorizing of foreign policy to integrate politics and economics and all their myriad manifestations. It will, however, not be sufficient for this retheorization to be carried out merely in terms of the empirical content of (assumed) scientific theory, or even in terms of the empirical *and* the analytic (covering hypotheses, explanations and theoretical models': Lapid, 1989, p. 239). In order fully to capture the empirical reality of Europe, retheorizing *must* include metaphysics (reality-defining assumptions, epistemological premises, ideology).

It is a measure of the continued hegemony of positivist thought in the study of IR that such an argument even has to be made, for as Rob Walker has recently pointed out, 'It is not a matter of arguing about ontological and epistemological issues in the abstract. Philosophical commitments are already embedded in concepts like state or state-system, typologies like the level of analysis distinction and utilitarian accounts of rational action' (Walker, 1989, p. 178). Unless the philosophical commitments that underpin the analysis of foreign and foreign economic policy are examined, we run the risk of being increasingly out of touch with the political community emerging in Europe today.

The results of retheorizing of FPA/FEP would not be to negate or decry the empirical work done to date, but to examine, evaluate and interpret this work within an expanded notion of what constitutes the appropriate framework, of what constitutes science. As suggested above, the core tenet of any such re-evaluation should be 'that significant theoretical modifications and choices must always take into account the supportive meta-scientific domains in which they are holistically embedded' (Lapid, 1989, p. 240).

The problems and limitations of FEP as currently theorized have been briefly considered here along the three dimensions or axes that together now define the structure of science as knowledge. On each of these dimensions I have argued that the simple application of existing FEP theory is problematic. Modification is not simply a question of adjusting the empirical content and referents of FEP theory, although this is clearly necessary. Nor can modification be successful if only concepts, models and explanations are changed, although again this too is necessary. Retheorizing entails the careful consideration of the metatheory of FEP/IPE (because the two fields are indistinguishable at this level). And on this dimension there are important questions concerning FEP's ability to capture the reality of policy and political economy, not just in Europe but at the global level. The heart of the problem is the insistence on the separation of subject and object, whether it be called positivist or neo-positivist, and the consequences that this epistemology has for the range of possible ontologies so legitimized. The denial of the reality of intersubjective meaning for political economy consequent upon such ontologies severely reduces our chances of understanding *and* explaining foreign economic policy.

Following from the above, some possible contours of a re-theorized FEP for Europe may be as follows.

Metatheoretical
A post-positive theory is needed which is reflexive and properly considers the reality of intersubjective meaning in policy and arena. This should allow a greater range of possible ontologies, particularly through the historical specification of concepts and the understanding of historical structures (Cox, 1987; 1989). Within these ontologies greater sensitivity to questions of causation, of agent and of structure should be possible with a move to consider the processes of structuration; i.e. it should be possible to move away from explanation being privileged in terms of the rational actions of individuals. It should also be possible to move away from an ontology that privileges, or makes silent, any section or sector of global population (e.g. class or gender).

Models and explanations
The expanded conception of foreign policy made possible by new ontologies should include a move away from foreign policy solely linked to the notion of territory – as is already the case in non-orthodox international political economy. Expanded conceptions of foreign policy should include considerations of identity and the practices of creating 'the other' (see Campbell, 1992); this is particularly significant in the processes of change now taking place in Europe. They should also include a re-evaluation of the nature of political economy which does not unquestioningly accept the core assumptions of a historically defined and ideological conception of economics that is claimed as scientific.

Both on a policy level and a system level, models should incorporate the global production of manufactures, services, ideas and knowledge as a necessary and long overdue response to the liberal fixation with trade. Equally important should be the bringing together of a political economy whose agenda is determined by economics and a foreign policy whose concern has primarily been defined in terms of military/political security.

Empirical content
The range of empirical investigation would need to be expanded. Much of the problem in trying to measure the impact of

international production is that governments do not constitute statistics in such a way as to enable analysis of inter-firm trade, i.e. the knowledge produced in the form of trade statistics underpins a state-centric model of IPE – not surprisingly. The United Nations has begun to expand the range of information, but with limited success. The questions asked should determine the empirical evidence utilized, and not vice versa.

The incorporation of intersubjective meaning does not require the abandonment of empirical evidence, just the asking of different questions and the searching for different evidence. As Robert Cox points out, 'Historical structures, the cumulative result of innumerable often-repeated actions, are discoverable through the common understandings and common expectations of behaviour that provide the common framework for actions', that is they 'are revealed as intersubjectivity' (Cox, 1989, p. 38). The constitution of intersubjectivity is part of structuration and, in principle, can be empirically investigated in the same way, with the same contingency, as any other phenomenon.

The sum total of the suggested changes is indeed to make the present theorization of foreign economic policy very much a questionable category where Europe is concerned. The consequences of a failure to understand and analyse the European political economy at this historical juncture are severe, particularly for those later generations who often have to pay (literally) for this failure. The American government is not unique in failing both to understand the nature of the global political economy and the interactions between domestic and international, and to take adequate domestic and foreign policy action based on that understanding: for example, the total cost of the Savings and Loan and federal banking crises may eventually be as high as US$400 billion. The question the theory of political economy asks in situations like this is: who benefits?

Notes

1 As well as the support and advice I have received from all members of the group, I have benefited in particular from discussions with Gerd Junne and Mike Smith on the form and content of this chapter and with Steve Smith over a period of many years on the nature of IR theory.

2 For a discussion of the way in which orthodox IPE marginalizes Marxist political economy, see Maclean (1988).

3 These dimensions constitute the defining characteristics of scientific knowledge in the restructured philosophy of science that has been developed in the last ten years; see Lapid (1989).

4 As mentioned earlier, the term 'neo-positivist' applied to IR/IPE is used by John Odell (Odell, 1990), but I have yet to see an extended discussion of the nature and content of such an epistemology, although an outline was offered by John Odell at the session we shared at the APSA Conference, Chicago, 1992.

5

Multinational Enterprises as Actors

Gerd Junne

The dominant realist paradigm depicts international relations as the outcome of the interaction of states. One of the important points of critique has always been that such an approach leaves other important actors out of the picture. Among these other actors, a prominent role is often accorded to multinational corporations (MNCs). If states are demoted from their position as principal actors, however, the debate on the most appropriate level of analysis will not be solved. Hollis and Smith (1990, p. 42) have recently pointed out that the problem of explaining versus understanding applies no less to transnational corporations or other units than it does to states.

Hollis and Smith extend the level of analysis problem from the famous two-level distinction to at least four levels: the levels of the international system, the nation-state, bureaucracies and the individual. The same levels could be distinguished in the analysis of the impact of multinational enterprises, which can be approached at the system level (the world market), the unit level (company), the subsystem level (divisions) and the level of the individual (manager). I want to illustrate in this contribution that all four levels are relevant for foreign policy analysis.

While following the basic outline of all chapters in this book, the different sections will at the same time address different levels of analysis. The description of the empirical domain in the first section will deal with the systemic level of world capital flows to underline that the internationalization of the economy very much limits the menu of choices for foreign policy decision-makers. The second section mainly discusses theories of the impact of the expansion of multinational companies on the process of European integration. This interaction has been studied only at a highly aggregate level. At this level, only statements about functional relationships can be made. The third section illustrates that one needs to descend to the actor level to understand the why, how and when of specific developments. The original contribution of the present chapter, in the fourth section, is that in order to grasp fully the impact of multinational enterprises on (European) foreign policy, the unit of the MNC would have to be disaggregated as well (as the state has to be in meaningful foreign policy analysis).

A focus on multinational corporations could in principle break up the dichotomy between the two subfields of the discipline of international relations which Rosenau (1988, p. 22) sees characterized by 'mutual boredom'. The dominant focus of international political economy (IPE) is on 'macro problems sustained by macro processes derived from macro structures in which the controls can only be marginally affected by the intervention of micro actors'. The comparative study of foreign policy (CFP), on the other hand, 'proceeds from the initial premise that its domain involves international problems in which micro actors participate in macro processes that can shape and (occasionally) even control other micro actors as well as their macro structures and processes' (Rosenau, 1988, p. 22). An analysis of the role of multinational corporations could perhaps build bridges between the two fields. According to Rosenau, IPE practitioners 'all share the assumption that trade, production, supply, demand, labor, and investment variables derive from the behavior of large aggregates of individuals whose common activities are responsible to macro structures and processes over which none of them can exercise meaningful control' (1988, p. 22). However, if more attention is paid to multinational enterprises, we see that a few companies often account for a substantial share in these aggregate flows. Their decisions, therefore, in many cases do have a more than marginal impact on the direction of macro processes. The more this is the case, the more IPE should open up for a CPF approach in order to improve our understanding of the individual decisions taken at the top of large corporations.

However, with the rapid internationalization of the economy, this argument may have become less valid. The reason is, perhaps paradoxically, the very proliferation of multinational enterprises. In the early 1970s, when the international discussion on multinational corporations got up steam, there was still a relatively small number of them. Since then, not only large but also numerous small companies have set up operations abroad – to such an extent that it has become less important what any individual company is doing. What acts as a constraint on the making of foreign policy is not so much the direct interference by one or a few companies but more often, again, the structures that have come about as the result of their collective actions, for which no individual company alone can be held responsible.

Acceleration of economic internationalization

The early 1980s have seen an extraordinary acceleration of different forms of economic internationalization. For example, during the first seven years of the 1980s more money was invested abroad world-wide than the accumulated stock of foreign direct investment throughout history until then. This process has not yet been sufficiently reflected in theories on international relations in general or theories on European integration in particular.

The present section will provide a short account of a number of changes in the international economy which have a far-reaching impact on European integration. It deals with (1) the steep increase in foreign direct investments, (2) the proliferation of strategic alliances, (3) the explosion of portfolio investment and (4) the increasing volatility of international monetary markets, and discusses some consequences of these changes for the process of European integration.

The spectacular increase in foreign direct investment

Annual investment flows reached an absolute level of $196 billion in 1989. At the end of that year, the total world-wide stock of foreign direct investment (FDI) stood at approximately $1.5 trillion. The bulk of this is of very recent origin. It stems from investments made since the mid 1980s. After having nearly tripled between 1984 and 1987, world outflows of foreign direct investment continued to increase by another 20 per cent in both 1988 and 1989. Foreign direct investment in the highly industrialized countries alone has grown at the remarkable average annual rate of 46 per cent since 1985 (UNCTC, 1991, pp. 3, 33).

Both the United States and the European Community (EC) account for more than one-third of the stock of outward foreign investment, but recent outflows from the EC reach more than twice the outflows from the US (UNCTC, 1991, p. 32). The share of the EC in world inward investment has somewhat declined (though absolute figures still show an annual increase of 8 per cent a year). While the relative importance of the EC as a host region has diminished, its relative weight as a home region has considerably increased.

In the statistics cited above, the EC is taken as one single economic unit, without counting *intra*-regional foreign investment. Intra-EC FDI increased from one-quarter of total inward stock in the EC in 1980 to 40 per cent in 1988. Intra-EC investment flows grew by an average of 38 per cent a year from 1980 to 1987, while flows from the EC to the rest of the world grew at only 17 per cent a year (UNCTC, 1991, pp. 33–4). However, EC investment in the United States grew even more rapidly. With $194 million of accumulated inward stock from the EC, European companies have still more invested in the United States than they have in other European countries ($160 billion).

Japanese investment flows to the EC increased to such an extent that in the two years between March 1988 and March 1990 they were 13 per cent higher than the total flows over the previous 36 years combined. Japanese investment in the EC in 1989 surpassed for the first time Japanese investment in the United States in terms of the growth of inward flows from Japan. Compared with this rapid increase, 'the low levels of investment into Japan stand out as a striking imbalance' (UNCTC, 1991, pp. 41–4).

The above figures substantiate a number of expectations regarding the future of European integration:

1   The share of foreign direct investment in EC countries that comes from other EC countries has significantly increased. This fact suggests that the EC has gained more cohesiveness.
2   Given the ever-closer links with the United States, it seems unlikely, though, that the EC will develop into a 'fortress Europe' and become a more self-contained economic unit.
3   The imbalance in investment flows to and from Japan adds to the political friction resulting from the imbalance in trade flows.

The proliferation of strategic alliances among firms

Latent conflicts among the major trade blocs are currently cushioned by the large number of strategic alliances among firms which have mushroomed during the 1980s. These are long-term agreements between otherwise competing firms to cooperate in specific fields of their activities (e.g. research, marketing) without necessarily involving equity participation in the partner firm or a subsidiary or affiliate (cf. Mytelka, 1991; Lorange and Roos, 1992). The MERIT data bank counted almost 4000 such inter-firm agreements up to 1988, four-fifths of them having been concluded after 1980 (Hagedoorn, 1990).

Most of the European companies involved in the early 1980s, at least in technology-intensive sectors, had concluded agreements with American and Japanese firms, rather than other European companies (Mytelka and Delapierre, 1988, pp. 129, 138–9; Dunning and Robson, 1988, p. 18). Very often they were the junior partner in such partnerships. The European Commission feared that such a position might have a negative impact on their future competitiveness, because it might keep these companies in a permanently inferior position with regard to their partners overseas.

The potential political importance of these alliances is obvious. In a world with strong neo-mercantilist tendencies, domestic pressure in favour of protectionism may be contained if competing companies not only do not regard each other as enemies but cooperate in other areas. This could limit the chance of trade wars or at least help to avoid uncontrollable escalation.

The explosion of portfolio investment

While long-term engagement in the form of direct investment has more than doubled during the 1980s, short-term engagement in the form of portfolio investment really skyrocketed from SDR2640 million in 1980 to SDR156,816 billion in 1988 – a sixtyfold increase (Zacher, 1992, p. 86) (SDR: special drawing right). This underlines how much more the financial sphere has become integrated internationally than has the trade in goods.

The tremendous increase in short-term financial flows across borders is reflected in the trend in deposit banks' foreign liabilities, which almost tripled (in constant dollars) from $1877 billion in 1978 to $4822 billion in 1988 (Zacher, 1992, p. 84). The 'ease with which savings have since [the early 1980s] been able to scour the globe for the highest returns (and the lowest costs) . . . has set at loggerheads governments, borrowers and financial centers which ten years ago gave each other barely a thought' (*Economist*, 1990).

International money markets

The expansion of multinational enterprises has a direct impact on the internationalization of money markets, the stability of the international monetary system in general and developments towards a European monetary union in particular. The volatility of money and exchange rate movements increases the need to fix exchange rates at least on a regional basis. But at the same time, it destabilizes any agreement reached as soon as there are indicators that the fixed rates might need adaptation.

Most international money movements are not the work of individual speculators that try to profit from a realignment of currencies, but are the result of careful cash management by multinational banks and enterprises which have to protect themselves against turmoil on currency markets. The resulting situation was well illustrated by the problems in the European monetary system in the autumn of 1992, before the markets enforced major exchange rate changes for the pound sterling and the Italian lira. In spite of the fact that British Prime Minister Major had committed his government to defend the current rate of the pound, the government had to let the pound float, after European central banks had spent some $150 billion on the defence of the existing exchange rates (*NRC Handelsblad*, 3 October 1992). This underlines, again, that the leeway for governments to freely decide on the modalities of European integration is indeed limited.

The European monetary union and other parts of the Maastricht treaty have given rise to harsh critiques of past achievements and plans for the future. Many reactions to the resulting crisis of European integration have underlined that the protest may adjourn the integration process, but that integration will proceed nevertheless. This expectation builds on the premise that structural changes are under way that will sooner or later force governments and the general public to face the political consequences: 'It is a perception fundamental to serious thinking about modern politics: that a crucial range of constraints on modern political possibilities is given by the working of a global system of production and exchange' (Dunn, 1990, p. 19). This is not to say that economic developments would *determine* political decisions. They do, however, constitute major constraints, which governments can only neglect temporarily and at considerable cost. They create a need for political action. There are still choices to be made: different decisions may clear bottlenecks in different ways and may constitute functional equivalents of each other. But the contradictions that force governments to react and the definition of the available options are very much structured by the collective decisions of non-governmental actors.

Theoretical explanations

If we look for links between the rapid internationalization of the economy on the one hand and the process of European integration and its implications on the other, there are at least three different causal relationships for which an explanation may be sought in existing theories. First of all, we may want to look for the determinants of economic internationalization. Secondly, we may look for theories explaining the impact of economic internationalization on the process of political integration. And thirdly, we may look for theories that provide us with some clue with regard to the influence of the internationalization process on the EC's foreign policy towards third countries.

Determinants of rapid economic internationalization

Economic theories about the determinants of foreign direct investment or foreign trade fill whole libraries. Most of them are not adequate to explain the *acceleration* of foreign direct investment in the 1980s and the *geographical concentration* of investments on the highly industrialized countries.

There is no doubt that the prospect of a common integrated European market has attracted considerable foreign investment, as the formation of the European Community stimulated many American companies to invest in Western Europe in the 1950s and 1960s. The integration process can explain some but not all flows into Europe. But it cannot explain the equally if not more important outflow of foreign direct investment from the EC to third countries.

Where does the new dynamic of FDI among highly industrialized countries in general come from? Some important determinants have been put forward in the half descriptive, half prescriptive study on 'triad power' by the Japanese McKinsey consultant Kenichi Ohmae (1985). The point of departure of Ohmae's argument is the acceleration of technological development as a result of the introduction of new technologies (first of all microelectronics) since the 1970s. This acceleration has led to a dramatic shortening of product life cycles, i.e. of the time span between the market introduction of a new product and the point at which it becomes outdated and is replaced by another new product.

In order to keep pace with their competitors, companies have increased their R&D investment to such a degree that, on average, they invest more in R&D than in new factory buildings and machinery. Given the short life-span of new products in technology-intensive areas, companies have to embark on new strategies to recuperate the large outlays for R&D. It is no longer feasible for companies to launch a new product first in their home market, and, if it succeeds, next to penetrate the regional market and finally to go overseas. By the time the product is introduced overseas, it will already have been replaced by a new generation of products.

Companies therefore have to launch a new product immediately on the world market. This world market mainly consists of those markets with the largest purchasing power, i.e. the 'triad' markets of Western Europe, North America and Japan. Since most markets in developing countries demand intensive attention to realize comparatively modest sales, companies increasingly concentrate their marketing efforts on the markets of the triad.

To be able to market new products in all triad areas simultaneously, companies have to be well represented in all three areas. This explains a good deal of the wave of FDI among highly industrialized countries, as it makes a contribution to a better understanding of the proliferation of strategic alliances among firms in technological development and marketing. Actual patterns of foreign direct investment correspond to such a degree with these ideas that the United Nations Centre on Transnational Corporations gave the *World Investment Report 1991* the subtitle *The Triad in Foreign Direct Investment.*

It is important to note that the determinants of foreign direct investment according to this approach lie outside the realm of state action. The major incentive would be neither the desire to avoid regulation in the home country, nor programmes to attract foreign investors in the home country. The drive for non-European investors to invest in Europe would exist independently of any progress in European integration, though this could be an additional incentive.

The impact of economic internationalization on European political integration

Theories of the impact of economic internationalization on political integration all have a functionalist[1] character. A crude theory of this kind was the one put forward by Ernest Mandel in the 1960s (Mandel, 1968). He maintained that international competition with American companies (cf. Servan-Schreiber, 1967) would lead to cross-border mergers in Europe (like the pre-war mergers creating the Dutch-British firms Unilever and Shell) in order to create European enterprises of a similar stature to their American competitors. These European companies then would actively press for European integration in order to create state structures which would correspond with the new economic structures in Europe. This development would finally lead to a European superstate.

History took a somewhat different course. The three most famous cross-border mergers to which Mandel referred (the Dutch-German steel company Estel, a merger of Hoesch and Hoogovens; the German-Belgian AGFA-Gevaert company; and the French-Italian alignment between FIAT and Citroën, creating the largest 'European' concern) were either dissolved (Estel, FIAT-Citroën) or became a fully owned subsidiary of one parent company, firmly entrenched in one country (AGFA-Gevaert, now a fully owned subsidiary of Bayer).[2] Nevertheless European companies grew quickly, not as a result of cross-border mergers, but rather as a consequence of *national concentration processes* which led to national champions in many sectors during the 1970s. As a result, European companies on average have a similar size to their American counterparts,[3] but they are still companies with a predominantly *national* rather than *European* base. This, however, is currently changing as a closely knit network of international joint ventures, subsidiaries and cooperation agreements is giving many companies a more European posture. Observers conclude that:

> The outcome of EC-wide industrial restructuring may be a shift from an economy characterized by a set of 'national champions' which were protected on a national level, to one which would look to the EC rather than the home nation as their principal market and their relevant policy and investment arena. (UNCTC, 1991, p. 34)

Although Mandel's predictions in the 1960s failed to materialize, the present-day integration process shows a number of characteristics which correspond well with Mandel's ideas (see below).

Another equally functionalist interpretation was put forward by Murray, whose article 'The Internationalization of Capital and the Nation State', though first published in 1971, is still one of the most inspiring sources on these matters. Murray started from the 'problem of territorial non-coincidence' which came about as the result of the internationalization of firms: 'business everywhere is outgrowing national boundaries and, in so doing, is creating new tensions between the way the world is organized politically and the way in which it will be increasingly organized economically' (*Fortune*, 15 August 1969: cited by Murray, 1971, p. 85). His analysis was much more cautious than the one by Mandel. He perceived the emergence of a European state as just one of several possible developments which would reduce the tensions described. He differentiated between different state functions (such as guaranteeing of property rights, economic liberalization, economic orchestration, provision of labour, land, capital, technology, and economic infrastructure, intervention for social consensus, and management of external relations) and instruments used in the performance of these functions. He then analysed which functions have to be internationalized to match the internationalization of firms. His conclusion was that different functions could be fulfilled by very different actors: by a regional state, by regional or global international organizations (like the IMF, the World Bank or the BIS), by multinational corporations themselves, or by powerful national states acting in the international interest. World-wide American intervention to enforce respect for property rights and further liberalization of the economy would be a case in point.

From this point of view, economic internationalization is less directly linked to political integration, because international state functions could be performed in alternative ways. Such a view is much less deterministic than that of Mandel. It lends itself much better to an explanation of the conjuncture of European integration.

Drawing on Murray's ideas, one might explain the pause in European integration in the 1960s by the continuing American hegemony which ensured that a number of international state functions were fulfilled by the United States. The European integration process, therefore, could be limited to negative integration, i.e. to pull down the obstacles to internal trade without much further economic orchestration at the European level. But with the proven inability of the US government to fulfil major international state functions any longer, some of them had to be taken over by other bodies. This was an important reason to increase the responsibilities of European institutions.

Theories of international hegemony are linked in a number of ways to theories on economic internationalization, leading to different explanations of the integration process. Robert Gilpin saw the expansion of American multinationals largely as the other side of the coin of American hegemony. European integration, supported by the US government mainly for *political* reasons, remained acceptable to American interests, because it improved the profitability of their own companies operating abroad (Gilpin, 1975, p. 108). For many Europeans, however, the integration process was perceived not as a stepping-stone to a universal or Atlantic system, but as a strategy for the revival of European power and influence *against* US hegemony. This stream of thought could only become more prominent during the 1970s, when American hegemony had indeed weakened.

Impact on external relations with third countries

For an analysis of the impact of multinational enterprises on the EC's relations with third countries, it is obvious that a distinction has to be made between firms from third countries (mainly the US and increasingly Japan) and firms from member countries. As long as American foreign investment was of primary importance (cf. Dunning and Robson, 1988, p. 10) and American hegemony beyond doubt, an even-handed treatment of foreign and European companies remained a particular feature of EC policy (Dunning and Robson, 1988, p. 8). The activity of MNCs did not create much additional tension in the relations between the United States and the EC.

But after 1973, the European market became increasingly penetrated by outside producers. Until then, the EC's policy towards MNCs had been dominated by anti-trust considerations (cf. Lemaitre and Goybet, 1984, vol. 1, Chapter II). Relations had been adversarial rather than cooperative. For that period, the European institutions can certainly not be blamed for having been nothing else than the instrument of European corporations. Under the influence of the economic crisis in the 1970s, however, EC policy became less dominated by considerations of competition policy. Instead, it started to facilitate the restructuring of European industry, which often involved further concentration (Robinson, 1986). The more responsibility the EC took for the restructuring of European industry, the more it started to discriminate against firms from third countries. This has obviously intensified conflicts with the United States and Japan. The degree of protectionism has differed from one sector to another (cf. Milner, 1988). These differences can only be understood as an outcome of the bargaining among the firms involved. To understand the degree of protectionism of the EC in different sectors, it would therefore be necessary to start the analysis at the level of the individual firm (cf. Ruigrok, 1991).

Deficiencies of existing explanations

Functionalist explanations alone can never be sufficient (cf. Hollis and Smith, 1990, p. 47). The mere fact that a specific development would be functional for another does not yet bring such a development about. Functional explanations normally cannot explain *how* the expected outcome comes about, *when* exactly it happens and *which obstacles* have to be overcome in order to make it happen. They only explain why specific developments are more likely than others (because they would cause less friction).

In the case of the new dynamics of the European integration process in the second half of the 1980s, functional theories would have difficulties in explaining why it found new momentum in the mid 1980s. In order to give an explanation, we have to descend to the actor level. This does allow us to understand the steps taken at that time which changed the dominant mood in Europe from 'Eurosclerosis' and 'Europessimism' into a far more optimistic outlook.

Launching the ESPRIT programme
The European technology programmes, starting with the pilot phase of the ESPRIT programme in 1983, have played a crucial

role in this process. The common technology programmes, whether effective or not, made an important contribution to changing the public image of the EC inside and outside Europe. At the same time, they were instrumental in creating a large constituency of Community beneficiaries among business and academic elites. Given the fact that it has often been doubted that the technological benefits from these programmes outweigh their costs, one might be inclined to think that their symbolic function has been as great as their immediate contribution to the improved competitiveness of the companies involved.

The European Federation of Industries (Union des Industries de la Communauté Européenne, UNICE) had urged the EEC in the mid 1960s to facilitate inter-company cooperation at the European level. When the competitiveness of the European microelectronics industries declined dramatically in the 1970s, representatives of European information technology companies and national governments came together and discussed the future of European microelectronics in 1976–7. No European support plan was put forward, though, because the larger member states insisted on strict budgetary rules (commitments on a year-to-year basis only).

In the late 1970s, the twelve largest European electronics companies formed a 'round table'.[4] Some internal contradictions of the companies who fiercely competed with each other had to be overcome. As a consequence, it took several years before common action was taken. In 1983, the twelve sent a pressing letter to the European Commission in which they presented a dramatic view of the competitiveness of the European information technology industry and underlined that the national programmes of the large European countries were not sufficient to safeguard Europe's position in the long run. In close cooperation with the companies concerned,[5] the Commission then elaborated the European Strategic Programme for Research and Development in Information Technology (ESPRIT), which was accepted in record time by the Council of Ministers (cf. Van Tulder and Junne, 1988, pp. 213–16).

The ESPRIT programme has become a blueprint for the other recent European technology programmes (such as RACE, BRITE, FLAIR etc.). The experience with ESPRIT also contributed to the creation of the EUREKA programme, which is only loosely linked to the EC technology programmes and is not restricted to the pre-competitive phase of research.

In the decision-making process on the technology programmes, a new coalition come to the fore that helped to speed up the process of integration: a coalition between the Commission on the one hand and large companies on the other which were influential in the different member countries (cf. Robinson, 1986; Sandholtz, 1992, pp. 173–80). National governments were thus exposed to concerted pressure from two sides: from the EC Commission and, probably more importantly, from members of their national business communities which could flex considerable muscle on the domestic political stage. These coalitions can only be understood when the strategy of individual companies is looked at in detail.

Towards an integrated European market

(Neo-)functionalists saw their predictions discarded when the forecasted spillover did not materialize, and the integration process changed into low gear in the second half of the 1960s and the first half of the 1970s. Many disillusioned integration theorists left the field. Some of their disappointment, however, may have been due to their impatience with the pace of historical processes, rather than the fact that their theories were basically wrong. Spillover processes still play an important role in European integration, although the automatism hoped for in the 1950s has been disproven.

Immediately after the first technology programmes had been launched, it became clear that the development of new technologies alone would not increase the competitiveness of European companies, unless they were able to produce and sell the resulting products in large numbers. The programme for the common internal market, therefore, is a complementary element in the strategy which led to the European technology programmes. It would be an exaggeration to describe the programme for an integrated European market as a spillover effect to ensure the success of the technology programmes; but the awareness that the technology programmes alone would not help European industry enough has been an important element in decision-making on market integration.

The momentum towards an integrated common market has its roots in initiatives taken by individual companies. A crucial programmatic step in this direction was taken by the president of one of those firms which had also been instrumental in launching the European technology programmes. Wisse Dekker (president of the Dutch Philips company) delivered a speech in November 1984 on the occasion of the presentation of the programme 'Europe 1990 – An Agenda for Action'. He reminded politicians and businesspeople that Europe had not finished the homework given in Rome in 1957, namely to establish a common market, and to achieve a more convergent economic policy of the member states

(Article 2 of the Treaty of Rome). According to Dekker, time for a European answer to the American and increasingly the Japanese challenge, especially in information technology, was running out. Against the background of this analysis, the relevant Philips staff departments had drawn up a five-year plan covering the years 1985 to 1990 as a pragmatic aid to bringing the common European market in 1990 closer to realization (Dekker, 1984). The target year was changed from 1990 to 1992, but the main points in the Philips programme were reflected in the Commission's plan for an integrated market.

Monetary and political union

A common market necessitates common economic and monetary policies. Large European companies have always been in the forefront of those in favour of monetary integration. Stability of exchange rates within Europe or – even better – one single currency would reduce the operating costs (of accounting, labelling etc.) of many companies about as much as the abolition of customs formalities at the borders between member countries. It would facilitate their internal planning and reduce the risk in their operations. In the mid 1980s, companies like Philips were therefore already in favour of the use of the European currency unit (ECU) by private entities, something opposed at that time by national central banks (*NRC Handelsblad*, 4 June 1985, p. 17).

Europe's leading industrialists have recently underlined their preferences when they called for an acceleration in both the widening and the deepening of the European Community. In a report issued on 19 September 1991, the European Round Table of Industrialists, representing 45 of Europe's largest companies with a total turnover of more than $600 billion, 'appealed for the urgent completion of the single European market and rapid progress towards a single currency . . . The Community should extend full membership to all seven countries in the European Free Trade Area (EFTA) before the end of the century. This process should be accompanied by a strengthening of Community structures, and the development of a foreign and security policy' (*Financial Times*, 20 September 1991).

Large European companies were an important driving force behind the political process which led to the treaty of Maastricht. They were, therefore, highly critical when the results achieved were put at risk by the decision of President Mitterrand to hold a referendum on the ratification of the treaty. They even broke with their tradition to refrain from open criticism of European politicians when they blamed Mitterrand for trying to boost his domestic support at the risk of a crisis of the European integration process.[6] For the analysis of national policies towards European integration in the aftermath of Maastricht, the position of individual companies is, indeed, an important aspect in the policy-making process.

MNCs: the need for further disaggregation

Multinational corporations influence policy-making in a double way: through their economic activity, and through their political interventions. On the one hand, with their own investment decisions, private companies give shape to structures of the world economy which form the framework in which political decisions are taken. They have an impact on policy-making, because the resulting structures influence the definition of the respective national interests and politicians' leeway for political manoeuvre. In an open world economy, a government which makes a country lose its attractiveness for foreign investment will sooner or later have to change its policy or will itself be replaced by a government of a different orientation. The economic structures do not directly determine policy-making, but they act as *constraints* that (more or less clearly) define the policy space within which politicians can move.

Direct involvement in policy-making

On the other hand, company officials often participate or intervene directly in policy-making. If we want to understand the concrete political measures which governments take at a specific point in time, we have to incorporate a study of the activities of individual companies into the analysis. As has been described, they played a leading role in relaunching the process of European integration in the mid 1980s, and they continue to have a large say in foreign economic policy, which has moved to centre stage since military security issues have diminished in importance as a result of the end of the Cold War.

The relationship between companies and the Commission (and national political bodies) implies more than that of the normal lobbyists who try to impose their vision on government. Representatives of MNCs are often called in by government (or the Commission, for that matter) because of their in-depth knowledge of specific affairs, which civil servants would lack. Public authorities are often as demanding as MNCs. Representatives of MNCs get directly involved in political decision-making either when their interests are immediately at stake, or when the implementation of specific measures would need their direct cooperation. An example of the first type of issue would be trade policy; an example of the second type may be international environmental diplomacy.

Trade policy is a main instrument of foreign policy (Praet, 1987, p. 38). With regard to some countries or regions, EC foreign policy, for all practical purposes, *is* trade policy. EC policy towards Japan is a case in point. In the formulation of trade agreements with Japan, industry plays a leading role (cf. Rapoport, 1992). But companies have also been closely involved in policy fields which touch upon security issues. An example is the strategic embargo policy.[7] European governments tried to ensure the permanent involvement of the business firms concerned in the technical parts of the control process (Roodbeen, 1992).

An increasingly important new issue in foreign policy is international environment policy. In the negotiations on measures to prevent the depletion of the world's ozone layer, which resulted in the 1985 Vienna Convention, the 1987 Montreal Protocol and the 1990 London revisions, the European Community 'followed the industry line', according to the head of the American delegation: so much so that when the EC delegation charged that the Americans were complicating the negotiations by adding new chemicals, these views were put forward in a paper under the letterhead of Atochem, the French CFC and halon producer (Benedick, 1991, p. 78).

MNCs: no longer unified actors?

MNCs can be important political actors, indeed. But they themselves actually undergo internal change which may be very relevant for their political influence in the future. The realist image of the world has often been criticized for its unrealistic assumption of states being unified actors; it has been pointed out that large corporations can be important international actors as well, pursuing their own interests, independent of those of home or host governments. There is now the irony that it is actually increasingly questioned whether MNCs themselves can still be regarded as unified actors.

In spite of increasing concentration in many branches, we see that international competition has stiffened in most fields. This is due to, among other factors, the globalization of markets, trade liberalization, international standardization, and the blurring of the boundaries between different branches of the economy. Increasing competitive pressure has led to an acceleration in technological development, highly volatile markets and rapidly changing patterns of international cooperation and alliances. This, together with the quickly changing political scene, confronts large companies with the *problems of gigantism* more than before. These problems include: bureaucratization, elaborate hierarchies, lack of motivation, slow reaction to outside changes, loss of touch with the market, and too large a spread of research and development efforts.

To cope with these problems, companies have been forced to *decentralize*. This can be done in several different ways. It can be done by terminating some activities and relying more on subcontractors. It can be done by splitting a company into more independent subsidiaries, and it can be done by shifting responsibility down the line to lower management levels. More and more companies split up into a multitude of profit centres, dealing with each other at arm's length. They flatten corporate hierarchies, leave space to 'intrapreneurs', and slim down corporate headquarters. But this implies that they have to create room for diverging internal interests. As a result, it may become more difficult to define the common interest.

With more profit centres operating independently of each other, it may become increasingly difficult to put the weight of the company behind specific proposals. Since different *internal* interests (e.g. with regard to more or less protectionist measures against Japanese competitors) may neutralize each other, company spokespersons will more often keep silent and will not make any effort to influence the political decision-making process. Or different interests from within large companies may *compete* for political influence, because they are unable to nail down their own corporate headquarters on one specific strategy. In order to understand specific actions (or non-actions) by MNCs, we therefore have to disaggregate them as well.

Items for a research agenda

It is obvious that the interaction between global economic developments on the one hand and European policy-making on the other needs much more elaborate analysis.

More research is necessary not only on the direct involvement of MNCs in European policy, but also on the impact of *structural* change (brought about by investment decisions of MNCs) on the freedom of action of European policy-makers.

Another important research topic would be the analysis of the impact of international strategic alliances among firms on international relations – especially on the choice between a 'fortress Europe' and an 'open Europe'. How far do the alliances really soften international trade conflicts? Are most of these alliances nothing else than the continuation of competition by other means, which do not reduce the level of conflict between the countries involved?

As far as the direct involvement of MNCs is concerned, it would be desirable to differentiate between issue areas[8] with more or less MNC influence, and between the influences of companies from different industries, and to analyse some intervening variables which have an impact on the success of MNCs in influencing European (foreign) policy-making.

Finally, more empirical research is needed on the role of MNCs as unified actors. Is their capacity to exercise political influence reduced by their own strategies of decentralization? Or, will this tendency not impede company headquarters in formulating comprehensive strategies and bringing their influence to bear on public authorities?

Notes

1 Federalists start from the assumption that common institutions can be created *before* there is a concrete economic need. For them, the internationalization of the economy plays only a marginal role in so far as it may contribute to creating the political will to proceed with the integration process.

2 Lemaitre and Goybet (1984) underline that for the first 25 years of the EC, its major industrial firms gave little support to the idea of cross-border collaborative ventures; indeed they 'turned up their noses' at such attempts (cf. Dunning and Robson, 1988, pp. 13, 18).

3 In the *Fortune* lists of the 100 largest industrial companies in 1965, 69 were US companies and 29 were European. In 1980, 45 were American and 42 European. Of the 45 American companies, 20 were oil companies. If these are left out, the majority of the large companies came from Europe.

4 These were Siemens, AEG and Nixdorf from Germany, GEC, ICL and Plessey from the United Kingdom, Olivetti and Stet from Italy, Philips from the Netherlands, and Thomson, CGE and Bull from France: cf. Mytelka and Delapierre (1988, pp. 140–7) and Sandholtz (1992, pp. 163–6).

5 The technical director of General Electric Company explained in a statement before the UK House of Lords: 'I find it very difficult, as a member of GEC or any other of the 12 companies, to say that we do not think the shape of the programme as defined was sensible because we had excellent opportunity to influence it and in many areas I think we did . . . it is not a programme dreamt up by Brussels bureaucrats and forced on us, it is our programme' (House of Lords, 1984, p. 37).

6 See the comments by Umberto Agnelli of FIAT or Etienne Davignon of the Société Générale before the referendum. The chairman of the Round Table, the Frenchman Jérôme Monod, president of Lyonnaise des Eaux-Dumez, underlined that a European monetary union would have to come as soon as possible (*NRC Handelsblad*, 19 September 1992).

7 The US Assistant Secretary of Defense, Richard Perle, complained after a visit to COCOM: 'I learned more about the organization than I did about the subject they were discussing. Philips from Holland had a representative at the meeting. The British delegation also had private industry people with them, ICL and others. This is a regulatory institution with the regulees present' (cited by Roodbeen, 1992, p. 151, n. 162).

8 Policy at the European Community level is even more fragmented by sector than at the national level, 'although *within* sectors a great deal of informal coordination, among national bureaucrats and interest groups, takes place' (Keohane and Hoffmann, 1991, p. 13).

PART III FOREIGN POLICY ACTORS IN THE NEW EUROPE

6

The Evolution of the EC/EU as a Single Foreign Policy Actor

Ben Soetendorp

The transformation of the European Community (EC) into a single foreign policy actor through the formation and implementation of a common foreign and security policy has been a continuous goal of the member states. The challenges of the new Europe and the post-Cold-War era have offered the opportunity to boost the international performance of the EC as a unified actor. The process of transformation has been greatly accelerated by two events: first, the challenge of completing a single European market in 1992 and the prospect of a single European currency; and secondly, the unification of Germany.

The implementation of a single European market and the prospect of an economic and monetary union (EMU) has made the Community a major international power in its own right. Consequently it became essential to have an independent European identity and a more unified performance in the international arena. At the same time, the unification of Germany triggered a process of negotiations among the twelve countries on major institutional and political reforms leading to a political union. Responding to German unification, political union had the undeclared aim of reinforcing the integration of Germany into the EC, thus constraining the freedom of Germany to act alone.

As a result of these negotiations, the twelve heads of state and government adopted the Treaty on Political Union during the summit at Maastricht in December 1991. The treaty has made a common foreign and security policy one of the three pillars of the newly established European union (hereafter called 'the union'). But the Treaty on Political Union has not created a European superstate with a single foreign policy. While the EC is increasingly perceived by non-members as a would-be state, and is expected to behave as a state-like actor, it has not reached that stage yet. On the one hand the twelve countries reinforced their obligation to formulate and implement a common foreign and security policy and to act on their own only in cases of imperative need, arising in the event that the Council of Foreign Ministers fails to reach agreement on a common decision. But, on the other hand, the wish of some member states to retain national sovereignty in the field of foreign policy remains a major hindrance for the twelve to act as a decisive and cohesive force in international relations.

The member states were unable to reach any agreement on significant institutional change such as introducing majority voting with respect to certain issue areas, granting the Commission the (shared) right of initiative in some areas of foreign policy, and integrating the EPC Secretariat (which helps to manage the process of European Political Cooperation) into the existing EC institutions. While the member states discuss the option of a European central bank, the start of some kind of a European foreign ministry (within the Commission or the Council of Ministers) is not even considered. The title of a 'common foreign and security policy', as Hill (1991, p. 190) noted, suggests singularity rather than pluralism and is therefore of symbolic importance. The joint actions taken by the member states so far, dealing with conflicts in the Middle East, South Africa and Yugoslavia, raise some doubts as to whether the EC is playing as one actor. Moreover, the substance of this policy is in essence of symbolic value. As Hill indicates, it often means agreement to hold a common view or issue an agreed declaration, and does not necessarily mean agreement to act in the sense of devoting resources or projecting power (1991, p. 191).

The outcome of the year-long negotiations on the treaty of Maastricht raises, therefore, the question as to whether the willingness of the member states to act in international affairs as a single foreign policy actor has reached its limits. The willingness to share national sovereignty is an imminent condition for the capacity of the EC to effectively manage common foreign policies.

Enlargement of the Community in the future, and the expected reluctance of some neutral states to take part in all joint foreign policies, also raises some doubt as to whether the transformation of the EC into a unified actor will gain further momentum. In this chapter we will try to understand the gradual transformation of the EC into a single foreign policy actor with the help of the relevant dominant international relations theories and foreign policy approaches. The aim is to examine the relative utility of these approaches in providing an explanation for the gradual evolution of the EC into unified actor, and the prospects for the continuation of this process in the new Europe.

But first we will reflect very briefly on the main schools of thought in this respect: realism and neo-realism; neo-functionalism and regional integration theory; interdependence theory and regime theory. In the short overview that follows, we will focus on the question of what the most prominent scholars of each approach say about the phenomena under consideration in this chapter.

The relevant theoretical approaches

Realism and neo-realism

A starting point for our excursion into the relevant theoretical approaches, which can help us to understand the evolution of the member states' individual foreign policies into a single foreign policy, is the school of thought called realism, the most dominant theory in the field of international relations (Vasquez, 1983).

Realists stress that nation-states are the most important actors within the anarchic international system. International relations consists, according to the realist perspective, of the interaction between sovereign states in pursuit of their foreign policy goals. Non-state actors, like multinationals and other transnational or domestic interest groups, are of secondary importance. The realists view states as being unitary rational actors, which operate solely for their own interests. States calculate costs and benefits and seek to maximize their own power, which is in the realist view the ultimate goal of states (Vasquez, 1983, pp. 26–7; Sullivan, 1990, pp. 8–9; Stein, 1990, pp. 4–5).

The influential realist scholar Morgenthau (1951; 1952) argued that, because all politics is a struggle for power, securing national sovereignty has to be considered as an irreducible national interest, a fundamental value that shapes the basic foreign policy goals of each nation-state. But despite the basic assumption in his writings that national sovereignty will continue to be a central driving force in the international system, he does not rule out the willingness of states to transfer their national sovereignty to supranational organizations. However, he makes such a willingness conditional upon the mutual recognition of the national interests of the nations concerned, and an expectation of benefits that outweigh the loss of the nations' freedom of action (Morgenthau, 1952, pp. 972–3).

Morgenthau viewed the establishment of the EC as an attempt by the member states to compensate, through united effort, for the loss of power of the individual European nations, as well as an endeavour by France and the other European states to solve the natural superiority of Germany among the nations of Europe. After the failure to counterbalance the superior power of Germany by a system of alliances, which resulted in two world wars, France and the other nations of Western Europe are trying, according to Morgenthau, to draw Germany into their arms in order to disarm it and to make the superior strength of Germany harmless (1973, p. 509).

Another leading realist thinker, Waltz (1979), who is also labelled neo-realist, argued that progress towards the unity of Western Europe cannot be understood without considering the effect that followed from the changed structure of international politics. Emphasizing that changes in the behaviour of states have to be explained in terms of the structure of the international system, Waltz suggested that the creation of the EEC was made possible after World War II because the international system changed from a multipolar into a bipolar one. So long as European states were the world's great powers, he noted, unity among them could only be dreamt of. The emergence of the Russian and American superpowers created a situation in which Britain, France, Germany and Italy realized that war among themselves would be fruitless. Once the possibility of war among states has disappeared, Waltz explained, they are more willing to be engaged in an enterprise which is more beneficial to some parties than others. This is partly in the hope that other activities will reverse the balance of benefits, and partly in the belief that overall the enterprise itself is valuable. Economic gains may be granted by one state to another in exchange for expected political advantages, including the benefit of strengthening the structure of European cooperation (Waltz, 1979, pp. 70–1).

Waltz (1986, p. 343), in an answer to his critics, however, qualified his statements with respect to the extent to which the structure of the international system determines the behaviour of states. Although structures condition behaviours and outcomes, explanations of behaviours and outcomes are interdeterminate because both unit-level and structural causes are in play. In Waltz's view, one cannot say for sure whether the structural or the unit-level cause is the stronger. Structures shape and shove, he notes, but they do not determine behaviours and outcomes, not only because unit-level and structural causes interact, but also because the shaping and shoving of structures may be successfully resisted (Keohane, 1986, p. 343).

Hedley Bull, a major contributor to realism, rejected the notion that the state system is in decline because of the tendency of some states to seek to integrate themselves in large units. Discussing the phenomenon of European integration, Bull (1977, p. 264) makes the observation that, although the member states of the EC have not ceased to claim territorial sovereignty, they have gone some distance in a process of integration which might lead to the loss of their national sovereignty. But such a process of European integration, Bull argues (1977, p. 266), would result simply in the creation of a new European superstate which is in Bull's view simply a nation-state 'writ large'. However, Bull doubts whether the EC would reach the stage of a European state. It might result in a hybrid entity, with some sharing of sovereignty between national governments and the organs of the Community.

Neo-functionalism and regional integration theory
Haas, the most distinguished thinker on regional integration and associated with the neo-functionalist approach to international relations, believed that pure self-interest was one of the main reasons for the transfer of power and sovereignty from national governments to a new centre of authority. In his view 'integration' is conceptualized as resulting from an institutionalized pattern of interest politics, played out within existing international organizations (Haas, 1964, p. 35). According to Haas (1958, p. 13), a shift of loyalty will take place only if more satisfaction is expected from the new institutions of the Community than from the existing institutions of the nation-states. All progress towards integration has to be based, in the view of Haas, on agreements between the political elites of the member states, reached by an accommodation of individual interests. Haas (1964, p. 111) distinguished three patterns of compromise: accommodation on the basis of the minimum common denominator, typical of classic diplomatic negotiations; accommodation by splitting the difference, prevalent in the negotiations of international economic organizations; and accommodation on the basis of upgrading the common interests of the parties. Haas considered the latter mode of accommodation the most effective method of stimulating cooperation in one area that will lead to cooperation in other areas: a spillover of integration from one policy sector to another.

In an attempt to clarify this basic theoretical rationale which underlies the neo-functional approach to the study of the integration process, Schmitter indicated that spillover refers to the process whereby members of an integration scheme attempt to resolve their dissatisfaction with their attainment of the collective goals they agreed on, by resorting to collaboration in another related sector. Schmitter (1969, pp. 162–3) explains that by extending the number and variety of policies subjected to collective deliberation, spillover enhances the possibilities for combining sacrifices and benefits in intersectorial 'log-rolls'. In Schmitter's view, log-rolling or package-dealing permits intergovernmental bargains in which concessions are exchanged across several policy areas.

Complementary to the spillover process is the likelihood that the member states will be engaged in the formulation of a common foreign policy. Once agreement is reached and made operative on a policy or set of policies, Schmitter suggests that externalization is a likely outcome. Member states will be forced, according to Schmitter, to hammer out a collective external position. Schmitter argues that in the process of externalization, the member states will probably also rely increasingly on the new central institution of the Community (1969, p. 165).

Neo-functionalists later modified their theory and adapted it to the realities of the integration process. Lindberg and Scheingold (1970, p. 32), for instance, suggested that integration should be seen as a merger of national and Community decision-making systems. Instead of thinking in terms of the Community's capacity to impose decisions forcibly on the member governments, integration has to be considered as some sort of symbiosis between the Community and national systems. As a result, actors tend more and more to define their roles in terms of joint problem-solving rather than as agents of one system or another.

Moreover, neo-functionalists also developed a more updated view with respect to the outcome of the integration process. Reflecting on his earlier writings, Haas (1970) recognized that regional integration involves both a process and an outcome. However, in his view regional integration theory focused on the process of integration and neglected the possible outcomes of this process, the dependent variable. Haas therefore introduced three ideal types which might be used as possible temporary dependent variables. The first possible outcome of the process of regional integration is the 'regional state', which is an analogue of the national state. The second possible result is the 'regional commune', which lacks central authority. The third possible outcome, the 'asymmetrical regional overlap', might be considered as a synthesis of the two other types and more likely than the other possibilities. It has a centre with some authority, but the units also retain authority and are related to one another and the centre asymmetrically (Haas, 1970, pp. 634–5; Kaiser, 1972, p. 215).

In an analysis of the European integration process after the completion of the internal market in 1992, Schmitter also focused on the possible end-states of this integration process, that is the definition of its dependent variable. Arguing that the EC is not just another international organization, or a continental nation or a superstate in embryo, Schmitter (1991) treats the EC as a new form of political domination and integration. Schmitter discusses three possible end-states into which it might develop, which he calls a 'confederatio', a 'condominio' and a 'federatio'. A strict fulfilment of the 1992 obligations, that is the elimination of all barriers to the movement of goods, services, capital and persons, without establishing a single central authority to regulate these exchanges or to redistribute their effects among member states, will result in a confederatio. A condominio is created when the national states, in addition to the removal of all barriers to the exchange of goods, services, capital and persons, agree to establish sectoral agencies to regulate the conditions for these exchanges. The next possible outcome, the federatio, stresses the establishment of a single centre with overarching authorities (Schmitter, 1991, pp. 7–10). In Schmitter's view, the condominio is the most likely outcome. It would have advantages for the incorporation of new states, given the diversity of prospective members. But it would lead to a proliferation of functional institutions, which will increase the difficulty in coordinating policy outputs, and in representing the EC as a whole in negotiations with external powers (Schmitter, 1991, p. 9).

Interdependence theory and regime theory
Interdependence theory and its offshoot, regime theory, dominate the current study of contemporary efforts to establish cooperative networks and build communities beyond the state. The interdependence approach considers the implications of the emergence of transnational and other non-state actors on the global stage, as well as the increased international transaction among countries and between actors in different countries.

The interdependence or transnational view of international politics moved from the realist assumption that military security is the sole goal for all states, and that military statecraft is the dominant foreign policy instrument in international relations. Adherents of the interdependence framework felt that because of increased interdependence among states and the growth in international organizations, new issues such as the environment, health and fraud were added to the foreign policy agenda. Economic statecraft became a major foreign policy instrument. The transnational perspective also contributed to the erosion of the separation between foreign and domestic policies and the artificial distinction between high and low politics. It also contributed to the recognition that foreign policy is not made by unitary actors but is an outcome of bureaucratic politics and organizational outputs. It is also influenced directly and indirectly by domestic and transnational interest groups as well as by various international governmental and non-governmental organizations (Sullivan, 1990, pp. 9–11).

The interdependence and transnational literature highlights the importance of change in the decision-making structure of foreign policy. Because of the increased emphasis in interstate relations on trade problems, monetary politics and other economic issues, it is not only the foreign ministry which involves itself in foreign policy activities. Such a development creates what the two most outspoken interdependence theorists, Keohane and Nye (1977, p. 34), have called a transgovernmental policy network, and Karl Kaiser (1970, p. 358) described as multibureaucratic decision-making. Under 'complex interdependence' (a term used by Keohane and Nye to contrast with a realist view of international politics), because of the existence of transgovernmental networks, the importance of the national interest as a guideline for national policy-makers diminishes. The two authors assume that national interests will be defined differently on different issues at different times and by different governmental units (Keohane and Nye, 1977, p. 35).

Moreover, the contacts between national bureaucracies may change the officials' perspective and perception of their interests and lead to a different interpretation of the national interest. Keohane and Nye argue that governmental bureaucracies charged with the same tasks may lead to transgovernmental coalitions on particular policy issues. To improve their bargaining position officials may even bring actors from other governments or countries into their own national decision-making processes as allies.

But the politics of interdependence will not necessarily lead to cooperation. Reflecting upon their writings, Keohane and Nye (1987, p. 730) argued that, from a foreign policy standpoint, the problem facing individual governments is how to benefit from international exchange while maintaining as much autonomy as possible. To regulate international behaviour under interdependence and control its effects, networks of rules, norms and decision-making procedures are created. Keohane and Nye (1977, p. 19) called these 'international regimes'.

The concept of regime is extensively developed in Keohane's other writings, using theories of rational choice to explain the creation, maintenance and evolution of international regimes (1984, pp. 65–132; 1989, pp. 101–31). In a world of many issues, egoistic governments seek to form international regimes on the basis of shared interests. A hegemon may help, according to Keohane, to create shared interests by providing rewards for cooperation and punishments for defection. But cooperation can also develop among egoists without a hegemon, because international regimes perform the valuable function of reducing international transaction costs, reducing uncertainty and facilitating negotiations, leading to mutually beneficial agreements among governments.

The view that self-interest of states is the driving force behind the creation and existence of international regimes has also been suggested by other students of regime theory. According to Krasner (1983), egoistic self-interest, that is the desire to maximize one's own interests and power, is the most important incentive for states to cooperate. Stein (1983; 1990) argues that sovereign states have a rational self-interested and calculated drive to abandon independent decision-making in favour of joint decision-making. Regimes arise, according to Stein (1990, p. 39), when states are confronted with the dilemmas of common interests and common aversions. In both cases, jointly reached outcomes are preferable to decisions made independently.

Such a joint effort can be made through either collaboration or coordination. While regimes were created in order to solve the dilemmas of common interests which require collaboration, those established to deal with common aversions need only facilitate coordination. However, in both cases the creation of regimes has a most important effect on the criteria by which national decisions are made. The institutionalization of coordination and collaboration may lead governments to recognize the importance of joint decision-making, thus making governments joint-maximizers rather than self-maximizers (Stein, 1990, p. 51–3). Such an understanding is crucial for the maintenance of regimes, which might change as a result of shifts in the international distribution of power, affecting in turn the pattern of interests of the actors involved.

The assumptions of regime theory are incorporated in the approach Keohane calls 'neo-liberal institutionalism' (1989, p. 2). This perspective on international politics keeps states at the centre of world politics, but stresses that state actions depend to a considerable degree on prevailing institutional arrangements. Keohane argues that institutions, defined as 'persistent and connected sets of rules (formal and informal) that prescribe behavioral roles, constrain activity, and shape expectations' (1989, p. 3), both constrain states and make their actions intelligible to others (1990b, p. 734). International institutions have three regulative and constitutive aspects. They affect the incentives facing states, make it possible for states to take actions that would otherwise be inconceivable, and affect the costs associated with alternatives that might have existed independently. International institutions may also affect the understandings that leaders of states have of the roles they should play and their assumptions about others' motivations and perceived self-interests (Keohane, 1989, pp. 5–6).

To sum up, the theoretical approaches discussed so far have provided us with some insight into the obstacles to and opportunities in creating a single European foreign policy. Perhaps not surprisingly, realism and interdependence theory differ with respect to the impact of the attributes of the international system on the willingness or unwillingness of states to collaborate. Realism considers the anarchic character of the system basically as a disincentive to integration, while interdependence, on the contrary, sees in the interdependent structure a crucial incentive for co-operation. Both neo-functionalism and regime theory agree that self-interest is the basic driving force behind the willingness of the states to cooperate, though such a motivation is made conditional on the expectation that the gains from cooperation far outweigh the costs of uncooperative behaviour. We will turn now to the question of whether these approaches adequately account for the gradual development of a single European foreign policy, and the prospects for the future continuation of this process.

The relative utility of the approaches

Before proceeding to examine the relevance of these approaches in providing an explanation for the gradual evolution of the EC into a unified actor, we have to emphasize that our analysis deals not with the integration process as a whole, but only with one part of this process, namely integration in the area of foreign policy. The creation of the European Economic Community (EEC) in 1958 established a new entity which, under international law, has a separate legal existence from the member states (Twitchett, 1976). Although the Treaty of Rome does not mention a common foreign policy, a number of articles deal with the external dimensions of the EEC. Most important is the obligation of the member states to set up a common external policy. The provisions of the treaty give the EC the exclusive competence to represent the member states in matters of external trade. Consequently, the member states have gradually transferred most of their sovereignty in the field of foreign trade policy to the Community. The EC acts as one bloc in the major international trade negotiations under the General Agreement on Tariffs and Trade (GATT). It also concluded (as one entity) a number of trade agreements with third countries, to soften the discriminatory effects of the formation of the EC for non-member states. As Hine (1985, p. 6) indicates, it helped the EC to gain international acceptability, and gave the Community greater confidence in its ability to act as a single, very powerful actor in world trade affairs.

Without the existence of the EEC, however, there would have been no European Political Cooperation (EPC) in the field of foreign policy. It was not until the creation of EPC in 1970 that the evolution of the EC as a single foreign policy actor gathered momentum. During the last two decades the EPC has gradually evolved into a collective decision-making body, capable of presenting a common European view on international issues and of taking joint action. With the signing of the Single European Act (SEA) in 1986, EPC became treaty based and its task and procedures received a legal basis. But as the outcome of the negotiations on a European union indicates, the integration effort in the field of foreign policy still follows a separate road.

External incentives

There is little doubt that the need for the coordination of various national foreign policies in the 1970s, and the strong demand for a single European foreign policy in the 1980s, were intensified by sudden changes in the structure of the international system. The Arab use of the oil weapon in 1973 demonstrated the vulnerability of the member states to external events, and the necessity to improve control over the economic effects of the foreign policy decisions of its member states in an increasing interdependent world. The Middle East War in 1973 worked almost as an external federator (Regelsberger, 1988, p. 14), enforcing the member states, for the first time, to reach consensus and produce joint policy statements under the pressure of a major international crisis, and the most serious threat to their economic prosperity since the Second World War.

By the same token, the collapse of the Soviet Union's power and the decline of American power at the end of the 1980s, combined with the challenge of a possible American retreat from the European continent as a result of the end of the Cold War, and the likelihood of an enlarged Community in the 1990s, could be considered important motivations for the present attempts to reinforce foreign policy cooperation among the member states. As neo-realism and interdependence theories suggest, changes in international structure were indeed favourable to the creation of the EPC and the current endeavour to deepen the institutional framework of the EPC machinery. Nevertheless, efforts to erase the distinction between 'high politics' to be discussed within the EPC intergovernmental framework, and 'low politics' to be dealt with by the EC institutions in accordance with the specific decision-making rules of the EC, remain unsuccessful. Although all member states support the common goal of strengthening an independent collective European identity in international politics, they are unable to agree on major institutional reforms, such as a merger of the EC and EPC systems of decision-making and, consequently, the introduction of majority voting in the area of foreign policy. To understand this behaviour we have to examine the actors' incentives and disincentives for foreign policy cooperation.

Neo-functionalism and regime theory provide us with the most important incentive for member states to cooperate in the joint making of foreign policy. In the scholarly discourse of both schools of thought about the motives for integration and cooperation, the concept of egoistic self-interest occupies a prominent place. It is obvious that the benefits of the economies of scale were the most important reason for the member states to join the Community, to pool their resources and to establish a common commercial policy for their external trade. Compared with the United States and Japan, only the pooling of economic resources makes the Community a world economic power in its own right, improving the competitiveness of EC industries on the world market and expanding the Community's powerbase (Sjöstedt, 1977, p. 226). It has made the EC an economic power bloc that commands the largest share of world trade of any state or grouping (Hill, 1990, p. 35). Hence, the cost to member states resulting from the loss of sovereignty with respect to foreign trade policy was compensated by the benefit of being a member of the trade bloc with the largest share in world trade. It serves the members' interests by creating a large and exclusive internal market on the one hand, and protecting trade interests in the outside world on the other, offering them opportunities to exploit economics and politics on a larger scale (Ginsberg, 1990, pp. 67–9). The emergence of the EC as a coherent powerful trading bloc has given the EC at least as much potential bargaining power in international trade negotiations as the United States (Keohane, 1984, p. 211).

It goes without saying that the smaller member states have gained in international status from the addition of a foreign policy dimension to economic cooperation, either from representing the EC as a whole when they occupy the EC presidency, which rotates among all members every six months, or simply from being members of the Community. While this observation applies to the larger states as well, EPC served, in addition, some very specific interests of the larger states. France used the EPC framework from its very start as an instrument of exercising leadership in Europe, and exploited it as a tool to check the potential influence of Germany on the one hand, and to resist the United States' political influence on its Western European partners on the other. Germany also used EPC to give international legitimacy to a more active foreign policy orientation which began with Willy Brandt's *Ostpolitik*, and to cover up for Germany's international assertiveness under Kohl and Genscher.

There is little doubt that the changing status of the EC, and the perception it has acquired in the minds of the outside world as a unified powerful economic actor, have caused spillover from economic policy areas into foreign policy. As indicated above, the necessity to improve control over the economic effects of foreign policy decisions of individual member states started and reinforced the development of a joint foreign policy. The EPC was created to serve as an instrument for the exchange of information, consultation, harmonization of views, coordination of positions and the taking of joint actions by the member states. The rise in the economic power of the EC generated new impulses towards improving the international performance of the EC as a unitary actor. The central role which was granted to the EC as a coordinator of Western economic aid to Eastern Europe, as well as the increased involvement of the EC in institutionalized international meetings at the highest level (such as the meetings of the Group of Seven or the biannual meetings between the President of United States and the EC leadership), pointed up the difficulty of maintaining a dual system of foreign policy-making in the Community.

Internal constraints

However, there is as yet no institutional spillover from the EC into EPC. Contrary to the expectations of neo-functionalists and interdependence theorists, there are no indications of the member states' readiness to abandon the intergovernmental structure of EPC decision-making which requires unanimity, and therefore places every member state in a position to block a decision. In the early days of EPC a sharp distinction was made between foreign policy activities to be dealt with by the EPC machinery, and international economic matters to be handled by EC institutions. But as Hoffmann and Keohane note (1991, p. 27), international politics are increasingly played on the chessboard of economic interdependence, where the Community decision-making method predominates. For political and practical reasons, it has become increasingly difficult to maintain the artificial separation between the two systems, as the ministers of foreign affairs have to change continually their EPC and EC hats. In practice, therefore, an interlocking partnership has evolved between EPC and EC policy-making. The SEA and the Treaty on European Union stipulate that the external policies of the EC and the policies agreed upon in EPC must be consistent, but it carefully distinguishes the competence of the two, thus codifying the practice of duality.

Proposals for a major institutional reform aimed at the merger of the EC and EPC decision-making structures have again been discussed during the negotiations leading to the EPU treaty. Some member states are ready to lessen the distinction between the two institutional frameworks, but almost no member state is inclined to abolish the separation with regard to jurisdiction, competence and powers. The establishment of the European Council of heads of state and government as an overarching ultimate decision-making body in fact institutionalizes the existing separation between the EC and the EPC frameworks.

Thus, in line with the realist view of international politics, the fear of states losing control over the conduct of their foreign policy conditions the evolution of the new established European Union into a single foreign policy actor. The willingness of member states to pool their national sovereignty has been made from the very beginning conditional upon a mutual recognition of each other's interest. Faced with the dilemmas imposed on the member states by the international system, self-interest dictated that the member states cooperate in a common foreign policy, enjoying the benefits of economics and politics on the larger scale. But the shape this cooperation has taken was prescribed by the importance of safeguarding the individual interests of the member states.

Until the signing of the SEA, this principle also prevailed within the EC method of decision-making. As a result of the first institutional crises in the EC in 1965 the member states agreed that, whenever a member state considers its vital interests to be at stake, it has the right to veto EEC decision-making or, as the Luxembourg compromise says, the debate must be continued until unanimous agreement is reached (Ifestos, 1987, pp. 314–15). The convention that no member state should be overruled by its partners (contrary to the provisions of the EEC Treaty, which do not impose the principle of unanimity in all matters) ended with the ratification of the SEA. To overcome the possible unwillingness of a government to compromise on issues with respect to the implementation of a single market, the member states agreed to apply the voting rule of qualified majority to all the decisions concerning the completion of the internal market. In the Treaty on European Union, the principle of qualified majority voting was extended to other policy areas. This principle implies that the member states accept the notion that their interests could be sacrificed.

This is precisely why the twelve countries were unable to reach agreement on the proposal by the Commission and some member states to introduce decision-making by qualified majority vote in some foreign policy issue areas. The treaty still says that the Council of Ministers, the Community's decision-maker, has to decide and act on the basis of unanimity. Only when a decision has been taken unanimously may the ministers agree, again unanimously, that certain decisions to implement the common policy should be taken by qualified majority.

The prospects for institutional change
What then are the prospects for the continuation of the process of developing a single European foreign policy? As we have demonstrated, in spite of the opportunities offered by the transformation of the international system, national self-interest imposes certain limits to the further development of the EC into a unified foreign policy actor. However, studying the process of institutional change in which the member states have so far been engaged provides a more promising future.

The pattern of change in EPC is best described as adaptation through incremental growth (Haas, 1990, pp. 97–108). In such a process of change in international organizations Haas argues:

> The organization is created by states who decided that their separate interests cannot be adequately met without some mechanism for collaborative, programmed or joint action. The initial task of the organization is the elaboration of a program and a set of rules of

conduct to bring about such joint action . . . Adaptation by increments is usually informal; constitutions are not at first formally changed. Only later are formal rules and procedures brought in conformity with the actual changes. (Haas, 1990, pp. 97, 99)

Over the last two decades such a process of incremental growth has led to continuing progress in the institutional arrangements for the formulation and implementation of a European common foreign policy. Beginning in 1970 with some meetings of foreign ministers and their political directors, and the setting up of a network of national officials to exchange information and coordinate EPC activities, it has evolved into a complex foreign policy machinery which is led and coordinated by the country that holds the EC presidency. This process has created a network of informal contacts between national officials involved in foreign policy-making. The institutionalization of coordination and cooperation with respect to foreign policy matters has created a habit of cooperation. As a rule, the member states consult each other on all important foreign policy issues and adherence to this rule depends on the members' goodwill. But as a former policy-maker states: 'A kind of unwritten law has developed among the member states. There are no penalties attached, of course, but there is tacit recognition of a rule which may be broken from time to time, but which nevertheless exists' (Ifestos, 1987, p. 272).

This repeated practice, which has been coined by observers of the EPC as a 'coordination reflex', is an illustration of how actors involved in joint decision-making change from self-interested actors into joint problem-solvers and from self-maximizers into joint maximizers. In the long term such cooperative behaviour can prevail over the egoistic self-interests of the foreign policy bureaucracies and elites within the member states. These formal and informal decision-making rules and procedures were successively codified in the Single European Act and the Treaty on European Union.

Conclusion

Contrary to those observers of EPC who believe that the development of a machinery that leads to a single foreign policy has reached its limits (Ifestos, 1987, pp. 256–7), we expect that the process of incremental growth will help the member states to overcome their resistance in accepting some kind of merger between the EC and EPC decision-making methods. In overviewing the last two decades, one has to acknowledge that a large leap forward has already been made. In the early days of EPC, ministerial meetings within the two different frameworks had to be convened in two different capitals on the same day, simply to underline a clear-cut distinction between EC and EPC activities and to avoid any links between the two institutions. Today, the practice of interaction between the two frameworks has led to a growing participation of the Commission in EPC activities. The President of the Commission and the Commissioner of External Relations take part in the European Council summits. The Commissioner is present in all EPC ministerial sessions and participates in the activities of the Troika, especially in contacts with third countries.

A common foreign policy has not necessarily to be made by a supranational authority in order to reach a further stage. As mentioned earlier, regional integration theorists like Haas and Schmitter have already modified their expectations with respect to the most likely outcome of the current European integration process. As we have seen, both foresee not a single centre with overarching authorities, but a system in which national governments and the Community institutions share authority. Keohane and Hoffmann remind us that, for Haas, a supranational style of decision-making was more important than the domination of Community institutions over national governments (Keohane and Hoffmann, 1991, p. 15). Majority voting is an essential component of such a supranational style of decision-making and is currently exercised in a number of policy areas, thus enabling the member states to gain experience with this method.

The lessons so far indicate that introducing the principle of qualified majority voting has not diminished the importance of negotiation and the consensual settlement of issues that are formally subject to majority voting. This practice corresponds with findings in studies of other institutions where the need for consensus is emphasized even in situations where formal decision rules would permit majority decisions (Scharpf, 1990, p. 318). We believe that this experience will in future permit institutional reforms to introduce majority voting to the field of foreign policy. In the past, the two most outspoken opponents to majority voting, Britain and France, supported their willingness to accept the application of the principle of majority voting in other areas with the argument that 'the Europe of the twelve could not be administered as was the Community of the six and must adapt its decision-making mechanism to this new enlargement' (Keohane and Hoffmann, 1991, p. 21). After the expected enlargement of the Community to about twenty members, this rationale applies even more, and then the foreign policy area cannot be excluded.

7

Tensions in Sovereignty: Foreign Policies of EC Members Compared

Frank Pfetsch

With the formation of the European Community,[1] the foreign policies of the member states have become a two-track enterprise: on the one hand the members act like traditional independent policy-makers, and on the other they act like representatives of the EC/EPC. In other words, in the first case the EC is an inter-governmental organism and in the second case it is a supranational single actor. These are the two extremes, with many more behavioural possibilities in between.

The foreign policy behaviour with regard to European integration evokes the following questions. What are the motives and expectations of the various states for joining the EC? In what respect has foreign policy become internal European policy? How far is the EC an intergovernmental organization, and to what extent a single actor? How far are the different national interests being harmonized? To what extent have the various European states given up national sovereignties, and to what extent do the constitutions of the European states allow such a transfer of sovereignty to international bodies? To what extent have the foreign policies of European member states been changed since the founding of the EC, and to what extent do traditional foreign policy patterns prevail? Who were the agents of the integration processes: governmental elites, supranational organisms, elites in the Commission, in parties or in business? Is there a difference between high politics and low politics? How can we explain the rapid progress of integration during the 1980s (the Single European Act of 1986 for a European union, the Maastricht agreement of 1992 for a monetary union)? How can the more positive (i.e. the Netherlands, Luxembourg, Italy, Germany etc.) and the more negative (i.e. Great Britain, Denmark, Greece etc.) attitudes towards an integrated EC be explained? How can the two processes of deepening (European union) and widening (joining of EFTA countries and eventually at a later stage of some East

European countries) be evaluated? Is the EU sufficiently equipped for the challenges ahead (migration, new nationalisms, local wars etc.)?

In this chapter I want to concentrate primarily on the different attitudes and performances of the EC member countries towards European integration and how these different forms of unitarian and communitarian behaviour can be explained.

Theoretical explanations and shortcomings

In answering these questions we want to consult theoretical explanations existing in the field of comparative foreign policy analysis and international relations. A great variety of explanatory orientations exists at different levels of abstraction (metatheories, middle-range theories, empirical generalizations), at different levels of analysis (national, subnational, regional, international) and with different empirical scopes; also, the empirical domains to which they are related vary considerably. It is, in this regard, important to differentiate between several aspects.

The last decades have seen several theoretical debates about the integration process. These debates were between broad meta-theoretical schools: the functionalists started their attack on the realists; then the neo-functionalists had their encounter with the neo-realists and lately also with regime theorists; in Germany the opposing fronts were the economic functionalists on the one hand and the constitutional federalists on the other. It seems that opposing parties converge at least partly in what is called the new institutionalism (Keck, 1991). Moravcsik suggests that European integration in the 1980s was furthered by two phenomena: supranational institutionalism (i.e. EC institutions like the European Parliament and the Court of Justice), transnational business lobbies and initiatives by the Commission; and inter-governmental institutionalism, meaning the bargaining processes between governments marked by the finding of a common denominator in order to protect sovereign rights (Moravcsik, 1991).

A main analytical distinction for theories in comparative foreign policy (CFP) is that between internal and external, where *internal* refers to theories related to domestic factors of a given nation-state, and *external* refers to those related to the systemic structure of the outside world, called the international system or environment (Hermann et al., 1987). In principle, the comparative foreign policy literature focuses on the first set of variables and the international relations theory on the second, acknowledging that in reality boundaries often do not exist and interaction of internal and external factors marks the foreign decision-making process.

The distinction between high and low politics is important for the understanding of integration processes. *High politics* refers mainly to governmental politics in the field of foreign and security policy, and *low politics* to economic and more technical issues to be dealt with by governmental and non-governmental agents. The long run of European integration shows that, in the field of high politics, consensus among the EC governments has been difficult, if not impossible, to achieve; whereas in low politics, where transnational interests operate, governments have been more willing to consent. Because of the differences in the vested interests of governmental actors, there has not been that much spillover from low to high politics.

The stock of existing theories can be further divided into two sets of theoretical orientations, one in the field of *comparative foreign policy* and the other in the field of *integration*. The separation may be too artificial, but the perspectives are different: one starts from the nation-state and the other from an integrated entity. Here, too, the boundaries are shifting: is the internal market policy still foreign policy or has it become domestic policy?

Another distinction is made between theories referring to different stages of the integration process, i.e. the periods of *formation*, of *functioning* and of *future developments*. Interdependence and integration theory, constitutional theory, economic theory of federalism, needs theory, cybernetic learning theory and national interest theory primarily concentrate on the process leading to an integrated entity, whereas organizational theory, group theory, coalition theory, decision-making theory, bureaucratic analysis, collective action theory and regime theory are mainly concerned with the functioning of a political organization.

A final distinction has to be mentioned, the neglect of which sometimes causes confusion. Politicians follow *political strategies* which are not identical with the *theoretical orientations* mentioned; hence an action-related concept like the so-called magnet effect was primarily a political strategy proposed by the US and Western Germany to overcome the division in Europe, and was not a theory at any level of abstraction. Theories of the type mentioned above have not become political programmes.

In this regard, European politics can be considered to be composed of two streams of approaches, of which one may be called visionary and the other pragmatic. Visionary conceptions like that of the United States of Europe put forward by Victor Hugo, Coudenhove-Kalergi or Winston Churchill give guidance to politics. Pragmatic politics means the step-by-step approach to the realization of integration. Somewhere between are the constitutional proposals for a European union made by various EC commissions and individual elites.

The theory of comparative foreign policy as presented in the impressive book by Charles F. Hermann, Charles W. Kegley and James N. Rosenau (1987) has the merit of presenting the state of the art in American foreign policy analysis but shows two major deficiencies. One is the almost complete neglect of the historical dimension. How can we understand the revolutions of 1989 in Eastern Europe, and the dramatic changes occurring in the former Soviet Union or in the former Yugoslavia, without taking into consideration basic historical processes, the national, religious and ethnic patterns of long-term durability which now surface again? The cybernetic approach by Karl W. Deutsch,[2] developed in the 1960s, may help to fill the gap. He states that emphasis should be placed on interaction processes; governments have to deal less with problems of power and more with the problem of steering, i.e. with communication and control. A decision-making system consists of three types of communication flows: one about its environment, another about its past history and a third about itself. It is this second type of information which accounts for the long-term experiences of a social group or of an entire country. Another valuable addition comes from international regime theory, and compensates for a second shortcoming of Hermann et al. (1987). This is the distinction between internal international regimes which primarily regulate the patterns of behaviour among the members of a regime, and external international regimes which primarily regulate the patterns of behaviour of the regime members towards third parties (Zürn, 1987, p. 237). Applied to our study, this is exactly what we want to enquire: how was and is the foreign policy of the actual EC member states organized with respect to their integration policy, and how was and is the foreign policy of the members of the EC shaped as unitarian towards the outside world?

A new theoretical focus on the performance of European policies

The concept to start an analysis of foreign policy behaviour is that of the national interest in the tradition of the realist school of thinking, especially since it fits other theoretical approaches which do not neglect national interests; they only differ with respect to relevant actors (state versus non-state actors, national versus international or transnational actors) and in their emphasis on different policy fields and issues. Neo-realists try to show that under certain conditions it is in the mutual national interest of states to cooperate with each other (see Stein, 1990). Integration theory, e.g. by Karl W. Deutsch, states that the members that form a community must benefit from the integration process. In other words, the ideal result is a positive covariance for each of them; both should receive a value added or at least not lose or become worse off than before union (Deutsch, 1976, p. 8).

For our analysis the realist approach in its most original form must be modified and extended in three ways. The first is to open up the black box of a unitarian nation-state and take into account subgovernmental groups and parties. Being a unitary actor also means that the so-called national interest is determined by the calculations of governments, which only take into consideration domestic demands and supports. Secondly, in enlarging this solitary monadic view of a single actor, Richardson proposed a dyadic approach, meaning that decisions taken by an actor A also depend on the decisions taken by an actor B. Hence not only are domestic factors of importance, but also the behaviour of external actors (see Richardson, 1987, pp. 161–77). A third modification of the realist school of thought refers to the importance given to foreign policy issues. Whereas for Morgenthau the security issue is of primary importance, in the neo-realist version, like that of Arthur Stein, other issues are considered to be equally important. Nevertheless, according to realist thinking, the policies of the various European countries follow a certain pattern which can be described as a set of national or vital interest elements.[3] The joining of the EC is, in this view, in the interest of nations, and a coordinating body serves national interests. This again is a complex composition of geopolitical facts, power status, historical experiences, and the personal preferences of individual politicians and others.

In analysing the foreign policy of the EC member states, I want to concentrate on the *performance* of governments and other agencies with regard to European integration. A systematic frame of analysis of foreign policy behaviour can be found by asking what kinds of behaviour are possible and – following this – what views on the future shape of Europe do exist. We propose a classification of five possible forms of behaviour ranging from an independent national policy to a uniform supranational or federative policy:[4]

Table 7.1 *Relationships between behavioural patterns and types of integration*

Types of behaviour	National state	Union	Confederation	Supranational	Federation
1	x				
2		x			
3		x			
4			x		
5				x	x

Header note: "Types of integration" spans the columns National state, Union, Confederation, Supranational, Federation.

1 traditional behaviour of a national independent actor;
2 supportive behaviour, i.e. a single actor pursues national policies in the traditional way but with the support of, or acceptance by, member states;
3 joint action of some selected members in some specific situations, i.e. selective cooperation;
4 coordination and harmonization of policies with other members, i.e. mutual recognition;
5 uniform behaviour conducted by a supranational or federative organism determined by laws, i.e. standardized treatment.

These forms of behaviour are not mutually exclusive, but vary in time and from one policy issue to another. They can be related to various types of integration (Table 7.1). The *nation-state* is characterized by the centralization of executive, legislative and judicial competences in almost all policy fields. No government proposes this model for the regional integration of European states. *Unions* form an entity in relation to the outside world in a particular field (i.e. EFTA as a customs union), without central legislative competences but removing barriers among the composing entities; this model was proposed by free trade liberals at the beginning of the discussions on European integration. A *confederation* possesses a delegated single authority with limited competence. Its source comes directly from national authorities. The Council of Ministers represents this idea, and the EC of 1993 with the removal of internal restrictions has approached this type of governmental structure. *Supranationality* goes beyond this by giving competences to the central authority on its own, a model which finds its expression in the Commission of the EC. Finally, a *federal* system has a single centre with overarching authorities, but is based on the principles of subsidiarity, horizontal division of power, parliamentary control of the executive, a two-chamber system of legislation, decentralized fiscal systems etc. According to these criteria the EC is still a pre-federal construct, but the aspirations of some member countries are towards a federation.

The different forms of behaviour of the various European countries can be demonstrated in some important areas of post-war European policy. In the following examples we discuss European integration as an intra- and inter-community process, and as the dominant systemic structure in East–West confrontation. The other cases refer to German unification as a key problematique in post-war Europe; and to the Gulf War, a crisis situation outside Europe, as a classical foreign policy issue.

How are these selected case-studies related to our concept, and what do they say about the behaviour of the various member countries?

The national interest strategy

The national interest approach most explicitly prevailed in political crisis situations in which the European state acted outside Europe. A major example is the Gulf War. The different behaviours of the various European countries showed that there was no common or integrated policy of the EC. The efforts to build up a common platform succeeded on broader terms but not on specific issues. The EC had not developed a standpoint of its own, but more or less consistently followed the line of the US government and the Security Council. There was a harmonization of policies in specific areas, but no unified action.

Another case in this category is that of German unification. At first, the French government under Mitterrand showed traits of traditional European power policy. The President's visits to Poland in December 1989, and to East Germany shortly before the collapse of the Honecker regime, were meant to counter-balance the Federal Republic. Mitterrand's insistence on the acceptance of the Oder-Neisse border and Germany's commitment to European integration have been part of French national interests since the days of De Gaulle, in which the concentration was on independence and security. Mitterrand's concern with European integration and national security is clearly consistent with these national interests.

The British government under Thatcher was, as on other occasions (e.g. the Gulf crisis), very much in line with the US government. Germany should remain a member of NATO; and, in line with the Soviet government, the process of unification should be an evolutionary rather than a precipitated one. The Bush administration, compared with the other Western governments, showed the most positive attitude towards German unification.

Other fields of action where an independent national policy prevailed were the policies of member states with regard to newly independent former colonies.

The national interest supported

Supportive behaviour by the EC countries for a member country can be observed in the later stages of German unification. As an example of an inter- and intra-European issue, the reactions towards German unification after the collapse of the communist regimes by different countries – governments as well as public opinion – varied according to their own national interests and according to their specific historical experiences with Germany in the past. The closer the countries were situated to Germany and – consequently – the more affected they had been by Nazi expansionism, the less favourable they were and the more afraid they became of a strong new Germany. The governments accustomed to two German states were at first more reluctant and hesitant but adapted themselves relatively quickly to the new situation.

In various international crises the so-called special relationship between the US and the UK is another example of supportive behaviour. The Gulf War did show this close relationship and simultaneous moves as well as the insistence on the NATO membership of a united Germany.

In a wide range of continuously practised policy actions, individual member countries negotiated with third countries as representatives of the EC which strengthened their bargaining position. This repeatedly adopted strategy of negotiating based on an EC consensus was practised by EC governments, particularly in relations with the former Soviet Union.

Coordinated national interest

The joint action of selected countries can be observed in various Franco-German cooperations like that of a Franco-German initiative of 1984 or that of the Franco-German brigade of 1992. Other cooperative actions were taken by Genscher and Colombo in 1981, a German-Italian initiative for the promotion of the EC, which later led to the Single European Act.

The idea of cooperation between individual member countries in selected fields and on selected issues is the basis of the concepts of 'abgestufte *Integration*' (graduated integration), of 'l'Europe à géometrie variable', of 'l'Europe à deux ou trois vitesses', that is a Europe with different speeds. This means that the integration process can be accelerated by a certain number of member countries that later on will be joined by the others (see Scharrer, 1984).

Coordinated policies

Coordination and harmonization of policies take place in the frame of European political cooperation. Especially in the UN forums and in the world conferences, the EC often speaks with one voice.

In their attitudes towards the dominant systemic structure of East–West confrontation, governmental actions in the post-war era are shaped by the bipolar relationships of the superpowers with phases of tension or *détente*. The common denominator was a more or less explicit anti-communist line amongst the member countries' post-war governments. Depending on their geopolitical positions, historical experiences and potential capabilities, the various European countries did adjust themselves differently and did, therefore, show differing attitudes to the United States and the Soviet Union.

Whereas France was ideologically more open and flexible, Britain was more in line with the US, i.e. being tough on ideological issues and pursuing the Cold War on one clear-cut side. West Germany for its part had a more ambivalent position. On the one hand it pursued the Western policy of integration, but on the other hand it tried more than the others to bridge East and West by promoting *détente* policies. West German interest in unification or at least in the improvement of living conditions for East Germans could only be realized in a climate of *détente*. Therefore, in times of crisis, it acted as a mediator or 'translator' (Helmut Schmidt) between East and West. The national goal of unification was understood from the beginning in a European context. The two-plus-four negotiations about German unification were a demonstration of a coordinated policy.

The EC as a single actor

European domestic policy is dominated by economic issues of the European market. The year 1993 showed that European institutions, like the Commission or the European Parliament, act as third parties with competences of their own. Not only has the EC become a powerful trading bloc in international negotiations with comparable bargaining power to Japan or the United States, but the Commission represented by Jacques Delors showed, especially in the 1980s, initiatives with far-reaching consequences,

Table 7.2 *Countries by dominant behavioural patterns*

	Types of behaviour				
	1	2	3	4	5
Belgium				x	x
Denmark			x	x	
France	(x)	x	x		
Germany			x	x	x
Greece		x		x	
Ireland				x	
Italy		x		x	
Luxembourg				x	x
Netherlands				x	x
Portugal		x	x	x	
Spain		x	x	x	
United Kingdom	x	x		(x)	

like the single market and the European Monetary Union. However, the economic theory of federalism tells us that the EC internally is still a pre-federal construct. Although the Maastricht treaties apply some federal principles, like that of no internal frontiers, the regulatory triangle of free movement, a minimum of harmonization, mutual recognition, regulatory competition, efficiency-motivated transfers and subsidiarity as the assignment principle, the budgetary part of the EMU is radically different from existing federations. The chances for a move in the near future beyond pre-federalism seem to be slight (Pelkmans, 1992). To the outside world, however, the weight of the EC has, measured by the recognition from other trading partners, constantly increased and will do so after 1993.

Condensed empirical findings

Empirical findings show the country-specific patterns in Table 7.2. These behavioural patterns of the various European countries are influenced and, at the same time, determined by the views that countries have of the ultimate form of an integrated Europe. The more that national considerations prevail, the looser the Community is supposed to be (i.e. intergovernmental); the weaker are national considerations the more countries are committed to a tighter form of integration (i.e. supranational, federal). These different views on the shape of the EC are also influenced by the experiences of various countries with certain forms of government. Besides Germany, there are now three EC countries with quasi-federal structures: Belgium, Spain and,

Table 7.3   *Views on the shape of Europe by the EC countries*

	Intergovernmental confederation	Supranational	Federation (union)
Belgium			x
Denmark		x	
France	x		
Germany			x
Greece	(x)	x	
Ireland		x	
Italy			x
Luxembourg			x
Netherlands			x
Portugal		x	
Spain		x	
United Kingdom	x		

increasingly, Italy. Pressures to decentralize are on the increase in several other countries. These domestic experiences are well reflected in the views of the future Europe (see Table 7.3).

Explaining foreign policy behaviour

This empirically different behaviour, the perception of European governments, and the expectations concerning the form of government of the EC, all have to be explained.

The theoretical literature in comparative foreign policy distinguishes analytically between internal and external factors, meaning that foreign policy is influenced by domestic structures and actions and by those structures and actions coming from the external environment. International external regimes are determined by the coordinated actions of individual countries versus the outside world; hence, the approach tries to identify factors from within a region and not from the outside. It is in this sense that we want to deal with the external relations and commitments of the EC member states.

Internal factors

Domestic factors in foreign policy are considered to be important in all of the theories, i.e. Marxist as well as liberal and – to a minor degree – realist theories. To the Marxists the domestic class struggles, and to the liberals the elites of organized social groups and firms, are relevant actors in the foreign policy process (Keohane, 1990a, p. 165). To the realists, the individual non-governmental actors are not relevant, but the national interests represented by the respective governments are nevertheless bound to domestic considerations.

A hypothesis with regard to European integration states that the range of action (*Handlungsspielraum*) that a government possesses in foreign policy is dependent on the domestic structure: the more a government in its foreign policy actions has to take into account internal social groups and political parties, and the more the internal sociopolitical structure is segmented and fragmented and ideologically split, the more its foreign policy shows a low profile, i.e. it is hesitant to take major decisions without the consent of the relevant groups in the constituency.

Before discussing the operational procedures for these three domestic determinants, i.e. social structures, party systems and ideological consensus, we must consider how the influence of the normative frame of the constitutions of the various member states gives a first indication of the openness of countries to integration. Do the constitutions or jurisdictions of the member countries allow for the transfer of sovereignty to a supranational institution? Is there a 'standardized treatment' (Schmitter, 1991) of European concerns within the various member countries?

Since constitutional law emanated from the nineteenth-century closed nation-state, national sovereignty is the constituent element of all constitutions of the EC member states. The principle of national sovereignty was modified after 1945 by two constitutional provisions: firstly by integrating international law into national constitutions, and secondly by opening up the possibility of transferring national competence to international organizations. By contrast, in some manner all constitutions (except Belgium's) allow the transfer – in one way or another – of national competence to international institutions. Almost all of the constitutions state that international law is either part of or even superior to national law. However, some do not mention explicitly such a transfer of legal procedures or are very vague about the willingness to give up national competence.[5]

All constitutions are characterized by ambivalence or even contradiction over the link between national sovereignty and international orientation. This can be an obstacle when political groups hostile to integration use this ambivalence in their favour. It is because of this that constitutional prerequisites differ in some cases (Luxembourg, Belgium) from empirically verifiable behaviour, although most integration-friendly countries like Germany, Italy and the Netherlands (see Tables 7.2 and 7.3) possess explicit constitutional provisions.

As to the internal explanatory variables, i.e. party structures, Hagan has tested the following hypothesis: 'Pronounced political divisions within a regime and the occurrence of strong political pressures threatening to remove the regime from power are likely to have a broad impact on . . . a regime's conduct of . . . two decision-making dynamics: controversy avoidance and consensus building' (Hagan, 1987, pp. 348–9). This is also what democratic concordance theory states, namely that internally fragmented and segmented societies develop cooperative strategies and, as a consequence, can develop a policy of neutrality (see Lehmbruch, 1969). Another variation of the same idea is the consociational approach of Donald Puchala, who states that units with cleavages such as language, religion or ethnicity can develop joint and consensual decision-making strategies which can be achieved by the establishment of grand coalitions of representatives of each of these segments (Puchala, 1981, p. 238). Other theoretical approaches like those of corporatism and neo-corporatism, bureaucratic theory and incrementalism, also focus on the elements of the internal political process and could be applied to foreign policy decision-making. Hagan's test shows that the very positive commitment to European integration in countries like Italy, Germany and France was, contrary to the hypotheses, not constrained by fragmented party regimes. The same holds for the vulnerability aspect. In the countries mentioned there was no dramatic change in government. The same results were obtained by Hagan on a much broader empirical basis and show positive correlations between regimes' attributes (fragmentation, vulnerability) and policy commitments. Hence, multiple-party constellations – to use a softer term for fragmentation – do not matter in foreign policy and, in particular, do not explain the direction in which commitments are given. These theoretical statements are not satisfactory in explaining external relations. Other factors have to be considered.

External factors

The other sets of variables influencing foreign policy behaviour and elements of theoretical explanations relate to the outside world. Two sets of variables can be distinguished: those of the international system and those related to alternative foreign policy orientations *vis-à-vis* other countries, namely what are called internal and external international regimes.

As to the variables related to the external international system, the theoretical literature focuses mostly on security issues (threat), power structures (hierarchy), anarchy (homogeneity), etc.

As to variables related to the internal international regime, the policy agenda has various policy alternatives which may be ordered along priorities and which are linked to each other. In the case of France the commitment to European integration goes along with security *vis-à-vis* Germany and – in the years following World War II – with expectations of being politically influential on the Continent. In the case of the Federal Republic of Germany, policy towards European integration was complementary to the policy of unification; hence, integration was in the national interest of Germany (defined in terms of unification) as much as it was of France (defined in terms of security).

Another external hypothesis relates integration policy in a given period with foreign policy orientations in former and present periods. The more a country was/is engaged outside the European Community, a field in which it can play independent national power politics, the less it was/is willing to engage itself in a system of interdependence. The test of this bilateral versus multilateral hypothesis results from the comparison between the bilateral external orientations and the multilateral commitments to Europe by the twelve European countries. In their orientations, countries differ widely. Great Britain, France, Portugal, the Netherlands and Belgium had rather strong colonial engagements; Greece, Ireland and Great Britain had bilateral commitments; only Italy, Denmark and Luxembourg were relatively free as to bilateral engagements. Some champions of European integration like France had in the founding period of the European Economic Community rather strong commitments in trans-European affairs: *la communauté française* with colonial and former colonial countries, a network of military bases, agreements, programmes from Cape Verde to the Comoro Islands, from Dakar to Djibouti, the Indo-China War, the Algerian War, the Suez debacle, etc. All these engagements and events could have led France away from Europe. But its national security interests in Europe prevailed and let France opt for a multilateral engagement in the form of European integration. Geographically close interests were given priority over remote national interests.

In addition, the extra-European engagements were in decline and partially substituted by the US role; with the dissolution of colonial empires and the absolute and relative decrease in their potentialities, Europe became a new frame of action for those with formerly strong colonial engagements. Europe was then closer and more vital to national interests. These and other extra- and intra-European engagements and commitments did not prevent France or Belgium from joining the European Community at the very beginning, but made Britain and Portugal hesitant; nevertheless, the different external commitments help to explain the degree of Community commitments by the different countries. The general as well as specific situations of Britain and France, and later, Portugal, explain their governmental or intergovernmental approach towards European unification and the more integrative approach by Germany and the smaller European states.

Extending the theoretical approaches
Why is it that countries with strong links outside Europe turned nevertheless, and partially in contradiction to our hypothesis, to European integration? Several factors, both common and country specific, must be mentioned as modifying the theoretical statements.

General theoretical orientations include the following:

1   Structural approaches such as those by Hagan neglect completely the agent variable and fail, therefore, to explain observable foreign policy behaviour. The agent–structure debate has to come in here (see Wendt, 1987; Dessler, 1989).
2   Theories of political economy grasp the post-war situation: the war weakened all European states regardless of winners or losers; the destruction of human and economic resources diminished the power bases and made great power policy impossible.
3   The conception of power of Morgenthau, among others, describes the evaluation of this loss of power in absolute terms and in relation to the new superpowers.
4   Learning theories conceive of the search for something beyond nationalism after the intellectual and moral failure of European nationalism.

Country-specific theoretical orientations include the following:

1   Rational choice or substitution theories and the realist approaches grasp the change of the foreign policy agendas of former major European powers: traditional foreign policy orientations had to be given up in favour of European orientations.
2   Theories of collective needs may incorporate security as a collective good: in the era of the Cold War, security was not defined in national terms any more; the forming of alliances and the building up of integration schemes proved to be an appropriate solution.

3   The dyadic approach of Richardson covers mutually related policies of member countries: some countries had special relations with specific countries and/or bilateral engagements like Portugal and Spain, Ireland and the UK, Greece and Turkey, the UK and Germany with the United States etc.; their action can only be understood by reciprocal reference.

4   The neo-realist approach and integration theories help us to understand why, for Germany, Europe constituted not only a substitute for nationalism, but also a frame for the solution of the so-called national question.

Conclusions

If we follow our scale of five behavioural attitudes, we may say that the individual member countries can be identified with each of the possible behavioural attitudes depending on the specific issue. On the whole the EC, in most of the cases examined, acted as a coordinated flexible governmental entity over broad issues and general positions. On specific matters, national political interests prevailed and differences became clearly visible.

As to theoretical explanations for the five forms of foreign policy behaviour, the applicable concept is certainly that of national interest, which is in the centre of the realist school. However, we have to use this concept in the modified and extended version of the neo-realists in combination with the liberal schools of interdependency together with learning and image theory. This means that internal structures and processes, put together with agent–structural links as well as the combined and interrelated external actors' behaviour, account for foreign policy decision-making. Past experiences, perceptions of the behaviour of other actors and that of new international constellations, country-specific situational facts and economic interests, are relevant determinants.

Regarding the relevance of theoretical constructs to explain reactions to events (positions on particular policy issues), we have come to the conclusion that the neo-realist approach together with integration theory is best suited to explain the behaviour of the EC member states. Besides the concepts of individual and common interests put forward by the realist and neo-realist schools, other conceptions like learning theory (historical experiences of each of the countries), the dyadic approach (importance of reference societies), liberal economic theories (expectations of economic advantages, economies of scale), and perception and image theories (threat of internal and external communist forces) have to be considered.

The hypotheses on the relations between domestic structures (constitutional provisions, party structures) and external behaviour, and on the relations between bilateral extra-European engagements and intra-European communitarian behaviour, could not be verified with the help of domestic structural theories in each of the cases tested. Our discussion suggests that other indicators of the description of the internal structures, potentialities, historical experiences etc. have to be taken into consideration.

Looking at the prospects of the European Union for the 1990s, our analysis has shown a strong commitment by national governments to national interests defined in terms of geopolitics, history, economic and political expectations etc. These factors counterbalance the communitarian drive of a single market and the strengthening of supranational agencies; they will not lead automatically to a common foreign policy of the EU member states in other policy fields except the economy. The spillover effects proposed by the functional school do not work in the way they were expected to. We observe a parallelism of supranational and intergovernmental institutionalism, where a redefined realism plays its part.

Summing up the value of theoretical constructs for the explanation of the behaviour of individual states of the EC, there are various theories at different levels of abstraction existing independently and referring to different empirical domains. So far, theories and theoretical orientations cover only partially the empirical field of European integration. An integrated theory remains on the CFP and IR research agenda.

Notes

1 In this chapter we deal neither with security issues (NATO, WEU, CSCE, Genscher-Colombo initiative 1981, Franco-German proposal 1990 for a European defence policy, Franco-German brigade initiative 1992 etc.) nor with other political and economic organizations with European participation like GATT, OECD, G7 etc. We understand European Political Cooperation (EPC) as part of the EC, now EU, though their organizational schemes are not (yet) finalized.

2 See a clarifying version of his cybernetic model by Dieter Senghaas (1966, pp. 252–76).

3 With some reservations it can be said that the theoretical development in the field of comparative foreign policy is a process of increasing differentiation of the concept of *Realpolitik*: differentiation as to state and non-state actors, as to policy fields (security versus economic, social, cultural etc.), as to levels of action and levels of analysis etc.

4 We incorporate Schmitter's (1991) three behavioural principles and practices into our five behavioural patterns.

5 More particularly, as to the transfer of national competence to international organizations, the most explicit constitutions are those of the Federal Republic of Germany (Art. 24,2, Art. 23), Denmark (Art. 20), Greece (Art. 28), Ireland (Art. 29,3/4), Italy (Art. 11), the Netherlands (Art. 92), Portugal (Art. 8,3) and Spain (Art. 93). More restrictive are the constitutions of France (only procedural prerequisites are mentioned) and Luxembourg (only temporal transfers are allowed); Belgium and the United Kingdom have no explicit provisions.

8

After Maastricht: Explaining the Movement towards a Common European Defence Policy

Alfred van Staden

This chapter seeks to explain the recent expansion of the European integration process into the hitherto uncharted areas of military security and defence. The frame of reference is the negotiations among the twelve EC countries which took place in 1991 and resulted in the treaty of Maastricht by the end of the year. The treaty created a European union with a separate pillar for foreign and security policy. The implementation of the treaty provisions, as far as security and defence are concerned, is likely to lead to enhanced European roles, responsibilities and contributions in the management of international crises and contingencies in which military capabilities may be required. In view of the European Community's traditional abstinence from military affairs as well as NATO's virtual monopoly of dealing with threats facing the West, one can hardly fail to recognize the significance of the development, even though it may be true that, as the impotence and disunity of Western European states towards the tragic events in the former Yugoslavia have borne out, the twelve are still far removed from a real common defence. But, as Alfred Pijpers writes: 'The tailpiece of a European federal order, a Community defence, seems to have entered the realm of serious options' (1992, p. 283).

To put the analysis into theoretical perspective, two rival theoretical approaches will be discussed: neo-functionalism, stressing the internal dynamics of the integration process; and structural realism, focusing on the challenges arising from changes in the international system. An attempt will be made to assess to what extent each of these two approaches accounts for the current drive for European defence cooperation.

The juxtaposition of both schools of thought, in the context of the subject under discussion, might appear a little surprising. Indeed, functionalism and realism (the intellectual predecessors of the two) represent the principal antithetical perspectives on world politics (Nye, 1988). Whereas functionalism perceives wide opportunities for international cooperation owing to the growing economic and technological interdependence among states, realist theory considers competition and conflict to be permanent features of international politics. Prominent realist writers like Arnold Wolfers and Hans J. Morgenthau have argued that the dynamics of world politics can best be understood in terms of the perennial struggle for power among states guided by a rational understanding of the national interest. Realist analysis starts from the assumption that, as a result of the absence of a central authority in the world, anarchy prevails in international relations. International anarchy prevents governments trusting each other and embarking on cooperative endeavours, because misjudgements about the peacefulness and goodwill of other states may damage the national interest or even jeopardize national survival. Also, in an interdependent world cooperation is supposed to be difficult to bring about since states are more concerned with *relative* than with *absolute* gains (Grieco, 1988).

In contrast, as A. J. Groom and Paul Taylor (1975, p. 2) have suggested, functionalism 'begins by questioning the assumption that the interests of governments prevail and proceeds to the active consideration of schemes for cooperation; it is peace-oriented and seeks to avoid a win–lose stalemate framework'. Functionalist ideas have been embraced extensively to analyse the early development of European integration in the 1950s. However, the subsequent decade seemed to refute most functionalist assumptions since the political leaders of some Western European states (first and foremost France) became increasingly reluctant to relinquish their national sovereignty and to accept the expanding authority of the European institutions. After being discarded as a useful explanatory framework in the years of stagnated integration and so-called Eurosclerosis, functionalism received renewed attention after the mid 1980s when the EC countries succeeded in causing a *relance européenne* and were heading for the single integrated market in accordance with the famous 1992 scheme. To quote Paul Taylor again: 'The student of the EC in the 1980s needs to return to the writings of a group of scholars – the neofunctionalists – whose writings have for many years been unfashionable' (1989, p. 23). As the twelve, in their parallel negotiations about the economic and monetary union and the political union, have been able to move further along the road of European integration, one may add 'the student of the EC in the 1990s' as well.

Regarding the relevance of structural realism to explaining the movement towards a common European defence policy, one should bear in mind that the latest expansion of the European integration process has occurred in a rapidly changing international environment. The chain of events since the fall of communism in Europe and the breakup of the Soviet Union has been so profound and so unique in its ramifications that no observer can overlook with impunity its consequences for the European unification process. Undoubtedly neo-realism, and especially the brand of structural realism elaborated by Kenneth Waltz, offers several valuable insights into the relationship between international system change and the parameters of the growth of integration.

The main thrust of the argument underlying this chapter is the notion that the process of European integration may be seen as a two-level game in that the pace and direction of unification are circumscribed by both the internal dynamics of economic, technical and social changes, and the pressures arising from the international environment (Wallace, 1990). It is also contended, however, that no full explanation for the security arrangements in the Maastricht treaty can be found without taking into account the previous processes of bargaining among the European political leaders. The results of the negotiations clearly reflect the power and interests of the larger EC states.

European integration and security: past and present

The history of the European integration process is marked by a striking paradox. On the one hand, initial efforts to create greater unity in the western half of the European continent were driven to a significant extent by considerations of security. Thus, the major motive underlying the plan for the European Coal and Steel Community of the early 1950s was to guarantee a lasting peace between France and Germany. War between the two was to be made not only 'unimaginable' but also impractical by developing webs of interdependence. On the other hand, the actual expansion of European integration evolved at the level of economic and social needs rather than at the level of high politics (i.e. foreign policy and defence). Collaboration in the field of military security was emphatically ruled out under the provisions of the Treaties of Rome, giving birth to the European Economic Community and the European Atomic Energy Community in 1957.

The abortive attempt some years before to establish a European defence community, arising from a pressing need to integrate Western Germany into the Atlantic alliance, did not fail to affect the future course of the integration process. The major reverse it caused put security firmly at the bottom of the agenda of European integration (Gambles, 1991). The military protection of

Western Europe became or rather remained the sole responsibility of NATO, with the European countries (except for France) accepting the political leadership of the United States. The predicament of structural dependence on American military protection may be interpreted as one of the main reasons why the European Community did not succeed in achieving a fully fledged political community (Calleo, 1987). Yet, it has also been argued that it was only because of the protective shield raised by the United States that the former warring states of Western Europe were able to bury their hatchets and to successfully pursue their integration objectives (Joffe, 1984).

After the eventual failure in 1962 of a renewed French attempt to achieve closer political and military cooperation within the framework of a political union (the so-called Fouchet proposals), no official plans bearing on the question of security were launched until the beginning of the 1980s. European Political Cooperation (EPC), which was created in 1970 on a strictly intergovernmental basis outside the formal community structure, tried to achieve cooperation on matters of foreign policy by means of extensive policy consultation and exchange of information. Although EPC also became engaged in coordinating the positions of the twelve on, for instance, CSCE-related issues, discussions (let alone decisions) on military hardware remained the *domaine réservé* of NATO. Thus, for example, the Genscher-Colombo initiative of 1981, which was designed to extend EPC to matters of defence, drew a negative response from several EC members. The Single European Act (SEA) of 1986, which has been heralded as a major step towards further integration, provided EPC with a formal status (under Title III, Article 30) but was very cautious on the issue of security. It referred to the parties' readiness 'to coordinate their positions more closely on the political and economic aspects of security'. In fact, the SEA meant 'nothing more than the formalization of what already existed in EPC practice, plus an EPC Secretariat' (Pijpers et al., 1988, p. 29).

The rather scholastic distinction between the political and economic aspects of security on the one hand and its military aspects on the other proved to be untenable in reality. The political crisis which broke out in Yugoslavia in the course of 1991 is an instructive case in point. Having started its involvement with the war-stricken country by making strenuous political mediating efforts, the EC decided to impose economic sanctions and to send observers to monitor the cease-fires agreed between the fighting factions. The observers were recruited from both military officers and civilian officials of the EC countries, and provided with military transport facilities. As soon as it became clear that the EC observers were quite unable to keep the peace, discussions began as to whether the Community should turn to the WEU, demanding the dispatch of a peacekeeping force. The final decision to organize such a force under the auspices of the United Nations does not alter the fact that during the Yugoslavian crisis joint diplomacy among EC members had become a policy in itself, and that the sending of observers to an explosive situation had brought the Community to the brink of direct military intervention.

Meanwhile, France and Germany deserve credit for putting the issue of security and defence once again high on the EC agenda. Their combined actions led in December 1990 to the decision of the European Council to mandate the so-called intergovernmental conference (IGC) with starting negotiations on the establishment of a European political union, in parallel to negotiations on economic and monetary union. Apart from the objective of achieving more effective decision-making in the EC, a better balance between its institutions, and more democratic control, the negotiations were mainly focused on seeking new arrangements for tightening EC cooperation on foreign policy and defence. As implied above, the Maastricht Treaty on European Union has paved the way for the union to deal also with the military aspects of security. Under Title V, Article J4(1), it is stated that '(the) common foreign and security policy shall include all questions related to the security of the European Union, including the eventual framing of a common security policy, *which might in time lead to a common defence* (italics added).' In the first stage, however, it is for the Western European Union – as the European union's defence components – to formulate a common European defence policy and to carry forward its concrete implementation through the further development of its operational role. Article J4(2) defines WEU as 'an integral part of the development of the European Union' and lays down the WEU, upon the request of the European Union, will elaborate and implement decisions and actions of the union 'which will have defence implications'. In spite of the cautious approach followed in the Maastricht treaty, it is of more than symbolic importance that the idea of a common European defence is no longer anathema at the official EC level.

Internal dynamics versus external pressures

Integration theory stands apart from other theoretical approaches to international politics in that it assigns causal significance to the process of integration itself. It postulates specific political effects stemming from the internal logic of integration (Sandholtz and Zysman, 1989, p. 98). This observation especially applies to neo-functionalism, the most influential school of regional integration over the past decades. In foreseeing a gradual expansion of integration 'from within', neo-functionalism builds on the basic tenets of classical functionalism as developed in the writings of David Mitrany and others. At the heart of the functionalist idea lies the assumption that, as the modern world becomes more interdependent, the present nation-states are less capable of solving problems facing humankind. The nation-state is believed to be particularly lacking in its ability either to preserve peace or to improve the social and economic well-being of its inhabitants. Pointing to the urgent need for organizing collaboration across national borders, functionalism holds that joint concerns of poverty and deprivation, regarded as the main roots of war, can be dealt with cooperatively by establishing international organizations run by technical experts rather than by conventional politicians. The transference of functions to these organizations is supposed to lead to a shift of public loyalty from the national to the international level. As the web of functional cooperation grows more dense, the freedom of state action is expected to become more constrained and national sovereignty to be eroded.

The essence of functionalist theory is, of course, the notion that successful collaboration in one technical field engenders collaboration in another. This is what Mitrany's famous doctrine of ramification is about: it is based on the plausible thought that cooperation result from felt needs, and that the satisfaction of those needs generates needs for cooperation in functionally related areas. Thus, as the history of the European Community reveals, the decision to create a common market not only implies measures to abolish national trade barriers (such as tariffs and quotas) but in due course is also likely to trigger pressures for fiscal harmonization and monetary cooperation. For this chapter's subject it is important to note that the functionalist argument has been carried outside the sphere of low politics to that of high politics. In other words: cooperation bred in socioeconomic fields eventually will also spill over to foreign policy and defence.

Basically, neo-functionalists have continued the functionalist line of thought that integration proceeds through the 'expansive logic of spillovers'. One of them, Philippe Schmitter, defines this mechanism as 'the process whereby members of an integration scheme – agreed on some collective goals for a variety of motives but unequally satisfied with the attainment of these goals – attempt to resolve their dissatisfaction either by resorting to collaboration in another, related sector (expanding the scope of mutual commitment) or by intensifying their commitment to the original sector (increasing the level of mutual commitment) or both' (1969, p. 162). Furthermore, spillovers have been compared to a learning process in which the occurrence of benefits in certain situations leads to the learning of certain types of behaviour connected with these situations (Clark and Welch, 1972, p. 375).

Leading representatives of neo-functionalism, such as Haas (1958), Lindberg (1963) and Nye (1971), concur that integration processes have the best opportunities in functionally relevant sectors with wide social ramifications, e.g. trade, energy, agriculture and transport. However, they differ from classical functionalists not only in the emphasis they place on supranational institutions, in contrast to the less tightly knit international organizations envisaged by Mitrany. They also differ because of their common view that integration should never be conceived as a spontaneously proceeding process which is started more of less automatically and fuelled by a momentum of its own. Much more than its intellectual predecessor, neo-functionalism is mindful of the political dimension of integration processes, i.e. the inevitable conflict of interests, bureaucratic clashes, and endless negotiations with direct interference from political authorities. Some social and economic conditions may favour integration and others may not, but additional steps towards integration are essentially dependent on political decisions, that is acts of political will.

Of crucial importance here are the expectations of gain or loss held by major groups within the unit to be integrated. Haas (1958, p. 13), in particular, focuses on the role of governmental and non-governmental elites who support integration for mainly selfish rather than altruistic reasons. If elites and interest groups have expectations of gain from activities within the new framework, they are likely to coalesce with like-minded elites across national borders. It is these transnational networks that become powerful actors in the integration process by making demands and raising support. Unlike Mitrany, Haas does not assume that international cooperation, as advocated by technocrats, bureaucrats and representatives of business and labour organizations, bypasses politics. He contends that, as a consequence of the actions taken, there will be a gradual politicization of those actors' purposes which were initially regarded as technical or non-controversial.

Later, having reflected on the disappointing development of European integration in the 1960s (and on the phenomenon of de Gaulle), Haas (1967, p. 324) admitted that 'pragmatic interest politics concerned with economic welfare has its own built-in limits.' He came to speak of the need for a shared commitment between major elites and government leaders if integration is to move forward smoothly. It was pointed out that 'the functional logic which leads from national frustration to economic unity, and eventually to political unification, presupposes that national consciousness is weak and that the national situation is perceived as gloomy' (Haas, 1967, p. 331). If the latter is not the case and integration has not gone far enough, the role of the strong political leader becomes crucial. He or she can either press forward the integration movement or allegedly weaken it by offering rewards at the national level which satisfy pragmatically inspired proponents of integration.

As Dougherty and Pfaltzgraff (1981, p. 435) indicate, by the mid 1970s Haas developed even greater reservations about the logic of incrementalism and spillover, especially in the European Community context. He introduced a new concept termed 'fragmented issue linkage', which is said to occur 'when older objectives are questioned, when new objectives clamour for satisfaction, and when the rationality accepted as adequate in the past ceases to be a legitimate guide for political action' (Haas, 1976, p. 178).

Several other scholars have made an effort to refine the original neo-functionalist concepts. A main theme in the modifications and amendments is the recognition that functional links among tasks do not always lead to spillovers, but could have an adverse effect on integration. Thus, among other things, the concept of 'spillback' was introduced.

In spite of all these refinements, neo-functionalism has been criticized on several counts. Next to undue optimism about the putative spillovers from social and economic integration to political integration, neo-functionalist writers were blamed for having laid insufficient emphasis on the impact of the international environment (Hoffmann, 1968). This impact is, on the contrary, fully recognized in neo-realist theory, which starts from the assumption that the behaviour of states can best be explained by taking into account the configuration of power in the international system. Kenneth Waltz, the most authoritative advocate of neo-realism, depicts as 'reductionist' those theories that focus on the internal attributes of states to understand their actions and policies. Reductionist theories are said to be fundamentally flawed as they fail to come to grips with the continuity of state action, despite changes in the agents that seem to produce it (Waltz, 1979, p. 39). Making clear that in international relations the results of state action seldom correspond to the intentions and aims of governments, Waltz contends that causes not found in the individual character of states do operate among the actors collectively. Only systemic approaches, i.e. theories that allow for the interaction of states and consider the distribution of power among them a centrally important variable, can explain the similarities and variations of the outcomes of state behaviour. According to Waltz:

> Systems theories . . . are theories that explain how the organization of a realm acts as a constraining and disposing force on the interacting units within it. Such theories tell us about the forces the units are subject to. From them, we can infer some things about the expected behavior and fate of the units: namely, how they will have to compete with and adjust to one another if they are to survive and flourish. To the extent that dynamics of a system limit the freedom of its units, their behavior and the outcomes of their behavior become predictable. (1979, p. 72).

The structure of the post-war system, i.e. the prevailing pattern in the power configuration of international relations since World War II, has been quite clear. For several decades international politics was controlled by two superpowers, who accounted for a considerable part of the military and economic capabilities available in the international system. The bipolar system gave rise to two opposite regional security complexes (NATO and the Warsaw Pact) whose members were so closely related to each other that 'their national security problems cannot reasonably be analyzed apart from each other' (Buzan et al., 1990, p. 13). But in Waltz's view this structure also significantly contributed to European unification:

> So long as European states were the world's great powers, unity among them could only be dreamt of. Politics among the European great powers tended toward the model of a zero-sum game. . . . The emergence of the Russian and American superpowers created a situation that permitted wider ranging and more effective cooperation among the states of Western Europe. They became consumers of security. . . . The new circumstances made possible the famous 'upgrading' of the common interests. . . . Not all impediments to cooperation were removed, but one important one was – the fear that the greater advantage of one would be translated into military force to be used against the others.

And he continues:

> Politics among European states became different in quality after World War II because the international system changed from a multipolar to a bipolar one. The limited progress made in economic and other ways towards the unity of Western Europe cannot be understood without considering the effects that followed from the changed structure of international politics. (1979, pp. 70–1)

but this chg. is not permanent!

In contrast with the neo-functionalists, who neglect the role of coercion as an integrating force, Waltz underlines in this context the crucial role of external pressures. The acuteness of the Soviet threat overshadowed primal conflicts among West European states, whilst the predominance of the United States worked as a catalyst of European integration. However, one may point to an interesting paradox of bipolarity. On the one hand, the impact of the bipolar system may explain why the European states managed to accomplish certain forms of economic integration; on the other hand, it may also explain why, until recently, they did not succeed in making real progress in politico-military collaboration. As it happened the EC members have not been unanimous in their acceptance of post-war bipolarity and the ensuing primacy of the United States in Western defence. France, in particular, has sought to accelerate tendencies in the international system towards multipolarity. As Stanley Hoffmann (1968, p. 401) holds, France's ambivalence towards European integration reflected the attitude that 'integration is good if it leads to an entity that will emancipate Europe from any bipolar system, bad if it does not' and merely chains France to the United States. As for Germany, it seems obvious that the country found in European integration a framework to regain a place of respectability in the family of Western nations as well as an outlet for national energies. On the other hand, Britain's attitude towards European integration used to be strongly influenced by global perspectives of foreign policy and the special relationship with the United States, the latter making it – in the perception of France – the Trojan horse in the group of Western European states and the caretaker of American interests. Hoffmann (1966, p. 865) takes the view that the political relations among West European states have been 'subordinated to their divergences about the outside world'. Also other writers have regarded the differences in international outlook as the main reason why the EC countries were not able to realize a common foreign and security policy. A quite unconventional position has been taken by Alfred Pijpers. He suggests that the West European countries have deliberately renounced the option of building a defence community in order not to disturb the central balance between the United States and the Soviet Union:

> Our presupposition is that the absence of a powerful European defence, and the modest degree of political and military cooperation in Western Europe thus far, is prompted by the wish of the Western European countries to maintain the existing power equilibrium between East and West, and the related situation of peace, security, stability, national

independence, and prosperity in Western Europe as much as possible. (Pijpers, 1990, p. 105)

The collapse of the post-war bipolar order compels a reappraisal of the position of the West European states.

Widening the perspective: the role of inter-state bargaining

Should one attribute the arrangements for security and defence to the internal dynamics of the ongoing integration process, as neo-functionalist theory suggests? Or has the recent expansion mainly been triggered by external pressures derived from changes in the international system, as the structural realists would have it? Not quite surprisingly, a case can be made for both explanations. We start with the first line of thought. By its very nature, the 1992 project of creating the single integrated market clearly set off the right momentum for the twelve to advance where progress was long overdue: economic and monetary as well as political unification. The years of Europhoria set in. Thus, as early as 1989 (two years after the SEA had become effective), the 1992 project was extended by the Delors plan for an economic and monetary union, and one year later it was supplemented by a Franco-German proposal for the establishment of a political union. The functional linkage between the internal market and the economic and monetary union seems to be self-evident. Indeed, it is hard to conceive of a real internal market without the harmonization of national economic and monetary policies. On the other hand, the relationship between economic and monetary unification and political unification is less obvious. Yet as, for instance, the discussions about aid to the former Soviet Union and the countries of Central and Eastern Europe have amply shown, economic issues and questions of international security are often interconnected. This view was voiced by the President of the EC Commission, Jacques Delors. Speaking about the virtuous circle of one thing leading to another he argued that the security dimension was logically related to the economic and monetary union:

> It is not difficult to envisage the consequences of the Community, with its single currency, playing a major international role to deal with factors liable to disturb financial and foreign-exchange markets. By throwing all its weight behind greater monetary stability – which implies world responsibilities for the European currency – and by calling for a more equitable apportionment of financial resources between rich countries and poor countries, the Community could make a meaningful contribution to strengthening security worldwide. (1991, p. 103)

However, it was not only the success of the 1992 programme that unleashed a drive for yet further integration; major international developments also underscored the need for moving beyond the limits of traditional economic collaboration. The Gulf War was another demonstration of the limitations of EC diplomacy; the lack of independent military power undermined the Community's ability to act. The conflict enhanced the sense of urgency among EC governments in finding arrangements to achieve closer military cooperation. Furthermore, the end of the Cold War as well as the collapse of the Soviet Union precipitated a considerable reduction of the American military presence in Europe. The uncertainties about the long-term continuation of transatlantic security bonds, and also the growing pressures in American society to give priority to solving domestic problems, reinforced the awareness in EC countries that Western Europe should be willing to carry a larger part of the common Western defence burden and assume wider security responsibilities.

Another important international change arose from the rapid German reunification process, which caused fears in some parts of Western Europe (particularly in France) of a future Europe being dominated by a new powerful Germany. After World War II European integration has been advocated, and rightly so, as the best way to deal with any revival of the so-called German question. The Franco-German initiative on political union may be used as the logical continuation of post-war efforts to anchor Germany as much as possible in the structure of West European cooperation. By framing a common foreign and security policy (including military defence) the likelihood of a German *Alleingang* or new German territorial ambitions could be diminished. Apparently, the German and the French leaders had different motives for their common initiative. Whereas the Kohl government sought to reassure Germany's neighbours by making a new commitment to European integration, President Mitterrand tried to neutralize enhanced German power by strengthening the bonds of bilateral cooperation.

The above observations about the impact of both internal dynamics and external pressures on the advances to defence cooperation seem to be consistent with the analysis of Buzan et al. Suggesting that the development of Western European integration can be explained to a considerable extent by the EC's position in the international system, they write: 'The history of integration should not be written solely as a slow internal process of learning the "necessary" cooperation and overcoming nationalist inertia – but as a dialectic between this process and the pressures on Europe from other actors, notably the United States, to pull itself together' (1990, pp. 147–8).

On reflection, however, one cannot fail to admit that neo-functionalism and structural realism fall short of explaining the whole story. Processes of integration are not the prisoner of deterministic forces. Internal dynamics and external pressures may set favourable conditions and create opportunities for moving ahead; they do not 'cause' responses by the political actors. As indicated above, neo-functionalism assumes that transnational governmental and non-governmental elites are the prime movers of unification movements. But the point is that neither pan-European interest groups nor EC officials played a prominent part in the discussions and negotiations on the political union. Foreign policy and defence have no clear constituency in Western European societies; consequently there are no well-organized groups to make demands for further cooperation in the field. It is true that the EC Commission has attempted to contribute to the public debate by publishing a draft treaty, but the position of this body is much weaker concerning foreign policy issues than economic matters. In contrast with the provisions on the economic and monetary union, the Commission was hardly able to set its mark on the treaty of Maastricht as far as foreign policy and security were concerned. Thus, for example, the Commission's proposal to bring all provisions related to external aspects – foreign policy, security, economic relations and development cooperation – on one title of the treaty was actually ignored by EC ministers and their aides.

We need to pay special attention to the position of the EC's principal external actor, the United States. As has been pointed out several times in this chapter, in the past the United States has played a positive role as a catalyst of European integration. Although the US administration went on to pay lip-service to the necessity for more European unity, it did not hide its reservations about plans for organizing European defence outside the NATO framework. Thus, for example, in March 1991 Undersecretary of State Reginald Bartholomew sent a harsh note to European capitals, encouraging a European voice within NATO but taking issue with a European caucus which would negotiate as such with the United States. American concerns about a European ganging-up in matters of defence were to cast a shadow over the IGC political union negotiations. The US weakened efforts by especially France to put the Western European Union into a position subordinate to the European Community.

If the neo-functionalist point of view focusing on the internal logic of integration, and the structural realist point of view highlighting international system changes, cannot carry the full burden of the explanation looked for, what alternative approach might do the rest of the job? In his seminal article on the birth of the SEA Andrew Moravcsik (1991) challenges the popular view that the successful 1992 project resulted from a coalition between the EC Commission and the leadership of the European multi-national corporations (associated in the Roundtable of European Industrialists). Rather, he argues, the EC reform package was the outcome of inter-state bargains between Britain, France and Germany. In elaborating his argument Moravcsik develops an explanatory approach, which is called 'intergovernmental institutionalism'. This approach stresses the central importance of power and interests, with the latter determined not simply by position in the international system but also by the preferences of domestic political actors. It is based on three principles: (1) intergovernmentalism, (2) lowest-common-denominator bargaining, and (3) strict limits on future transfers of sovereignty. The first principle refers to the heads of governments being the main actors in EC decision-making. Backed by a small group of ministers and advisers, they initiate and subsequently negotiate major initiatives. Holding that each EC government views the EC through the lens of its own policy preferences, Moravcsik believes that the primary forum of their political expression remains national, even when societal interests are transnational. The principle of lowest common denominator is related to the fact that the bargains struck in the EC reflect the relative power positions of the member states. While small powers allegedly can be bought off with side payments, larger states are said to exercise a *de facto* veto over fundamental changes. This explains why bargaining tends to converge towards the lowest common denominator of large-state interests. The third principle assumes that policy-makers safeguard their countries against the future erosion of sovereignty by demanding the unanimous consent of the parties involved. Rather than granting open-ended authority to supranational bodies such as the Commission and Parliament that may infringe on their sovereignty, national leaders prefer to work by means of intergovernmental institutions such as the European Council and the Council of Ministers.

In underlining the autonomy and influence of national leaders *vis-à-vis* international institutions as well as the importance of power resources in determining the outcome of intergovernmental bargains, Moravcsik's approach clearly deviates from neo-functionalist ideas. How do his ideas relate to structural realism? Certainly, the emphasis on states being the principal actors in international politics, pursuing their own interests, perfectly fits the realist pattern. But Moravcsik's intergovernmental institutionalism differs decisively from structural realism 'in that it locates the sources of regime reform not only in the changing power distribution but also in the changing interests of states' (Moravcsik, 1991, p. 27). Here Moravcsik strikes the familiar note of the importance of the domestic sources of foreign policy.

If traditional notions of convergent national interests, inter-state bargains, and protection of sovereignty provide clues for understanding the success of the negotiations on the SEA, these conceptions are bound to be helpful in explaining the negotiations on the political union. Probably they are even more relevant in the context of foreign policy and defence than in the realm of economic liberalization. Firstly, the framing of the political union negotiations in the format of an intergovernmental conference implied that those negotiations were conducted by representatives of national governments. The main issues were settled at the level of government leaders and foreign ministers. Indeed, the role of the EC Commission and European officials hardly exceeded that of interested observers. Secondly, the negotiations were dominated to a great extent by the larger European states. As mentioned before, the main input in the IGC was the Franco-German proposal, presented on the eve of the European Council meeting of Rome in December 1990 (a second draft followed in February 1991). The proposal met with firm resistance by Britain (and by smaller states like the Netherlands and Portugal) because Mitterrand and Kohl wanted, in pursuance of a common European defence policy, to forge an organic relationship between the political union and WEU under the common roof of the European Council. Echoing American views on maintaining NATO's core functions and establishing a European defence pillar only inside and not outside the Atlantic alliance, the UK government refused to endorse a one-sided orientation towards the European Community. Shortly before the French and German leaders took a new personal initiative to keep the idea of European defence cooperation alive, Britain along with Italy, in a bid to overcome existing disagreements among the EC members, released in early October 1991 a document on European security and the implementation of a European defence identity. The central message of this memorandum was to keep WEU at equal distance from the European Community and NATO. Thus, WEU was intended to function both as the defence component of the political union and as the vehicle to strengthen the European pillar in NATO. Meanwhile, the US administration went on to exert pressure particularly on the German government to protect the interests of the Western alliance. Washington apparently succeeded in persuading Bonn not to support arrangements that might pave the way for independent European security policies. On 2 October 1991 the American Secretary of State, James Baker, and the German Foreign Minister, Hans-Dietrich Genscher, issued a joint statement in Washington expressing the view that 'NATO will work to adapt its structure to encompass European desires for a distinct security identity within the Alliance and will encourage greater European responsibility for European defence.' At no stage during the negotiations were the smaller countries able to significantly affect the direction of the discussions about foreign policy and defence, in spite of Luxembourg holding the EC presidency in the first half of 1991 and the Netherlands in the second.

The final outcome of the bargaining among the larger European nations can hardly be regarded as an instance of 'upgrading the common interest'; actually it was a classical compromise between conflicting national positions. The Maastricht treaty provisions on security and defence met the aspirations of France (and to a lesser extent those of Germany) because WEU could be considered the defence arm of the European Community. On the other hand, Britain could boast that as a result of the agreement the policy of the European Union would be compatible with the policy of NATO.

Thirdly and lastly, the treaty provisions on the common foreign policy and security policy are a perfect illustration of Moravcsik's principle of strict limits on future transfers of sovereignty. More than any other policy field, security and defence strike at the heart of national sovereignty. For the foreseeable future none of the EC members can be expected to commit itself to majority decision-making or to accept the authority of a supranational body on questions of life or death. Hardly surprisingly, the kind of cooperation envisaged in the Maastricht treaty with respect to the area under discussion is intergovernmental cooperation without the usual Community procedures (Wellenstein, 1992). Thus, there is neither a monopoly of proposal for the Commission not any real influence for the European Parliament. The Commission is merely associated with the work of the Council of Ministers, and the Parliament is only entitled to regular debates and to have its views taken into account. The Court of Justice, obviously, does not come into play at all. Finally, the Council takes its decisions unanimously, unless it decides otherwise.

Although the course and outcome of the IGC negotiations can be adequately analysed by means of Moravcsik's general approach, some nuances have to be made as to the position of the larger and the smaller EC members. It may be true that the larger European states are especially anxious to defend their sovereignty; nevertheless there is some diversity in their general attitude. Germany (and for that matter Italy) is less reluctant to strengthen the authority of the EC's supranational bodies than Britain and France. Conversely, it would be false to believe that all smaller EC members are staunch supporters of a federal development of the European Community. Thus, for instance, the proposal presented by the Netherlands (acting in its capacity as EC president) in late September 1991, aiming at a European federation as a long-range goal, was supported by Belgium only. Denmark, in particular, firmly opposed the creation of such a federation.

Conclusion

In this chapter the movement of the European integration process towards a common European defence policy has been analysed from the perspectives of neo-functionalism and structural realism. The internal dynamics or logic of integration processes was seen as the essence of the former theory; the external pressures originating in the international system were seen as the central tenet of the latter. Neo-functionalist theory predicts that successful integration in one field is likely to generate needs for further integration in functionally related areas and that transnationally oriented elites will convert those needs into political demands. On the other hand, one can deduce from the assumptions of structural realism that the parameters of integration processes are circumscribed by the international configuration of power and that fundamental changes in the power structure are likely to affect national commitments to cooperative state action.

Our observations suggest that both approaches are valuable but can only claim part of the truth. Neo-functionalist explanations for the recent agreements on security and defence make sense to the extent that those agreements may be regarded as the result of the momentum created by the implementation of the Single European Act and the subsequent proposal for economic and monetary union. Structural realist explanations for the same problem are equally plausible to the extent that the relevant provisions of the Maastricht treaty were triggered by international developments such as the end of the Cold War, German unification, the altered American–European relationship and the Gulf War. The conclusion is that both the internal integration dynamics and the international changes created favourable political conditions for moving the European integration process ahead, but that in the final analysis the two approaches fail fully to grasp the political processes set in motion by the successes of previous integration steps and by the challenges of the new international setting.

More specifically, neo-functionalist explanations in the context of security and defence are flawed because European bureaucrats and technocrats played no prominent part in this arena. But structural realist explanations are also deficient because they overlook the importance of differences in national traditions and domestic political preferences. Both kinds of explanations have to be supplemented by taking into account the intricacies of bargaining at the level of national political leaders. By the same token, no understanding of the compromises underlying the treaty of Maastricht is possible without paying due attention to the conflicting interests and views as well as relative power of the larger European states, eager to protect their sovereignty. Of special importance was the position of the United States. By actively interfering in the negotiations among the EC states the American administration was able to back up the position of Britain and to prevent the Franco-German coalition from controlling the outcome of the negotiations. Finally, the quest for a common European defence policy in the near future is not likely to transcend well-defined boundaries of intergovernmental cooperation.

9

Testing Weak-Power Theory: Three Nordic Reactions to the Soviet Coup

Hans Mouritzen

The failed Soviet coup of 19–21 August 1991 and the ensuing dissolution of the Soviet Union and its ideology provide excellent opportunities to investigate to what extent shifts in the balance of power in weak states' salient environments can account for their policy changes. Typically, theories stressing the balance-of-power factor are at a disadvantage compared with most other theories seeking to explain foreign policy, because visible changes in their core explanatory factor happen so infrequently that the factor is easily forgotten or, at best, is ascribed the status of a parameter surrounding more dynamic factors. The best opportunities to challenge balance-of-power theories occur in connection with wide-ranging *and* sudden power shifts. The short time span implies that other explanatory factors have fewer chances to blur the impact of the balance-of-power factor. This means typically dramatic turning points in world history such as major wars, or the collapse of empires in the wake of revolutions.[1] An example would be studies of the 'turn of the tide' during World War II and how it affected the position of a number of weak powers and their foreign policy strategies (see Baker Fox, 1959). The shift in the Central European balance of power in late 1989 and the beginning of 1990 with the Eastern European revolutions and German unification also seems sufficiently wide-ranging and sudden to provide promising analytic opportunities.[2]

I think that even better opportunities are presented by the situation analysed in this chapter. For a number of weak powers, the balance of power in their salient environments changed dramatically and suddenly. The communist coup implied that the Soviet Union seemed to be re-emerging as a *military* superpower during those couple of days when its success seemed likely. Ideological bipolarity was re-established, and Western reactions strongly condemning the coup could lead one to expect a future conflictual East–West relationship in general terms. In other words, the amorphous and sleeping bipolarity that had existed prior to the coup seemed to have become real bipolarity. As the failure of the coup became evident on its third day (Wednesday 21 August), not only did this polarity melt away as quickly as it had emerged, but the status quo prior to the coup did *not* get a chance to re-establish itself. The Communist Party was suspended in the Russian republic, and soon the rest of the republics followed suit. Even though President Gorbachev was restored, his power base was rapidly undermined, as declarations of independence were issued by the various Soviet republics one after the other during the week that followed. The independence of the Baltic republics won wide international recognition within a couple of weeks after the coup. The conservative forces within the KGB and the army which had initiated the coup seemed to be eliminated, thus significantly reducing the risk of another attempted takeover. Within one or two weeks, therefore, bipolarity manifestly re-emerged and was dissolved again, and then the actor that was one of the potential power poles seemed to disappear, paving the way for something approaching EC/Western unipolarity (as to the 'Europe as a pole' scenario, see Buzan et al., 1990 or Mouritzen, 1993). It is an understatement to say that this was a wide-ranging shift in the balance of power, given the fact that post-war bipolarity actually *disappeared*. Moreover, this happened during an even shorter time span than the 1989–90 events mentioned above. So the opportunities to challenge a theory on the balance of power between the strong and the policies of the weak seem to be favourable.[3]

Anti-balance-of-power behaviour: concept and theory

More specifically, I want to challenge a modified version of Baker Fox's hypothesis on small states' 'anti-balance-of-power behaviour' (1959, p. 187). Instead of trying to restore the so-called balance of power (like the classical holder of the balance would do), the small state's support is rendered to the probable winner. Through this form of bandwagoning, or weathercock policy as critics would say, a contribution – however modest – is made towards an even more askew balance of power. Top priority is given to safeguarding the small state's core values in the short run; otherwise, there may be no long run to bother about. It cannot afford the luxury of trying to safeguard its long-term interest in a more balanced polarity (Baker Fox, 1959, p. 181; see also Rothstein, 1968, pp. 11–12; Handel, 1981, p. 29).[4]

Being somewhat vaguely formulated, a number of specifications for and comments on this hypothesis should be made initially. There are no aspirations here to observe or measure any 'balance' whatsoever. What is possible, however, is the observation of clear-cut *trends* in this balance, including major turning points. Correspondingly, it is possible to analyse trends, including major shifts, in weak-power policies regarding the relevant issues. In other words, the concept of anti-balance-of-power behaviour (ABPB) is only meaningful diachronically. 'Supporting the winner' refers, hence, to the trend winner (who may be the underdog in absolute terms), and 'support' may actually mean a less hostile attitude than previously.[5]

Secondly, in order to focus on 'pure' bandwagoning behaviour I shall require that the weak's support is rendered for reasons that can be traced, directly or indirectly, to the balance-of-power trend, i.e. not to any alternative source of foreign policy behaviour.

Baker Fox tends to see ABPB as characterizing small states *generally* (whereas great powers are seen as being in favour of a balance of power: 1959, p. 187).[6] My assertion here is that the occurrence of ABPB depends on which type of constellation the weak power belongs to, being understood as its basic set of relationships to the strong powers in its salient environment (Mouritzen, 1991, p. 218). Examples of weak-power constellations could be a roughly symmetrical position between the two strong powers, an alliance to one of the poles, a satellite relationship, or an adaptive acquiescence constellation (Mouritzen, p. 221).[7] The balance of power between the strong in the salient environment of a weak power differs according to which constellation it belongs to. However, the basic set of relationships that the constellations refer to are more than sheer geopolitical power relationships to which the weak are subject. The weak are ascribed a certain, more or less pronounced, element of *choice* (for instance on the question of joining an alliance or staying outside).[8]

Among the three specific constellations that I shall be interested in, I assume ABPB to be strongest in the adaptive acquiescence constellation, medium (relatively speaking) in the symmetrical constellation, and lowest in the alliance constellation (to be qualified below). In the adaptive acquiescence constellation, the weak is in a geopolitically higher dependent position *vis-à-vis* one of the power poles. This paramount power possesses significant negative sanctions that the weak anticipates (manifest threats are usually redundant). As the balance of power tips in favour of the paramount power, its negative sanctions have also increased, and the assets of the weak are not requested to the same extent as before. Unilateral dependency has become more marked than before. In order to prevent the negative sanctions from materializing, i.e. in order to retain status quo, the weak will have to sweeten the status quo for the paramount power more than before. In other words, in addition to a favourable balance-of-power development, the paramount power is rewarded with some extra benefits. This is ABPB as stipulated above. Conversely, if the balance tips to the disfavour of the paramount power, inverse tendencies will be found. The weak power may even be able to jump out of adaptive acquiescence to, typically, the symmetrical constellation. Also this is ABPB: the strong power is punished for its weakened position, so that it may be further weakened.[9]

In the symmetrical constellation, the weak is in a roughly similar relationship to the two strong powers. Non-commitment in relation to both poles is the core strategy. If the balance of power tips in one or the other direction, the weak must, in order to stay roughly symmetrical, move somewhat in this direction. But this is obviously ABPB, as the strengthened power pole will be a bit further strengthened in this way. However, this type of behaviour will be less pronounced than in the former constellation: owing to its symmetrical position, the local balance of power will never shift as dramatically as it may do close to one of the poles. Also, too much weathercock behaviour could easily undermine its actor credibility, a factor vital to its core strategy of non-commitment.

The weak allied power will not typically engage in ABPB, I assume as a first impulse. Its reason for joining the alliance in the first place is typically to borrow military or other counterweight from a strong power, in the face of an increasing threat from a conflicting power. This is actually the opposite type of behaviour, in the sense that a contribution is offered towards the *restoration* of an existing balance of power – though in no way for altruistic reasons, of course (balance-of-power behaviour, BPB).

However, the freedom of manoeuvre is typically more significant for the weak allied power than for the weak power in the two previously discussed constellations (except, of course, for allied satellites). The range of behaviour hence is broader, giving more leeway for the influence of, for example, domestic factors in a rather unpredictable direction. One factor, however, that one can consider *a priori* in a systematic way is the weak ally's threat perception. Let us assume that it can be high, medium or low. In the former case, the weak *has to* be extra loyal to its pole and thereby usually rather hostile to the threatening power, for fear of being abandoned. In the latter case, the weak can *afford* such an attitude. It is in a position to express its identity or other values that will typically be in conflict with those of the perceived enemy (its reason for joining the alliance originally). With a *medium* threat perception, however, a more cautious attitude of non-provocation is called for. The weak has a lot to lose in this situation; there is no reason to provoke high tension in its own salient environment, thereby ultimately turning its own territory into a battlefield. Now, what is interesting here are diachronic trends. With three levels of threat perception, we get six changes proper, and three constants (e.g. from low to low threat perception). If the reasoning above is plausible, we get two developments (out of six) that will cause ABPB: from medium to low threat perception, or from low to medium. In the latter case the balance of power has shifted to the advantage of the perceived enemy, and this has entailed, specifically, that the weak has become more exposed. Hence, it has lowered its profile and become more cautious in its behaviour *vis-à-vis* the perceived threat. This is a way of rewarding the trend winner, in other words ABPB. Conversely from medium to low threat perception: as the balance of power has shifted in disfavour of the perceived threat, and specifically has reduced the weak ally's threat perception from medium to low, the weak can now abandon its former attitude of non-provocation. In other words, the perceived enemy is punished for being a trend loser. This is also ABPB. The rest of the transitions need not be commented upon here; they will lead to either BPB or unaffected behaviour on the part of the weak ally.[10]

The apparent effects of the Soviet coup and its aftermath on three weak-power foreign policies will be analysed below, one for each of the stipulated constellations. Finland will represent the adaptive acquiescence constellation, Sweden the symmetrical constellation, and Denmark the alliance constellation (for justifications of these classifications see Mouritzen, 1991). Regarding Denmark, I believe that its threat perception *vis-à-vis* the Soviet Union developed from low to low during the period of concern here. In other words, I do not believe that even the few days where the coup seemed to succeed led to any significant threat perception, given the shift in the Central European balance of power that had taken place since about 1988 (including the retreat of the Soviet Union from Eastern Europe). In the light of the above reasoning, we should *not* expect Danish ABPB in the period. The expectations concerning Finland and Sweden can be established from the constellations solely. Taken together, hence, we should expect significant ABPB on the part of Finland, no such behaviour from Denmark, and a middle position from Sweden. The actual shifts, if any, that took place in each of the three policies will be confronted with the expectations, and deviations from the expectations will be sought and accounted for by referring to alternative explanatory factors, should such be available.

The policy shifts will be inferred from analysing the three weak powers' official statements concerning the coup, their attitudes to the recognition of the Baltic states, their attitudes to EC membership and to the concept of neutrality (Sweden and Finland), and their attitudes to the Friendship, Cooperation and Mutual Assistance Treaty (FCMA Treaty below) with the Soviet Union (Finland). These were the major issues that were on the agenda during the two weeks selected for study.

The Soviet coup and disintegration 1991: three Nordic foreign policy reactions

Statements regarding the coup
On the first day of the coup, Monday 19 August, the Finnish government issued a rather brief statement, in which it was regretted that 'the proclamation of Martial Law has brought the democratic development in the Soviet Union to a halt'. Furthermore, it was hoped that 'a return to normal condition will take place as soon as possible' ('Regeringens ställningstagande med arledning a situationen i Sovjetunionen', Helsinki, 19 August 1991). The latter formulation was sufficiently vague to allow Finland good relations with whatever regime might take control. The takeover was not described as a coup or as unconstitutional as in most other Western reactions. As late as the evening of Wednesday 21 August, when it seemed that the coup had failed, the word 'coup' was still avoided, and there was no condemnation of the takeover, for instance from the standpoint of the CSCE process (the Paris charter on democracy).

On 20 August a statement strongly condemning the *coup d'état* was issued from an EPC meeting in The Hague ('Declaration on the Situation in the Soviet Union', EPC Extraordinary Ministerial Meeting, the Hague, 20 August). The EC countries described the coup as an 'unconstitutional act' that also violated the Soviet Union's obligations in the CSCE process. It was demanded that President Gorbachev be reinstated in his functions. Most important, perhaps, EC willingness to conclude association agreements with Hungary, Poland and Czechoslovakia in the 'near future' was emphasized, together with support for the reform processes in the rest of the former Eastern Europe. Within the Soviet Union, special concern was expressed for the situation of the Baltic states. Finally, the EC suspended its economic and technical assistance (except for humanitarian emergency aid).

Not only had Denmark signed the EPC statement, there were also various Danish comments that gave the impression of Denmark cultivating a high profile. Already on 19 August, Foreign Minister Uffe Ellemann had declared that humanitarian food aid should *not* be exempted from suspension. Eastern European security should be supported. The Danish Prime Minister was one of the first Western leaders to declare that the coup could easily fail: 'Diplomatically, we now have a different relation to the Soviet Union than before, because its leadership has come to power through a *coup d'état*. . . . It is impossible for us to deal with (them) . . .' (*Politiken*, 21 August 1993).

In view of these Finnish and Danish attitudes, the soil was hardly fertile for a common Nordic statement at the meeting of Nordic foreign ministers in Skagen (Denmark), the very same day as the EPC statement had been issued. A statement was made, however, that was a little higher than the lowest common denominator (the Finnish attitude). The word 'coup' was omitted, and no demand for the reinstatement of President Gorbachev was formulated. As a compromise, the Soviet development was 'deeply regretted' (instead of simply 'regretted') and the Paris charter was emphasized.

The statement, however, became more of an object of inter-Nordic rivalry than an expression of mutual solidarity. The differences of opinion between Finland and the rest of the group came out in the open. Not only was Uffe Ellemann anxious to emphasize that the EPC statement represented the 'real' Danish attitude; also the Swedish Foreign Minister Sten Anderson distanced his country from the Nordic statement by saying that Sweden could actually have signed the EPC statement.

On 22 August, when the coup had definitely collapsed, President Koivisto held a press conference, where the phrase *coup d'état* was used for the first time in Finnish rhetoric, and where the coup's violation of CSCE principles was emphasized. Koivisto stressed that Finland had actually for the first time criticized internal Soviet affairs; this was due not only to the uniqueness of events, but also to his own good personal relationship with Gorbachev.

Attitudes to Baltic independence

Regarding the Baltic states' independence, Denmark was in the forefront (as had been the case, along with Iceland, in the recognition of Lithuanian independence in February 1991) (Jonson, 1991, pp. 134–5). At a press conference during the coup in connection with Latvian Foreign Minister Jurkans's visit to Copenhagen regarding the formation of an exile government, Ellemann stated that he would work for international recognition of Baltic independence, particularly within the EC. Also, Ellemann took credit for the special mentioning of the Baltic states in the EPC declaration of 20 August. Moreover, this Danish avant-garde position was illustrated about a week later, as the EC had finally decided to recognize Baltic independence: 'for more than a year, we have encouraged the EC to support the Baltic states' independence. But nobody has listened to us before now' (*Dagens Nyheter* (*DN*), 28 August).

Iceland and Denmark were the first countries in the Western world to recognize Baltic independence; the rest of the Nordic countries followed closely on their heels. Regarding Sweden and Finland, however, this happened after relatively slow starts. Sten Anderson declared on 22 August that negotiations between Moscow and the Baltic states concerning independence should now be resumed. In other words, the unilateral Baltic declarations of independence should be neglected until the Balts had come to terms with the Soviet Union. The next day, however, it was said that Swedish recognition might come within a week. An agreement with Moscow would be preferable, 'but not a condition from the Swedish side . . . having waited for 50 years, we should be able to wait an additional week' (*DN*, 24 August), as expressed by the Under-Secretary of State. However, this proved impossible. On 24 August, after Yeltsin had announced Russia's recognition of Estonia's and Latvia's independence, the Swedish Foreign Minister consulted the other Nordic countries (except for Finland!). On 25 August, it was declared that the Baltic countries would be recognized as independent on 27 August, as they had now 'sufficient control over their territories' (*DN*, 26 August) (*full* control being the normal Swedish condition, supported by international law).

Finland started out from roughly the same position as Sweden. As emphasized by Koivisto at the press conference on 22 August, 'there is no reason to revise our Baltic policy . . . they must first negotiate with the central authorities' (*Hufvudstadsbladet* (*Hbl*), 23 August. This view was also held by Foreign Minister Väyrynen on Saturday (*Hbl*, 26 August). The next day, however, it was announced that conditions had changed rapidly and that the cabinet would decide on 26 August. A few hours later, though, a meeting was held between the cabinet's foreign committee and the President. It was announced that 'the view of the Russian republic in the matter [i.e. Yeltsin's recognition] will also be that of the

Soviet government.' It was admitted, though, 'that we have no clear impression of the attitude of the Soviet central government' (*Hbl*, 26 August). It was emphasized, furthermore, that Finland had already recognized Baltic independence in the 1920s, and that this recognition had never been cancelled. So only the practical re-establishment of diplomatic relations was at stake.

Attitudes on EC membership, neutrality, and the FCMA Treaty

The first two of these issues were, naturally, only on the agenda for Sweden and Finland, and the third issue only for Finland.

Sweden applied for EC membership formally on 1 July 1991. This application had been preceded by heated controversy as to whether membership in a future, yet unknown, EC union was compatible with continued Swedish neutrality (cf. Andrén, 1991; Ross, 1991; Carlsnaes, 1993b). In the application as such, no mention was made of neutrality, but the concept was simultaneously strongly emphasized in a parliamentary speech by the Prime Minister. At a press conference immediately after the initiation of the coup, the Prime Minister declared that 'the coup in the Soviet Union affects in no way Sweden's decision to apply for EC membership, based on the parliamentary decision regarding continued neutrality.' In view of the security political role that the EC played during the coup (cf. the EPC statement referred to above), along with its role simultaneously in Yugoslavia, the membership/neutrality dilemma was highlighted (e.g. Nycander, 1991). However, the newly established polarity proved so short-lived that no official Swedish decision-makers were forced into more precise statements.

Turning to Finland, President Koivisto declared at the above-mentioned press conference that 'events in the Soviet Union do not affect . . . Finland's view of European integration. My views remain unchanged. This means that our country still strives for an EEA agreement . . . A debate on full EC membership would not be improper, though' (*Hbl*, 23 August).[11] On 27 August the Minister of Foreign Trade Salolainen (Conservative) distributed a press release saying that Finland should make preparatory investigations for a decision on EC membership, adding that the membership option had at no time been discarded. Prime Minister Aho (Centre Party) reacted promptly by saying that the statement was 'surprising' and hinting that it contradicted the government programme (*Hbl*, 28 August). Salolainen replied that a decision on membership might have to be made during the spring of 1992. Exactly one week later, the Prime Minister spoke in front of the Paasikivi Society. It was now said (*Hbl*, 4 September) that an EEA agreement with the EC had never been seen by Finland as an *alternative* to membership. This statement was elaborated the following day in a speech by Foreign Minister Väyrynen (*Hbl*, 5 September), discussing the relationship between membership and Finnish neutrality. A common security and defence policy in a future EC union would create problems for Finnish neutrality. The common EC foreign policy declarations would hardly cause difficulties; but regarding decisions on sanctions, interventions and common troops, the neutrals applying for membership would have to consider the matter carefully. 'The core of neutrality is that the state in question does not belong to military alliances and that it keeps decisions on its defence in its own hands.' Hence, the membership/neutrality dilemma that we saw in the Swedish case was approached here by hinting at a significant watering down of the concept of neutrality (and even more of the Finnish version of neutrality).[12]

A related theme was the FCMA Treaty with the Soviet Union. Even though its military paragraphs had been regarded as outdated by several observers in public debate, official statements in this direction had never been made. However, both Aho and Väyrynen hinted that the treaty was outdated: 'The thinking in terms of coalitions and military guarantees that prevailed in the post-World War II agreements has lost its significance' (*Hbl*, 5 September). It should be added that Aho's and Väyrynen's speeches were the first official Finnish statements in which relations eastwards were not given special priority compared with, for example, the EC, Norden and the CSCE.

Interpretations of diachronic trends: Finland

We shall now see for each of the three Nordic cases whether the diachronic trends in their policies can be regarded as ABPB or not. As I have chosen to understand this type of behaviour, it is required not only that support for the trend loser is waning (or conversely that the winner is increasingly supported), but also that this happens for pure power (trend) reasons. This is, of course, difficult to prove on the basis of overt evidence; still, by comparing diachronic trends in the salient power structure with trends in overt behaviour, I think that reasonable arguments can be provided in one or the other direction.

Regarding Finnish statements about the coup, the turning point was obviously Koivisto's press conference on 22 August, i.e. the day after the coup had collapsed. The word 'coup' was used for the first time, and reference was made to the CSCE process. One may ask, of course, why this turning point had not occurred the evening before, when Aho and Väyrynen talked to the press (*Hbl*, 22 August) and when it seemed obvious that the coup had failed. However, they may have wished to consult the President before shifting rhetoric and, of course, to wait and see for a little longer. All things considered, it seems that there was a neat correspondence between the two turning points: one in the salient power structure and the other in Finnish rhetoric regarding the coup.

As to Baltic independence, the major speeding up occurred on Sunday 25 August. What requires an explanation in this matter is why publicly declared criteria of recognition like full territorial control and agreements between the Baltic states and the Soviet Union were suddenly abandoned. The timing of this abandonment indicates that Yeltsin's recognition on 24 August was important (this was openly admitted by the government). Compared with the other Nordic countries' speeding up, the timing also hints that we are actually dealing with a kind of Nordic race in this question (officially denied, of course, by all governments involved). In the Finnish press, it was actually compared to a bicycle race: the riders lying in wait, carefully watching each other, and one rider suddenly initiating the spurt, trying to take the rest by surprise. Iceland was 'allowed' an early spurt, whereas Denmark was not: the others followed closely in its track, making it a close race at the finish. The explanation underlying this race hypothesis clearly involves the opinion of the Nordic peoples and their pro-Baltic attitudes. They would hardly allow their respective governments to lag significantly behind the others in the race. Unlike Sweden, there was no imminent election in Finland, but still it would be troublesome for the government in domestic debates to lag behind the other Nordic governments, especially in view of Finland's historical and linguistic ties with Estonia (see the editorials of *Hufvudstadsbladet*, 27 and 30 August). Another explanation underlying the race hypothesis is probably concern for good future relations with the new independent Baltic states: lagging too much behind the other Nordic countries could be symbolically unfortunate in future dealings with Finland's new neighbours.

This apparent sensibility to public opinion and to future relations with the Baltic states is, however, something entirely new in Finnish foreign (security) policy after 1944. As expressed by President Paasikivi (1946–56), 'Foreign policy is too difficult for the "man in the street". The leaders must courageously assume responsibility and guide public opinion' (see Mouritzen, 1988, p. 322). Even though a democratization of foreign policy had taken place during President Koivisto's periods in office, the participation in a Nordic popularity race like the one described above would hardly have occurred during Finnish adaptive acquiescence – that is, as long as the Soviet Union and the old polarity seemed likely to persist. Finland has traditionally been among the most reluctant states in the Western world on the question of Baltic independence (as opposed to Finnish popular sentiments); as late as 10 January 1991, in connection with the violent events in Lithuania and Latvia, Koivisto said that 'we do not interfere, evidently, in the internal affairs of the Soviet Union. Finland has *de facto* recognized the annexation of the Baltic countries and we stick to all those agreements that we have made internationally' (*Helsingin Sanomat*, 26 August). In other words, Finland has never allowed itself the freedom of contributing to the likely dissolution of the Soviet empire, through initial support for Baltic independence. However, after the breakdown of the old power structure and with the trend pointing in the direction of the dissolution of the Soviet Union and Baltic independence, Finland could allow itself to take other considerations into account, including public opinion. It was quite clever to say in the new situation that Finland had never *legally* recognized the Soviet annexation; the fact, however, that this legal circumstance had never been mentioned before only serves to indicate the importance of the salient power structure.

Regarding EC membership, neutrality and the FCMA Treaty, the speeches on 3 and 4 September represented the most far-reaching shifts ever to occur. As Finland interpreted Soviet views and its neutrality during the old power structure, EC membership was totally out of the question; Finland had to strive hard for its free trade agreement with the EC (and its membership of EFTA) (Hakovirta, 1988). With the dissolution of the Soviet Union that could be discerned on 3 and 4 September, not only was traditional EC membership seen as being compatible with neutrality, but possibly also membership in a future political union with a common security policy. Also, it seems hardly accidental that the first Finnish official statement indicating distance from the military paragraphs of the FCMA Treaty occurred so soon after the collapse of the old power structure.

The various power interpretations offered above on a whole range of major issues are mutually supportive. The fact that several crucial turning points occurred simultaneously, roughly speaking, supports the interpretation that they were caused by one and the same phenomenon: the breakdown of the classical power structure in Finland's salient environment.

The first-mentioned prerequisite for ABPB to apply, namely that the apparent trend winner is increasingly supported (or, conversely, the trend loser is disfavoured), was also clearly fulfilled in the Finnish case. The initial, extremely cautious rhetoric was replaced by less cautious formulations, as the power trend shifted. Subsequently, as the Soviet Union began to disintegrate, it was 'punished' through Finnish recognition of Baltic independence, the opening of a door to Finnish membership of a Western political union, the watering down of neutrality, and the official outdating of the FCMA Treaty in its military aspects. We can conclude, hence, that *both* defining characteristics of ABPB as here understood have been fulfilled in the case at hand.

In view of our trend focus, various absolute labels are of minor importance here. What deserves to be said, though, is that Finland definitely jumped out of adaptive acquiescence (Mouritzen, 1988; 1991) during the two weeks that have been considered above. The classical paradigm that had prevailed since 1944 had been sustained, notably during the latter part of the 1980s and the early 1990s, by strong forces of inertia (Mouritzen, 1988, part IV).[13] As has often been seen in the past, modes of adaptation required a forceful and sudden injection for their termination, i.e. setting the factors of inertia out of force. The coup in the Soviet Union and its aftermath proved to be such an injection: firstly, the classical behaviour of the old paradigm was called forward and then, suddenly, its power basis melted away. This, of course, exposed the responsible politicians to accusations in the Finnish press of weathercock behaviour. The termination of adaptive acquiescence in Helsinki almost came to look like a mini version of the simultaneous liquidation of communism in Moscow.

Interpretations of diachronic trends: Sweden

When it comes to Sweden, it should be possible to be more brief, as there are fewer trends to interpret. Regarding official statements about the coup, it can hardly be ABPB; quite the contrary. For Sweden to publicly distance itself from a common Nordic declaration (a quite unusual thing to do in diplomacy, and also hurting the Finns) and to declare that it could have voted for the EC statement (Tuesday during the coup), there must have been strong reasons. It was actually tantamount to putting Swedish weight into the Western side of the scale in the re-established East–West polarity that seemed to exist for a few days. If anything, this amounts to BPB rather than the opposite. There is no diachronic trend in this question; there were no significant amendments later on.

Turning to the question of the recognition of the Baltic states, I have already mentioned the bicycle race metaphor in the above section (along with Yeltsin's recognition, which was also crucial for Sweden). Sweden also participated in the bicycle race, and probably for the same reasons as Finland: popular sentiments (even an ongoing election campaign) and the desire for a good symbolic platform for future relations with the new Baltic neighbours. Allowing such reasons to play a role in Swedish Baltic policy is, however, far from the traditional course. Apart from the old sins of originally recognizing Soviet annexation and handing the Estonian and Lithuanian gold reserves to the Soviet Union, Sweden has traditionally held a low profile over the question (at the government level, that is). A certain modification occurred in connection with the previously mentioned violent events in early 1991, but it was still the Swedish view that independence should be agreed upon between the respective new states and the Soviet Union (together with other requirements). Hence, it was a significant shift of policy that took place on 24 and 25 August, notably by joining the race. As expressed in a Swedish editorial (*DN*, 28 August): 'Suddenly the principles of international law were irrelevant. . . . The legal strictness has been sacrificed, as politics and emotions have taken over.' The question is, however, whether this represents ABPB. One prerequisite is clearly fulfilled, in the sense that the trend loser, or what was left of it, was disfavoured by the step. It is an open question, at least to the present author, whether the other prerequisite is fulfilled: was the rapidly changing power structure part of the explanation, as a necessary condition, or were the above-mentioned reasons sufficient? Would they have caused a shift also with a more stable situation in the Soviet Union?

On the question of membership of a future political union and neutrality, it is impossible to discern any diachronic trend whatsoever. If ABPB had been involved, Sweden should have played down the question of its membership application during the coup. This did not occur, as we have seen; on the contrary, the membership application was reaffirmed (with continued neutrality). Hence, ABPB does not apply here.

To sum up, ABPB could *possibly* be found in the Baltic issue. But the opposite type of behaviour occurred as regards official statements about the coup.

Interpretations of diachronic trends: Denmark

I have previously described in detail how Denmark accompanied its signing of the EPC statement with a range of comments on the coup and its implications: the taking of credit for certain parts of the statement, telling Finland what it should have said, etc. This Danish hyperactivism actually placed Denmark among the hawks as regards Western reactions to the coup. As ironically expressed by the Finnish editor-in-chief Keiho Korhonen (*Hbl*, 24 August): 'Denmark is a Great Power. We can in no way afford what Denmark can.'

Also, as regards Baltic independence, we noted a Danish avantgarde position. Denmark did not follow the criteria of international law for recognition, but took a purely political stand. Not only might this help the Baltic states by drawing further recognitions with it (as actually happened); there was also unanimous domestic political support behind this posture. As with declarations about the coup, a purpose may also have been to heighten Denmark's international profile in general, a purpose which seems to have played a role for some years.

This being said, it should be obvious that no ABPB can be found in the Danish case. In contrast, BPB was at stake, as Denmark chose to be at the forefront among Western reactions and initiatives from the very beginning.

Expectations versus observations: theoretical implications

We thus expect, on the basis of Baker Fox's theorizing on small states' anti-balance-of-power behaviour and the modifications regarding constellations that have been added here, that Finland would exhibit significant ABPB during the period selected for study; that such behaviour would be absent as regards Denmark; and that Sweden would be found in an intermediate position. How do these expectations relate to what has been observed above (as summarized in Table 9.1)?

It should be obvious from the above conclusions that expectations and observations fit neatly in the Finnish and Danish cases. By stipulating *two* criteria for ABPB and ensuring that both were fulfilled in the Finnish case, I dare say that not only could such behaviour be found superficially (i.e. decreased support to the trend loser), but also it could be seen to be carried out for the right reasons, namely power trends. This, of course, corroborates the theoretical reasoning.

The fit between expectations and observations is more dubious in the Swedish case. Superficially speaking, the Swedish case is intermediate or 'medium', as there is less bandwagoning than in the Finnish case, and less BPB than in the Danish case, from an aggregate point of view. But it is hardly medium on each of the

Table 9.1   *Three Nordic reactions to the Soviet communist coup
and the subsequent disintegration of the Soviet Union, 1991*

Issues	Finland	Sweden	Denmark
Statements regarding			
the coup	ABPB	BPB	BPB
Recognition of			
Baltic independence	ABPB	ABPB?	BPB
Attitude to EC			
membership	ABPB	0	–
Attitude to			
FCMA Treaty	ABPB	–	–

Notes:
ABPB   anti-balance-of-power behaviour
BPB   balance-of-power behaviour
0   unaffected
–   irrelevant

three issues that have been considered. From the point of view of the credibility of the theoretical reasoning, therefore, I should be able to offer reasonable explanations for the deviations that have been found on two of the issues. One explanation, I think, was the ongoing election campaign; parliamentary elections were to be held on 22 September. In view of general popular sentiments, a forceful posture had to be taken *vis-à-vis* the Soviet communist coup. If the Skagen declaration had been the only Swedish manifestation, this would unavoidably have been exploited by the bourgeois opposition. The same would have happened if the government had distanced itself from its EC application. It had been of vital importance to the government's election strategy that a decision on EC membership had been made (late autumn 1990) and that the formal application had been handed over to the EC well before the election (1 July 1991) (Sundelius, Chapter 10 of this book). Opinion polls indicated solid pro-EC attitudes among the voters at this time.

Another likely explanation, I think, was concern for the Swedish image in the EC Commission and among EC member countries. In view of the Swedish application for membership, it was crucial to seem mature and sufficiently Europeanized (Mouritzen, 1994) – not least in foreign and security policy issues that would probably be crucial in a future EC union (EU). This explains, I think, why Sten Anderson felt it necessary to take the unusual step of describing what Sweden would have done in a hypothetical situation (i.e. vote for a statement that Sweden had no opportunity to vote for). And it also explains why it was necessary to stress, almost demonstratively, that the Swedish application was unaffected by events in the Soviet Union.

Sweden had been accused of weathercock behaviour in connection with the EC membership decision in late 1990 (and also previously in this matter: see Hakovirta, 1988, p. 251). As late as May 1990, the Prime Minister had declared that 'concern for the credibility of our policy of neutrality is the reason why we are not applying for EC membership.' A new revision, this time in the opposite direction, could have undermined Sweden's general credibility both in the EC and among Swedish voters.

Each of these explanations, the EC connection and the election campaign, would I think be sufficient to account for the observed deviations. However, the sin of explanatory overkill must be permitted here, where we have access to overt evidence only. The two deviation explanations have, I think, saved the theory from being damaged by the Swedish case. But it has not really been corroborated either.

The bicycle race explanation, being relevant in all three cases, deserves a few comments. It actually refers to the phenomenon of diffusion, well known in most segments of social life between the Nordic countries (Karvonen, 1981; Nielsson, 1990). It should not be seen as an explanation rivalling the status of the balance of power; rather, it served as a catalyst for this more basic explanation, determining, to a large extent, the exact *timing* of ABPB behaviour in the Swedish and Finnish cases.

The Danish and Finnish cases have corroborated the theory, as argued above. In particular, I think that the explanatory power of the notion of constellation has been demonstrated (even with such a relatively broad trend definition of ABPB as has been used here). As I have also argued elsewhere (Mouritzen 1991, 1993), the concept of a small state (or a weak power) is simply too broad to allow for common theory-building – as attempted in the so-called small-state literature (see note 7).[14]

The always dangerous and insidious sin of circularity is not committed in the present analysis. The theoretical reasonings behind the belief in ABPB are based on such general principles as rationality, states as actors, and the importance of positive and negative power sanctions. Moreover, the empirical inspiration that *may* have played a role for Baker Fox (1959) or Mouritzen (1988) mostly stems from World War II cases (and the cases in Mouritzen, 1991 derive from the early 1980s). Hence, the confrontations that have been made here between a theoretically derived hypothesis and empirical observations can hardly express circularity, i.e. that the hypothesis should have been made with the same cases in mind as those that are used in the confrontation.

There are rich opportunities to provide fruitful challenges to the theory from contemporary cases, in view of the wide-ranging and rapid shifts in European balances of power that have taken place in recent years. For instance, can the shift in the Central European balance of power that took place during the autumn of 1989 and the first half of 1990 (together with the EC integration that had been seen from about the mid 1980s) explain the Swedish 'conversion' on the EC membership question that took place during the autumn of 1990 (making reasonable allowance for inertia in the Social Democratic Party) (Ross, 1991; Sundelius, Chapter 10 of this book)? This conversion should then represent ABPB in a symmetrical constellation (like, probably, the Austrian reorientation on the same question). Or, can the very same balance-of-power shift also explain the new high profile in Danish foreign policy, for example entailing that the classical post-war non-provocation line eastwards has been abandoned (ABPB in the alliance constellation, as the threat perception has changed from medium to low)? For instance, Danish reactions to the introduction of martial law in Poland in 1981 were extremely cautious compared with its reactions to the violent events in Lithuania and Latvia in January 1991.

Should EU unipolarity continue to characterize the European power structure in the future, it can be expected to encompass plenty of ABPB behaviour. Logically, a unipolar structure makes the symmetrical and the alliance constellations obsolete, as they both presuppose two poles as a minimum. The unilateral dependency that is involved in the adaptive acquiescence constellation should be all the more widespread – even in view of the historically rather unique character of the EU pole. Following the thesis of this chapter, I would therefore expect more ABPB behaviour in Europe and less, or negligible, BPB behaviour. Whether this is true empirically, is evidently difficult to say. It seems, though, from a superficial glance, that the ABPB way of thinking is widespread among non-EU members in Central and Northern Europe (which are all weak powers compared with the pole). The EC/EU and its institutions being the trend winner, it is better to adapt today than tomorrow, as increasing pole strength will make it more and more costly and uncomfortable to remain intransigent. This is not to deny popular reluctance, of course. As everyone else is adapting, there is not even a modest alternative platform to the EC in sight, as with EFTA or Norden previously. This way of thinking can be traced back to the mid 1980s, when the EC increased its low-politics attraction, but it seems to have been exacerbated by the definite collapse of bipolarity in 1991.[15]

What makes ABPB an interesting focus of inquiry is, firstly, that it forces us to study the major turning points in world politics (which one would seldom do in bureaucratic politics or in the study of decision-making processes). Secondly, it is an intriguing focus because it cuts through the rhetoric of those responsible for the policy. ABPB is never openly admitted, because it tends to undermine the long-term credibility of the actor in question (the current 'race to Brussels' being an exception, though). There are several ways to try to conceal this type of behaviour (e.g. various delaying tactics), but this means, in turn, that it is tempting to try to unravel it.

Who are the true weathercocks?

The underlying reasons for the Danish–Finnish contrast *vis-à-vis* the Soviet coup and disintegration, as corroborated in this chapter, seem to be shared implicitly by former Finnish Prime Minister Kalevi Sorsa (*Turun Sanomat*, 27 August): 'Can anything be more admirable than Danish verbal courage? Is there anything that can beat these challenging voices that are heard from Aunt NATO's embrace far away behind our back?' This is another way of stressing the importance of constellations (with a certain ironical/ humorous flavour, apparently). In this chapter, I have in no way wished to take sides in the Danish–Finnish 'dispute'. There are good theoretical reasons for the policy of both weak powers in the period being considered. Evidently, the Finnish policy has been exposed as bandwagoning or 'weathercock policy' in the circumstances. However, there is no reason to believe that Danish politicians should be any less weathercocks than their Finnish colleagues. The point is simply that the wind force was so much stronger in Finland's salient environment than in the Danish one.

Notes

1 On the need for macro-historical commentary in general in the present situation, see Deudney and Ikenberry (1991b, p. 225).

2 Knudsen (1991) discusses the effects of the Soviet retreat from Eastern Europe from about 1988 on a number of small powers: the neutrals, the former Warsaw Pact allies and the Baltic states (not independent at the time).

3 The level of tension (conflict) between the two poles varied dramatically even during the short time span we are considering here. Hence, the balance-of-power factor was not alone on the stage. However, as I have shown elsewhere (Mouritzen,

1991), the tension factor affects the weak powers' level of activity rather than the substance of their policies that we shall consider here. Therefore it does not really blur the picture, as one might have feared.

4 As expressed by Rothstein (1968): 'Small Powers threatened by neighboring Great Powers, or intent on securing benefits for themselves in the course of Great Power conflicts, were forced to play a perilous game: moving quickly from the lighter to the heavier side of the balance as soon as an apparent victor in any contest could be discerned. If power corrupts, so does the lack of it' (p. 11).

5 With this trend stipulation of 'bandwagoning', I differ from the literature referred to above, and also from the recent article by Labs (1992, p. 409, n. 2).

6 She is a bit doubtful, though, regarding the applicability of this hypothesis to small states after World War II.

7 The so-called small-state literature is rich in discussions concerning the proper definition of 'small state' (or 'weak power') (for a survey and discussion, see Christmas-Møller, 1983). The focus on constellations here instead of size makes it unnecessary to delve into the essence of smallness (or weakness). We can, for example, happily ignore the question of whether Finland, Sweden and Denmark are really weak powers or not. The point is simply that they are all significantly weaker than the two power poles in their respective constellations (which, in all three cases, happen to be the Soviet Union and the West). With the rather broad definition of bandwagoning used here, one can probably also find this phenomenon among powers not typically regarded as small states.

8 The constellations should not be mistaken for 'modes of adaptation' (Mouritzen, 1988, Chapter 5), even though the two are related.

9 The trends described here are evidently exacerbated if the paramount power constitutes the essential *dynamics* of the balance-of-power shift: for example, if it goes through a rapid rearmament process or, conversely, if its power base is being undermined or even disintegrated.

10 I do not find it necessary for my purpose to distinguish between various *types* of alliances (see Rothstein, 1968). There are, of course, many other determinants of choice regarding alliance posture (Snyder, 1984, pp. 471–5) than the one emphasized here. However, as our interest pertains to the occurrence of ABPB, the weak's threat perception is seen as the most crucial factor. Another factor that might deserve consideration is the level of tension between the ally and the adversary (see Mouritzen, 1988, pp. 385–9).

11 EEA refers to the European Economic Area on which negotiations were taking place at the time between the EC and the EFTA countries (including Sweden and Finland). Its main idea was to extend EC internal market principles to the EFTA area.

12 The Finnish version of neutrality has implied stricter requirements of symmetry in viewpoints between East and West than the Swedish version. In conflict issues, it has often entailed silence (e.g. voting abstentions in the UN). To put it bluntly, one can say that whereas Finnish foreign policy has striven for neutrality in much of the post-war era (an effort not always recognized by the Soviet Union, e.g. Penttilä, 1991, Chapter 8), it now seems to be moving *away* from the straitjacket of neutrality (by watering it down, apparently). For a conceptual analysis of 'neutrality' see Carlsnaes (1993b). As to various European neutralities during the old power structure, see Hakovirta (1988).

13 Notably in government (foreign ministry). One crucial mechanism here has been uncertainty avoidance. As expressed by an anonymous foreign ministry civil

servant (*Hbl*, 30 August) regarding the FCMA Treaty: 'It would be highly irresponsible in the current unstable situation to propose negotiations for a revised treaty. Nobody knows what those negotiations might lead to. Even if the Soviet future is in doubt, Russia will always remain a Great Power and Finland the weaker party. If we have managed with the treaty so far, why start negotiations and jump into the unknown? Stability is valuable.' It would be interesting to compare the factors of inertia in Finland with those in Sweden 1942–3 (Mouritzen, 1988, Part IV). As to Finnish and Swedish foreign ministry inertia around 1989–90, see Karvonen and Sundelius (1991) or Sundelius (Chapter 10 in this book).

14 I agree with the article by Labs (1992) that bandwagoning is not a general type of behaviour for weak powers – not even a frequent type as believed in the literature on bandwagoning that I referred to initially. However, neither is it as rare as suggested by Labs. But that difference of opinion is probably due to the fact that I find a broader definition of bandwagoning more fruitful than the one followed by Labs (see note 5).

15 After the completion of this chapter, I have carried out the kind of analysis suggested here pertaining to a unipolar structure; cf. Mouritzen, 1993, in particular pp. 391–402.

10

Changing Course: When Neutral Sweden Chose to Join the European Community

Bengt Sundelius

In this short study, an existing state-of-the-art scheme for the analysis of foreign policy change is used to examine the decision-making processes of a recent case of policy redirection in Europe. The chosen theoretical approach is a scheme for explaining foreign policy change suggested by Charles Hermann (1990). This is a good example of the predominantly North American, behaviouralist-oriented approach to the comparative study of foreign policy. Many of the strengths and weaknesses of that well-established tradition of scholarship are evident in this specific approach. Following the ensuing case application, some reflections will be made regarding the utility of this type of theoretical approach for the further development of foreign policy analysis.

The empirical case to be examined is the recent shift in Swedish policy towards the European Community. Traditionally, the official position has been that membership of the Community would not be compatible with the long-standing Swedish security policy based on the doctrine of no alliances in peace, aiming for neutrality in the case of war. As late as May 1990, the then Prime Minister, Ingvar Carlsson, articulated this restrictive government position in an authoritative article in the leading Stockholm daily. In October 1990 the government, as part of an economic reform bill, declared its ambition to join the Community as soon as the contextual circumstances would allow. In December, this position was reaffirmed in a parliamentary declaration, which also shifted the wording from ambition to intent. During spring 1991 an internal Foreign Ministry group examined the potential membership issue in great depth. On 14 June the Prime Minister read to Parliament a statement outlining a new government policy on the membership issue. On 1 July 1991 an application for membership was submitted to the Chair of the Council of Ministers of the Community in The Hague. This remarkable policy transition over approximately twelve months represents one of the most fundamental shifts in Swedish post-war foreign policy. The case has important implications also for relations between the EC and several other states, such as Norway and Finland.

This chapter should contribute to an understanding of the twists and turns of foreign policy now overrunning the dynamic European scene. Secondly, it should help illuminate the potentials and limitations of mainstream theoretical schemes in the foreign policy field, particularly as they concern analysis of the European setting. Much of the modern scholarship on foreign policy builds on a theoretical departure point as well as on an empirical reference base drawn from the particular national setting of the United States or some other major state. The evolving European scene is composed of several smaller states with contextual settings very different from those leading states. In many instances, their government leaders have had only limited exposure to the conventions and practices of international politics. An analytical approach which focuses on the dynamics behind decisions for or against foreign policy change within such smaller units of world politics may be a timely complement to other prevalent perspectives on the logic of small-state behaviour in international affairs.

The decision-making approach to foreign policy redirection applied here is initially placed in the context of other prevailing analytical approaches to the field of small-state foreign relations. Before an examination of the Swedish case is embarked upon, two well-established, structurally focused approaches will be briefly discussed. In the first and classical perspective, the weight of the international power structure on a small state's foreign policy is seen as a primary explanatory factor. In the second and more recently developed approach, the enduring character of domestic structures is regarded as the proper focus of explanatory foreign policy analysis for small states. Before this theoretical discussion, however, the main elements of the chosen, critical case of European foreign policy redirection will be presented.

Credible neutrality or Community membership

Traditionally, Swedish neutrality was conceived in narrow terms of national survival. It was an instrument by which the state sought to remain outside any armed confrontation in its vicinity. Its basic function concerned wartime conditions, such as during the two world wars or after 1945 in a superpower military conflict. One vital aspect of this wartime focus became the credibility of this articulated desire and demonstrated ability to remain neutral also under the pressure of international crises. Swedish involvements with other states or commitments to international organizations were carefully assessed with regard to the implications for this credibility. In the domestic setting, the requirements of neutrality were used as the primary reference point in political debate and inter-bureaucratic rivalries over national security policy. The Ministry of Foreign Affairs served as the only legitimate interpreter of this doctrine within the state. The dominant Social Democratic Party was its primary protector against potential deviations to the left or to the right. The significance of the present case of policy redirection must be understood in the light of this background.

The issue which during recent years has stirred most domestic debate on the meaning and implications of neutrality is European integration. The prospect of being left outside the united West European market after 1992 has become an unacceptable vision for most political groups and business leaders. The image of turning into a small, marginalized nation on the northern fringe of a dynamic European continent haunted the domestic scene as the Delors target of 1992 approached.

In 1989 Sweden, together with the other members of the European Free Trade Association (EFTA), began negotiations with Brussels about the establishment of a European economic area comprising both the EC and the EFTA member states. The invitation by Delors in January 1989 to such a joint European undertaking struck a highly positive chord in Sweden. It was hoped that this arrangement would give the EFTA countries access to all forms of economic exchange within the EC without membership. The question of how to secure some influence on EC decision-making concerning the rules for this internal market was left ambiguous until the final phases of the negotiations in 1991. At that time, some judicial problems appeared after the treaty text was reviewed by the European Court. The Swedish government declared repeatedly during 1989–90 that it was not seeking full membership of the Community. Ingvar Carlsson stated in May 1990 that 'concern for the credibility of our policy of neutrality is the reason why we are not applying for EC membership' (*Dagens Nyheter* (*DN*), 27 May 1990).

Several arguments were presented for this restrictive official position. The supranational character of the EC, which by limiting state sovereignty also impacts on neutrality, has been a factor. The security and defence policy aspirations of the Community have been viewed as incompatible with a posture of neutrality. Further, it is often argued that the Swedish international role as mediator and bridge-builder in various global conflicts would become less credible if the government were to subject itself to the collective will of the Community. The visible foreign policy profile of Sweden, including its unique development assistance programme, would be eroded through membership.

Much of the early domestic criticism against the Swedish policy of rejecting EC membership was based on a pessimistic view of the so-called EFTA track. Critics either did not believe that these multilateral negotiations would result in anything concrete, or they feared that the resulting treaty would make EFTA a powerless stepchild of Brussels. In this view, the promised EEA agreement was not a sufficient base for competitive Swedish business involvements in the anticipated economic dynamics of the 1990s and beyond.

Some critics went even further, questioning the applicability of neutrality in the international politics of Europe altogether. According to these critics of the established dogma, a major structural shift had taken place in international relations. The state-centred view, on which the concept of neutrality is based, would no longer be a valid operative framework in this new structure. International exchanges now primarily take place at various transnational levels without the central involvement of sovereign states. The accelerating multilayered developments within the EC are seen as the prime example of this transition in Europe. Consequently, foreign policy is no longer a matter of governments choosing sides or remaining neutral between state-based blocs. Rather, a multitude of transnational actors pursue specific interests in a complex setting of considerable pluralism and overlapping loyalties. This sceptical view of the future relevance of neutrality as a guide for Swedish government policy was formulated in November 1989 in a pointed poem (Sundelius, 1990, p. 123): 'If there is no East and no West, where should the neutral come to rest?'

The government leaders answered their critics both directly and indirectly through intermediaries, such as retired ambassador Sverker Åström. After a season of academic exchanges and newspaper debates on the subject, Ingvar Carlsson in May 1990 set in writing the parameters for involvement by the Swedish state in the European Community:

> Should the EC choose to proceed towards such a far-reaching coordination [of foreign and defence policies] it will become impossible for Sweden to consider membership. The definitive limit lies here. The credibility of our policy of neutrality would be called into question if we were to adapt to a binding cooperation of the kind that an EC membership appears to presuppose. (*DN*, 27 May 1990).

In contrast to the direction of the above statement by the then Prime Minister, the Swedish government's position on this issue evidenced a clear slide over the next twelve months. At the end of this transition period, it favoured Swedish membership of the European Community, but with the retainment of neutrality. This relatively speedy departure from the traditional argument that credible neutrality is incompatible with membership was made possible through an increasingly positive interpretation of the European security setting. Several steps in this reformulation of doctrine are discernible.

In an authoritative statement at the opening of the annual parliamentary session on 2 October 1990, the Prime Minister presented a vision of an evolving Europe 'with a new peace order and where the bloc divisions have disappeared'. In this security setting, it would be possible to 'combine Swedish EC membership and continued neutrality policy'. Later the same month, in an economic reform package to forestall further balance-of-payments problems, the government articulated an even clearer ambition to begin negotiations for membership. This statement of intent was followed by a request to Parliament for an official declaration supporting a Swedish application for membership. In early December 1990, such a parliamentary resolution was passed. It stated that membership with retained neutrality was in the Swedish national interest. In this multipartisan declaration, it was argued that this new important step was possible because of the positive developments in Europe during the previous year. In addition to changes in eastern Europe, the importance of the CSCE framework as a conflict resolution instrument was mentioned.

This widely supported pro-Europe formula was based on the assumption that EC membership could be combined with credible neutrality. Following the December 1990 parliamentary decision on this critical point, Åström noted in a newspaper article that Sweden through this articulation of intent had entered a journey into the unknown without any clear understanding of what might lie ahead. In his view, the implications of EC membership for the requirements of neutrality from the second half of the 1990s onwards had not yet been examined. Several political leaders in a similar fashion argued for a comprehensive review of this major question prior to joining the Community. In February 1991 the Prime Minister suggested that the planned membership nego-tiations should be followed by a binding national referendum, possibly in 1994.

During spring 1991 a high-level Foreign Ministry working group drafted versions of a public declaration favouring membership with retained neutrality. The final text was approved across party lines after some personal involvements by the leaders of the major parties. On 14 June this important and pre-approved document was read to Parliament on its last day in session before the forthcoming national election. An application was formally submitted by Ingvar Carlsson to the Head of the EC Council of Ministers in The Hague on 1 July. Following the September 1991 election defeat of the Social Democratic government, the Conservative Party leader Carl Bildt assumed the position of Prime Minister. In his October 1991 cabinet declaration to the new Parliament, he reaffirmed the Swedish intent to seek membership of the EC.

Structural approaches to small-state foreign policy

A well-established scholarly tradition exists which links the direction of foreign policy by small or weak states to fundamental structural conditions bearing upon their external profiles. Many students of small states have emphasized the impact of the international power structure for the position of the small, and therefore weaker, units of international politics. Among notable North American contributors to this genre are Baker Fox (1959), Rothstein (1968), Handel (1981) and most recently Labs (1992). Comprehensive reviews of this tradition have been presented by Europeans such as Baehr (1975), Amstrup (1976), Lindell and Persson (1984), Väyrynen (1983) and Platias (1986). In Chapter 9 of this volume, Hans Mouritzen builds the analysis of small-state foreign policy adjustment upon this structural perspective focused on the international power configuration.

The recent Swedish reorientation towards membership of the European Community can be explained in terms of an adjustment to the drastically shifting power balance in Europe. Building on the premise, first articulated by Annette Baker Fox (1959, pp. 186–7), that small states tend to go with, rather than move against, the international power balance, the dramatic redirection of Swedish EC policy during 1990–1 can be understood in terms of the impact of international structure. As long as the European post-war balance of power was defined by two relatively equally endowed military blocs, the traditional Swedish posture of avoiding any open military-political entanglements with either side was widely regarded as a prudent national security position. Maintaining an international appearance of independence also *vis-à-vis* the (West) European Community was one element of such a balancing security posture.

After the emergence of a more dynamic European Community, the sudden collapse of the Warsaw Pact, and the rapid and peaceful reunification of Germany, the defining international power constellation shifted. With a military and financially strong Germany at the centre of the envisioned European union, Sweden could best enhance its national interests through a closer affiliation with this new and unrivalled power pole in its vicinity. The power of attraction of Germany became highly visible once again to the small state on the northern fringe. Still, the very real possibility of highly chaotic political developments within the former Soviet empire required that the new Swedish commitment to the German-centred EC also included a caveat, in case of a sudden power balance reversal. Russia could return to a position of power projection along the eastern shores of the Baltic Sea and in the far north. Thus the enduring value of the traditional Swedish neutrality posture was emphasized by the Prime Minister in the June 1991 announcement of the decision to apply for membership.

It seems that the new Swedish EC position can be explained as a national policy adjustment to the European power balance emerging after October 1990. The June 1991 statement, however, also included an appreciation of the still tenuous character of this new constellation. In this explanatory approach, the altered international political structure is seen as the primary force behind the outcome in this case of foreign policy redirection. The logic of this type of analysis is strikingly based on common sense: it permeates journalistic and practitioner accounts of these developments. This explanation also fits well within the realist and neo-realist school of international politics. It seems to capture the essence of the dynamics behind the national policy shift in a parsimonious manner. In the ensuing empirical analysis, using a decision-making approach to foreign policy redirection, this international structural perspective is incorporated as one external stimulus affecting the processes behind the decision to alter official policy.

At the same time, the relatively simplistic, structurally focused approach sidesteps any examination of how the readily observed international changes filter into national policy-making processes behind the subsequent decision choice in favour of a revised policy position. By stressing the direct linkage between the international, situational context and the resultant policy action, the analyst dismisses other pertinent but also more complex elements behind a major redirection of established governmental policy. If a logic of international structure bearing down upon nation-states was uncritically accepted, one would not be able to explain the domestic political agony, the considerable internal party bargain-ings, and the organizational strife experienced during this season of movement towards a new policy formula. Observers of these events in Sweden have noted that the domestic dimension must be included in order to explain adequately the eventual policy outcome on this important issue.

This observation in this recent Swedish case is reinforced by the more generalized conclusion by two of the foremost international relations theorists working on the relationship between inter-national structure/process and foreign policy. Robert Keohane and Joseph Nye, reflecting on their previous landmark book *Power and Interdependence*, argue that 'we have paid too little attention to how a combination of domestic and international processes shape preferences . . . research at the systemic level alone may have reached a point of diminishing returns' (1987, p. 753). Obviously, one must penetrate more deeply inside the Swedish national setting to be able to explain why the recent shift in EC policy occurred.

National attributes, such as domestic structures, form another well-established focus for students of the foreign policies of small states. Maurice East (1978, pp. 124, 133) has developed this explanatory perspective through his claim that 'differences in the national attributes of nations will be related to differences in the foreign policy behavior patterns of these nations.' National attributes consist of the amount of resources and the ability to use resources, which together form the capacity to act. Together with another national attribute, the predisposition to act, the capacity to act shapes the foreign policy behaviour of the nation. East has applied his scheme to such different small states as Uganda (1973) and Norway (1981).

A more sophisticated and historically sensitive version of this domestic structure perspective has been put forward by Peter Katzenstein (1984; 1985) in his celebrated works on how small states 'confront the dilemma of how to balance their quest for autonomy with the fact of interdependence'. He concludes that their 'economic and political successes derive from their capacity to combine economic flexibility with political stability' (1984, p. 256). The pivotal role of close-knit elite networks across the traditional state–society divide is emphasized. The European small-state success stories have been built on these crucial domestic structures. Katzenstein's academically influential thesis parallels arguments presented by native scholars about the foundations of public policy-making in Sweden.

In this second structural perspective, the recent Swedish policy redirection towards Europe can be explained through a significant change in the national capacity to act. This internal structural shift occurred as national elite networks redefined their positions on how to handle the classical dilemma between autonomy and interdependence. The social organization for the effective use of the shrinking material resource base was affected, leading to a reduced capacity to act. According to many observers, domestic economic constraints, and even panic, formed the contextual background to the shift in preference by industry, labour unions and political parties, and eventually to the October 1990 governmental announcement of a revised view on the membership question. In the terminology of the Katzenstein thesis, the domestic structures supporting the traditional policy line, emphasizing autonomy, were eroded in favour of a new constellation of interests promoting a different solution to the acute challenge of economic dependence. The subsequent foreign policy redirection is in this perspective seen as the logical outcome of such an internal adjustment process. It was triggered by international developments, but it can only be explained through an analysis of the shift in domestic structures, which define the national attributes behind any foreign policy position.

Yet, the focus in the prevailing small-state literature on international or domestic structures, interests and realignments is not a sufficient analytical departure point if one holds to the belief that individuals make decisions and shape governmental policy. Foreign policy does not simply evolve from structural features abroad or in the domestic setting. Like other forms of human or social behaviours, it is the result of some purposeful act. Accepting this agency-driven view of foreign policy, the analyst must proceed beyond the two structural perspectives outlined above. In the ensuing Swedish analysis, these wider defining features are incorporated as external triggering stimuli behind the more closely examined decision processes leading to the new official policy posture.

Certainly, agents are affected both positively and negatively by the structures surrounding their definitions of problems, their comprehensions of goals and alternatives, and their choice and implementation mechanisms. Occasions for decision are not set in concrete by nature or by social structures. They are defined through complex and often drawn-out structuration processes, which include a varying degree of consciousness of this cognitive dynamics among the individuals involved. It is hoped that in this case-study the dynamics behind policy redirection can be traced in close proximity to the experienced reality of the relevant actors. It is argued that their subjective views of the strategic problem facing the nation, and the decision occasion confronting them, form a key element behind the goals and means chosen to deal with this recognized challenge. A structural, in contrast to an agency-focused, perspective cannot offer the necessary analytical guidance needed for this particular research task.

After a review of the scant scholarly literature dealing with foreign policy redirection (George, 1980; Goldmann, 1982; 1988; Holsti, 1982; Hallenberg, 1984; Väyrynen, 1987; Hermann, 1990), it has been found that the framework presented by Charles Hermann, initially as his 1989 ISA presidential address, constitutes the most comprehensive attempt to focus on the processes of foreign policy change as an agent-driven activity. This abstract scheme is worthy of empirical application in a specific case, such as the one chosen here. The primary purpose of this short pilot study is to evaluate the wider utility of the scheme as an explanatory approach to a highly pertinent research focus for scholars concerned with the future of Europe.

Other similar cases of recent European foreign policy redirections could easily be identified and examined with the analytical tools used here. For example, several other traditionally neutral member states of the European Free Trade Association (EFTA) have recently redefined their preferred relationships with the emerging European union. The basis exists here for a cross-national project on the dynamics behind this significant policy redirection across Europe. The strategic question of whether such an empirical research programme would be a meaningful activity for European specialists on foreign policy analysis will be addressed in the final section of this chapter. The next task is to examine the Swedish pilot case of foreign policy redirection with the assistance of the chosen analytical scheme developed by Charles Hermann.

Hermannizing the Swedish case

Hermann (1990, p. 5) defines foreign policy as a goal-oriented or problem-oriented programme by authoritative policy-makers directed towards entities outside the policy-makers' political jurisdiction. Four graduated levels of change are suggested: adjustment change, programme change, problem/goal change, and international orientation change. What type of foreign policy change does the chosen case represent? It cannot be said to represent a redirection of the entire Swedish orientation towards world affairs, i.e. the last type. Likewise, the 1990–1 shift involved much more than an adjustment in the level of effort or in the scope of recipients, i.e. the first type.

The purposes or goals behind the established policy line were not replaced by new objectives. A concern for the goal achievement of the fundamental national objectives of prosperity and physical security could be seen as one motive for the dramatic change in foreign policy. The traditional doctrinal relationship between EC membership and the requirements of credible neutrality had to be redefined. This was necessary in order for this established policy doctrine also to enhance these basic policy goals in the future. This recent Swedish case would not seem to fit Hermann's definition of a problem or goal change. Rather, a redirection was made in the means by which the long-standing policy goals were addressed. A qualitative shift occurred as a new formula for combining neutrality and prosperity was found, i.e. a programme change. The new official line was articulated in the statement to Parliament on 14 June 1991.

Hermann is identified with the decision-making approach to foreign policy studies. In the analytical scheme drawn upon here, the observed policy change is assumed to be initiated by some activity external to the decision-making process within the government. The primary focus is upon understanding the activities inside the so-called black box. However, before one digs into the decision-making process proper, one must consider the external stimuli activating these internal mechanisms. Four such sources are identified by Hermann (1990, pp. 11–13). The so-called change agent can be leader driven, based on bureaucratic advocacy, brought on by domestic restructuring, or stimulated by external shock. It is also noted by Hermann that these types of stimulating sources may work in tandem. The next task is then to identify the primary change agent in the Swedish case under examination.

According to many accounts of the developments leading up to the final policy shift in summer 1991, this process was not initiated or driven forward by the cabinet leader or by any strong advocacy segments inside the relevant bureaucracy, i.e. the Ministry of Foreign Affairs. In fact, one can find several conflicting public statements on the doctrinal issue in the 1990–1 period. In some announcements by government leaders, such as the Prime or Foreign Minister, openings towards a membership were made. In other comments, the many remaining obstacles for such a new course were stressed.

Inside the Foreign Ministry, considerable confusion was evident at middle and junior career levels. Several leading diplomats testified privately to their frustration over the uncertainty surrounding this essential element of their professional *esprit de corps*. A sense of disappointment and even betrayal over the political opportune slide at the top level of the ministry was also articulated in private by some career officers with intense personal stakes in the traditional definition of the core of Swedish security policy. In their view, the neutrality doctrine became secondary to the perceived partisan necessity to safeguard prosperity and domestic political tranquillity. Neither the leader-driven nor the bureaucratic advocacy sources seem to have served as primary change agents in this case.

External shocks are large events in terms of visibility and immediate impact on the recipient. Several such relevant events unfolded during the traumatic years of 1989–91. The collapse of Soviet dominance in Central and Eastern Europe became a clear reality during 1990. The new importance of German strength was evidenced by its speedy unification in October 1990. In that same month, the first Swedish official articulation of a change towards EC membership was made. In November, this historical German event was followed by the symbolic signing of the Charter of Paris indicating the promise of a new European security order. The following month, the Swedish Parliament went on record supporting the previously announced plan to join the Community.

In autumn 1990 a sense developed in Swedish public debate, as well as inside some relevant policy-making circles, that the traditionally strict interpretation of the requirements of credible neutrality was becoming irrelevant to the foreign policy problems of the 1990s. In fact, the persistent pursuit of a seemingly outmoded neutrality doctrine could lead to unnecessary material sacrifices without any matching security gains. The changing international setting made previous policy increasingly obsolescent. A significant policy adjustment would be the logical step following the momentous international transformation, it was argued. A static position on neutrality and EC involvement in the face of such overwhelming European developments could very well lead to a significant future policy failure. Thus the proposed policy change was not driven by a sense of failure with the previous posture between the blocs, as stressed in the Hermann scheme. Rather, new realities abroad required a revised national policy for the now approaching significant national issues.

The confidential deliberations inside the Foreign Ministry during spring 1991 largely concerned the possibilities for various alternative developments in the European security setting. Were the changes permanent? How likely and severe could a setback be?

Could Sweden credibly shift position again if the emerging European peace order did not materialize or collapse? How likely was an upsurge of violence across the Baltic Sea? These difficult questions did not concern primarily the immediate situation. They focused more directly upon the plausibility of various more or less threatening futures. Naturally, such discussions were also driven by considerable uncertainty among specialists. Disagreements over the most likely future, and over the most proper Swedish policy course in these possible scenarios, would seem a natural consequence of the structure of the situation. The externally driven source must be included as a significant primary change agent in this case of policy redirection.

Hermann's fourth primary change agent is labelled domestic restructuring. It refers to the politically relevant segment of society whose support a regime needs in order to govern, and the possibility that this segment of society can become an agent of change. This rather ambiguous category in the applied scheme is further narrowed for the purposes of this examination. Here, it will be limited to considerations of any apparent shifts in the domestic political support of the established policy position. Such shifts could be evidenced through the positions of opposition parties, leading interest groups, and public opinion surveys. Assuming that a government prefers to pursue policy positions which have domestic support, or at least tries to avoid antagonizing significant segments of society, it may be useful to examine any recent shifts in domestic support for the traditional government rejection of EC membership.

It has been well documented that the parties in opposition, particularly the Conservative and the Liberal Parties, were well ahead of the party in government, the Social Democrats, in adjusting their views on the matter of EC membership. Until summer 1991, both of their leaders could claim special roles as enthusiastically pro-Europe. They could also label their main rival, Prime Minister Ingvar Carlsson, as much less serious on this issue. With a national election scheduled for September 1991 and with the clear possibility that the opposition parties would turn the EC membership issue into a major campaign theme, it would make good sense for the party in office to defuse well in advance this potential election problem.

Surveys of public support for the political parties are regularly conducted in Sweden. Over the 1989–91 period, the party in office suffered historically low support rates. The parties to the right with more active pro-Europe positions fared better in the polls. If these survey results were to be manifested also in the election of September 1991, the Social Democratic government would have to leave office. Considering this precarious political base, it would seem important for the survival of the cabinet to avoid creating additional targets for attacks from the right prior to the forthcoming election. In September 1990 for the first time a majority of those surveyed in a public opinion poll expressed a preference for EC membership. By then, both the Conservative and the Liberal Parties had come out in favour of eventual membership. The Social Democratic government still held to a more traditional position regarding the restrictions inherent in the neutrality posture. A similar survey in December 1990 indicated that two-thirds of the public then favoured Swedish membership of the Community. These trends in domestic support for a revised government position suggest that one factor motivating considerations of a policy change was the anticipation of a domestic restructuring at the polls, if the current official line were retained in the face of an opposition offensive in favour of membership.

The positions of the major Swedish interest groups also underwent significant changes during 1989–91. Until this period of rapid European transformations, even the Federation of Industry held on to the established policy line, in spite of its previous advocacy in favour of Swedish membership. The leading unions, such as the Federation of Workers (LO) and the Federation of Salaried Employees (TCO) representing blue- and white-collar workers respectively, traditionally have been sceptical of the European integration effort. To them, the EC has lacked a social dimension and has shown an inadequate interest in the concerns of workers and consumers. Significantly, the positions of these leading unions began to shift during 1990. It then became evident that Swedish industry would join the anticipated European internal market with or without any government membership of the Community. Leading firms invested heavily in the EC nations to the possible detriment of their Swedish-based production and service operations and research and development facilities. A clear risk of massive capital flight and eventual loss of employment among the members was at hand.

Considering the traditionally intimate relationship between interest group heads and the leadership of the Social Democratic Party, this growing union concern would soon also affect the deliberations inside the party and within the cabinet. At the Social Democratic Party Congress of September 1990, some discreet and vaguely phrased signs of a possible change of party policy on the EC issue surfaced through the media. In October, the balance-of-payments condition seemed to require not only a major domestic economic reform package but also a public commitment towards a formalized involvement in the Community. The resulting statement by the Ministry of Finance was met with approval by the leaders of the major interest groups, such as the LO, the TCO and the Federation of Industry. It was not cleared in advance with senior civil servants in the Ministry of Foreign Affairs.

It seems that the primary change agent category of domestic restructuring was of significance in this case. However, the resulting decision-making process in favour of a policy change was not initiated by an actual restructuring in society. More appropriately, the decision-making process was stimulated by the anticipated restructuring of domestic preferences against the government and in favour of a different position from the one officially articulated. Naturally, this domestic drift was related to the external shock of a radically different European security scene. As suggested by Hermann, the primary agents of external shock and domestic restructuring interacted in this case to serve in tandem as the primary sources of the initiation of decisions to change direction in foreign policy. It was previously noted that the resulting policy output can be characterized as an example of programme change.

Intervening between agents of change and the actual foreign policy change is decision-making. The next step is then to outline the phases of the decision-making process through which information about possible policy failure is transformed into new government policy. The seven proposed stages are as follows (Hermann, 1990, p. 14):

1   initial policy expectations;
2   external actor and environmental stimuli;
3   recognition of discrepant information;
4   postulation of a connection between problem and policy;
5   development of alternatives;
6   building authoritative consensus for choice;
7   implementation of new policy.

Initial policy expectations, either generated by the policy-makers themselves or imposed upon them, create standards for subsequent judgements of success or failure. Policy can be changed for various reasons but policy-makers must accept some kind of causal connection between what their policy will do and the state of the problem of concern to them. The traditional definition of the EC problematique in Sweden was based on the assumption that economic benefits were possible without formal membership. It had been argued that the hoped-for EEA agreement could provide the necessary prosperity inducing connections with the European internal market. Similar benefits had come from the 1992 free trade agreement.

It was also assumed that a primary consideration in this superficially economic issue must be the implication for credible neutrality between East and West. The traditional problem structuring was to a large degree defined as a national security matter. Although membership would yield greater economic advantages, this opportunity was considered foreclosed owing to its negative consequences for the critical core of established security policy. For example, the 1972 free trade agreement was negotiated by Sverker Åström, who at the time had no particular expertise in international trade issues. However, he was considered well in tune with relevant thinking on the requirements of neutrality and Western entanglements. His previous posting had been as Swedish ambassador to the United Nations.

During the rapid transformation in Europe, the empirical foundations for this well-entrenched national problem definition began to crumble. According to Hermann, when explaining a decision to change policy, one must understand the characteristics of the environmental stimuli in terms of how they are perceived by policy-makers. It appears that the relevant Swedish policy-makers only slowly picked up on the new developments in Europe. These did not fit well with their schema for understanding world politics or the Swedish role in superpower relations. As one foreigner observed, a certain nostalgia for the more well-structured bloc conditions of the Cold War era seemed evident in Stockholm at that time. I have elsewhere (Karvonen and Sundelius, 1990) argued that this reluctance to redefine the basic premises behind Swedish security policy in the light of the rapid transformations abroad can be understood as an effect of the weight of a domestic decision regime built around the doctrine of neutrality.

One crucial external stimulus behind the eventual movement towards a restructured Swedish problem definition was the October 1990 reunification of Germany without any apparent Soviet protest. This fundamental alteration of the security and economic structures of Europe may have triggered the subsequent Swedish commitment to an application for EC membership. Prior to this event government leaders articulated ambiguous caution regarding the compatibility between membership and credible neutrality. After German reunification, the public declarations became more precise. The spring 1991 internal Foreign Ministry group assessing the plausibility of a return to the traditional superpower frost in

Europe decided in its conclusions to emphasize more the opportunities to be seized in the new Europe rather than the possible setbacks and risks.

Hermann argues that for major foreign policy change to occur it is necessary for authoritative policy-makers to conclude that their prior formulation of the problem, their mode of dealing with it, or both, no longer accommodate information received from the environment. After the critical German settlement, it became obvious that a new mode of dealing with the classical dual Swedish problem formulation of prosperity and security was required. One had to find a revised policy formula for achieving the still important joint objective of continued prosperity and adherence to the deeply entrenched security posture. In the terminology of the applied scheme, the policy-makers concluded that their traditional policy was ineffective in dealing with the problem, as presently defined, making the problem worse, generating new problems (i.e. in the domestic election arena) and costing much more than anticipated.

The impression from media reports is that a painful decision-making process took place within the Social Democratic government during the 1990–1 parliamentary session. On 14 June 1991 the policy-makers were locked into a new mind-set of almost equal rigidity as the one which recently had been abandoned. For example, Ingvar Carlsson's spontaneous comment during the early phase of the August 1991 Soviet coup attempt is illustrative of this new analytical closure. He then claimed that despite this setback the favourable superpower conditions allowing Swedish membership, with retained neutrality, had not changed sufficiently to reassess this recent commitment to integration with Western Europe. The policy-makers were soon fortunate enough to see the Soviet domestic military intervention fail. No sudden change in the Soviet domestic political system shattered the newly found formula for Swedish prosperity and security.

The next suggested stage of the decision process leading to foreign policy change is the development of alternatives. In this particular case, the focus was on the possible means by which the fundamental, and still intact, policy objectives could be fulfilled. One of the traditional obstacles to any deep Swedish involvement in the European integration process, with its potential economic benefits, had been the perceived costs to a credible neutrality posture. Also during the initial years of the recent European transformation period, this limiting aspect was stressed by authoritative government leaders and Foreign Ministry officials. In his May 1990 newspaper article, the Prime Minister reaffirmed this restrictive, official position on the boundaries for credible neutrality.

Following the dramatic year of European transitions, the government could solve its Community membership problem by declaring that this traditional restriction was no longer relevant. It could be argued that the preferred policy line of the Social Democratic government could now be realized as the international setting had significantly changed. With the favourable prospects for a European order of common security, the Swedish government could join in this important regional enterprise. According to this logic, the government line was not manifesting any radical shift in preference. Instead, it realized a long-standing Social Democratic ambition, which has been hampered by the unfortunate security restrictions imposed by the requirements of credible neutrality.

In Swedish politics, building an authoritative consensus behind major policy initiatives is an important ingredient of successful decision-making. In this particular case, the elaborate process of consensus-building spanned the 1990–1 parliamentary session. It involved finding support and analytical rationales inside the government machinery for the new position. It required considerable effort to get the Social Democratic Party leadership behind the offensive towards participation in European integration. Within both the relevant government bureaucracy and the party machine, considerable resistance to a swift policy change was encountered. Some internal critics articulated their scepticism towards a potential redirection of policy through the media. Within the cabinet, the Minister of the Environment voiced some concerns over the relevant Community record. To some Social Democrats, the unique Swedish international role, including its progressive development assistance profile, would be endangered through membership of the EC.

Outside the government and party in office, a primary target for consensus-building was the Centre Party, one of three non-socialist parties forming the loyal opposition. Traditionally, the Centre (formerly Agrarian) Party has safeguarded the primacy of secure neutrality, when confronted with schemes for international entanglements. The Left Party (former communists) and the Green Party were also opposed to the pro-EC policy line. However, it was not seen as necessary to bring these two small fringe parties behind the planned policy shift. Their parliamentary votes were not required to pass a bill on the EC issue.

In order to reach a consensus-based formula for the pro-EC position which could include the Centre Party, proponents made references to the continued importance of the well-established policy of neutrality in any great-power conflict. This aspect was also important to the guardians of security policy inside the government machinery. In May and early June 1991, such commonly agreed language was found within a select working group composed of the Prime and Foreign Ministers and the other major party leaders. The subsequent letter of application by the Kingdom of Sweden of 1 July was based on a multiparty consensus of both the left and the right. Only the small Left and Green Parties remained opposed to this new formula.

One motivating factor behind the prolonged consensus-building effort was to diffuse a potentially difficult election campaign issue. The EC membership question did not figure prominently as a divisive issue in the September 1991 election. All major parties declared their support for the agreed pro-Europe line. The Conservatives tried to take the credit for pushing the Social Democratic government forward on the issue, while the latter asked for a renewed mandate to work for a better people's Europe. The two small parties opposed to the EC suffered election losses together with the party in office. The Conservative Party as well as two new pro-EC parties gained parliamentary seats. The new Prime Minister, Carl Bildt of the Conservative Party, is recognized as strongly favouring a Swedish return to its European economic, political and cultural base.

The final stage in the decision process behind policy redirection, as suggested by Hermann, is implementation of the new policy. In one sense, this step was completed through the 14 June public declaration and the application for membership on 1 July 1991. However, the implementation stage could enter into this case in more complex ways in the future. For one, the constitution must be altered prior to entering the Community, as this step involves transferring some sovereign powers to this larger entity. Constitutional revisions can only be enacted through two legislative steps, with a national election between these parliamentary decisions. A special commission of parliamentarians and relevant experts is at work on formulating recommendations for the necessary constitutional revisions.

Further it has been agreed that, following the planned negotiations, a referendum on the membership issue should be conducted prior to accepting formally a new treaty relationship with the Community. To hold such a national campaign on the issue was decided long before the more recent Danish and French referenda on the Maastricht treaty were conducted. It is said that this Swedish referendum must be held in 1994 if possible membership should take effect on 1 January 1995. One likely date is in conjunction with the next scheduled parliamentary election in September 1994. The level of public commitment to the new formula will thus be tested before the nation is locked into a qualitatively new international relationship with obvious implications for its economy, social structure, foreign policy profile and traditional neutrality posture.

If placed in opposition for the entire 1991–4 parliamentary period, the Social Democratic Party may, in the September 1994 election and referendum, take a different line towards the ensuing negotiation results than it would have done as the party in office. Possibly, its commitment to European integration is precarious. The support inside the party for this position could crumble if partisan gains seem likely among voters still opposed to a deeper Swedish involvement with the Community. After all, considerations of the implications for the domestic political context seemed to be one important stimulus behind the recent pro-Europe shift in official policy. The Left Party has continued its opposition to membership, as has the now ousted Green Party. The Centre Party is a member of the present coalition cabinet, but it remains a more reluctant proponent of the official pro-EC line. If this issue became a subject of domestic controversy and cabinet conflict, the government of Carl Bildt could fall well before the next national election in September 1994. Considerations of domestic partisanship could very well enter into the Community-relevant calculations of the central decision-makers again. If so, the implementation stage of this case of foreign policy redirection is not yet completed, but may remain a subject of analysis for some years to come.

Lessons of wider significance

According to Charles Hermann (1990, p. 20), we 'need a perspective that views major change not as a deterministic response to large forces operative in the international system, but rather as a decision process'. His scheme was constructed to aid the scholar wanting to characterize the conditions that can produce decisions for dramatic redirection in foreign policy. At the same time, it is clear to Hermann that 'a characterization of the analytical stages of the decision process that may be necessary for the emergence of a new direction in foreign policy does not provide a theory explaining such changes.' Rather, the intended contribution of his essay is the presentation of 'a scheme for interpreting decisions in which a government decides to change policy direction' (1990, pp. 19–20).

One is struck in these quotes by the seemingly modest level of explanatory ambition by one of the foremost representatives of the so-called behaviouralist tradition of foreign policy analysis. The scheme is viewed as a useful tool for interpreting decisions. It is not regarded as having explanatory value as it lacks any theoretical underpinning, Hermann admits. The ambition to 'interpret decisions' is in striking contrast to his earlier attempts to build a scientific base for the comparative study of foreign policy through the use of rigorous explanatory models and the collection of events data. This primarily North-American-based tradition of scholarship was evaluated in Hermann and Peacock (1987). The more limited aspirations of this recent analytical scheme can be deplored as defeatist, if one adheres to a more positivistic orientation towards social science than the one Hermann embraces in this essay. Others may find the new modesty becoming and more fitting for this field of study than the scientific pipedreams of some decades ago.

For a scholar with an interest in mapping the evolving events and involvements of the principal actors in a specific case of foreign policy redirection, the analytical scheme used here proved to be of considerable value. The primary purpose of this effort was to illuminate a chosen case rather than to generate explanations of decisions for policy change which would be valid across time and space. The scheme brought several insights into the dynamics of the Swedish decision processes during the eventful 1990–1 policy transformation. It could very well form the basis for a research programme on the recent foreign policy redirections in Europe, including the experiences of the neutrals.

Many significant questions were raised through the use of this comprehensive but also detailed approach to examining the research problem. It is quite possible that parallel examinations of other cases in Sweden and elsewhere could help the originator to refine further this already valuable framework for showing how foreign policy redirection is an outcome of a complex governmental decision process. Such policy change cannot be properly understood or explained if it is viewed simplistically as the natural adaptation to structural alterations at home or abroad. The chosen emphasis on actor-driven decision processes proved a valuable research focus. However, some limitations of this approach should be noted.

As predicted by the Hermann framework, the impact of domestic restructuring was an important element behind the Swedish decision to change policy direction. Similarly, during the lengthy process of building political and bureaucratic support for the proposed new policy line, the structure of the European security setting was one important background feature. Apparently, structures at home and abroad were conditioning factors in this case of policy change. However, the outcome was not triggered by any domestic restructuring *per se*. Instead, the anticipated future restructuring of Swedish domestic politics through the election process loomed large in the minds of the decision-makers. Also in the discussions about the international setting, the focus was primarily on the possible futures for European security. The declaratory outcome of that collective, analytical process was to take note of the promises offered by the favourable trends abroad, while downplaying any serious risks. The structural aspects cannot be seen as prior to or even separate from the agency-based decision processes. Policy choices were made which could help shape the domestic political structure, or at least reduce the likelihood of the anticipated unfavourable election outcome.

Prediction was an important element of the decision-making process in this case. Both the concerns over the possible election outcome and the expectations for a peaceful Europe, which were part of the determination behind change, are examples of the use of predictions as central signposts in policy-making. In Swedish security planning, for example, considerable effort is devoted to exploring alternative futures and their implications for specified national goals. In a sense, when the policy-maker chooses a particular future as the baseline for further deliberations about policy alternatives, the parameters for the seemingly major choices over goals and means have largely been set. Hermann has not included this dynamic, forward-reaching aspect in his scheme. One reason could very well be the limited knowledge in the field about the role of predictions in decision-making (Stenelo, 1980). Yet, without adding considerations of the anticipated future to the frequently used 'lessons of the past' perspective, the analyst will overlook one key aspect of the operational setting for national leaders involved in foreign policy redirection.

One of the assumptions of the applied scheme is that new policy measures are developed in response to perceptions of failure of previous means towards given goals. One striking observation in this Swedish case was the remarkable lack of any sense of failure. Rather, the new policy line was regarded as the logical consequence of a new situation. The term 'the only way' was even coined during the September 1991 election campaign by the successful Conservative Party. The previous restrictive membership policy was likewise a success as long as the international security setting remained bloc focused. Obviously, these public statements are good illustrations of attempts to rationalize the outcome of a decision-making process.

Still, one may wonder to what extent this potential refusal to consider the possibility of a policy failure actually influenced the deliberations behind the eventual policy redirection. The lesson to be drawn from this case appears to be that policy-makers do not accept failure lightly, if at all. They simply move along to the next occasion for decision and again choose the 'only logical' policy direction considering that particular situation. Practitioner insight into the weight of the feedback loop in decision-making was not a trademark of this Swedish case. How can an observer then apply the yardstick of failure in analysis, when this potential decision process component may not enter into the mind-set of the participants? The analytical departure point of the Hermann scheme seems to be in question if one examines more critically the place of this key element in his input–output model for decision-making.

The strength of the Hermann framework is its penetrating focus on the so-called black box between problem recognition and decision outcome. In contrast to other prevalent modes of analysis dealing with foreign policy adaptation, Hermann has recognized the voluntaristic basis for decisions to alter or to retain established policy. The surrounding international or domestic structures do not compel any redirection in a deterministic fashion, in his scheme. They may however serve as strong stimuli towards a decision to change policy. The important analytical distinction, recognized by Carlsnaes (1992, p. 254), between the intentional, dispositional and structural dimensions of foreign policy explanations can be maintained when using this broad scheme. One shortcoming is, however, that the threat or opportunity which triggers deliberations within the black box is treated as a given. The decision-maker enters a rather passive mode of adaptation in an input–output type of processing chain after the given occasion for decision is identified.

Hermann also notes that in the foreign policy field one often faces ill-structured problems. This element of the triggering setting complicates the processes behind decisions for or against policy redirection. Picking up on that observation by Hermann, one may assume that decision-makers frequently have considerable latitude in their interpretations of the so-called occasion for decision. As these are ill-structured, they can be defined in various ways by alert decision-makers or policy advisers. Thus, threats to be met and opportunities to be seized are largely created through the process of interpreting a complex and ambiguous operational setting. In the Swedish case at hand, the leaders of the Social Democratic government initially saw little of particular policy interest in the evolving Community. The continental developments seemed to be outside the parameters for meaningful foreign policy action. In contrast, the party leaders on the right noted the opportunity to batter the government over its inability to take a lead on an issue which could be said to concern the economic survival of the nation. Two competing schemata of the European future, and its consequences for Sweden, were constructed out of one ill-structured occasion for decision.

One lesson of this application seems to be the existence of an active problem definition mode among the Swedish decision-makers. They recognized the enabling character of any given occasion for decision, as well as its manipulative potential. When engaged in considerations of policy change, one is also actively involved in choosing an image of the future. This process begins prior to the point where the so-called triggering occasion enters the black box, as outlined in the Hermann scheme. This early phase of the dynamics behind policy redirection is not included in the framework used here. It appears to have been an important part of the processes of the Swedish case examined. This problem formulation phase involved many aspects, such as prediction, wishful thinking, and even active manipulation of the image of the future.

Looking beyond this Swedish case of policy redirection in 1990–1, it is striking how Europe over the last few years has become an arena for competing visions of the future. During the second half of the 1980s, two European models confronted each other. Delors's view of the internal market after 1992 was one important and highly influential alternative. Gorbachev's notion of a 'European home' became for a time another preferred future structure for the Continent. Both concepts served as instruments of manipulation in the processes of forming the evolving new political context. It appears that the Delors perspective proved more enduring than the aspiration for a European home.

Today several such images of the European future compete for dominance in the mind-sets of national political leaders and publics at large. Two security-relevant perspectives stand out in particular. In one pessimistic view, Europe will slide into great-power rivalries linked to regional conflicts reminiscent of the pre-war era. In another image, European common security will be established through the shared governance of collective institutions, such as the CSCE and NACC. Each of these perspectives has important implications for national policy choices and party preferences. Will

Sweden remain secure in its traditional reliance on military neutrality in a European context of great-power rivalries? Will Swedish security be enhanced as part of a new collective governing structure transcending traditional bloc divisions? What consequences will these two alternative future security settings have for Sweden as a member of a European Community moving towards a European union?

Depending on the adopted defining perspective of the future, Swedish decision-makers will choose a national security policy pointing in a different direction. At the same time, this choice will in part shape the larger European security context and eventually feed back into the national decision processes. Structure and agency are hopelessly intertwined through such forward-feeding processes and feedback mechanisms. The obvious conclusion is that in order to be able to explain the fundamental transformations now under way in Europe, one must examine the processes behind decisions for or against significant policy change inside the relevant nations. This pilot study has shown that, although not without its own limitations, the analytical scheme developed by Charles Hermann (1990) could serve as an appropriate starting point for such a Europe-focused research programme on foreign policy redirection.

11

Context and Action in the Collapse of the Cold War European System: an Exploratory Application of the Agency–Structure Perspective

Olav F. Knudsen

In 1989, the structure of the East European system was suddenly gone with the wind: practically all of the relatively long-term relationships between states within the Soviet sphere of influence were uprooted. Before long, the East–West structure started coming down as well. World politics left the bipolar system behind and entered a new systemic condition which – though variously described as unipolar and multicentric – is still not clearly defined or definable. That is not an obstacle here. The empirical aim of this chapter is to study the process of structural change itself, as it has been described by leading decision-makers of the region.

The foreign policy behaviour of states, as conducted by their governments, is determined partly by influences from the domestic political system, partly by the impact of specific characteristics of the bureaucratic system and personalities of decision-makers, and partly by influences from the external political environment, notably the international system. My concern here is exclusively with the third type of influence. In particular I want to study the significance of changes in the mutual relations of great powers, which constitute the general political environment for all other states in their day-to-day existence.

The subject, in short, is the influence of the environment upon foreign policy behaviour, exemplified by the recent changes in European and international relations following the Soviet withdrawal from Eastern and Central Europe and the fading of the power of the Soviet Union itself. The question is how the Central European states related to this upheaval. Government leaders in these countries had long known pretty much what they could and could not do in their foreign affairs. Over the years Soviet and Western governments had demonstrated to each other standard ways of dealing with recurring problems. New problems always had to be handled within the framework of set ways. Superpowers were 'free'; other states had to treat the pattern as given.

In 1989 it suddenly became possible for Soviet client states to think that they could break the rules and go their own way. The thought of alternatives in itself undermined not just the policies of Eastern and Central European states, but the very legitimacy of their regimes: they fell.

The governments which replaced them started off by assessing the new foreign policy environment. All adjusted their foreign policy course accordingly. This process of policy formation in the first half of 1990 is the main focus of the empirical section.

The theoretical setting

The general empirical phenomena just described may be classified as *contextual* effects on behaviour (Galtung, 1969): whether and how a change in the states' most general political surroundings leads to changed behaviour on the part of the states' governments, and how to tell that it has (see also Hollis and Smith, 1990, pp. 7ff., 97ff., 104–18, 197–216). In recent years this question has most often been referred to – because of a post-behavioural interest in explaining action – as 'the agent–structure' issue. My use of a different term implies no dissent where the explanation of action is concerned, but a wish to emphasize that the usage regarding structure is remarkably fuzzy (see Giddens, 1984, p. 16). Context, as used here, encompasses both (a) structure in the sense of patterned behaviour, and (b) situational factors in the sense of transient characteristics of the actors' environment.[1] It will be argued below that under conditions of structural change, as patterns of behaviour become uncertain, situational characteristics tend to predominate in conditioning action.

Contextual puzzles are by no means specific to international politics; they represent an old issue in social and political science (Ruggie, 1986; Wendt, 1987; Carlsnaes, 1992). Kenneth Waltz presented the relevance of context to international politics in his thoughtful essay, *Man, the State and War* (1959). Waltz has subsequently played a leading role in the further development of thinking in the field of international relations pertaining to contextual – or, as he calls it, *systemic* – analysis, as we shall see below.

Stated simply, the analytical objective involved is to use characteristics of a more encompassing environment (or higher level) to explain action undertaken within that environment (i.e. on a lower level; again see Hollis and Smith, 1990). In international politics, contextual reasoning is perhaps most familiar from balance-of-power theory, according to which states (lower level) align and realign themselves in response to the overall constellation of power (higher level) so as to oppose potentially dominant powers or coalitions.

However, we must not forget that all studies of state action, and in particular foreign policy decision-making, involve multiple contexts:

1 an immediate institutional context for the individual decision-maker;
2 a wider administrative (bureaucratic) context within the government for the decision-making institution;
3 a broader domestic political environment for the government as actor;
4 an environment external to the state when conceived as actor.

It is only the last which will be discussed here, and among such external environmental factors I shall concentrate on those which can be associated with the power structure, or in Waltz's terms the 'capability distribution'.[2]

Contextual reasoning coexists and competes with other lines of reasoning. Explanatory variables may be fetched from higher levels, the same level or lower levels than the variable to be explained. In international politics it is useful to sort variables descriptive of the higher levels into two classes: those which are the same for all states (e.g. the structure of global power), here termed *contextual* but also called systemic; and those that vary with whatever other state or group of states the acting state has relations, usually called *relational* variables (East, 1969).

Theories are rarely all contextual or non-contextual. Individually, they may combine different elements of reasoning regarding the levels at which variables are defined. Indeed,

> there is no such entity as a distinctive type of 'structural explanation' in the social sciences; all explanations will involve at least implicit reference both to the purposive, reasoning behaviour of agents and to its intersection with constraining and enabling features of the social and material contexts of that behaviour. (Giddens, 1984, p. 179)

The ambiguities of structure must be remembered. Giddens has no separate conceptual place for transient situational aspects; they blend into the context.

Statements of the balance-of-power theory usually involve relational reasoning for major states and contextual reasoning for minor states. Governments of major states which assume the role of balancer, like the traditional British policy, do so on the basis of contextual thinking. Other theories compete with the balance-of-power theory. Some theories use relational aspects of characteristics of the states themselves to explain policy.

The so-called bandwagoning principle employs a relational explanation. It says that small states do not dare to counterbalance ascendant states, but join them for protection instead (Fox, 1959; Waltz, 1979; Ruggie, 1986). This is not a contextual explanation, but rather one that explains with reference to the direct relationship between the small state and an ascendant state.

When developing contextual arguments, theorists often use the term 'structure' to refer to the contextual element, as already pointed out. Prominent attention has been given to the writings of Kenneth Waltz on this subject, but the relevant literature is much greater than that, even within the narrow field of international relations theory proper.

In an influential early contribution, Morton Kaplan (1957) dealt with the significance of a system's structure for its stability, kicking off a scholarly debate which lasted throughout the 1960s. The key issue was whether war was more likely to occur in one kind of system or environment than another. Because wars are made by states through the decision of their governments, the contextual element was at the heart of this debate. Significant theoretical contributions were made by Waltz (1964), Deutsch and Singer (1964), Rosecrance (1966) and Young (1968). The empirical research of Singer and Small, Rosecrance and others has since contributed to our understanding of such contextual effects while also revealing a need for more in-depth work on specific issues.

Still, the aim of the studies just mentioned was not to explain state action, but to understand the conditions of systemic stability. More directly relevant theoretical advancement in agency–structure research began with Kenneth Waltz's provocative book *Theory of International Politics* (1979). Waltz argues that

> It is not possible to understand world politics simply by looking inside of states ... Since the variety of actors and the variations in their actions are not matched by the variety of outcomes, we know that systemic causes are in play. Knowing that, we know further that a systems theory is both needed and possible. To realize the possibility requires conceiving of an international system's structure and showing how it works its effects. (Waltz, 1979, pp. 65, 69)

In Waltz's conception,

> Systems theories, whether political or economic, are theories that explain how the organization of a realm [such as international politics] acts as a constraining and disposing force on the interacting units within it. (Waltz, 1979, p. 72)

To Waltz, anarchy and the capability distribution among the system's principal actors (great powers) are the two structural characteristics that count in international politics. Since anarchy is an invariant characteristic of international systems, the distinguishing structural trait becomes the capability distribution: bipolarity or multipolarity. States behave differently under bipolarity than under multipolarity. However:

> Structures do not work their effects directly . . . In itself a structure does not directly lead to one outcome rather than another. Structure affects behavior within the system, but does so indirectly. The effects are produced in two ways: through socialization of the actors and through competition among them. (Waltz, 1979, p. 74)

Although Waltz's discussion is thorough and well exemplified, it leaves many questions unanswered, or answered only in general terms. The book gave rise to a great debate in the field. Much of the argument was presented in the pages of Keohane's edited volume (1986), which collected some of the more important reviews of Waltz's book. (The concerns of that debate were much broader than just the contextual one dealt with here.)

However, not until Wendt's (1987) article was the issue examined in a more focused way. Wendt's contribution whipped up a whole new debate (Dessler, 1989; Wendt, 1991; 1992b; Hollis and Smith, 1991; 1992; Carlsnaes, 1992) which has served to clarify a number of important subjects.

The ability of theories adequately to explain recent events

Only the works dating from 1986 and later will be discussed here. The Keohane volume (1986) was rather inconclusive on the issues which concern us, although Ruggie and Keohane contributed useful discussions.

Wendt's (1987) article, while commendably penetrating, was nevertheless too broadly conceived, contrasting the world structure theorists (such as Wallerstein, 1974), who are not doing contextual analysis, with Waltz. The point of world systems analysis is to study effects over time on the whole emanating from its parts, or effects on specific traits of the whole at a given stage caused by other characteristics of the whole at some earlier stage. The fact that constituent units of systems are treated as effects of the system is Wendt's basis for including the world system approach on a par with the approach of Waltz (see Dessler's critique, 1989). However, this seems an unimportant criterion as long as the analytical emphasis is elsewhere and the contextual relationship is postulated by assumption.

The emphasis of these works (except Keohane's) has been heavily on the philosophical side. Contrasting views of central issues are presented in an exchange in the 1991–2 *Review of International Affairs* between Wendt on the one hand and Hollis and Smith on the other. While clarifying, much of this is only of limited use to those of us who are engaged in empirical research, as emphasized by Dessler (1989, p. 443). Dessler's sensible standpoint on this score is not, however, followed up in his own article. His distinction between 'positional' and 'transformational' conceptions, furthermore, seems to be of secondary significance.

Wendt's presentation of Giddens's 'structuration' theory (see also Giddens, 1984), on the other hand, points to a promising broader perspective on the relationship of action to structures, even in the study of international politics. Despite some important objections offered by Carlsnaes (1992), structuration theory will remain a fruitful perspective for thinking about contextual effects. (A rather critical essay on some of Giddens's ideas is found in Archer, 1985.)

Where empirical research is concerned, only Giddens (1984) and Carlsnaes (1992) in my opinion provide guidance. Giddens usefully underlines the need for 'detailed investigations of agents' reasoning' and gives extensive examples from other areas of social research (Giddens, 1984, pp. 310ff.). Carlsnaes offers suggestions relevant to the study of foreign policy change. Otherwise there is still a remarkable lack of empirical work.

In the following I shall make a preliminary effort towards an empirical application. *The reasoning of agents* tops my agenda. We need to understand in what way the context constrains or enables the behaviour of states. The question is how actors take structures into account and relate to them. To make sense of what we are dealing with we shall have to reach back to basics for a definition of 'structure'. In Giddens's language,

> [structure] has tended to be used as a received notion. But there can be no doubt how 'structure' is usually understood by functionalists and, indeed, by the vast majority of social analysts – as some kind of 'patterning' of social relations or social phenomena. (1984, p. 16)

From this Giddens proceeds to launch his concept of 'structuration', which I find theoretically overdeveloped for my present purposes.

Fundamentally, we are dealing with the structuring of social relations, and the consequences thereof. In the following, structures will be understood as recurrent patterns of behaviour, or stable expectations about putative behaviour in given social settings, in the case of inter-state relations in Eastern and Central Europe.

The understanding of the agent–structure linkage itself must be spelled out. From one perspective, context (or structure) may be said to have causally affected behaviour if it is possible to show that behavioural change was preceded by structural change, and if one can rule out alternative explanations of behavioural change.[3] There is no need to demonstrate intermediary links, according to this view.

A rival perspective emphasizes the role of individual decision-makers. Causal links, according to this view, can only be established via human consciousness and international behaviour. If structural change 'causes' state behaviour to be modified, a link must in principle, at least, be traceable to individual actors, decision-makers who *occupy formal roles* on behalf of states and *pursue goals* on behalf of states. Such individual actors must perceive an altered setting for action in which their expected goal achievement on behalf of the state is affected; moreover, their subsequent action on behalf of the state must be linked to this perception if a causal link is to be held plausible. This latter view is also my position.

Social context (structure) as conceived here is not of interest except as it exists in the minds of men and women; social context has relevance for social action only to the extent that pre-existing patterns are recognized by the agents. The existence of social structure is indicated by – and observable in – regularized, patterned, repetitive behaviour. It is also observable to the extent that explicit utterances are made by social agents describing such structures.

For example, the main contextual trait of international politics in the neo-realist mode of thinking is said to be anarchy and the consequent continuous search for ways of survival and self-preservation. Some thinking along such lines must be present in actors' minds if the notion of anarchy as a structure has any worth. Another example, pointed out by Raymond Aron many years ago (Aron, 1964), is that great powers rely on their reputation for power to establish 'power structures' or hierarchies of power. Instead of repeatedly fighting wars, they exercise their accumulated power by utilizing the impressions they have previously made on other international actors. In this connection I accept Giddens's view that

Structure has no existence independent of the knowledge that agents have about what they do in their day-to-day activity. Human agents always know what they are doing on the level of discursive consciousness under some description. (1984, p. 26)

In other words, to be conceived to have constraining or enabling effects on actors, structures must somehow be perceived by them and be part of their practical thinking, in international politics as in other social relations.

Structures are reflected both in the form of *descriptive statements* and in the form of expressed *expectations* among actors in the system *that behaviours will be repeated* and in their *notions as to why* this is so.

My idea here is to seize the opportunity offered by the transitional period in 1990 to search for traces of the relationship between structure and action in statements by decision-makers in Central and Eastern Europe. I want to recapture how the actors on the European scene recognized that the world was now a new one, and came to the explicit conclusion that their governments had to act accordingly.

The main reference points in terms of policy change are easily definable: starting from Hungarian demands for Soviet troop withdrawals, via Soviet offers of unilateral (partial) withdrawals, Gorbachev's demands for East European reform, Soviet military restraint in the face of massive popular protest in East Germany, through Hungarian, Czechoslovak and German demands for complete troop withdrawals, to Warsaw Pact reform (demilitarization) and Soviet acceptance of a reunited Germany in NATO.

Data and method

Foreign policy will here be studied in the shape of public utterances which I shall call 'diagnostic statements'. By 'diagnostic' I mean that the statements in question convey an assessment or evaluation by a country's official leaders of *the kind of situation they are facing*. Diagnostic statements thus may be said to give a record of the leaders' reading of their most salient environment.

Using diagnostic statements as data for analysis involves some of the same problems as the use of other public utterances. Like statements of motivation, such assessments may be shaped or timed by tactical considerations, and may give an incomplete and possibly erroneous picture of the speaker's actual perceptions and thoughts. Nevertheless, diagnostic statements are less liable to have been manipulated than statements about the speakers' own motives and intentions, because they are not nearly as closely tied to his or her behaviour.

Given the problems being dealt with here, I shall seek out indications of the extent to which political leaders see *systemic structural* change as the key to new situations they are facing. The data will consist of such diagnostic statements on the part of governmental elites of Czechoslovakia, Hungary and Poland.

A second type of statement gleaned is *expressions of expectation*, especially as regards possible great power intervention. We may define expectations in this context as the actor's future-oriented images, explicitly expressed, of his or her action environment. When expectations are firm, as in a stable system whose structures have long remained unchanged, those expectations are often taken for granted and are thus rarely stated explicitly. When the system is ostensibly undergoing change, expectations may be stated openly more often and more tentatively, as if the actor wants to persuade him- or herself and others that this is indeed the kind of world in which he or she lives.

The statements *about* structure are taken to reflect the *actual* structure. It is important to note that making statements *at the same time* in itself represents *action*. There is, in other words, a partial overlapping of analytical function between two concepts, variously described as 'reflexive monitoring of action' or as 'duality of structure' by Giddens (1984, pp. 5, 23ff.). To the extent (allowing for some variability) that action conforms to a pattern, it reinforces that pattern. To the extent that it breaks the pattern, it contains the seed of a new pattern.

Nevertheless, and contrary to Archer's critique (Archer, 1985; see also Carlsnaes, 1992), it is not the case that action and structure in this conception become coextensive. The structure itself exists in the minds of each of the actors as perceived patterns of prior behaviour. Action is taken with that perception in mind as well as on the basis of other influences.

There is thus no predetermination, or logical identity, involved in this way of conceiving the relationship between structure and action. In the empirical analysis, however, no attempt is made explicitly to identify 'structure' and 'action', as this would be a case of misplaced concreteness.

Empirical application

During the 1970s and 1980s, the perceptions of structural constraint on state behaviour in the area of the Warsaw Pact (WP) were linked to the following specific issues:

1   the existence of the Pact;
2   the Brezhnev Doctrine legitimizing interventions of 'fraternal assistance';
3   the stationing of troops on the territories of Czechoslovakia, East Germany, Hungary and Poland;
4   the issue of the leading role of the party in each member state.

The process of change discussed in this chapter can be traced through the crumbling of all these constraints during 1989 and 1990. The crumbling took place in two stages, here labelled Acts I and II. Considerations of space prevent me from presenting both stages here. I shall focus on early 1990.

Mostly, the crumbling occurred in one of the following ways:

1   Statements were made by East European governments to the effect that the constraint ought to be changed, or that it no longer applied, etc.
2   Statements were made whose implication was contrary to the constraints.
3   Other action was taken in breach of constraints, e.g. the Polish military oath in the summer of 1988 (see below).

In both 1 and 2 no opposition was voiced from Moscow; or, if Soviet opposition was expressed, the statements were nevertheless repeated.

Act I: challenging the old structure, 1988–9

Briefly, Act I begins with the Hungarian demands for troop withdrawals, first broached as early as 1986 and resumed in the spring and summer of 1988. Poland started stirring at this time. In June 1988 the Sejm unanimously voted to remove from the military oath of Poland the pledge of 'fraternal alliance with the Soviet Army'. President Gorbachev started troop withdrawals from Hungary the following winter. In May 1989 Hungary took away the barbed wire on the border to Austria. Gorbachev declared in Strasbourg in July the end of the policy of Soviet military intervention in Eastern and Central Europe. In October and November, orders were given to Soviet military commanders not to fire at demonstrating crowds in Leipzig and Prague (Skak, 1992).

Act I ends – in the present conception – with the peaceful installation of Vaclav Havel as president of Czechoslovakia and the violent overthrow of Ceausescu as president of Romania.

As has been shown elsewhere (Knudsen, 1992), statements from two sides – power pole and small state – engaged each other throughout Act I in an uncertain dialogue. Gradually, the thinking of political actors changed.

Act II: struggle over the definition of a new structure and the burial of the old

Straightforward diagnostic statements are rare in the wealth of material available. An early allusion to a new structure was made by Polish Prime Minister Mazowiecki upon taking office as the first non-communist leader of an East European government. On 12 September 1989 Mazowiecki elaborated his understanding of Poland's place in the international structure:

> During recent years, Poland's situation has largely been determined by tensions and conflicts in world politics. Today, when the era of the Cold War is coming to an end, the opportunity arises [for us] to realize our national aspirations in consonance with the future trends of world politics. (*Europa Archiv*: translated by the author)

Even after New Year 1990 diagnostic statements were often shaped as queries. The following was made by Hungarian Prime Minister Nemeth on 29 January 1990:

> It is our task to ask this question over and over again: are we ready to accept, in our minds and our hearts, that a historical epoch of Europe has come to an end? That a new structure will replace the divided Europe, that even if lines of division may continue to exist, they are now located elsewhere? That this new structure inevitably will change Europe and the foreign relations of this continent? (address to the European Council in Strasbourg: *Europa Archiv*)

Prime Minister Nemeth also revealed explicit structural thinking in this statement, made during the same speech:

> We are now removing the artificial confrontation between the eastern and western part of our continent. It is not only the Iron Curtain and the Wall which are being torn away, but also the underlying ideological values and political structures in Eastern Europe, as well as the planned economies. (*Berlingske Tidende*)

However, such explicit references to structure were exceptional. It is typical of the period that diagnostic statements are few and closely intertwined with argumentation. There is a lot of tugging and hauling at the structure: in other words, there are argumentative attempts to gain acceptance for one's own description of the world, to create a new set of expectations which in time – if and when those expectations stabilized – would constitute a new international structure.

The spring of 1990 saw the two-plus-four negotiations on the reuniting of Germany (including the difficult question of the alliance status of the new Germany), the integration of East Germany in the Federal Republic and the European Community, and the attempts by Lithuania and later Estonia and Latvia to gain Western recognition. The Lithuanian case offered a welcome opportunity for the Soviet military to illustrate how they proposed to deal with wayward friends. It began to dawn on many that even if Gorbachev were indeed a genuine reformer, many around him – and below him, in positions to implement his decisions – were not. At a meeting of the CPSU Central Committee in early 1990 the conservatives accused the Soviet leadership of having sold out the socialist community (Skak, 1992, p. 39: reported 8 February 1990).

Such reactions behind the scenes may have encouraged the Soviet military to continue their resistance to a new order. In Central Europe, the CPSU assessment was rebutted by Hungarian Socialist Party Chairman Rezso Nyers, who said that Hungary no longer belonged to the old, Soviet-dominated Eastern bloc (reported on 13 January 1990). Nyers also said the Warsaw Pact should change from a military organization based on inter-party relations to one of inter-state cooperation (Reisch, 1990a, p. 16).

Although Nyers's statement was in accordance with declared Soviet policy, the disagreement as to that policy's true meaning continued. For the Soviet military, international disarmament negotiations provided an arena in which they could still make strong plays to serve their interests in this larger debate. Obvious complications arose in connection with the CFE talks, which were built on the old assumption of a united Warsaw Pact. Prime Minister Nemeth reported from a meeting in Sofia with Nikolai Ryzhkov that

> the two sides had agreed . . . that even though the presence of Soviet troops in Hungary was neither politically nor militarily justified, the matter should be discussed only in connection with the CFE talks in Vienna. (Barany and Reisch, 1990, 24: report published 9 February 1990)

On 18 January 1990 Hungary formally asked the USSR to withdraw its troops from Hungary by the end of 1991 at the latest (Barany and Reisch, 1990, p. 24).

Early 1990 was also a time for first approaches to 'Europe', meaning letters and visits to Brussels. In a letter to EC Commission President Jacques Delors, Prime Minister Calfa of Czechoslovakia described European unity as a dominant factor in the new Europe, in which Czechoslovakia sought for itself a firm position (*Frankfurter Allgemeine*, 22 January 1990).

However, Germany dominated the agenda. With greater freedom came the need to tackle new – and old – local concerns. In the Polish case, the fear of Germany overshadowed everything, including the Soviet troop presence. Soviet authorities declared their willingness to discuss the question of Soviet troops in Poland 'if the Polish authorities express a desire to do so' (according to *Izvestia*, 4 February 1990: see Stefanowski, 1990, p. 16). But the Poles left the issue in the air. The difference between the situation of Poland and the others was obvious in geopolitical terms. As long as Germany was full of Soviet troops, they were likely to remain in Poland as well.

> President Wojciech Jaruzelski has ruled out a Soviet military withdrawal from Poland until 'an overall solution' to the East–West division of Europe is found that would guarantee that a reunited Germany would not seek to regain territory it was forced to give up to Poland at the end of World War II. (speech 4 February 1990 in Davos, Switzerland: cited in Stefanowski, 1990, p. 15)

On 26 February 1990 a new defence doctrine for Poland was made public by the National Defence Committee, chaired by President Jaruzelski and with Prime Minister Mazowiecki and Foreign Minister Skubiszewski among its members. According to the new doctrine, the defence agreements Poland has signed, including its membership in the Warsaw Pact, continue to be important elements of national security. However, these elements may change with the creation of the new European security system. Poland would remain in the Warsaw Pact until this new system is established, but

> under no circumstances will Poland commence military action against another state or alliance of states, or participate in a war unless it or its allies become the target of armed aggression. (Sadykiewicz and Clarke, 1990, p. 21)

Sadykiewicz and Clarke conclude that,

> In effect, the text of the Polish defense doctrine annuls Poland's adherence to the 'Statute of the Joint Armed Forces [of the Warsaw Pact] and Organs of their Command in Wartime' . . . This statute stipulated that, in times of war or the threat of war, the Soviet Supreme High Command, with the Soviet General Staff as its sole executive agent, would assume leadership of all non-Soviet armed forces. (Sadykiewicz and Clark, 1990, p. 21)

Sadykiewicz and Clark sum up their assessment thus:

The new doctrine
* is an important step in Poland's transition from a Soviet satellite to a truly sovereign state;
* is the first official document that provides evidence that the Warsaw Pact is no longer an operational military alliance;
* could well serve as a model for other countries in Eastern Europe. (p. 22)

Less than a week later, on 1 March 1990, President Havel warned the WP members that 'wild steps' such as switching from one camp to another or proclaiming neutrality would solve nothing (Reisch, 1990c, p. 18). NATO's Manfred Wörner said in an interview published 6 March 1990 that 'the Western alliance was interested in closer contacts and dialogue with the Warsaw Pact but was not trying to dissolve it. He said that NATO should remain even if the pact were to be dissolved and that the NATO allies were opposed to a neutral status for the future united Germany' (Reisch, 1990a, p. 17). We can see the emerging disagreement over Germany's affiliation with NATO.

On 2 March 1990 Czechoslovak Foreign Minister Dienstbier, in connection with a visit to EC Commissioner Andriessen in Brussels, made it clear that there is unlikely to be any long-term future for his country with either NATO or the Warsaw Pact. 'We need to replace these structures of confrontation with new structures of European unification' (*The Guardian*, 3 March 1990).

On 11 March 1990 Hungarian Foreign Minister Gyula Horn stated that it was an 'illusion' to expect the two alliances to dissolve simultaneously. The unification of the two Germanies would undoubtedly take place, leading to a new balance of power in Europe. As a result, political and military cooperation could develop between members of the former opposing camps, Horn said, adding that it was in Hungary's clear interest to have its security guaranteed multilaterally (Reisch, 1990a, p. 19).

At the WP foreign ministers' meeting in Prague on 17 March 1990, there was open disagreement as to a united Germany's future status. Czechoslovakia, Poland and Hungary agreed that a neutral Germany would be 'the worst alternative' (Dienstbier), and that NATO membership for a united Germany would be to the advantage of the East European states. Horn said the point was the coordination and control mechanisms available within NATO and absent in the case of a neutral status. Shevardnadze was alone in opposing NATO membership for a united Germany (Reisch, 1990a, pp. 19–20).

President Havel continued to stick to a position closer to the

Soviet than the American one. At a press conference in London on 22 March 1990, Havel said it was 'unfortunate to keep on insisting on NATO', as the European situation was changing rapidly. President Havel declared his preference for a common security system subsuming both NATO and the Warsaw Pact. Within a few weeks, his position changed.

Note that by March 1990 diverging opinions in WP meetings are permitted, and the opportunity is eagerly seized. As the old structure departs, there is no convergence of expectations about the character of the new world. The Warsaw Pact is still there: the most visible sign and symbol of the old order.

May and June 1990 saw the final struggle which ultimately sealed the fate of the Warsaw Pact. There had been confusion and disagreement in Central Europe ever since the preceding autumn as to the preferable role for the Warsaw Pact. Initially, Shevard-nadze's call in October 1989 for a political, not a military, pact had seemed benign. Now, however, with communist regimes more or less gone, the idea of a political pact appeared more threatening than a straightforward military alliance of the traditional kind. Polish Foreign Minister Skubiszewski stated on 26 April 1990 in a speech to the Sejm:

> We are treating the Warsaw Pact as a defensive alliance in accordance with the United Nations Charter and not as an instrument to influence the system and political and economic order of the member states. The pact has lost its ideological role . . . So long as it exists, it is essential, from the point of view of Poland's interests, that it be transformed from a military-political alliance into a consultative-military one. (Clarke, 1990a, p. 41)

In May, the scene shifted to Hungary. On 9 May 1990, on the historic occasion of the first ordinary session of the first freely elected Hungarian parliament after the Cold War, the first speaker, Miklos Vasarhelyi of the Alliance of Free Democrats, proposed

> that the parliament pass a resolution reinstating the decision of Hungary's revolutionary government on November 1, 1956, to withdraw from the [Warsaw Pact] and declare Hungary's neutrality . . . Thus, Vasarhelyi said, the parliament should call upon Hungary's new government to declare its intent to withdraw from the Warsaw Pact, to start negotiations immediately with the Soviet Union and the other pact members, and in the meantime to suspend the country's participation in the military element of the pact. (Reisch, 1990b, p. 24)

The proposal touched off a stormy debate in Hungary, and a series of comments by interested parties abroad, primarily the USSR, demonstrating the extent to which the old structure still had a hold on the participants.[4] The following day, 10 May, acting Foreign Minister Gyula Horn again criticized the proposal to leave the Warsaw Pact. He said it involved 'an extremely high number of risks' and warned that the international balance of power based on the Warsaw-Pact/NATO relationship would certainly be affected by the announcement by a member state that it was withdrawing. Horn said an entirely new situation was emerging in Europe in the wake of the democratization still taking place in the countries of Central and Eastern Europe. It was too early to predict whether this process would result in those countries being left out of the current bipolar alliance system. For Horn, a new collective security system outside the two alliances was hardly imaginable and could even be harmful (Reisch, 1990b, p. 26).

The soon-to-be Foreign Minister Geza Jeszenszky said that

> even though the reasons for the pact's creation had ceased to exist, it was nevertheless better to modify an existing international treaty and organization through negotiation and to bear in mind the Soviet Union's legitimate security interests. (reported 11 May 1990: cited in Reisch, 1990b, p. 27)

The future status of Germany was still hanging in the balance. President Havel, speaking in Strasbourg, by now agreed with his Foreign Minister regarding the Western alliance. In his 10 May 1990 speech to the Council of Europe, Havel said that NATO, 'the structure which makes more sense, is more democratic, and simply works better [than that of the Warsaw Pact]', had the best credentials for being transformed into the nucleus of a new European security system. However, he added that NATO should rename itself and change its military doctrine. As for the Warsaw Pact, Havel said that once it lost its role as 'a political instrument for European disarmament and an escort to some countries on their way back to Europe', it would be deprived of any reason for its continued existence and would eventually be forced to disband (Obrman, 1990, pp. 10–11).

The Hungarian proposal remained at the centre of the debate. The first Soviet reaction arrived: Commander-in-Chief of the Warsaw Pact forces, General Petr Lushev, also Soviet Deputy Minister of Defence, said

> that it was possible to imagine a member of the pact deciding to withdraw from the alliance before a new European security system had been created to replace the two dissolved military alliances. Although it was their right to do so, said Lushev, these states should also be aware that by changing the structure of the Warsaw Pact and NATO they

would greatly modify the international balance of power and could actually impede *détente*, the stability of Europe, and the creation of a 'European House'. The balance of forces in Europe was an elementary condition for East–West cooperation and the maintenance of the military alliances was justified until a new security system took their place. (reported by Radio Budapest, 11 May 1990: cited in Reisch, 1990b, pp. 27–8)

As it happens, 13 May was the date on which the Warsaw Pact was signed in 1955. The moral standing of the Pact was at one of its low points. On this occasion Czechoslovak Minister of Defence Miroslav Vacek declared that the Pact had been a 'neo-Stalinist organization' which had restricted the sovereignty of its members. He recalled the negative consequences of the invasion of his country in 1968 by five Pact states. Czechoslovakia supported the transformation of the Pact into a political organization (Reisch, 1990b, p. 28).

The anniversary gave the Soviet side an occasion to respond. General Petr Lushev in another interview (Soviet Army Daily *Krasnaya Zvezda*, 13 May 1990) said

the Warsaw Pact should not be disbanded yet and would become unnecessary only when the armed forces of the 'opposing blocs' could no longer launch large-scale offensive operations. Lushev denied that the pact was in a state of decline and said it contributed to the stability both of Eastern Europe and Europe as a whole. (Reisch, 1990b, p. 28)

Not surprisingly, the Soviet commander was backed up by his Defence Minister, Dmitrii Yazov, who was interviewed by *Izvestia* (13 May 1990). Yazov said he rejected the statement of some politicians and publicists who were saying the Warsaw Pact was disintegrating. Yazov did not mention Hungary, but claimed that all Pact members had reaffirmed their support for the alliance. The talks on transforming the Warsaw Pact and NATO into political alliances were in his view reaching a practical stage and the democratization of Eastern Europe had made it possible to discuss a new European security structure. To disband the Pact before such a system had been created would be 'irresponsible and narrow-minded', Yazov said (Reisch, 1990b, p. 28).

A new non-socialist Hungarian government was about to take over. It signalled a decisive shift in policy regarding WP membership. Prime Minister designate Jozsef Antall, in a speech on 22 May 1990 announcing his new government's programme, said with regard to the Warsaw Pact that 'Hungarian participation was [Antall's own words:] "contrary to the will expressed by the nation in 1956 and reaffirmed in the latest election"' (Reisch,

1990b, p. 30). The new Minister of Foreign Affairs designate Geza Jeszenszky, testifying to the Foreign Relations Committee (21 May 1990), 'called for Hungary's withdrawal from the Warsaw Pact and said that putting an end to military blocs was a prerequisite for establishing a new collective European security system' (Reisch, 1990b, p. 30).

Revelations about secret military commitments to the USSR entailed by the WP membership contributed to the Hungarians' determination to move ahead with their proposal. The process of undermining the Pact was accelerated. On 30 May 1990 Geza Jeszenszky declared that

> Hungary had not joined the Warsaw Pact of its own free will . . . and it believed that the organization was no longer needed. Since it could not be denounced unilaterally, Hungary wanted talks on either canceling the treaty or on its own withdrawal from the pact in mutual agreement with the other member states. (Reisch, 1990b, p. 31)

Some time in mid to late May the decision must have been made in Moscow to have a meeting of the Warsaw Pact's highest organ, the Political Consultative Committee, on 7 June (Reisch, 1990c, p. 17). Czechoslovak Foreign Minister Jiri Dienstbier stated before the summit (5 June 1990) that it was important that the Soviet Union not be pushed out of Europe and that a reformed Warsaw Pact would play a role in preventing this. Hungarian Prime Minister Jozsef Antall said efforts to exclude the USSR from Europe should not be tolerated. He said Hungary did not wish 'to shift the line dividing Europe today more toward the East' (Clarke, 1990b, p. 35).

The meeting itself brought significant movement towards a new solution. An intergovernmental commission was to propose a new structure for the Pact, based on sovereignty, equality and democratic values. However, there was no clear settlement: 'At a press conference in Prague after the [7 June 1990, Moscow] meeting, Havel said that the pact, in its present form, had not shed its heritage of Stalinism, since all the armies of the member states were subordinated to the Soviet army' (Clarke, 1990b, p. 36). On the other hand, in connection with the 7 June summit, 'Havel later emphasized that his country had never considered withdrawing from the pact. His objective was to change it radically from inside' (Clarke, 1990b, p. 35). To this end Czechoslovakia had played an unprecedented role behind the scenes, pushing to rewrite the Soviet draft for the final communiqué, along with Poland and East Germany.

The battle was not yet over. The military side had to be brought into the bargain as well. Warsaw Pact defence ministers met a week later, on 14 and 15 June in East Germany. There was reportedly a great struggle over the communiqué. The Soviet representatives seem to have succeeded in keeping the proposed abolishment of all military structures out of the text (Clarke, 1990b, p. 36). According to Clarke, it seemed clear that both the military obligations of the member states and the future of the Pact itself had been taken out of the generals' hands.

Their displeasure came out in other ways. Citing the new 'military-strategic situation', i.e. the prior cuts in troop levels combined with the recent political events in the region, especially the imminent reunification of Germany and the agreements to withdraw all Soviet forces from both Czechoslovakia and Hungary, the Soviet military announced in mid June that it would suspend withdrawals from Germany (Clarke, 1990c, p. 34). As we know, this rearguard action was only temporary, although it did continue for months.

In reality the struggle was over. NATO declared at its London meeting that the USSR and the WP were no longer seen as NATO's adversaries. The announcement on the occasion of Kohl's Caucasus visit in July 1990, of Gorbachev's agreement to the compromise bringing the reunited Germany under the wings of NATO, brought the process to its conclusion.

The alternative for Hungary could now be seriously discussed. Jeszenszky explained on this occasion:

> Neutrality is usually not a permanent state but a temporary one for a country in time of war. To some degree, a war [the Cold War] started in 1947 and now seems to have come to an end. As long as that war was waged, the possibility of neutrality for a country that was not a voluntary member of the Warsaw Pact was a very attractive idea. But if the Cold War is hopefully and happily really over and the Soviet Union and the West no longer regard each other as possible enemies, then it no longer makes sense to declare oneself neutral. Thus, neutrality is not something we would place much emphasis on. On the other hand, Finland, which voluntarily recognizes Soviet interests while maintaining and increasing its full national independence in every sense of the word, is a model for us, although not with regard to neutrality. (Reisch, 1990c, p. 18)

In view of the heated debates of the early summer, it must have seemed momentous when Antall could visit NATO's general secretary Manfred Wörner on 18 July 1990. German reunification on 3 October and the Paris summit of the CSCE in November 1990 were both remarkable events, but the main part of the groundwork had already been laid by July.

Towards an empirically based understanding of structure

Act I – not studied in detail here – showed the beginnings of change and brought the process to the climactic confrontations in Leipzig and Prague. Structural change, to which a long series of little events contributed, went on inside the heads of policy-makers. Giddens's description seems apt: 'Structure is not "external" to individuals: as memory traces, and as instantiated in social practices, it is in a certain sense more "internal" than exterior to their activities' (Giddens, 1984, p. 25).

Act I provided indications (Knudsen, 1992) that the Soviet leaders were mistaken about the true foundation of the structure when they pushed for East European reform in 1988–9. It seems that Gorbachev and Shevardnadze assumed that what held East Europeans in the fold – and certainly what they thought would hold them to the narrow path after reforms – was a normative commitment to the values of socialism. Compliance, in their view, came primarily from political convictions and commitment. It is more likely, however, that the structure was above all based on the expectation among East European elites that non-compliance would bring Soviet armed intervention.

Act II brought statements by new leaders of how they saw the situation. These statements only rarely demonstrated perceptions of existing structure. In a most natural way, however, given the circumstances of Eastern and Central Europe at this time, the statements gave evidence of a process of 'structural probing': agents presented tentative or conditional diagnoses. Such probing statements were made both by power poles and by small states.

Sequences of structural probing may be said to constitute a reflection of structure undergoing change, coming out as an indirect debate about whether the structure is indeed changing or not. When structural change was perceived to be in disfavour of one of the power poles, its government tried to maintain an image of 'no change', of business as usual. Smaller states who stood to gain from change pushed interpretations indicating change: 'The world is no longer what it was' etc.

Empirically, then, the data give evidence that the structure of the international system is a matter of the perceptions and expectations of those individuals who act in the name of states. Apparently, there is also empirical support for the notion that structure is *interactively* constituted, as assumed in the structuration approach (Giddens, 1984, p. 25; for a different but compatible view see Archer, 1985, p. 66).[5] Finally, it became abundantly clear that deviations from habitual patterns of behaviour contributed to the creation of a setting for action during the summer and autumn of 1989 which contained its own strong situational influences on East European governmental behaviour – notably the mobilization of crowds of peaceful demonstrators.

It is ironic to note that Gorbachev and Shevardnadze saw the norms of socialism as the true basis of the old structure, and hence as worth saving for a reformed system. Of course, those expectations turned out to be wrong, and they were most probably not widely shared even within the decision-making system of the USSR. But they do illuminate what happened and why the power apparatus of the USSR was not brought into the game to restore control.

Notes

1 The distinction between structural and situational elements is not clear-cut, and I cannot offer any simple criteria. It may be of interest to note in this connection that in a 1992 article in *International Studies Quarterly*, Walter Carlsnaes presents a model which, with a few exceptions, appears to be identical to another model introduced by him in his 1987 book *Ideology and Foreign Policy* (p. 108). The main difference between the two is that he alters the name used for the explanatory dimension in question from 'situational' to 'structural'. This is duly pointed out in a footnote to his 1992 article, but there is no explanation for the switch. Further comparison of the two versions of Carlsnaes's model reveals that there is no simple correspondence between the use of 'situational' in the one case and 'structural' in the other.

2 Contextual reasoning is also found in other approaches, such as those which emphasize hierarchical aspects of the international system, or world-wide/system-wide characteristics such as mode of production (capitalism), e.g. theories of imperialism, dependency theory and stratification theory. I regard world systems theory as a more dubious example of contextual reasoning.

3 The notion of a causal link does not imply that causation is direct. As pointed out above, structure can have only indirect causal effects.

4 It was part of the situation at this time that the Hungarian Socialist (formerly Communist) Party had just lost the first free elections, but the transfer of power had not yet taken place. It did during the following weeks, with noticeable effect on the government's foreign policy.

5 Archer makes much of Giddens's alleged insensitivity to the pre-existence of structure when actions are taken, subsequently transforming the structure (see also Carlsnaes, 1992). I feel Archer overdoes her critique of Giddens on this score. In my view, the observed patterns in Eastern and Central Europe during 1989–90 fit Giddens as well as they fit Archer.

PART IV CRITIQUES

12

What's New? Feminist Observations on the New Europe

Marysia Zalewski

From a quasi-post-modern stance, my initial observations on the new Europe take their cue from the silences, spaces and assumptions abundant in the contributions to this volume. Sometimes the silences are broken by an insightful reference here and there in some of the chapters: 'exclusions may be more interesting than inclusions' (Smith, Chapter 2); 'any evaluation of theory which does not consider the epistemological bases of that theory . . . reproduces the assumptions built into the meta-theoretical bases of that theory' (Tooze, Chapter 4); 'boundaries do not exist' (Pfetsch, Chapter 7). Indeed it is these unpursued insights that form the basis of my chapter.

It would seem that the twin revolutions of 1989 and 1992 (or more accurately the revolutions of 1989 and the evolution of 1992) have provided heady fodder for foreign policy analysts and international relations theorists alike. It does, of course, seem obvious that such momentous events and rapid changes are in need of explanation and analysis. In almost one fell swoop, such events have provided an opportunity to come up with illuminating insights on the nature of the new Europe as well as a good chance to ruminate on the utility of foreign policy theories. With that in mind, the task for the contributors to this volume was to identify an empirical realm, within the general parameters of the new Europe, and then apply some of the dominant FPA/IR theories to this realm in order to see how useful these theories are and whether they would stand up to the rigours of testing in this new world order.

It might therefore be assumed that my task in this chapter would be to adjust the empirical realm of the contributions to this volume to include women: add women and stir. The implication is that women have not been included (perhaps the reasons don't matter) and that this should be redressed. My empirical area would be women, presumably in any area of Europe I would wish to choose. As to theory, it is a little more difficult to imagine what I would choose as theories are generally supposed to be gender neutral or gender free.

It is the common practice of academic disciplines, particularly international relations and its subfield of foreign policy analysis, to strive towards simplification and categorization in order to try to understand, predict and control events allocated the 'high-politics' accolade. Efforts are consistently made to produce coherent, all-purpose theories to that end. Major issues such as wars (hot, cold, trade) and inter-state relationships are pared to the bone in an attempt to produce seemingly understandable slices (Waltz's *three* causes of war(s), Morgenthau's *six* principles of political realism, Singer's *two* levels of analysis). It is notable that the editors of this volume seem to be engaged in a battle between *two* levels or stories: actors versus structures. But as Sandra Harding points out,

> coherent theories in an obviously incoherent world are either silly and uninteresting or oppressive and problematic, depending on the degree of hegemony they manage to achieve. Coherent theories in an *apparently* coherent world are even more dangerous, for the world is always more complex than such unfortunately hegemonous theories can grasp. (Harding, 1986, p. 164)

It is my contention that looking at the twin revolutions that have given rise to the so-called 'new Europe' (the end of the Cold War and the increasing integration of West European states) with short-sighted, masculinist, hegemonic lenses is analogous to the tip of an iceberg: there is much depth that is completely obscured and massively underestimated but is undoubtedly there.

The silences that I am specifically concerned with are women and gender, but I am very aware that there are other silences which also scream out for attention, race being an obvious example (Doty, 1993). This is not the place for a step-by-step guide to the bias of the theories surveyed by the contributors to this volume. There is a rapidly growing literature on this (Grant and Newland, 1991; Peterson, 1992a; Tickner, 1992; Sylvester, forthcoming). What I intend to do first in this chapter is to make some comments about my supposed empirical area: women. Second, I will consider some of the effects on women of the end of the Cold War and then make some comments on the relationship between those effects and the end of the Cold War. Third, I will look briefly at some of the issues involved regarding women and gender and the increasing integration of Western European states. Finally, I will make some concluding remarks on the nature of theory and the role of gender in the construction of the new Europe.

The empirical realm: women

Immediately there is a problem. As implied in my introduction, adding women and stirring is not as simple as it first might appear. At one level it seems obvious to many feminists that it is vitally important to study women as a separate group. IR and FPA theories are notorious for the abstractions embedded within them. States are labelled as states; little attention is paid to the enormous differences between states, particularly by the more structural, realist theories. Individuals within states are actors; little attention is paid to the gender, race or class of the actors. Indeed human populations are often seen as irrelevant to the study of inter-national relations and foreign policy analysis. Individuals in the international political system are somewhat similar to passengers waiting to be picked up by a bus driver who is late; they simply get in the way. But for many feminists one of the most significant features of human societies, or indeed states, is the fact that the human populations that make them up are deeply divided on the lines of gender. Being defined as male or female markedly affects one's life chances, health, status, employment opportunities, financial security, education etc. etc. But historically, in IR and FPA analyses, little attention has been paid to this gargantuan fact. Individuals or human populations continue to be discussed either in the abstract (actors/individuals) or in the explicitly male form (he/him). The point that many feminists would make is that women's and men's lives are very different and any discussion of the effects of the twin revolutions of 1989 and 1992 which did not pay attention to the specific effects on women is simply inadequate and poor scholarship.

The *problem* with this is that analysing women as a separate group tends to give the impression that the study of women and gender is that of a special interest group, an option that one can either do or not do. It tends to reinforce the assumption that gender is not an integral and constituent part of the international system and FPA/IR theorizing. Studying women as a separate group and having a special chapter in a volume that pays scant attention to the issue of gender and women might, unfortunately, secure in the mind-sets of the contributors the view that the issues of gender and women are something that need not enter their analyses. However, for a problem to be recognized it has, at the very least, to be named and described. Additionally, drawing attention to the differentially gendered effects of the twin revolutions in terms of 'empirical' women should lead us to consider why women and gender are so easily left out. This in turn leads us to consider the question of the gendered construction of the states/blocs/communities that are the focus of IR/FPA analyses as well as the gendered construction of the theories that purport to explain what happens within them (see V. Spike Peterson, 1992a, p. 17).

The end of the Cold War

Many of the contributors to this volume express concern about the end of the Cold War, not so much simply because it has ended, more because it seems to lead Europe, however defined, into an unsure situation where the security of states is under threat and the spectre of war is very real. For Mike Smith (this volume, Chapter 2), the old European order was extraordinarily robust, reinforced by the polarization and rigidity between the blocs, whereas the new European order is essentially fluid and transitional and therefore less easy to predict. It is generally acknowledged by IR/FPA theorists that the Cold War, despite the zero-sum rhetoric it inspired in terms of the possibility of all-out (nuclear) war between the two superpowers, actually had a very stabilizing effect. But with the demise of communism, the fall of the Berlin Wall, the apparent capitulation by the East to Western-style capitalism and democracy, much of the predictability and stability has vanished. How has all this affected women? Let us look briefly at three important areas: political participation, employment and abortion rights.

Political participation and visibility
The rush towards the democratization of Eastern and Central Europe has largely had the effect of drastically reducing women's public political participation. Prior to 1989, women were active at all levels in opposition and dissident movements in Eastern and Central Europe. Examples would include Bärbel Bohley and Ulrike Poppe of Women for Peace in the GDR, who went on to become leading figures amongst the founders of New Forum and Democracy Now, which were two of the movements responsible for the 'turning point' in autumn 1989. But in all the cases where past dissidents formed or were important in the first democratically

elected governments (in pre-unification GDR, in Slovenia, in (the former) Czechoslovakia, and in Poland), it has been men, with very few exceptions (in the former Czechoslovakia and in Poland), who became government ministers (Einhorn, 1991, pp. 16–17). Yudit Kiss makes a similar claim about Hungary, claiming that the spectacular political changes of 1989–90 seemed to create a negative trend for women. They had been present at the 'big demonstrations, on the happy streets, but disappeared from the negotiating tables. In the heroic battle on behalf of the democracy, the male fighters tended to forget about the biggest, oppressed majority, "their other halves"' (Kiss, 1991, p. 51). Under the old regime, women were officially emancipated and indeed had a relatively large presence in official political office. Since the fall of communism, however, women's public political representation has plummeted. In Romania, women held a third of all parliamentary seats before 1989; they now hold only 3.5 per cent. In the former Czechoslovakia the drop was from 29.5 to 6 per cent; in Bulgaria from 21 to 8.5 per cent; in Hungary from 20.9 to 7 per cent. It is not surprising that one feminist scholar has characterized these new political structures as 'male democracies' (Siklova, quoted in Einhorn, 1991, p. 17).

Employment
The move from state-run socialism to embryonic capitalist democracies is not easy on much of the populations of Eastern and Central Europe and the former Soviet Union. Unemployment and the increasing cost of public services, such as transport and health, have made everyday life harder for many of these peoples. But, once again, women seem to be amongst the biggest losers. In Eastern and Central Europe, women now form the majority of the unemployed (Einhorn, 1991). In Poland, although women make up less than half of the workforce, almost 60 per cent of the 2.5 million unemployed are women. Employers now often advertise 'male' and 'female' positions, and of these only one of every 120 jobs is now offered to women (*The Economist*, 12 December 1991, p. 54). In Romania in September 1990, 85–90 per cent of registered unemployed were women. In Bulgaria and Albania, women represent 60 per cent of the unemployed (Watson, 1993, p. 78). The unification of Germany, arguably one of the most significant features of the end of the Cold War, has resulted in a worsening situation for women. Marina Beyer states that many East German women feared that they would lose many of their rights and social provisions upon unification, claiming that 'their fears were confirmed . . . women are suffering more than men when it comes

to unemployment: they are losing the childcare facilities they had
. . . and they are losing their presence in the political arena' (Beyer,
1992, p. 111). Industrial production in the former GDR decreased
in 1991 by 30 per cent, primarily within light industry, food
production and the textile industry – precisely the sectors in which
women have traditionally worked. In September 1989 women
constituted 48.8 per cent of the workforce but by February 1991
they represented 54.7 per cent of the officially unemployed (Beyer,
1992, pp. 111–12).

Abortion rights

This is an area of great importance for women: indeed, it is often
the starting point for rising feminist dissent. It has also proved to
be very important to the male leaders in these post-communist
countries. Amongst all the economic, social and political mayhem,
abortion has become a primary question in almost all such
countries. In Hungary, one of the first big discussions of the newly
elected parliament took place over a draft law to ban abortion
(Kiss, 1991, p. 53). Milica Antic, writing on the former Yugoslavian republic of Slovenia, claims that the previously liberal
abortion law, which allowed women the right to demand an
abortion till the tenth week of pregnancy without constraints, has
come under increasing threat. In Poland, possibly in Western eyes
one of the front runners towards democracy in the East, President
Lech Walesa put his signature to the new Polish bill to criminalize
abortion on 15 February 1993 (Einhorn, 1993a, p. 20). This new
law outlaws abortion except in cases of rape or when three doctors
attest to the 'severe' threat to the mother's life. Doctors performing
abortions for other reasons can be imprisoned for up to two years.
This law is indeed harsh but it is being seen as liberal by many
contemporary Polish politicians who expected that abortion would
be banned completely.

Interim remarks

What, I hear the reader ask, has all this got to do with foreign
policy analysis? The sensitive reader might be thinking that these
things are very interesting and/or important but are surely
irrelevant to the arena with which this volume is concerned. The
demise of women's political participation and visibility is surely
more to do with perhaps reactionary (paradoxically) male leaders,
or the natural/psychological inclinations of women to stay away
from high-pressure occupations. As to employment, this might
merely reflect more market-sensitive mechanisms which will tend to

result in larger numbers of unemployed than is the norm in state-run economies. Again, the increasing numbers of female unemployed probably reflect the fact that women are less qualified and are more likely to want to stay at home with their children. The sensitive reader might agree that these post-communist countries may lag a little with regard to equal employment legislation (despite communism's stated commitment to women's emancipation), but surely this has nothing to do with foreign policy analysis. And as to abortion, this may well be regarded by the reader as a personal, domestic or even moral issue, having nothing at all to do with foreign policy analysis and international relations.

But, to paraphrase Cynthia Enloe, the workings of the international system are far more complex than the experts would have us believe (Enloe, 1989). The construction of the Cold War, the continuation of the Cold War, the effects of the Cold War and the endings[1] of the Cold War rely on far more than conventional foreign policy analysts would ever consider. And gender, in its manifestations in terms of masculinity and femininity, in its guise as natural and/or domestic arrangements, plays a large part in turning the wheels of foreign policy actions and inter-state relations. In short, one can claim that the Cold War was, in part, the result of gendered ideologies. Its continuation depended, in part, on the playing out of certain constructions of masculinity and femininity; and its demise will eventuate in further reconstructions of masculinity and femininity which, let the reader be under no misapprehension, will have some very dire consequences for large numbers of women and men. Those scholars genuinely curious to know more about the Cold War and its endings will find their work lacking if they do not pay attention to gender.

Let me elucidate.[2] It is probably too easy just to accept that we live in an inherently conflictual world. Looking at the past and concluding that, because wars and conflictual inter-state situations have always existed, they are either natural or inevitable, as realist thinkers tend to do, is a much too simple way out. Bearing in mind Roger Tooze's insightful comment (Chapter 4) that 'any evaluation of theory which does not consider the epistemological bases of that theory . . . reproduces the assumptions built into the metatheoretical bases of that theory', we can start to think about the types of theories and the concomitant epistemologies that define and dominate much of IR/FPA work. Through feminist post-positivist lenses the claim would probably be made that oppositional thinking and epistemologies which create and reconstruct war scenarios are both masculinist and modernist. This claim, with its roots in both feminist standpoint theory and post-modern feminism, is not to be confused with the old biological reductionist equation of males/men with natural aggression, but is a more sophisticated theory based on psychological, material and social conditions (see Hartsock, 1985; Harding, 1992; Zalewski, 1993). This is not an uncontentious theory *but*, if scholars are genuinely curious to understand the nature of conflicts such as the Cold War, then they surely cannot afford to ignore it.

Let us move on from that brief foray in the arena of metatheory to the question of how the so-called domestic politics of states are affected by international events and processes such as the Cold War. Each bloc, fuelled by oppositional rhetoric which kept ideologies polarized, relied on perceptions of gender difference to construct and maintain certain domestic arrangements. Under state socialism, the goal of full employment coupled with the stated commitment to women's emancipation' (at least in the public realm) meant that women's role as *workers* was emphasized. Women certainly had to be mothers as well, but the stress on working in the public realm legitimized widespread day-care for children. This resulted in the notorious 'superwoman' syndrome in which many women spent all day out at paid work, only to come back and do a second shift at home (see Corrin, 1992). Now, with the ending of the Cold War, a particularly interesting issue is how ideas about gender difference are *reconstructed* according to the changing needs of societies instigated by an international process such as the end of the Cold War.

For example, with regard to political participation, employment and abortion rights, ideas and beliefs about gender, in the guise of women's (and men's) proper roles and purposes, abound in the construction of the new democracies. Take political participation. As Peggy Watson points out, one can hardly use the weary argument that women lack the expertise to explain the dearth of women in important political positions: in Eastern Europe nobody has expertise in running liberal democracies (Watson, 1993, p. 71). Additionally, as women and men have similar educational qualifications, that too cannot be claimed to be the reason for women's exclusion from political power. Instead 'radical claims of gender difference are the sole basis for the legitimacy of the rule of men and constitute an explicit justification of the exclusion of women from power in Eastern Europe' (Watson, 1993, p. 72). Watson gives an example of the type of rhetoric rife in Eastern Europe with this quote from the Polish representative on the

Council of Europe, Marcin Libicki: 'It is impossible to speak of discrimination against women. Nature gave them a different role to that of men. The ideal must still be the woman-mother, for whom pregnancy is a blessing' (Watson, 1993, p. 73).

Similarly, with employment rights, the introduction of market mechanisms does indeed create unemployment. But it is neither accidental nor natural that it should be women who suffer disproportionately. Rather it is the result of gendered ideologies which are now being used to give priority to male workers over female ones, particularly at senior levels. With regard to that putative private arena of abortion rights, the end of the Cold War has spawned an almost messianistic rebirth of gendered ideologies of a woman's proper role and place. Tales of Romania's pre-revolutionary enforced monthly gynaecological examinations on women to ensure the absence of contraceptive devices and the continuation of any existing pregnancies were greeted with horror. But in post-communist Poland there is increasing evidence that women are under surveillance by the 'gynaecological police'. Barbara Fraczek, Sejm (lower house) deputy and a member of Solidarity, has issued a demand to the director of the Tarnobrzeg-voivodship hospital to provide her with a list of all female patients seeking treatment for 'strange bleeding' (Watson, 1993, p. 77).

With the ending of Cold War polarization, the restructuring of Eastern European countries does not *only* depend on the introduction of free elections or market mechanisms. The reconstruction and construction of states/societies/blocs is so much more complex than that. International relations and foreign policy analysis scholars who genuinely want to try to understand something more about the workings of international processes and events should surely start thinking about their theories in different ways. We do live in a complex world. Theories of the past have tended to try to tame this complex world and reduce it to simple, if illusory, isolated pieces of fact and information. International politics and inter-state relationships depend on many complex interrelated issues. The politics of gender is just a starting place.

Religious ideology, too, plays an important role in East Central Europe, notably the Catholic church. This male-dominated institution has notoriously entrenched ideas about the proper role and place of women. It also has the power to enforce its ideas and has dome so pre- and post-Cold War. The Catholic church in Poland has waged a sustained campaign to eliminate sex education, one of its fairly recent successes being the closing of family planning centres in 1989 (Einhorn, 1993b, p. 89). Currently the Catholic church is trying to revoke women's rights to abortion partly by using some drastic tactics and terminology (Einhorn, 1993b, p. 94). Anyone attempting to make sense of what happens in any East Central European country would not be able to do so without considering the influence of the Catholic church.

Integration of Western European states

The European Commission's Vice-President in 1980, Henk Vredeling, once said:

> The picture now presented by the European Community is not inspiring and is hardly likely to create converts. There is, however, one area of the Community's work and responsibilities which we might describe as a pioneering one, and which gives a lead and generates enthusiasm – its efforts to banish from our society discrimination against women . . . In this area Community legislation represents more than merely deriving a common denominator of the laws applying in the Member States. It is ahead of their legislation. (quoted in Warner, 1984)

Since the inclusion of Article 119 of the Treaty of Rome in 1957, which stipulated that men and women should receive equal pay for equal work, it might be claimed that the prospect of the increasing integration of Western European states is necessarily advantageous for women, particularly if accompanied by a strong Commission, Parliament and Court of Justice. As Vredeling alluded in 1980, legislation on women's rights in member states was virtually non-existent. Indeed, in 1957 it was only France which had equal pay legislation. However, by 1984 historian Harriet Warner had good reason to conclude that despite the Community's efforts in this area (women's rights) 'there is no evidence to suggest that the Community has been able substantially to improve the position of its female citizens' (Warner, 1984, p. 142).

This probably seems counter-intuitive, especially to my imagined sensitive reader. Economic integration, following the Single European Act, promises the free circulation of EC citizens, services, capital and merchandise. Surely this is no more detrimental (if at all) for women that for men? The social and political integration of Western Europe enshrined in the Maastricht treaty has its fair share of opponents and adherents but, as former Vice-President Vredeling pointed out in 1980, EC legislation on women's rights is often ahead of member states. So at the level of social integration, at the very least, increasing integration must be positive for the female citizens of such states. There is, in fact, a special Standing Committee on Women's Rights (with permanent official status) which monitors existing equal opportunities legislation. Certainly, there have been a series of EC Directives which have become very important legal instruments for women in Community countries (e.g. Directives 75/117, 76/207).

But if we dig a little deeper into some of the values and beliefs which have informed the development of the Community of Western European states we can start to understand Harriet Warner's statement, quoted above, a little better. For example, Article 119 of the Treaty of Rome was introduced to protect France, which had just introduced equal pay legislation, from unfair competition from other member states which did not have this legislation and could therefore undercut labour costs by employing women at a lower rate than men (Duchen, 1992, p. 18). In other words, the basis of Article 119 was not women's rights but fear of undercutting profit margins. Of course, Article 119 did, if unintentionally, provide the basis for equality legislation in the European Community, which surely, for my sensitive reader, is a wholly positive move. To be sure, EC policy on women has, up to a point, had a considerable effect in bringing about reforms in some countries and in stimulating information networks (Hoskyns, 1985; 1986; 1992). But the principle on which such legislation is based is *equality*, which is problematic on at least two levels: first, it is unpopular with governments; and second, it is based on the standard of a male worker.

Do not underestimate the first point. As students of politics will know, policy implementation is at least as important as policy formulation. And the implementation of policy will depend a great deal on the underlying acceptance and belief in the policy or law and the values behind it. Gender equality, which carries with it substantial economic implications, is generally not acceptable to Western European governments. Community policy on women is very vulnerable to economic and political changes in member states (there may be resonances here with the changes in Eastern Europe: women's rights are often the first thing to go). This general statement has to be tempered with the knowledge that there are many differences between member states. Nordic countries are more likely to make some sort of effective commitment, for example to child-care facilities, than Greece or indeed the UK. It has recently been reported that Sweden may force public bodies to ensure that at least half the members of governing boards be women. The reason behind this move is the apparent failure of anti-discrimination laws to achieve the goal of sexual equality (*International Herald Tribune*, 18 May 1993). However, as Harriet Warner points out, we have to temper the EC's promotion of women's rights with much caution. Starting with the original lack of (gender equality) commitment in Article 119, there are many obstacles which will limit official policy (Warner, 1984, p. 162). It is very difficult for such policies to prevent indirect discrimination founded on entrenched beliefs in gender difference and natural roles. The recent move towards right-wing economic philosophies in many Western governments, where the emphasis is on the demands of the market, will do little to help.

Contrary to popular belief, the principle of equality is not accepted as the guiding principle behind gender justice for all feminist theorists (see Thornton, 1986; Phillips, 1987; Bacchi 1990). Indeed, the principle of equality can work against the goal of gender justice. EC policy on women's rights focuses centrally on women's rights as workers, one of the important rights being equal pay for equal work. But the problem with the stress on achieving equality via women's status as workers is that it assumes there are no important or relevant differences between men and women. Of course, liberal feminism has played a large part in trying to prove that women are just as 'good as men', but feminists of a more radical persuasion have insisted that women are different; their life chances are different from men's, their employment patterns are different from men's, and they arguably have different needs and requirements from men. Therefore to base a system of equality on the standard of a male worker necessarily disadvantages women. And, with the increasing integration of Western European states this problem is likely to magnify because there is a growing tendency to see the population of the European Community as workers rather than citizens. At the very least the *rights* of citizens in the new Western Europe will depend in large part on their status as workers. As Eleonore Kofman and Rosemary Sales point out, the fortress Europe mentality, with its xenophobic and anti-immigrant attitudes, will have serious effects on black and ethnic minority women (Kofman and Sales, 1992, p. 29).

The process of the integration of Western European states is on a much slower scale than the events in Eastern Europe, and the changes are probably less dramatic. In other words, the integration of Western Europe is really just more of the same whereas the democratization of Eastern Europe is very clearly not. To look at these international processes or events through gendered lenses does not simply mean either looking only at the position of women or claiming that these events can be understood wholly via one feminist theory or another. What I am claiming is that gender will play an important part in the construction, reconstruction and playing out of such international processes. Ideologies and beliefs about gender will inform policy-makers' beliefs about what constitutes gender equality – and the acceptance of male worker as norm will be central here. Beliefs about natural gender roles will dictate who is expendable in the workforce and who is not – encouraging the belief that a married woman is less in need of a job than others (Watson, 1993, p. 80). Beliefs about the need to, and naturalness of, controlling women will inform the construction of new laws and policies: the intense speedy concentration on the abortion law in Poland was partly because this was an area in which it was assumed something *could* be done (Watson, 1993, p. 75). I am not claiming that we can view all women throughout Europe as suffering from similar problems to which some sort of universal solution can be applied. Here I would concur with writers such as Susan Bassnett (1992) and Chris Corrin (1992), who claim that the homogeneity implied by such a term as 'Eastern Europe' or 'the women of Eastern Europe' is little short of absurd. Boundary-making is indeed a very useful device for concealing rather than revealing – a point I will refer to in my concluding section.

Conclusion

Steve Smith in his introduction (Chapter 1) claimed that his primary concern was to look at how the dominant FPA/IR theories explained the empirical realm, particularly given the changes implied by the twin revolutions of 1989 and 1992. But as no less a figure than Albert Einstein once pointed out, 'on principle it is quite wrong to try founding a theory on observable magnitudes alone. In reality, the very opposite happens. It is the theory which decides what we can observe' (quoted in MacKinnon, 1989, p. 106). Given this insight, perhaps it is more interesting and potentially illuminating to ask in what way the dominant theories create or construct the empirical realm.

In this sense FPA/IR theories define what issues are relevant and interesting to look at and where to draw the boundaries of what is and is not relevant. Many of the contributors to this volume have very clear views as to what the important and relevant issues are when analysing Europe. Walter Carlsnaes (Chapter 14) claims that there are three main issues in European foreign policy: the evolving role of the state in the new Europe; the development of the European union as an actor; and the role of economic relations. Alfred van Staden (Chapter 8) claims that the process of European integration is to be seen as a two-level game of internal dynamics versus external processes. Olav Knudsen (Chapter 11) claims that the foreign policy behaviour of states is determined partly by influences from the domestic political system, partly by the impact of bureaucratic systems and partly by the external environment in the international system. Clearly, the vast majority of the authors here do not consider gender as a relevant issue. The authors survey some of the theories available to them as IR/FPA analysts, highlighting strengths and weaknesses, claiming victory for some theories over others. But to use Thomas Risse-Kappen's trenchant reference to self-fulfilling prophecies (Chapter 3), defining boundaries in such rigid ways will only serve to reify the naturalness of the excluded, either theoretically as with gender, or empirically as with non-EC citizens in the looming 'fortress Europe'. Boundaries are not a natural phenomenon but are an intrinsic part of the politics of exclusion and domination (see Peterson, 1992b; Jan Pettman, 1992).

But my imagined sensitive reader appears in my mind's eye once again. Surely we cannot study everything? Some lines have to be drawn, don't they? Clearly the question of where the lines are drawn and who decides to draw them will resonate with those scholars even marginally on the 'post' side of the post-positivist debate. But if IR/FPA scholars do seriously believe that the old order has gone and that we are now in a state of flux and confusion, then perhaps old theories need to be treated with extreme caution. The tendency for FPA/IR theorists to sort out bits of this complex world into tidy, neat pieces, empirical and theoretical, is, I fear, not the most innovative way forward. Susan Bassnett quotes from a poem by Polish writer Katarina Turaj-Kalinska, which opens with the lines: 'Little daughter I'm going to teach you how to tidy up / which – in this world – means moving the garbage elsewhere' (Bassnett, 1992, p. 12). As Bassnett points out, it is so much easier to move the garbage elsewhere than to look into the whole complex process of how we generate it in the first place or at what the implications are of getting rid of it. The seemingly coherent theories of the past, with their emphases on making boundaries, defining exclusion zones, simplification and categorization, can only have limited application precisely because of those exclusionary and stifling mechanisms. If the world is complex then theories to explain it will necessarily be complex too. There is more involved in the making of inter-state relations or foreign policy than the list of 'usual suspects' put forward by scholars in this field. Gender is just one, though vitally important, issue which needs to be at least acknowledged as playing a part. Foreign policy scholars cannot go on ignoring the garbage that reifications of gender continue to spew out.

Notes

1 Cynthia Enloe spoke of the endings of the Cold War, as opposed to the ending of the Cold War, at a recent conference on gender and international relations held at the LSE on 15 May 1993. This emphasizes the awareness that the Cold War has different meanings for different groups as well as reminding us that the process of ending will vary greatly. Readers may wish to read her forthcoming book *The Morning After: Sexual Politics at the End of the Cold War* (University of California Press).

2 My elucidation, especially of the metatheoretical point, is painfully brief. Readers may wish to follow up the references.

13

Resisting the Temptation of Post
Foreign Policy Analysis

Ole Wæver

Being asked to comment on this project 'from a post-modern (or post-structuralist) angle', it is of course tempting to start playing with the idea of 'post foreign policy analysis'. In putting 'post' in front of this three-worded concept, one can interpret PFPA in several ways, and one soon discovers that it might mean almost anything (or nothing). Let me survey a few of these meanings; this might after all be a way to formulate a problematique for discussing the state of the art of foreign policy analysis. PFPA will in the following three sections be investigated first as (P)FPA, then as (PF)PA, and finally as (PFP)A.

(P)FPA: Post Foreign Policy Analysis

With the general assault on international relations which has been carried out through the 1980s by various types of reflectivists, post-modernists, post-structuralists, feminists and critical theorists, it would seem an almost too easy job to drag down FPA as well.

It has been pointed out by deconstructivists that international politics as a special sphere is constituted as a mirror image of domestic affairs. This contrast is not simply a coincidental after-the-fact difference, but reflects the way that the two fields are constituted. Our idea of the international is basically built on an idea of what it is *not*: domestic politics, rule of law, centralized. And this concept of domestic politics – as the unfolding of community and of enlightenment ideals about rationality and progress, peace and justice – is stabilized by having a field *outside*, where the other is pushed out, where all the anomalies, the contradictions, violence, repetition and regression, can be seen as spatially distinct, or as temporarily differentiated as that which is *not yet* covered by modernity's progress, where development and civilization has still to move. The field of international politics is the field where normal optimistic principles do not hold, where the different can only be controlled by the heroic statesman who dares to go to the border and handle that which is different, and then go back and teach the civilized people in the enlightened state that there is this world out there, which they should not naïvely treat as part of the world of progress. Out there history repeats itself, in archaic and brutal ways (Ashley, 1987; 1989a; 1989b; Walker, 1987; 1988; 1989; 1993; Wæver, 1994).

The basic principle structuring political space and time is the sovereign state. The organizing idea of state sovereignty was a powerful solution to the dilemmas posed by the waning medieval order, and consisted of the dual (mutually constitutive) principles of the *fragmentation* of global political life into autonomous units, which are internally *centralized*, holding a monopoly of power and authority over a specific territory. This split meant, in the words of R. B. J. Walker (1990, p. 10), 'an exceptionally elegant resolution of the apparent contradiction between centralization and fragmentation, or, phrased in more philosophical language, between universality and particularity'. Universal principles are applicable within, not externally. Difference, on the other hand, is concentrated outside: international relations is seen as essentially lacking community and therefore it can only with difficulty be analysed as *politics*. It is merely international *relations*.

In the light of this, the whole agenda of analysing foreign policy would seem to be seriously questioned. What is foreign policy if not that specific field of relations among states? Does the enterprise not inevitably partake in the reification of the state? On the surface it has, with its opening of the black box, been doing the opposite, but is the whole agenda not inherently linked to the conceptual bifurcation into domestic and foreign? Is the very idea of foreign policy meaningful without the basic inside/outside metaphor?

This line of argumentation seems almost too easy, and somehow not promising much either as to metatheoretical insights, or in the form of new approaches to the study of 'that which used to be called foreign policy'.

(PF)PA: Post-Foreign Policy Analysis

Post-foreign policy analysis? This is not another critical or alternative suggestion. No, this is what FPA actually *is*. FPA is basically a series of attempts to domesticate international relations by interpreting these as essentially excrescences on domestic society. It is policy analysis in a mode which tries to move foreign policy back from the field of the foreign to the field where policy analysis has established itself as a legitimate or even dominant approach. This policy analysis is post-foreign: (PF)PA.

There is in FPA a general disposition towards defining foreign policy *differently* from 'relations among states', as something like 'a set of goals, directives or intentions, formulated by persons in official or authoritative positions, directed at some actor or condition in the environment beyond the nation-state, for the purpose of affecting the target in the manner desired by the policy-makers' (Cohen and Harris, 1975, p. 385: quoted and commented on by Goldmann, 1988, p. 7). But it does still – I will claim – circulate around some basic idea of states acting towards other actors, the most important of which in the end are (perceived as something like) states. Thus, for all the attempts to reconceptualize the key object of study, the enterprise does draw its coherence from the connotations of the key term – foreign policy – which links back to the classical image. At the same time the language of FPA is that of domestic policy analysis.

In the interpretation of Ashley, international relations is constituted by a 'double move'. The first is the metaphorical reduction of community to its meaning in domestic society, which is to say its dominant meaning in Western rationalist discourse: community as eternal and universal identity. Incompatibility, rupture and violence cannot exist *in* community and are referred beyond its *margins*. Simultaneously, definitive limits for this community are unthinkable: by definition it tends towards integration of everything and everybody into the rational, universal identity. The second move is then grounded in a historicist consciousness. By reflecting on these abstract, rational principles, it notices their blindness to *history*: this belief of rationalism in the progressive inclusion of everything into community is blind to its own situation 'amidst the hazardous movement and potential resistances of an open-ended and decentered history' (Ashley, 1987, p. 414). Therefore the realists point to

> the historical margins of community, the margins that separate domestic political community from the resistant world beyond its sway. These margins define a spatial relation, a *difference* between domestic and international politics, but the move that constitutes these margins is also a temporal relation, a *deferment* of domestic community's essential project for a universal and timeless rational unity. (Ashley 1987, p. 414)

Thus, FPA can be seen as the opposite of the heroic statesman, the opposite of the realist creation of IR. FPA is simply the first move without the second, yet it still somehow remembers being told about the second move: i.e. there is a field out there which one has to deal with, but it can basically be done on the basis of domestic approaches and concepts.

In the self-conception of FPA this story is told heroically as the gradual overcoming of the restrictive assumptions of a distinction between the domestic and the international through a gradual sociologization of this question. It is transferred from a postulated difference to an empirical question (Lijphart, 1974, p. 15; see also Rosenau, 1980, pp. 125ff.). Alternatively, there is a classical realist version of the same story, probably best told by Hans J. Morgenthau (1946): owing to its domestic, historical experience, the liberalist bourgeoisie is unable to grasp *how foreign* is foreign policy.

Kjell Goldmann has noticed with what great noise it is announced, time after time, that international and domestic politics cannot be kept separate:

> Views such as these are occasionally put forward aggressively, as if major opposition needed to be overcome. However, at least in so far as the community of international relationists is concerned, few deny that international relations and domestic politics have much in common. (1989, p. 103)

This surprising repeated tilting against windmills should make us suspicious. Goldmann has pointed to one of the central rituals of FPA. It is in this sense an opposition against a fictional orthodoxy; really it is the opposition that is the orthodoxy.

A second remark on the foreignness of foreign policy and the attempt to tie foreign policy into the domestic universe is that, more or less explicitly in most foreign policy theories and certainly in most everyday talk on foreign policy, a topological assumption is made about the relationship between inside, outside and the voice of foreign policy. The implicit picture of foreign policy is that it stems from inside and travels towards the outside through the medium of a decision-making machinery. The sources of foreign policy in the explanatory sense can be external or internal, but the references, the motives and the interests are located internally. The ideology of foreign policy is that it is policy for the domestic society, and therefore, in some sense, the political process is directed from the inside to the outside. The voice of foreign policy – the statesman – is located in the midst of domestic society from where he collects the motives and drives for a foreign policy which is then conveyed to the outside world as abilities allow.

In a book like Henry Kissinger's *A World Restored* the perspective is radically different. The statesman is located neither internally nor externally but on the border, trying to mediate two worlds:

> It may be asked why Metternich had to choose a procedure so indirect ... Why not attempt to adapt the Austrian domestic structure to the national *élan* sweeping across Europe? But a statesman must work with the material at hand and the domestic structure of Austria was rigid, much more rigid, paradoxically, than the international one. (Kissinger, 1957, p. 28; see also pp. 62, 83, 297–313, 324, 329)

This is not a choice of succeeding internally or externally. A statesman has to succeed in both arenas; a failure in either place can be fatal. The option of manipulating one or the other is a pragmatic choice on the basis of a judgement of the conditions for action, the availability of a strategy for affecting change on either side. In fortunate conditions the two tasks are immediately reconcilable, but if not then the statesman (the regime, the decision-makers) has to act creatively. A policy – possibly even a grand strategic design – has to be devised that promises change on either side. Which side is chosen is not directly a product of the strength or size of the state, but depends mainly on where the options for manipulation or modification are least difficult. Austria at the time of Metternich was not the strongest power in Europe, but Metternich had to direct his energies towards elaborate and creative statesmanship on the European level because of the rigidity and frailty of Austria's domestic structure (including the personality of the Emperor). Austrian statesmanship had to attempt to create a European order on principles of legitimacy compatible with – or even actively supportive of – the domestic principle of legitimacy in Austria, the dynastic principle.

What should be noticed in this example is that the traditional perspective of foreign policy as tied primarily into the domestic side is partly a product of the general liberal-democratic ideology of what foreign policy ought to be. The Kissingerian conception is potentially more realistic and captures at the same time the creative, agency-driven nature of foreign policy which enables explanation of even radical, far-reaching designs that are hardly likely to emerge from traditional input–output schemes for foreign policy decision-making (Carlsnaes, 1993a).[1] A situation where the internal/external constellation does not immediately allow for a policy which can succeed simultaneously on both fronts necessitates a proactive policy which cannot be derived mechanically from these demands. It is not a product of the combined pressures but an attempt to modify structures domestically and/or internationally with the aim of creating a constellation where foreign policy and domestic order can return to a mutually reinforcing circle.

(PFP)A: The Analysis of Post Foreign Policy

How can we construct a mode of analysis for that which is no longer foreign policy but rather 'post foreign policy'? One approach was the Walkerian one of political theory suggested above, where one reconsiders fundamental theoretical and philosophical assumptions related to the constitutive distinction between international relations and political theory. Another might be to approach the study more sociologically, with the guiding interest being how processes unfold across borders in the dual sense of crossing state borders without being foreign policy (i.e. state-to-state relations), and at the same time crossing the border of domestic and international relations. The latter means to circumvent the conceptualization in terms of foreign policy at the same time as one operates where foreign policy used to be. (This is different from the Walker approach which, amongst other things, takes more seriously the fact that the world in some sense still *is* constructed on the principle of sovereignty. Any move beyond this is limited by our inability to conceive of world politics in other terms. This approach tries to study the very basic ways of conceiving of political time and space.) The less philosophical – sociological or political science – approach takes as a starting point that there now *is* a new field which is functioning in terms different from foreign policy and which should therefore be studied: (PFP)A.

Some ideas might be taken from Rosenau's 'post-international politics'. One of the basic premises of his (1990) analysis is a change in the nature of individual identity and attitude to authority which undermines the logic of the inter-state system of sovereign states. This state logic continues in some fields, but is increasingly challenged by a second world where actors are not bound by the principle of state sovereignty. Rosenau talks of 'sovereignty-free actors', but actually the image of these agents is very much that *they* become sovereign individuals (freed from *state* sovereignty). From a Walker-inspired perspective one discerns the well-known modern figure of the sovereign individual.

Among the limitations of this approach is that it is not well integrated as *theory*. More specifically, it does not designate very clearly the actors and the modes of operation in the new world of sovereignty-free actors (cf. Rosenau, 1990). If sovereignty is not the organizing concept, what is? Are we just talking world politics? If so, we will still be faced by the Walker-Waltz[2] question: how is it organized? What is the principle of separation and differentiation of functions among units? How is political identity defined? How is universalism and particularism distributed? Who are the we's, and how do they relate? How is estrangement mediated among whom (Der Derian, 1987)?

Michael Smith in Chapter 2 points out how 'the state in Europe no longer reflects the archetype of sovereign statehood', although the state is certainly still around and in many ways strengthened. Thus we have to think about the new kind of structures and relations that emerge among post-sovereign states. Although Michael Smith points out a central issue, he largely stays with rather formal, methodological questions of how to view the strategies of adjustment when the arena becomes this chaotic; these questions essentially are related not to the *changing nature of the state*, only to the changing *state strategies* given the changing (nature of the?) European order. But what is a state strategy when the state is not a state?

So far there has been no convincing framework for studying 'post foreign policy', no clear idea of a specific delineable and definable field which somehow replaces foreign policy and holds enough characteristics and dynamics to be studied as a specific subject. Thus, we probably would drift towards the more abstract perspective of Walker's political theory in an attempt to see the processes shaping the various types of political forms in a complex arena that *might* be changing its basic rules of the game, but where the attempts to define the new field are still extremely vague even at the structural level (Rosenau, 1990; Wæver, 1991; Luke, forthcoming; Ruggie, 1993). It can be called neo-medieval, post-modern, post-Westphalian or post-sovereignty, but knowing only what the units *no longer are* does not tell us much about the new principle of separation of units. There will be many and different units – but in the old sovereignty-based system there were also lots of other units beyond the states. The point about the sovereignty-based system was that sovereignty was its *organizing principle*, a powerful legal fiction (Bull, 1979), and states were the defining units (cf. Manning, 1957; 1962; Wæver, 1991; 1992). In the new system we do not know the nature of the defining units. These do not have to be necessarily one type of like units, but we need to have an idea of what kind of units we are talking about: distinguished in time or space, in territory or informatics, continuously of discontinuously, personalized or abstract, overlapping or exclusive, etc. Without such an idea, we will be even further removed from generating any kind of actor or unit theory.

So, the big question is: what is FPA? And what comes after it? What characterizes the (sub)discipline? Which assumptions, procedures and operations remain intrinsically linked to all FPA, and what would happen if one started to challenge these? We will not follow (immediately at least) the lead of PFPA and jump to any safe 'beyond'. Instead, we will stay for a while with FPA and only tediously work our way to somewhere else. The next section will attempt a characterization of FPA and a demarcation of its blind spots, while the section following it will present some contemporary modes of analysing foreign policy which actually operate from these blind spots, and therefore fall outside FPA despite their high degree of relevance for the understanding of foreign policy. This whole issue of FPA in the overall figuration of the IR discipline is the theme in the final sections: why are the various theories and approaches defined and categorized the way they are, and why might there at present be specific openings pointing towards foreign policy analysis in a new key?

What foreign policy analysis was and remains

The subdiscipline of FPA is (and has for very long been) marked by a fabulous diversity, containing approaches stretching from systems theory, decision-making models and bureaucratic politics through implementation analysis and decision analysis to psychological and cognitive approaches, not to mention the very general and ambitious theories explaining foreign policy from basic, objective variables. And yet! Yet, it seems that there are certain shared assumptions, or rather modalities and operators.

I will now go through some of the most prominent approaches, draw out some premises or characteristic traits, and then see if these are specific to a specific approach or are simply clearer there, actually holding for more or less the whole subfield.

A main strand has been interested in *decision-making*, which can be summed up as an interest in how the *how* influences the *what* (White, 1989, p. 15): how decisions are made influences the policy that comes out in the end. This characterizes all studies from the original Snyder framework through bureaucratic politics to implementation approaches. Studies like these are most often explained and argued as alternatives to the realist *rational actor*, where the *state* as such is reflecting in an abstract sense on the substance and arriving at a how-free what. The inclusion of the how also means a displacement of the who: it is not the state that thinks, but various actors (individual or collective) within or around the state. Thus decisions can only be understood if these within-the-state actors have been localized (who are they?), analysed (what does each stand for?) and positioned (what are the constellation, the power relations and the connections?). *Actors with interests, aims and calculations* are central to most of these studies; they are different actors from the state, and one has to study their inner drives and their relationships.

There is a rather significant group of studies which focus on (mis)perception, images, belief systems or psychological processes (e.g. Janis and Mann, 1977; Jervis, 1976; Lebow, 1981; Stein, 1988; Little and Smith, 1989):

> Over the past two decades a great deal of research has been focused on the *systematic characteristics* of human error. These studies, largely concentrated in psychology and organizational behaviour, treat humans not as omniscient and calculating rational actors but, rather, as beings with limited *information processing* capability, possessed of an uncanny ability to make unjustified inferences in disastrously inopportune circumstances and beset by a variety of historical, emotional, cognitive, and organizational blinders. (Schrodt, 1991, p. 1502; emphasis added)

Slightly simplified, it can be said that all these approaches share a conception of politics as information processing, and a picture of the human element as an information processing machine plus (to varying degrees) an emotional element which somehow yields weight to the elements collected in the memory. Despite their (self-) labelling as 'psychological' they are most often very far from any relationship to (continental) psychoanalytical traditions. Their notion of psychology is normally American and thereby much more dichotomous as rational/irrational, and the model ends up as one where a rational ego is at the centre flanked by irrational forces (not influencing the normal actor). This rational ego is not rational in the sense of the realist rational actor (maximizing state interests), but it is *predictable* and is ultimately conceived of in machine terms, an information machine. The input is information/ perceptions, that is data *about* the external world; and the internal side consists on the one hand of the inertia of previous input (images, perception, belief systems) and on the other of values which are the inner, untouchable drive of the unit, that is its motor, and thereby the ultimate source of direction for the theory. This cognitive psychology tradition has to keep the unconscious out of the theory; the I is kept intact, and language as well as most action is reserved for the rational I and kept away from the unconscious whereas language in Freudian psychology is just the place where the unconscious is able to show itself (Wæver, 1990a, pp. 339ff.). The contributions from these theories are mainly derived from the fact that some general laws of human perception, cognition and reasoning are discovered. These are not specific for individual persons, are not related to any inner irrational processes, but are basically processes that can be simulated or assumed. Thereby different actors (states or more often substate units) can be dealt with, since their mode of operating can be assumed to be known given the input into them from the external world. The individual in its all-too-human complexity (as a level of analysis with inside as well as outside) is not really studied, i.e. these approaches are cognitive rather than psychological. The unit is an idealized actor.

In studies on EC integration, there has been a tendency in recent years to rehabilitate realism as a theory/tradition to which one is allowed to talk. Then (Pijpers, 1990; Moravcsik, 1991; and in this book especially Soetendorp (Chapter 6), Risse-Kappen (Chapter 3) and Pfetsch (Chapter 7)) a constellation is almost inevitably constructed where realism is pulling in the rationalist, non-cooperative direction, and a counter-pull towards cooperation and integration is generated by the other tradition (labelled 'functionalism' (Pijpers), 'liberalism' (Moravcsik and Risse-Kappen), 'interdependence'/'regime theory' (Soetendorp) or 'learning theory' (Pfetsch)). This basic ordering for the game is seldom discussed or argued; it is taken for granted that these are the functions to be given the different traditions, that these are their dispositions. *Structure* is located outside the state, and *will* inside (the will to do that – integration – which the analysis presupposes to be progress). Limits are external and evolution internal; regress is in the international system and progress comes from domestic sources (learning, liberalism or spillover). Realism is allocated the system and the role of explaining away those cases where integration did not take place (and thereby realism can supplement and save liberalist integration theory, which cannot explain non-integration); while liberalist theories take care of the positive processes which ultimately stem from the inside, and therefore they become foreign policy theories. Only rarely do attempts to build foreign policy theory take off from realist assumptions or try to refine explicitly classical ideas from realism or other traditional speculation in IR. Rarely is realism merged with FPA, seldom is there an inner relation between realism and FPA instead of an external confrontation; the only instance in this volume is probably Chapter 9 by Mouritzen.

Studies from the FPA tradition have (as actually have most other studies) a problem in dealing with the simultaneity of unitness at the state level and at the EC level. They oscillate between dealing with one (EC foreign policy) and with the other (state positions on a common foreign policy). As we saw above, in FPA the level of analysis moved down to intra-state, but this was still interesting because it became translated into the action of (or in the name of) a specific type of unit: the state. Is it still implicitly so, that one thinks in terms of the sovereign state, i.e. that one level/unit is always crucial, and just doubles this thinking and operates it both at the European and at the state level? This produces an unclear dualism because one just adds a level without reflecting on the novelty of this. The analytical approach smuggles on board several assumptions related to sovereignty (i.e. that one level is unrivalled; cf. Wæver, 1991), and thereby one produces an unsettled dualism, with both state and EC levels studied as if they were *the* unit. The procedure is in practice that only one level at a time is foreign policy and the other is part of the environment. The other level is not dealt with as foreign policy too (foreign policy for partly the same people but at a different level of aggregation).

Preferably, one should study the simultaneity, the interplay, the contest and the differentiation between the state and the quasi-state, the EC. In this book, one finds discussions touching on these questions first of all in the chapters by Pfetsch (Chapter 7), M. Smith (Chapter 2) and Soetendorp (Chapter 6), but also with some interesting reflections by Risse-Kappen (Chapter 3). Frank Pfetsch's chapter – to concentrate on one – opens by directly stating the problem:

> the foreign policies of the member states have become a two-track enterprise: on the one the members act like traditional independent policy-makers, and on the other they act like representatives of the EC/ EPC.

Pfetsch proceeds by showing the continuum of forms from inter-governmentalism to supranationalism. However, in implementing this investigation the issue is resolved into one of explaining the evolution of national foreign policies: why does whom choose to go how far on the scale? But the independent dynamics emerging out of the other focal point, the EC as such, is not addressed. It is explained when and why a state chooses to proceed far in the direction of a joint EC policy. What then about the EC level? Also here we have policies more or less explained by way of subunit interests (e.g. states), but if the procedures of FPA are repeated at the EC level, one should also be concerned with the dynamics that emerge around this focal point as such: the way EC interests, the reasons integration and a European universe of social meaning have developed to the extent that the EC has become a state-like political unit. It thus deserves to be dealt with in parallel to the states, thereby generating unique and intriguing dynamics of competition between state logic at two levels.

The result of this survey of four strands of FPA is to displace the deciding unit from the state to a constellation of (smaller) units, where one has to take into account both the constellation and what each wants and does: a psychological reconstruction of decision procedures in the individual (or enlarged group individual); a tendency to see inner drives as dynamic and wilful and outer forces as limitation; and finally an inability to deal with multilevel foreign policy.

If all this is summed up, we find that it is all about a self, a subject which is not necessarily the state. Actually it is mostly *not* the state, because this would contain a danger that the system became short-circuited into the *state system*, the state as constituted and driven by the system (IR, realism). Therefore, the ideal type FPA builds on a *parallel displacement* of the subject (which has hitherto always been the state) to a subsubject. This can be psychological ('an anthropomorphism in which the ego is depicted as a sort of mini-agent', as Giddens has put it, 1984, p. 7), institutional-bureaucratic, systems theoretical, or organized around decision units or networks and spaces of several types of actors. Usually, it is larger than the individual and smaller than the state.

Any attempt at this form of generalization of course asks for counter-arguments of the type 'this is not true: it does not hold for such-and-such a theory or an author.' Having first tried to find some typical traits by commenting on some dominant (or conspicuous) foreign policy theories/approaches, I can cut the cake differently in a second round, by taking the national traditions as the unit of analysis. Following Steve Smith (1983; 1986; Chapter 1 of this book), we can contrast American and British (or European!) approaches, and we might (cf. Wæver, 1990a; 1990b) add a Scandinavian school.

The American school in FPA has been closely associated with the specific enterprise of comparative foreign policy (CFP), and beyond that it still has a special preference for on the one hand general theory (at a very high level of generalization), and on the other hand inductive (or at least very empirical) studies (Smith, 1983; 1986; Wæver, 1990a). Many Americans seem to *think* that this has changed a lot, but with a European eye it rather seems that they have changed from hard positivism to soft positivism (cf. the comments by Steve Smith in Chapter 1). Thus the American studies have moved from on the one hand CFP and on the other the study of basic variables (Rosenau's pre-theory etc.) and types of states (small-state theory, for instance) towards the complex studies to be found in for instance the *New Directions* volume (Hermann et al., 1987).

It still seems that American studies move on the two extreme levels of general theory and empiricism (Wæver, 1990a, pp. 335ff.; 1990b, pp. 153ff.). Most studies either generate findings that cannot be explained by any theory, or attempt to explore relationships that are so general that no relevant laws or data can be found. Comparativism, scientific methodologies and a wish for a limited number of factors remain the general organizing ideas. All this is held together by a very strong – often implicit and ultimately heroic – assumption that there is a very coherent reality, foreign policy, which can be studied. You could not proceed in these very indirect manners with large explanatory gaps unless it was assumed that foreign policy existed as a field of tremendous regularity and uniformity.

The British tradition is more for middle-range theory, case-studies and historical approaches. Paradoxically, these eclectic methodologies have produced a much more coherent school of studies, a number of relatively consistent edited volumes and a clear profile (Smith et al., 1988; Clarke and White, 1989; Little and Smith, 1989). This tradition was less ambitious than the American tradition and so had less far to fall. What unites this tradition? First of all the middle-range theories. The historical approach probably defined the British non-Americanness in the earliest years of FPA, but since the general ideas of the American FPA reached Britain, the historical approach has only been an addition, not the defining approach. Case-studies of course are numerous (in the US too), but they are by definition not very capable of controlling a field by their definitions and theories since they do not share any. Thus, the middle-range theories are the meeting ground. What then does British middle rangeism consist of?

These theories are all general regarding one factor (bureaucracy, belief system or decision-making, for instance) but without any intention of modelling the whole into a theory of foreign policy. They are general in trying to include whatever is necessary for understanding this factor (not the American insistence on a limited number of factors) but are limited in their ambition (in contrast again to the Americans) since the British middle-range theories do accept that they will not be able to combine a specific number of middle-range theories into a total theory. This is so because the different theories include more than their own compartments, and therefore the different theories are overlapping, including the same substance but defined differently. Thus the overall image is one of a big system with a number of interesting points or places along the way: you then choose to organize your study around one of these, and you include whatever you find necessary to study this *place*. Here we find almost more clearly than in the American tradition the typical FPA traits, the mini-agents etc.

What distinguishes the Scandinavian school (e.g. Goldmann, 1988; Carlsnaes, 1987; Mouritzen, 1988; Chapter 9 in this volume) is first of all a commitment to *weak theory*: neither the over-ambitious American grand theory and/or raw empiricism, nor the English middle-range theory and/or historical studies. Weak theory means that one stays away from the large explanations – with huge explanatory gaps – known from American theory, but also works differently from the British synthesizing of theories of something (images, implementation, bureaucratic politics). The Scandinavian studies organize around a theory (weak theory), a specific *idea, thesis, problematique*. This comes close to the Americans in focusing on a limited number of factors, and close to the British in staying away from the overall general theory of foreign policy (cf. Wæver, 1990a; 1990b). The distinguishing feature is the central place of one theory in each study, a theory with internal coherence even if this means that the theory is in some sense incomplete or only able to cover rather small explanatory gaps (not from deep causes to final effects). These studies still share the essential FPA traits, especially as they conceive of domestic politics either as psychological/cognitive structures or as agency; and as criticized by Carlsnaes (1993a), they often share the input–output conception of foreign policy-making. On several other dimensions, the Scandinavian school tends to move away from common assumptions. For instance see the studies that focus on change and inertia, where there is a bias in the direction of seeing dynamics as stemming from the external side and stability being constructed internally (Goldmann, 1988; Wæver, 1990b). See also the willingness to link up with classical realist hypotheses that become embedded in the FPA theory (Goldmann, 1988; Mouritzen, 1988; Chapter 9 in this volume).

The studies that are carried out in the three traditions follow different logics of science, but they study to a large extent the same questions, and use a lot of the same ideas. None of the three approaches militates against the general agenda of FPA. This consists of studying a self or a subject, which is mostly not the state but somehow comes to take the place of the state, and thereby constitutes subjectivity in international relations, which is lacking in the relations/system posing of the problem.

An explanation for this (beyond the epistemological and ontological biases of a certain science tradition, i.e. beyond the debate in terms of philosophical naïvety – why should it be particularly common in FPA?) would seem to stem from the *functions* that FPA has had, the *tasks* it has been given, the *location* it has always had in the *constellation* of IR theories, its place in the great debates. FPA was born in the so-called second debate and matured during the third. Therefore it has (a) a tendency to question strict lines between domestic and inter-national without being able to replace this conceptualization by any other basic concept, and therefore leaning still on it; (b) a belief in this domestic/foreign border being crossed first of all by one uniting factor, a general methodology for the study of social and political phenomena; (c) a role as counter-player to 'realism'. This implicit agenda suggests that foreign policy analysis means not the analysis of foreign policy – which could take place (and actually does take place) in numerous ways – but a certain bounded field which does certain things, and not certain others. So we now turn to some contemporary cases of what it excludes.

Approaches that are not FPA but might help us to analyse foreign policy

I have picked two examples that illustrate the point about how FPA relates to the overall positions in IR debates. These can be found in the texts of the present volume as obvious candidates that are not chosen, as close cousins that are still not seen as members of the family. Realism is often discussed, but then always with a specific role. Psychology and cognitive factors are popular at present, but a *structural* analysis of discourse is not welcome, it seems.

Neo-realist deduction

Since the EC is an in-between phenomenon, in some ways state-like and in others clearly not a sovereign state, one must as a realist first note that security dynamics operate on both levels: power balancing work inside the EC (against integration) and on the external side (possibly strengthening integration). Theory and history tell us that it will ultimately come to work mainly in one of the two places. If one asks a person from Ohio today about security (in a non-individual sense), he will not answer about the threat from Michigan, but start talking about Russia, the Middle East or Japan. This is because North America has been lifted to the higher level, excluding security dynamics among the states, and looking out on the external scene as its appropriate level. The same mechanisms can be seen operating on the EC (especially in relation to high-tech competition with the US and Japan), and in the conscious attempt to try to move the security dynamics; i.e. uniting in order to avoid re-emergence of *security competition* among the European states which is very close to the arguments given in the *Federalist Papers* for American unity.[3]

Thus it seems that the balance-of-power and security logic can contribute to an explanation of European unification. This stands in stark contrast to the way both Risse-Kappen (Chapter 3) and Soetendorp (Chapter 6) discuss realism in the present book. In their analysis, realism is the appropriate theory when one needs to explain the uncooperative behaviour of states, whereas integration is ultimately explained by liberal theories. This is part of the overall pattern for FPA (and integration theory), and it tends to narrow down the room for manoeuvre of realism – and the possibility for it to make valuable contributions.

The more specific theoretical tool used for organizing the analysis could be the Buzanian concept of 'security complexes' (Buzan et al., 1986, Chapter 1; Buzan, 1991, Chapter 5) as a tool for generating *scenarios*. A security complex can exist in four different conditions: (1) the 'normal' regional pattern of rivalry, balances and alliances; (2) external overlay; (3) centralization; and (4) insufficient coherence and interaction capacity to generate a complex. Derived from the current global power configuration (which excludes option 2) and the nature of societies in Europe (which eliminates option 4), it can be concluded that Europe at present faces two scenarios:

1   Integration: Western Europe as a pole. This scenario is about the replacement of the European security complex by an actor sufficiently integrated to constitute a pole of power in the international system. Within Europe, this means a pattern of concentric circles. The name of this game is centrality/distance: how far away from the core group will we land?
2   Fragmentation. This scenario is about the re-emergence of the European security complex. Here decisive relations are between a number of centres in Europe.

The logic of integration/fragmentation not only tells us the long-range options, but also explains important forces that shape foreign policies here and now. For instance, it is difficult to explain French and German policies in the 1992–3 ratification crisis over Maastricht without the force of this structural mechanism as well as the fear of it. If viewed in an economic perspective or on the basis of specific narrow national interests, it is hard to understand the plans that started to circulate in Bonn and Paris for how to respond to the potential situation of a second Danish 'no' in the May 1993 referendum on ratification (Holm et al., 1993). European security experts generally speculated about neither the continuation of a slowed-down integration on the basis of its economic rationale nor an enlarged all-European cooperation, but rather about either an unravelling of the EC (not only the union) through increasing nationalism and egotism or a tight mini-union with France, Germany and Benelux, if need be outside the EC framework.[4] These considerations and plans were structured by a specific construction of the potential outcomes for Europe after the Cold War. In this context it is less relevant whether the neo-realist scenarios are actually true or not. They are socially true enough to be self-fulfilling.

This is not the kind of realism discussed in most of the chapters of this book (state centred and anti-integrationist). In the present illustration, realism becomes a tool for analysis by using as its motor the multilayered nature of political authority in Europe, which has been shown above to be a main *problem* in the analysis for much of traditional FPA.

Discourse analysis on national discursive spaces

Another completely different approach to the study of foreign policy is to focus on those structures *in* the societies that play a major role in *shaping* foreign policy. They do not cause or trigger foreign policy, but they do explain the directions and forms that foreign policy can take for a specific state if it is still to remain politically meaningful in its national context.

National discursive spaces can be analysed in a structured manner with the use of discourse analysis (Wæver et al., forthcoming). It studies how some key terms like concepts of state, nation and politics are woven into an intricate constellation that can change dramatically but never freely; only certain rearticulations are possible. One can therefore construct a matrix for nation and state projects and from this deduce for instance the possible 'Europes' of France and Germany.

An advantage of this approach compared with psychological approaches studying perceptions and belief systems is that it stays totally clear of any relationship to what people really think. It is not interested in inner motives, in interests or beliefs; it studies something public, that is how meaning is generated and structured in a national context. If it is true that this has both a certain inertia and a relatively strong structuring effect on foreign policy, one has found a location for studying a domestic factor which is at the same time important and accessible.

Discourse in a post-structuralist perspective (Laclau and Mouffe, 1985) is by definition never settled; it is always open for rearticulation. There are always contradictions present, always fragments ready to be redefined and played out against the dominant discourse. Therefore, there are in practice always competing national discourses, and even quite radical transformations are possible (and do happen). The theory cannot predict *which* outcome will follow a radical change, but it can sense when a change is approaching and it can tell what are the most easily available options, and what are the almost completely excluded lines of action.

Henry Kissinger presents the question in terms of a state and its vision of itself (1957, p. 146: see also pp. 144, 171):

> This is not a mechanical problem . . . an exact balance is impossible . . . because while powers may appear to outsiders as factors in a security arrangement, they appear domestically as expressions of a historical existence. No power will submit to a settlement, however well-balanced and however 'secure', which seems totally to deny its vision of itself.

Today, the main question for the future of European stability is not directly the relations among the major powers, but rather the *inner* struggles over national identity and Europe projects in France, Germany and Russia. In each country, strong competitors have emerged to the project that functioned in the comprehensive *quid pro quo* of 1990 (Wæver, 1990c).

Discourse analysis is able to explain even grand designs, i.e. that which is often problematic in an FPA tradition which focuses on decisions seen as reactions to specific stimuli (Carlsnaes, 1993a). Articulating a vision for Europe (and thereby a vision for nation and state) is necessary for the domestic stabilization of an overall policy concept. For most major states a policy is not stable if it is not able to answer questions about, so the speak, the meaning of life: who are we, where are we going? Several very different answers are possible, but some answers are almost totally excluded since they go against the whole national repertoire of political key terms and connotations. And a non-answer is unlikely too. This is the cause of proactive policy, or non-linear reactions. If one line breaks down, at least for a medium or major power, it is likely not that one will just live with the ensuing vacuum, but that the question about the meaning of and future for the nation/state will generate a new concept that can lead to discontinuous developments in foreign policy. It will be a creative act from e.g. a French foreign policy leadership trying to shape a world, internally and externally, that is France compatible (Holm, 1993).

Various liberal theoreticians have stressed recently how a task for liberalist theory (where it should be able to improve on realist conceptions) is the *endogenization of interest formation* into theory without putting interests into a closed circuit with international structure. According to Alexander Wendt, liberals are at present characterized by attempts to argue that state action is influenced less by '"structure" (anarchy and the distribution of power)' and more by '"process" (interaction and learning) and institutions' (1992a, p. 391). In practice the proclivity of neo-liberalist foreign policy theory is roughly to treat interests as endogenous and identities as exogenously given. The formation of interests can be explained by a detailed investigation of domestic processes and by strengthening the state–society link (Moravcsik, 1992), while the *identities* of actors are given prior to politics. Thus it might be true that liberalism focuses on 'the interactions between domestic politics and international relations' (Keohane and Nye, 1993) but only in the superficial sense of political processes interacting (and thus in line with the tradition for domesticating *policy* analysis within FPA), and including neither the deeper questions of the formation of identities and the structural forces at the domestic level, nor the proactive political element of grand designs and purposive action. Discourse analysis emphasizes identity rearticulation and stresses in relation to interest formation the interpretative schemes that insert meaning into the many interests.

What, then, was the logic of picking these two approaches to the study of foreign policy? The first – and alleged – reason was that these structural approaches were modes of study that would not come naturally to FPA, since they break with the anthropomorphism of the constantly displaced mini-agent, the ontology of subject, will and agency. There is, however, a second agenda too: the basic constellation, in which FPA normally acts implicitly as the counterpart to a systemic theory of international relations and therefore with a strained relationship to realism, structuralism and non-subject-acknowledging approaches, might be changing.

Let us place foreign policy in the overall scheme of great debates in IR (following Wæver, 1992). FPA is marked by both the second and the third debates: the second (behaviouralism–traditionalism) debate gave FPA its methodological fixations, and the third (the inter-paradigm or structuralism–pluralism–realism debates) gave FPA the then (1970s) dominant conception of the IR landscape as one of incommensurable paradigms (Guzzini, 1988). It was assumed that the main line of debate remained that between realism and liberalism (now called interdependence or regime theory) and that the latter was the more hospitable towards domestic factors.

The constellation of IR theories in the 1980s and 1990s

The debate has changed, however. During the 1980s, realism became neo-realism and liberalism became neo-liberal institutionalism. Both underwent a self-limiting redefinition towards an anti-philosophical, theoretical minimalism, and they became thereby increasingly compatible. A dominant neo-neo synthesis became the research programme of the 1980s. No longer were realism and liberalism incommensurable; on the contrary, they shared a rationalist research programme, a conception of science, a willingness to operate on the premise of anarchy (Waltz) and investigate the evolution of cooperation and whether institutions matter (Keohane). Inside this we saw both the emergence of direct attempts at synthesis (Ruggie, 1986; Buzan et al., 1993) and a standard type of *International Organization* article operationalizing and testing realism and liberalism against each other in a specific field, but with a clear idea that they could be brought back into conversation.

In this environment, the main line of controversy shifted to the opposite direction as one between rationalists and reflectivists: the post-modernism debate. As the previous line of debate petered out, the secondary axis towards the radicals entered to fill the vacuum. Thus the two main poles became a neo-realist, neo-liberal synthesis and reflectivism. (Although the magic number 'three' kept reappearing, this should be the *fourth* debate, clearly different from the 'third debate' of the 1970s.) And within the synthesis a consensus seemed to evolve saying three things (Figure 13.1). First, the Waltzian idea of structure is sound but has to be enlarged, carefully, a little (preferably by taking in the second tier again: Ruggie, 1986; and possibly also by a differentiation of the concept of power, the third tier: Buzan et al., 1993). Secondly, the unit level has to be elaborated on, not remain the waste basket as in Waltz's conception (cf. Buzan et al., 1993). And thirdly, a third factor encompassing technological development, norms, degree of institutionalization, international society, and the like has to come in as the underlying, gradual, slowly emerging trend which causes from time to time systemic change. Whether it is called 'dynamic density' (Ruggie), 'process' (Keohane and Nye, 1987) or 'interaction capacity' (Buzan), it is essentially *the liberal factor* – all that

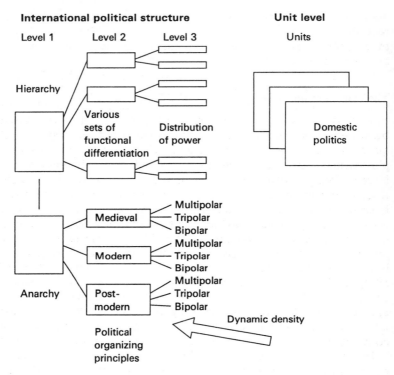

Figure 13.1   *Ruggie's reformulation of Waltz*

which liberal theory has always wanted to insert as giving hope for evolutionary but ultimately qualitative change, that is progress. Logically these elements are *systemic* but *non-structural* (not part of the positional arrangement of units). Attempts to put these into the structure have therefore correctly been resisted by Waltz, but his own conclusion of dumping it all to the unit level (including for instance nuclear weapons) is clearly unsatisfactory. Developments in technology, and the innovation and diffusion of nuclear weapons, are questions not only of who has what but also of the systemic effects of these factors entering the system.

In this situation one increasingly hears something like a call saying 'we need a foreign policy theory (a unit theory), but we don't like those foreign policy theories we have got.' There is thus a theoretical vacuum; demand is bigger than supply, and one needs to speculate about what kind of foreign policy theory could go together with this emerging synthesis. As suggested by Richard Little, it would be natural to see the problem as one of parallel internal and external structures that put demands on the reproduction of the state (in Buzan et al., 1993, pp. 120ff., 165ff.). One suggestion for the internal ones is then the discourse analysis outlined above.

But why do I take this emerging synthesis so seriously? I was supposed to offer the reflectivist comment on established theory. If it is true that the most promising approach to the unit level is the reflectivist one (discourse analysis) and the systemic level is covered by a fusion of realist and liberalist theory, we get the overall question of how to reconcile such different philosophical approaches. One reaction is to just accept their different wavelengths (Wæver, 1992). Another would be more aggressively to see whether one tradition can subsume the other under its perspective. It would here seem that realism or liberalism can hardly contain discourse analysis, but maybe a post-structuralist reinterpretation of realist structure is possible. After all, the reinsertion of the second tier by Ruggie already opened up towards something which is in some sense discursively constructed (Ruggie, 1986; Wæver, 1991), and it is also possible that anarchy can be seen as socially constructed (Wendt, 1992a; Jones in Buzan et al., 1993) without this meaning that it is false, only that it has to be studied differently. Also the third tier (distribution of capabilities) can be rearticulated as socially constituted (Knudsen, Chapter 11 in this book), which is in line with much classical realism. Even dynamic density does not translate automatically into political expressions but depends on discursive practice to establish new political categories (Ruggie, 1993). Thus, after all, the synthesis of the synthesis might happen increasingly on a post-structuralist or at least constructivist terrain. 'The problem with Waltz's theory is not the explanatory scheme it sets forth but the ontology on which it is based' (Dessler, 1989, p. 463). It is possible to attempt a reformulation of Waltzian structure in terms of rules, structures or practices and at least as a starting point to assume that Waltz's is still the best suggestion of *what* these rules are, of what the deep conventions actually consist of.

This discussion leads to the following conclusions:

1   Neo-realism actually has the major hold on international structure and it is a natural task for foreign policy analysis to try more open-mindedly to explore the potentials of neo-realist foreign policy analysis.

2   A privileged basis for foreign policy analysis proper (the domestic level) is at the moment the most surprising one: post-structuralist discourse analysis.

3   The liberalist contribution could try to change its agenda, no longer trying to monopolize theories of cooperation and learning (which are covered better by realism and discourse analysis respectively), but instead exploring its contributions at the systemic level. Explore the liberal factor: how do these deep forces of technology and enlightenment actually alter the system structure, and how can this be studied?

The price might be to leave foreign policy analysis to the post-structuralists!

Agency and structure, levels of analysis and a different story

The above presentation seems to contradict the emerging insights strongly represented in the present book by the agent–structure debate. Isn't it so that the domestic–international debate really is the expression of the problem of agency and structure? Isn't the real problem to conceptualize agency at the domestic level? Why then this overtly structuralist conceptualization? Because agency is not foreign policy on the domestic level.

The alleged debate on structure and agency is actually a loose constellation of at least three debates: (a) the relationship between objective and subjective; (b) levels of analysis; and (c) the structuration debate about the co-constitution of structures and agents.

Objective and subjective

At heart the structure–agency debate retains some relationship to the classical object–subject dichotomy. Structure is the (relatively more) objective side against subjective agency. Not surprisingly, one post-structuralist reaction to this debate will therefore be to refuse to accept the question.

Take for instance the writings of Michel Foucault. A sizeable part of his work can be seen as undermining the notion of an object to be studied – and in parallel denying the notion of the innocent, knowing subject seeing the object. Subjectivity is located in history as woven into specific conditions and discourses; it is no longer a given, privileged place from where we can talk. Concepts like 'man', 'the work' and 'the author' are dealt with in the same vein. None constitutes a closed system where we can search for an inner intention. Instead we study the structures of meaning that make possible such works. This is a theme in Foucault's early works, but in *The Archeology of Knowledge* Foucault makes it clear that the task is to substitute the study of things (given before discourse) by an interest in the regular production of objects that only emerge in discourses. Objects cannot be studied in themselves since the great question is how objects are constituted at all (for a given period or discipline) as objects. This in parallel dissolves the subject (1972, p. 12) since sovereign consciousness has as a condition the continuous history which enables it to control everything. Without the unity and transparency of history, rationality and the other preconditions of anthropology and humanism are undermined. Objects as well as subjects are unable to fulfil the function of a stable reference point, neither origin nor endpoint. They are both to be studied as the points of crossing discourses or, in the terminology of later works, as strategies.[5]

Similar stories can be told about the works of Lacan, decentring the subject, or Derrida, deconstructing the self-presence of the voice. However, for all that can be said about the trend in post-structuralism for the last 25 years, there is still a problematique of the object (the thing, the unarticulated, silence). And certainly one of the subject. The vibrant presence of the question was felt when Jean-Luc Nancy asked 'Who comes after the subject?' (Cadava et al., 1991). 'The critique or the deconstruction of subjectivity is to be considered one of the great motifs of contemporary philosophical work in France' (Nancy, 1991, p. 4). Nancy wants to suggest that 'such a critique or deconstruction has not simply obliterated its object' (p. 4) and therefore it points 'to the necessity, not of a "return to the subject" . . . but on the contrary, of a move forward toward someone – *some one* – else in its place' (p. 5). There is a living search for a new determination of the responsibility of the subject that can be called 'post-deconstructive' (Derrida, 1991, p. 104). In the present discussion, I will therefore retain as one element the level of the individual subject.

In the structure–agency debate as it is normally received, there is considerable confusion regarding the relationship between the strict individual type of agent and the more inclusive understanding of agents as possibly collective. Roy Bhaskar, for instance, grounded his discussion in *The Possibility of Naturalism* (1979) in the classical society/person problem, and he established society and the person as possible objects of scientific investigation and thereby showed the transcendental conditions of the social and psychological sciences. Thus elements of the structure–agency debate draw on literatures that actually speak about individual subjects, whereas other parts of the literature explicitly open up for collective agents (cf. e.g. Bertramsen et al., 1991, pp. 206ff.). Authors like Dessler and Wendt (with more of less explicit justification) take the state as the (main) agent. Wendt and Duvall (1989, p. 59) clarify that

> *Agents* are conscious, purposive, and socially recognized individual or organizational actors, the practices of which intentionally and unintentionally produce and reproduce social structures. State actors, for example, are agents in this sense; they are capable of reflexively monitoring and learning from their actions; they make choices; and they are socially recognized by other state actors as subjects of international life capable of engaging in a whole range of practices.

This interpretation takes us into the third type of discussion, and further treatment is reserved for then.

Levels of analysis

The second strand is the levels of analysis debate. Inside this we have to distinguish between two possible meanings: one is *sources of explanation*, the other *scales*. Barry Buzan (1994) argues that the sources of explanation have often been taken to be the content of the levels of analysis debate. Then why 'levels'? If the issue was where to ground explanations, there would be no necessity to end up on a scale of sizes with social units ordered unilinearily according to size. Then, the sources of explanation would ultimately – for me – be the places in Figures 13.1 and 13.2: unit (domestic structure), international political structure and interaction capacity (and to Buzan: structures, process, units and interaction capacity). A source of explanation is not necessarily located solely at one level. Sources are explanatory mechanisms and they might include factors that ontologically belong at different levels but together constitute a mechanism which is the source of explanation.[6]

This argument, however, can hardly replace the issue of levels of analysis since the very term 'levels' includes the scaling connotation. Furthermore, it can be argued (Buzan, 1994) that the different factors (for instance structure, process and interaction capacity) reappear at each level. Clearly the levels question in its topological sense has not disappeared with the clarification that sources of explanation can be different from levels. Thus we have to see the second meaning of levels of analysis as still scales, e.g. global, international, regional/subsystemic, state, bureaucracy/decision-making system, individual, subindividual. Approached empirically there is an indefinite number of possible levels. Analytically one can try to establish some as primary. This should involve a study of the morphogenetic cycles whereby processes of practice establish certain foci as primary levels. Thereby we approach the issue of the duality of structure and unit (agent) as mutually constituted.

Structuration

Third is the agency–structure problem as presented in more detail elsewhere in this book (Chapters 1 and 14). On the premise that the properties of agents and of structures are both relevant, one has the choice at the level of ontology between individualism, structuralism or structurationism.

The theory of structuration as developed by Anthony Giddens offers a specific solution to the agency–structure problem. Structuration means 'The structuring of social relations across time and space, in virtue of the duality of structure' (1984, p. 376), and the duality of structure refers to 'Structure as the medium and outcome of the conduct it recursively organizes; the structural properties of social systems do not exist outside of action but are chronically implicated in its production and reproduction' (p. 374). Structure enables as well as constrains action, and structure is the outcome and the medium of action. In this way the approach overcomes the traditional dualism by positing agency and structure as two sides of the same coin. This has invited the criticism of Archer and others for central conflation, for erasing any relationship between the two, and thereby disabling a study of the effects of one on the other over time (cf. also Dessler, 1989, n. 45, on Wendt).

As argued by Carlsnaes (1992), the counter-suggestion on the other hand underestimates the importance of Giddens's insight that structure and agency are co-constituted, that there is an internal relationship between the two. A possible way out is to operate at two levels (cf. Wendt and Duvall, 1989, pp. 60ff.)[7], perhaps best phrased by Wendt (1991, p. 390): structure and agency are both '"mutually constituted" *and* "co-determined"', the former referring to the internal relationship and the latter to relationships of causality.

There is a structural dimension, in which the clue is that structure and unit are co-constituted. The issue is here *internal relations* or constitutive principles, which generate 'socially empowered and interested state agents as a function of their respective occupancy of the positions defined by those principles' (Wendt and Duvall, 1989, p. 60). Structures and the interests and powers of actors are inseparable. Especially at this level, the approach is drawn towards a focus on *states* and on the relationship between state system and state (not any unit that also appears on the scene, but those that are involved in the defining move that generates a system with a core structure). There is also a systemic dimension, where we deal with structures that organize and regulate the interactions and select certain practices (Wendt and Duvall, 1989, p. 62). The constitutive level makes certain practices *possible*, the second makes them more or less *likely*. It is at the latter level that unit behaviour can influence state structures, and structures have an impact on units.

With structure and agency, we are thus talking about different *kinds* of properties (Bhaskar, 1979, p. 145). The international system has its, and the unit has other, emergent powers. What here appears as agent is not the *subject*. The concept of agent should be freed of its anthropomorphist connotations. The agent is in a sense also a structure, a patterning of practice that stabilizes as relatively inert and self-reproducing. What is particularly agential about agents is the 'faculty or state of acting or exerting power' (Webster's definition of agency, quoted in Buzan et al., 1993, p. 103). This, however, does not distinguish agency clearly from structure, especially not in a perspective of scientific realism where structures are endowed with emergent powers. If one is to avoid thinking of agents as enlarged individuals,[8] then the focus has to be on the way agential structures are empowered with specific qualities/abilities. Some qualities that we normally think of as human reappear in the specific cosmos of diplomatics (Manning, 1962). They are generated at the inter-state level where these terms become meaningful with reference to the relevant actors/members, the states. This, however, does still not mean that *all* subject qualities have been transferred to this collective level. The quality of being human in some senses still refers only to the individual.

Model formulation

It is now possible to turn back to my emerging synthesis, to look at the landscape of IR theory and the place in it for foreign policy theory.

Hayward Alker (1992) recently reminded us of the humanistic ideals and approaches that are part of the Renaissance to which our science is so indebted, and returned to IR the ideas of the complete individual and of civic virtue. The early modern and Renaissance ideal of the many-sided individual included the achievement and exercise of virtue, which meant, amongst other things, the civic humanism of engagement in the *res publica*. Public deeds are essential parts of one's *living*, and *living* means a totality of

> describing, arguing, self-discovering, world disclosing, difference recognizing, policy proposing, state constructing, interpretation criticizing, collectivity mobilizing, historical sense making, lesson drawing,

explanation seeking, and consequence inferring activities. (Alker, 1992, p. 366)

This aligns with Walter Carlsnaes's appeals (1987; 1992; 1993a) for putting back true human agency into FPA. Carlsnaes wants us to focus on 'sentient and self-reflective actors' (1993a, p. 12), decision-makers who can be powerful enough to make a significant difference as agents of change. This involves more fully adhering to Kegley's dictum: 'We should begin with individuals, because only persons think, prefer and act' (Kegley, 1987, p. 249; Carlsnaes, 1993a, p. 11). As argued above, the place of foreign policy is not the domestic standing *vis-à-vis* the international; the place is the boundary between the domestic and the international. It is that of the statesman struggling to survive domestically as well as internationally. Where the cross-pressures meet, you find individuals that make choices.

This real human actor is then not a *state* actor and is not to be treated as such: it is not the state materialized in an individual, or an individual treated only in its state role. Human actors are ultimately to be treated as individuals who are split as all individuals but strive to achieve an impossible reconciliation (Bhaskar, 1979, p. 144; Žižek, 1990). Thus there is a sense in which choice and agency are ultimately individual, driven by the individual problematique of reconciling outer and inner existence. This point is the ultimate source of *problematizing* and thus of non-linear change. Subjectivity, though historically constituted, can be seen in the perspective of the late Foucault (1987; 1988) as the work of subjects on themselves, employing and developing the techniques of the self, in care of the self. Change can still have all kinds of economic, political, meteorological or psychological origins, but the reaction hereto is decided by humans, who are individuals and therefore ask questions as part of their *life*, of their own inner–outer reconciling operation.

This points to the uniqueness of choice, of politics. If one synthesizes the different major strands of contemporary IR theory, the model that ensues can place international structure and domestic structure as parallel limitations, as structures from where one can make negative predictions about relative impossibility (Figure 13.2). These, however, cannot be seen as causal factors eventually interacting to produce an outcome. They only construct an arena for action. Ultimately these contradictory demands are handled in political action. And the different political actions interact in inescapably unpredictable ways (Arendt, 1958). We should respect the unerasable *political* – and thus open,

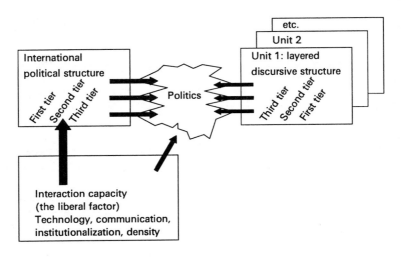

Figure 13.2   *An emerging synthesis in IR theory*

undecidable and strategic – nature of the final outcomes. This is in a theoretical perspective the meeting point of classical realism and post-structuralism.

The structures themselves are never objectively given laws of nature, but rather socially constituted. If one is to pick a metatheory for integrating these rather diverse strands of IR theory, it can hardly be one of the more rationalistic ones, but possibly a reflectivist one of a constructivist bent (Wendt, 1992a; Onuf, 1989). No structure is deep in the sense of existing independently of human practice. No change can be said to be totally impossible (which is after all what Wendt, 1992a, is arguing; see also Patomäki, 1992; Dessler, 1989, fns 55 and 87), but it seems to me rather self-limiting to construct theory mainly about what is in principle possible (the principled 0.01 per cent chance) instead of trying to construct a model which is able to do both the 99.99 per cent trick and the 0.01 per cent trick. There is a tendency with Wendt as well as with the deconstructivists to say: power political anarchy is socially constructed ('Anarchy Is What States Make of It') and therefore the mechanism of self-help is not given by nature; it surely is strongly self-reproductive, but *in principle it can change*. Well, sure it could, but it could also – much more likely – continue. That is, after all, worth analysing too. Why only study the limits to structure and not also their effects? If systems and structures have a certain inertia and even some inner logics of

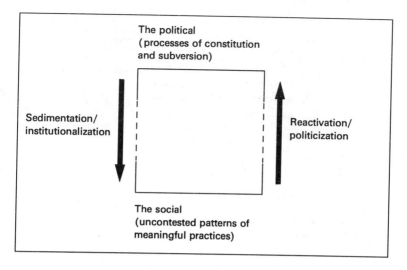

Figure 13.3 *The political and the social*

reproduction, how do we analyse that? If one attempts a kind of metatheory incorporating the insights from, for instance, Waltz, one should be able not only to do what he can't, but also what he can: explain how structures produce regularity and repetition.

Thus, it is necessary to include – as argued so often in the structure–agency debates – the duality of structure as constraining/ enabling and the actions that change/reproduce structure. One way of operationalizing this is to stress that structures are *layered*, that there are more superficial levels that can more easily be attacked by a political actor caught in an unstable or unacceptable squeeze between the meaning-giving inner structures and the international scene of political constellations. (On layered structures, see also Wendt and Duvall, 1989, pp. 63–6; and Dessler, 1989, p. 469.) If there is for the nation no 'vision of itself' available under current international conditions, the statesman will try to manipulate structures on either the domestic or the foreign side; at first those closer to the surface, and if necessary – and then with more radical effects – the deeper ones. One way of conceptualizing this could be to combine my first model (Figure 13.2) with the model (Figure 13.3) from Bertramsen et al. (1991, p. 30) of the relationship between the political and the social (derived from Laclau, 1990, pp. 33–6).[9] In this conceptualization, politicization means to problematize and articulate social structures and practices as

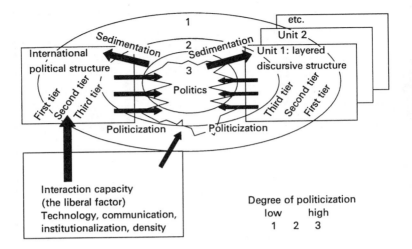

Figure 13.4   *Politics in the synthesis*

open to choice and modification. Decisions and practices on this basis then gradually sediment into becoming social in the sense of the taken for granted, the lived practices (*doxa*).

Then in the combined model (Figure 13.4) it is emphasized that the relationship between political action in the narrow sense (the central arena) and the structures is of the politicization/sedimentation form. This resolves the seeming tension of using the term 'political' in a dual sense. At one level politics refers to the inner arena where the structures never fully determine but only influence the final choices and interactions that are – in the Arendtian sense – irreducibly political. At another level, I use the Wendt argument which amounts to saying that no structures are outside the field of the socially constituted; everything is political in the sense of deriving from human actions and choices. This is, however, the same politics in the form of degrees. Everything is in principle open, but only the centre is politicized. The further one moves away from that arena, the further one sinks down into the sedimented deeper levels of structure: on the one side down through Waltz's third tier (distribution of power), through the second tier (principle of separation of units) to the first tier (anarchy/hierarchy); and on the other from the more visible elements of political structure to the deeper levels where key concepts of state and nation hold the politics of a national discursive space in a rather tight grip. The dimension of politics can therefore be represented as shading that lessens in intensity towards the edge of the figure.

In this way it seems perfectly compatible to insist on the role of agency and to take the domestic side of the model not as agency but as structure. This points to three major avenues of foreign policy analysis: (1) from international structure, (2) from domestic structure, and (3) jumping directly into the intricacies of political manoeuvring and interaction. Though structural, the first and especially the second will involve heavy doses of *Verstehen* research since the structures are grounded in and work through social practice. These insights have to be modelled in the form of schematic, layered representations of the structures in order to test whether they hold explanatory power in relation to actual political developments (cf. Wæver et al., forthcoming).

Doesn't this model deviate from the lessons of the structure–agency debate, as the figure splits structure and unit and treats them separately as framings for the action arena? No: structure (Waltzian international political structure) and agent (in the sense of the unit, e.g. state unit) are linked in two ways emulating the distinction between constitution and selection outlined by Wendt and Duvall (1989) and Wendt (1991) (cf. above):

1 The character of the units is present in the structure as the second tier of structure. Any major, principled change in the character of the units – between sameness/difference or between the basic principle of the separation of units – will be a deep structural change at the international level. There is thus a direct internal relationship.
2 Specific units can have structural effects – and vice versa. Here one has to follow the arrow from unit to politics and from politics to international structure.

Some final questions could be raised about the nature of the right-hand side of the model. Are units necessarily states? No: if for example the EC builds increasingly its own inner universe, generating its own agenda, self-limitations and drives, it has become state-like and should be added to the row of states with their inner depth levels in the upper right corner. Then states and the EC are overlapping units, not neighbours but aggregates on top of each other.

FPA inside/outside the new Europe

EC developments challenge the principle of the sovereign, territorial state. The depth of this change is difficult to see from a liberal perspective where sovereignty has always been declared dying, but from a more classical perspective where sovereignty is seen as very real in the form of organizing principle, the situation with overlapping authorities is unprecedented in the modern period and leads to the use of metaphors like neo-medievalism. Sovereignty has referred to a system where one level was always primary (if contested, a civil war had to settle the question) and operated on the basis of territorial exclusivity. In the EC world this is hardly true any more (Wæver, 1991; Ruggie, 1993). Elements of sovereignty seem to get dispersed at various levels, and civil war does not appear a relevant means for settling the ambiguity – so maybe the ambiguity will last. Maybe we are not simply on our way from one sovereignty-based order, with the national capitals as sovereign, towards another with sovereignty in Brussels; maybe we are on our way from one where sovereignty was the organizing principle to one where, at least in Europe, it is no longer. The most recent parallel is the Middle Ages, hence the increasing use of the medieval analogy.

The decomposition of formerly uniform and coherent units is also visible along another axis. In Western Europe, society presents itself more often as a self-reliant challenger for state logic. Nation and state go their separate ways, and we see for instance cases of the independent security policy of *nations* (societal security). For example protests against integration in the Maastricht ratification crisis of 1992–3 were expressions not of *reason of state* but rather of *reason of nation*. There was a clearly articulated concern about *survival* (hence security policy), but for a nation survival spells not sovereignty but identity (Wæver et al., 1993, Chapter 2). John Ruggie (1993) talks about the EC as a multiperspectival polity.

With the mediator perspective on the statesman it becomes less relevant whether the units are exclusive and territorially organized. Different sets of domestic discursive worlds are overlapping. The different insides do not relate to each other as geographically separate territories producing an exclusive and exhaustive categorization of the world. They can in principle be any kind of units that are in some way represented on the international, public arena by specific agents. Probably we should still retain some more restrictive definition in terms of *political* units, i.e. collectivities of some kind of 'we' character, that can be state, nation, tribe, city-state, empire, etc. – but not a multinational corporation, at least not until this takes a community quality? This is, however, a huge question waiting for further debate.

In relation to the empirical picture of Europe produced by the book, this commenting chapter tries to draw attention to the centrality and radicality of the multilayered character for the new Europe. It challenges basic assumptions of traditional FPA; it raises new questions, like the logic of interaction between state-like units at several levels (the motor of the neo-realist integration scenario); and it asks for the kind of foreign policy that will evolve among units that are increasingly unlike. Differentiated as to function, and maybe implicitly acknowledging suzerainty-like hierarchies, they will develop kinds of diplomatic relations and foreign policies that we best anticipate by reading about 'proto-diplomacy' in Der Derian's *On Diplomacy* (1987) and by searching even further away in time and space – among the empires of antiquity, the Chinese and Indian diplomatic traditions and many others – in Watson's *The Evolution of International Society* (1992).

This is post foreign policy, but is certainly not post-foreign.

Conclusion

It would have been easy – too easy – simply to reflect on post foreign policy analysis. Instead the 'post' perspectives (post-modernism, post-structuralism) have been presented and elaborated alongside a discussion of foreign policy analysis. The aim has been to work more carefully through the characteristics and traditions of FPA towards modes of analysis appropriate for an international system that contains elements of change that point beyond central elements of the modern state system as we have known it – and thereby to ask for an analytics able to deal with 'post foreign policy'.

The discussion in the first part showed that FPA in fact was not foreign enough, and 'post-foreign' actually did not point to a new mocking challenge but rather described FPA as it has developed: FPA is post-foreign in its attempt to domesticate foreign policy. On the contrary, we need analysis of policy towards the foreign – analysis which does not pull back towards reintegration in domestic familiarity. There is a need for PFPA in the sense of conceptualizing that which comes after foreign policy, that which replaces a system made up of states and inter-state relations.

On the way to opening up this it was first shown how the subdiscipline of FPA was actually not simply designating 'analysis of foreign policy' but a specific tradition with its implicit norms and perspectives. Then, two analyses of foreign policy were presented that would normally not qualify as FPA: neo-realist deduction and discourse analysis of national discursive spaces. Finally, these two were placed as dual structural framings of what was to remain the irreducible and unpredictable political space for action and interaction. Thus, domestic does not equal agent: the agent in its most classical sense is squeezed between domestic and international structure, and if no line of action is immediately available which is meaningful in both arenas, the result will be a more far-reaching innovative policy which attempts structural change at either side.

As a post/structuralist and de/constructivist (a post-structuralist with structuralist leanings, and a deconstructivist interested in recent attempts in constructivism) I was then tempted to suggest a synthesizing perspective which is still not a harmonizing grand theory. It retains the polyphony of the different strands of competing IR theories with their different tonalities, but it points to an emerging new *attitude* to their relationship, an attitude which is not here invented or suggested but actually can be heard from the voice of the discipline, that subject whose self-description this is all embedded in (Wæver, 1993b). The different schools move increasingly towards a division of labour instead of incommensurability and inter-paradigm debate. An overall reflection on the historical constitution of the main categories presupposes the deconstructivist understanding of the emergence of domestic/international as inside/outside and the potential – and possibly actual – transformations of these categories, not least in the new Europe.

Notes

1 Perspectives with the state located between domestic and international can also be found elsewhere, notably in neo-Weberian historical sociology such as Mann (1986), Halliday (1987) and Evans et al. (1985); in state-adjustment theory (Ikenberry, 1986; Mastanduno et al., 1989); two-level games (Putnam, 1988; Lamborn, 1991) and in parts of adaptation theory (Rosenau, 1981; Mouritzen, 1988). None of these however fully capture the Kissingerian dynamic of overall strategies related to the identity of the unit as well as the arena.

2 Walker-Waltz? Yes, Walker points constantly to the importance of the specific modern expression of political identity, the specific solution to the relationship between universalism and particularism that was achieved when merged with the distinction between inside and outside. And Waltz – or at least Waltz *à la* Ruggie (cf. Ruggie, 1986) – draws our attention to the question of principle of separation of units, which is essentially the same. In a Waltzian (but not Waltz's) perspective, the possible and relevant questions for structural change are, with increasing magnitude of importance and decreasing likelihood: change of polarity (distribution of capabilities), change in the differentiation of functions among and the principle of separation of units, and finally a change from anarchy to hierarchy.

3 Cf. Hamilton et al. (1911). The argument in this section is an extremely condensed version of that in Wæver (1993a; also appearing e.g. in Buzan and Wæver, 1992; and with less logic and more description in Buzan et al., 1990).

4 See the statements by Edwin Mortimer, Michael White, Dominique Moïsi, Pierre Hassner (who dissented), Peter Glotz, Michael Stürmer and Christoph Bertram in interviews with the Danish daily *Berlingske Tidende*, 9 May 1993, p. II:6. See also Bertram's comment in *International Herald Tribune*, 12 May 1993, p. 6.

5 Another post-structuralist reaction to the structure–agency debate is represented by Ashley (1989b, pp. 272–8). That reply rests on a somewhat problematic insistence on interpreting structurationism as based on a privileging of structure/theory over historicity and only using the other half of the dualism (the agency side) as supplement. A bit surprisingly, Ashley does not address the logocentric presuppositions involved in the structure–agency debate.

6 Ultimately the coherence of a mechanism is constituted in and by theory and thus the source for defining the different boxes is ultimately a sociology of science approach or more ambitiously a Luhmanian conception of the IR system as a reflexive and self-referential system where the study of the discipline and the study of IR cannot be kept separate. More on this in Wæver (1993b).

7 These two levels are related to the distinction between constitutive and regulative rules (cf. Dessler, 1989; Patomäki, 1992, pp. 39ff.).

8 To simply say that agents are collectivities that by dint of containing individuals include the human element of reasoning and purposive action is still to beg the question, since (the structure of) the international system also contains individuals. The units are not in any logical sense more subject-like than the international structures, but they are socially constructed *as* quasi-subjects, i.e. they are constructed as communities, as wes that are allotted collective ideas of interests, aims and fates (cf. Manning, 1962).

9 This was suggested to me by my students Claus Holm and Katrine Bom Hansen (cf. Holm and Hansen, 1992).

PART V CONCLUSION

14

In Lieu of a Conclusion: Compatibility and the Agency–Structure Issue in Foreign Policy Analysis

Walter Carlsnaes

In retrospect it can perhaps be argued that the agenda set for this volume was somewhat too ambitious, except in one respect: to bring and to hold together, over a two-year period, a number of European foreign policy scholars in order to produce a joint publication. To my knowledge the studies collected here are, in any case, the first successful effort of this kind. Thus, although this venture should in no sense be viewed as an exclusionary manifestation, our hope is that this will turn out to be but the first step in a continuous and increasingly active collaboration between European foreign policy scholars.

Given the range of issues discussed in the preceding chapters, and the fact that the new Europe on which they focus is still very much in the process of being reconstituted, there seems little point in using much space either to summarize the various contributions to the volume or to venture any substantive conclusions regarding the implications – empirical or theoretical – of these studies. In my experience concluding summations of this kind tend in any case to receive short shrift by the reader, if read at all; and this is certainly a fate which every self-respecting editor must try to side-step as adroitly as possible. Thus, in order to avoid the danger of ending this volume on a soporific note, I intend instead to use most of this chapter to discuss – and, what is more, to take issue with – two of the most fundamental questions raised by my coeditor in his introductory chapter. However, before doing so, I would like to take the opportunity of first suggesting, however briefly, some implications for future research of the substantive – as distinguished from commenting – chapters in this book.

First of all, these studies identify at least three broad *substantive* foci which, in my view, will continue to dominate the research agendas of students of European foreign policy. The first is the evolving nature and role of the state in the new Europe, a topic discussed most extensively by Michael Smith (Chapter 2). Clearly, given the fact that membership in the European Union (EU) *ipso facto* entails giving up substantial aspects of the full sovereignty – both internal and external – assumed in classical conceptions of statehood, this will continue to remain a seminal focus in the analysis of European foreign relations. Fortunately, it is also a highly topical issue in contemporary political theory and research on both sides of the Atlantic; hence this should be an area for considerable cross-fertilization between foreign policy analysts, political theorists and empirical researchers. The second topic is closely linked to the first, but has at the same time both a more specific *and* an amorphous focus: the development of the EU *qua* actor in the area of foreign and security policy (discussed above by Ben Soetendorp (Chapter 6), Frank Pfetsch (Chapter 7) and Alfred van Staden (Chapter 8)). Although the Maastricht treaty is purposely vague on the envisaged future role of the EU *vis-à-vis* the rest of the world, it is nevertheless clear that a strengthening of such a role is in the offing, and that this poses very intricate questions – both of a conceptual and of a substantive nature – for the decision-maker and foreign policy analyst alike. The third focus which, in my view, will remain crucial to an understanding of future foreign policy developments in Europe is the role of economic relations, broadly defined, in (and beyond) the new Europe (see, in particular, Chapters 4 and 5 by Roger Tooze and Gerd Junne). Here, as in the first two issue areas noted above, the need for theoretical rethinking and reconceptualization is considerable, particularly if the foreign policy scholar is to keep pace with the quickly changing economic realities of the 1990s.

In addition, I would also like to suggest three *analytical* issues which have been highlighted by the studies in this volume and which, in my view, will continue to concern the foreign policy analyst of the new Europe. The first is the need to get a firmer and more refined conceptual grip on the study of policy change itself. In their various ways Michael Smith (Chapter 2), Hans Mouritzen (Chapter 9) and Bengt Sundelius (Chapter 10) have each focused upon this topic; but I am sure that they will be the first to admit that much still remains to be done, given the implication that the study of policy change – foreign or otherwise – raises ontological and epistemological issues of the first order (Carlsnaes, 1993a). The second important analytic issue which I would like to point to here is the role of institutional analysis in the study of foreign policy change, discussed by both Thomas Risse-Kappen (Chapter 3) and Roger Tooze (Chapter 4). Although this approach has made considerable inroads into the field of international relations in general, it has yet to put a substantial mark on the study of foreign policy itself. My bet is that this situation will change rapidly, particularly in the face of the fundamental institutional changes which at present are undermining the traditional structures of the European nation-state system. Finally, although only Roger Tooze has broached this issue explicitly in the substantive chapters of the present volume, I am also willing to put a substantial wager on the increased future importance of discursive analysis in the study of European foreign policy.[1] This approach to our subject matter not only recognizes the innate inability of neo-positivism to capture the intersubjective nature of foreign policy *qua* intentional behaviour (as noted by Tooze), but also, when combined with an institutional focus, is significantly better (I would claim) at accounting for both the genesis and the evolution of institutional structures. The strength of this combination lies in its emphasis on the interactions between institutional-political practices and discursive frameworks, and hence on the reciprocal link between institutional and discursive transformations. Surely, this combination of analytic tools is precisely what is needed in order to understand and to explain a domain of reality as dynamic, variable and complicated as the current European scene, in which not only such institutions as the state are losing their traditional grip and meaning, but in which the language and concepts used in this transformation do not merely reflect piecemeal systemic and policy changes (as most neo-positivists would think) but are themselves, in the most fundamental sense, constitutive of such changes.

This adumbration of a linkage between institutional structures and intersubjective meaning provides a suitable point for passing on to a discussion (in the rest of this chapter) of the *agency–structure problem* and its implications for foreign policy analysis, suggested by my coeditor, Steve Smith, to constitute a crucial factor complicating – perhaps beyond redemption – the *compatibility* of the existing approaches to the study of foreign policy (some of which are exemplified in the present volume). As he has indicated in his introductory chapter, the two of us do not quite agree on either the nature or the implications of this problem for foreign policy analysis, even though both of us regard its resolution as absolutely fundamental to the future of such scholarship.

Although the agency–structure debate has been blessed with a most distinguished pedigree, it continues to remain a seemingly interminable dispute. Historically, it has signified a series of arguments typically defined in terms of dichotomies such as individual and society, action and structure, actor and system, part and whole, unit and system, individualism and holism, micro and macro, voluntarism and determinism, subjectivism and objectivism, and so forth, all of which are still highly topical today. These antinomies have been pursued within two essentially different types of discourses, the one – stretching back to the late medieval period – implicating classical questions of political philosophy, and the other involving fundamental issues within the philosophy of social science (and hence of a more recent vintage). Without wishing in any way to downgrade questions of the former type, I will here concentrate on the latter.

Within this metatheoretical debate there is, however, also a further division, involving what are essentially two different sets of issues, terminologies and intellectual traditions. The first debate revolves around the banner of the micro–macro linkage, and is currently most prominently pursued by American social theorists (Ritzer, 1990). The second – and more typically European – debate is about how, in the explanation of social behaviour, agency (or actor) and structure are to be related to each other (Ritzer, 1993). An essential difference between the two is that whereas the first can be subsumed under the broader rubric of the levels of analysis problem, the second is primarily concerned with the relationship between *purposive (or intentional) behaviour* – the defining characteristic of agency – and *social structures* on any level of social analysis. Although there is a substantial overlap between these two traditions in contemporary social theory, it is the agency–structure issue in this latter and more circumscribed sense that I will focus on in the discussion below.

The reason why these disputes matter in the present context is my coeditor's strong suspicion that in so far as accounts stressing agency cannot be combined with accounts stressing structure, the agency–structure debate is essentially unresolvable. Clearly, if this is indeed the case, its consequences for foreign policy analysis – as for the social sciences in general – are of the first order. In the face of this, I am perhaps not alone in experiencing the gut reaction that rather than forthwith resigning myself to an acceptance of this preliminary verdict, I must first give my coeditor's argumentation a good run for its money.

In barest outline, the argument in support of his diagnosis is in two steps. First of all, either social science can be pursued from the inside, in the form of accounts of human social behaviour in terms of the actors' intentions and definitions of the situation; or, alternatively, it can be grounded in outside accounts based on the model of the natural sciences, treating the human realm as part of nature and hence as *causally* rather than *intentionally* determined. As Steve Smith and Martin Hollis have argued in their widely acclaimed introduction to international relations theory, there are always two sorts of story to tell: the insider's, which is quintessentially that of understanding, and the outsider's, taking the form of explanations couched in the naturalistic language of external, causally determinative factors (Hollis and Smith, 1990).

Secondly, there is no way of combining these accounts. Or, to use the culinary metaphor which Smith and Hollis have launched in a recent debate with Alexander Wendt, the 'agent–structure problem is not settled by deciding what proportions to put into the blender' (Hollis and Smith, 1991, p. 393). Three fundamental types of reasons are posited in support of this claim. The first is *methodological*, and refers to the impossibility of finding a 'secure place from which to assess the relative potencies of the accounts', since each contains its own criteria of what is to count as evidence. The second argument is *epistemological*, implicating the question of what is to be regarded as knowledge in each type of account. Since inside accounts refer to agents' intentions and definitions of the situation, whereas outside accounts eschew all such reference to agential self-understanding in favour of strictly causal explanations of behaviour, it is simply not possible to blend what essentially are two mutually exclusive epistemologies. The third type of reasoning is *ontological*, referring to the question of whether social scientists give primacy to actors or to structures in their assumptions of how society is constituted. Agency accounts give such primacy to individuals (society or social systems being by-products of interactions between individuals), while structural accounts give it to social structures (within which it is the destiny of individuals to occupy roles not of their own provision).

How persuasive are these claims? Starting with the ontological argument, let me immediately admit that I am rather perplexed by why this choice has to be made in the first place. Undoubtedly, this response is due to a somewhat different reading of the agency–structure debate compared with that paraphrased above. As I have argued elsewhere, this literature not so much suggests that agency and structure are inextricably involved in an *ontological* zero-sum relationship as reflects an increasingly general insight – amongst a range of social theorists on both sides of the Atlantic – that human agents and social structures are in a fundamental sense dynamically interrelated *empirical* entities, and hence that we cannot account fully for the one without invoking the other (Carlsnaes, 1992). The problem is that although there exists a strong consensus regarding the need to synthesize agential and structural aspects when theorizing about social behaviour (Ritzer, 1993), we continue to 'lack a self-evident way to conceptualize these entities and their relationships' (Wendt, 1987, p. 338). The implication of this is *not* that the ontological issue is therefore unimportant to a resolution of the problem discussed here, since it is to a large extent precisely this factor which continues to sustain its Janus-faced character, presenting an action side to some and a structure side to others. However, it does imply that to insist on the necessity of making the ontological choice suggested above is to beg the very question lying at the centre of the problematique. It certainly precludes by fiat any serious examination of, for example, the claim that although social structures both constrain and enable the actions of individuals, they are at the same time the outcome (intended or not) of such purposive behaviour. Assuming, for the sake of argument, that this is *prima facie* a plausible view, how could we ever *know* what is ontologically – as distinguished from empirically – prior in a dynamic, reciprocal relationship of this kind? And furthermore: why should we bother to find this out?

This admission of the issue of knowledge into the discussion leads us straight to the epistemological argument against the possibility of resolving our problem. The question here concerns the feasibility of combining the two mutually exclusive epistemologies on which inside and outside accounts are based. Two lines of counter-argumentation are possible. The first is to call into question the epistemological argument itself; and the second is to focus on its relevance for the agency–structure debate as a whole. I shall very briefly attempt to do both, although at least the first deserves much more attention than it can be afforded here.

With regard to the epistemological argument itself, I am strongly inclined towards the view of those, like Wendt in his discussion of the Hollis and Smith volume, who stoutly resist being enamoured by the unadulterated either/or character of the two-stories view so eloquently defended in it. This scepticism can take various forms, for example in the naturalist claim that intentional behaviour is explicable in terms of both interpretative analysis *and* causal determination (Carlsnaes, 1987, pp. 32–8; Mäki, 1991), or – using Wendt's narrower argument – that 'at least on a scientific realist conception of science (which Smith endorses), thinking about world politics from the perspective of actors – from the "inside" – need not imply the abandonment of scientific or "explanatory" inquiry and its methodological entailments' (Wendt, 1991, p. 391; see also Shapiro and Wendt, 1992). However, Hollis and Smith have, sooth to say, not been persuaded by criticisms of this kind; but neither have they – at least in their response to Wendt – opted to argue for the rejection *in toto* of scientific realism and its implications for social theory (Hollis and Smith, 1991). Hence, in so far as the jury still appears to be out in regard to this issue, my suggestion is that there is at present no compelling reason to accept as final the verdict of the prosecution.

Nor, would I further argue, is there any compelling need even to wait for the return of this particular jury, since the relevance to the agency–structure debate of this argument – even if it were entirely persuasive as such – is by no means transparent. The question here is the following: why do we need to combine accounts stressing two mutually exclusive epistemologies in order to resolve the agency–structure problem? The logic of my coeditor is certainly most impeccable: two mutually exclusive epistemologies do not blend well. But do we really have to put two *accounts* – including their rival epistemologies – into the blender? If, instead, we define the agency–structure issue as a question not of combining two accounts but rather of the need for a *single integrative conceptual framework* in terms of which the *empirical interaction* of agential and structural factors in social behaviour can be properly analysed, then we can escape the implications of this harsh logic. What I am suggesting here, in other words, are two things: that given the terms of my coeditor's definition of the problem, it is indeed unresolvable, by definition; but that we do not have to accept these terms if we conceptualize the problem as having its roots essentially in the empirical rather than the philosophical domain. Our stories – of whatever kind – are always *about* something; and it is this something *qua* the agency–structure linkage which, as argued above, is the focus of analysis in this debate. In short, if our stories do not mix well, so much the worse for our stories.

This brings me, finally, to the methodological argument against the view that the agency–structure problem may have a solution. My coeditor's line of reasoning here is that since there is no position external to each account from which to assess their relative weight, it is impossible to know how much of each to put into the blender. Since each type of account has its own criteria for selecting evidence, it 'is simply not possible to say that empirical behaviour is in this instance 75 per cent agency and 25 per cent structure'. Here, once again, the argument is wholly in terms of the incompatibility of second-level *accounts* rather than in terms of the first-level *social domain* (despite the reference to empirical

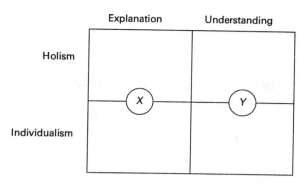

Figure 14.1   *Types of social theory*

behaviour in the passage quoted above). Hence, without taking issue with the claim that all data are ineluctably theory-laden (which underlies the above view, but the implications of which are not entirely self-evident), the force of this argument can nevertheless be questioned for the same reason that we questioned the epistemological argument above. Furthermore, it seems once again to beg the very question which an integrative framework for analysing the agency–structure linkage is intended to answer: the relative weight of agential and structural factors in any given concrete instance of social behaviour (such as the foreign policy of a state). In other words, I would here like to suggest that it is unfruitful not only to think in terms of combining two *accounts*, but also to assume that the question is one of putting predetermined proportions of our two basic ingredients into the pulverizing milieu of a high-speed *blender*. Clearly, it is possible to accept the argument that the two do not *blend* well without *pari passu* having to accept the conclusion that therefore something edible containing both cannot ever be cooked as *one* dish. If we must import our images from the kitchen, I would thus like to suggest that a more appropriate metaphor in this context would be that of a layer cake or – since my coeditor has already appropriated it for a different purpose – that of a layered casserole, a gastronomic invention much favoured in American homes.

However, before giving my own favourite recipe for such a dish, let me first add one additional comment to the above discussion. If, as has been suggested above, the agency–structure debate is not really about inside or outside accounts, what is it about? Here I would like to refer the reader to Figure 14.1, which is also the very first figure in the Hollis and Smith volume referred to above. They have explained it as follows:

> We have represented the holism–individualism range on the vertical axis and the explaining–understanding contrast on the horizontal, with the actors in their social capacities located on the dividing line, *where, one might say, structure meets action.* X is an actor in the spirit of the scientific tradition, Y the counterpart in the spirit of the interpretative tradition. *For both there is a pull in two directions.* On the one hand, X and Y are human beings with beliefs and aims, and we are interested in what is in their heads. On the other hand, their situation is structured, and . . . we are interested in the social constraints on their actions. (Hollis and Smith, 1990, pp. 4–5; my italics)

The italicized passages are, in my view, the key to the issue discussed here. Assuming that X and Y are actors whose actions we would like to account for, the debate (as I understand it) is both about the relative weight to be given to structures and actions in such an account, as well as about the relationship between these factors themselves. Furthermore, the figure – and the text describing it – also makes it clear that since the agency–structure debate in the sense represented here can occur within *both* explanation and understanding types of discourse, it cannot at the same time be a debate *about* the respective merits of the latter. These therefore have to be argued in terms of other considerations (which Hollis and Smith do, with great insight), although such arguments may, or course, include references to the respective consequences – supportive or not – which each type of account has for the agency–structure problem. In short, this figure indicates that given the *two* types of powerful intellectual traditions in the social sciences explicated in the Hollis and Smith book, the agency–structure problem has *two* variants – one for explanatory approaches, another for understanding approaches. One can thus, in principle at least, resolve the problem within the framework of the one tradition without resolving it for the other. This, of course, is not satisfactory if the ultimate aim is twofold: to integrate the explanatory and understanding traditions within social science *as well as* to resolve the agency–structure problem *tout court*.

This brings us back to my own favourite recipe, dubbed above as the casserole approach to our subject matter. Since I have discussed it in some detail elsewhere (Carlsnaes, 1992), only a very brief résumé – which the reader already acquainted with it may in good conscience skip – will be provided here. Before that, however, it should be made clear what this is intended to be a recipe *of*, i.e. the nature of the explanandum must first be specified. My premise here is that if and when we are speaking about foreign policy, we are dealing with *intentional behaviour* in some form or other; and hence that foreign policy belongs to the class of actions rather than to outputs in a broader sense. This ontological premise has fundamental epistemological implications with regard to the type of explanans which can be utilized in subsequent inquiry. The latter (and here I return to my recipe) can be grouped into three analytically distinct but conceptually linked layers of explanation.

The first can be termed the *intentional* dimension, invoking the thoroughly purposive character of all foreign policy behaviour. Before we can say anything else about a specific action, we have to establish the specific meaning signified by it in the particular context in which it occurs. However, we may also wish to go one step further, choosing to deepen such an essentially descriptive analysis by providing an analysis in which the factors characterizing the intentional dimension are themselves explained in terms of a question which the intentional dimension itself is inherently unable to accommodate, namely *why* the given choices and preferences defining the intentional factor are implicated in the first place. The distinction between these two levels can also be described in terms of an 'in order to' and a 'because of' – a teleological as opposed to a causal – dimension, where the former refers to the intentional sphere while the latter constitutes the link between this intention and *the having of it*, that is how a particular intention has become a particular actor's intention. I have chosen to call this second level the *dispositional* dimension of explanation, since it refers to all the factors disposing – psychologically or cognitively – an actor towards one type of purposive behaviour rather than towards another.

The third layer is based on the assumption that in so far as intentional behaviour is never pursued outside the crucible of structural determination, factors of the latter kind must always be able to figure in our accounts of the former. Thus, while I agree with my coeditor that theories premised on the rock-bottom assumptions of understanding and explanation are incompatible (at least as defined by him), I find it difficult to have to draw from this the conclusion that an interpretative account therefore cannot incorporate thoroughly *structural* factors as *causal* explanans. In other words, one can agree that as *accounts* – in the form, for example, of micro or macro *theories* – the two are incompatible, without having to agree that therefore an *integrative framework* for theorizing about the relationship between micro and macro *levels of social analysis* – for example, between personality and social structure – is beyond the pale of social science (Ritzer, 1990, p. 352). Such a link between structure and agency can be conceived as either of the constraining or of the enabling kind, causally affecting policy actions via its effects on the dispositional characteristics of the agents of policy. This implies that structural factors – such as institutions, bureaucracies, international regimes, the state of the economy, geopolitical emplacement, etc. – are *cognitively* mediated by the actors in question rather than affecting policy actions directly.

The above has been an attempt to indicate one way of integrating structural and agential factors into a single explanatory framework by essentially linking levels of social analysis in such a way that it becomes feasible for the researcher – by means of a logical, step-by-step procedure – to render increasingly exhaustive (or deeper) explanations of policy actions. However, it does not in itself contain a solution to the agency–structure problem, since the relationship between social structures and human agency is conceived not as reciprocal and dynamic but as entirely uni-directional, in so far as the former is assumed to affect the latter but not vice versa. In other words, the type of approach discussed here is essentially static, and as such it can serve to analyse any given single policy action but not the dynamic notion that decision-makers *qua* state agents not only make choices in response to particular issues or problems facing them but also are intimately involved in the collective production and reproduction of social structures, and that the latter process has far-reaching conse-quences – both of a constraining and of an enabling kind – for their subsequent actions.

One way of conceptualizing the above is to think in terms of the notion that structural factors – such as institutions – both pre-date and post-date any action or set of actions affecting them; and that a course of action – such as the pursuit of a policy – both pre-dates and post-dates the structural factors conditioning it (Carlsnaes, 1992, pp. 256–68). This view is based on the morpho-genetic notion of a continuous cycle of action–structure inter-actions, a process which not only serves to provide continuity and change to social systems, but also can be penetrated analytically as a consequence of its essentially *sequential* thrust in societal transformation. It thus indicates the interplay over time, in the form of developmental patterns, which exists between structure and action in any given foreign policy system.

In this perspective, actions thus not only are causally affected *by* structures, but in turn – in terms of both intended and unintended outcomes – subsequently affect them, and so forth, indicating the mutually dynamic relationship between the two over time as well as the inherently constraining *and* enabling character of the structural domain. In other words, to explain fully a policy action at a certain point in time, this conceptualization indicates the necessity of considering not only *its* underlying causal structures, but also previous actions and both the structural effects *and* structural antecedents of the latter.

The beauty of this type of solution to the problem discussed here is at least twofold. First of all, it provides both a *comprehensive* and a *manageable conceptual framework* for examining foreign policy change, showing how all relevant structural and agential factors can be analysed *qua* causally interrelated phenomena. Furthermore, since it does this in terms of three analytically distinct but logically related dimensions, it facilitates both a step-by-step and a bracketed conceptualization and examination of these causal mechanisms. For example, it can be used to examine the radical changes which have recently occurred in Swedish foreign policy in terms of a cyclical analysis involving all three dimensions over an extensive period (this would, so to speak, give us the full story); or it may, for example, focus exclusively on how recent structural changes in the international environment have causally affected the values and perceptions of current decision-makers (thus leaving aside – or bracketing – queries such as how these changes have manifested themselves in actual policy, or why they have had such effects in the current situation but not previously). It must immediately be emphasized, however, that both of these aspects refer to conceptual rather than to theoretical characteristics. In short, it is a framework and not a theory; and as such it can be used to penetrate causal mechanisms in a common-sense fashion without any substantive theoretical implications of this or that kind.

However, and this is the second advantage which I would like to stress, *theoretical claims* can be tendered on the conceptual foundation provided by this framework, e.g. in the form of theoretical elaborations linking particular types of bureaucratic organizations with specific types of dispositional characteristics of decision-makers, or how individuals can purposively create or modify regimes in order to affect processes of domestic or international preference formation. Thus, to take one example, although the framework itself is neutral with regard to how to explain regional integration, it can be used to provide a common frame of reference for explanations of a neo-functionalist, an intergovernmental institutionalist and a federalist kind (Keohane and Hoffmann, 1991). It can do this because it is based on the scientific realist notion that in so far as causal mechanisms in society can be both objective or subjective, the social scientist cannot afford to limit himself or herself to either outside or inside stories (see Shapiro and Wendt, 1992).

The above has been an attempt, in regard to the question of whether the relationship between agents and structures in social theory fundamentally hinders analytical compatibility between various approaches in the analysis of foreign policy, to end this book on a somewhat more hopeful note than the one sounded (albeit cheerfully) by my coeditor in his introduction. These two different views on such compatibility – and on the role of conceptual frameworks more generally – perhaps also reflect a characteristic difference, recently noted by one of our contributors, between a British and a Scandinavian approach to foreign policy analysis (Wæver, 1990b, pp. 153–4).[2] The former, Ole Wæver thus surmises, is typified not only by the finite ambition of aiming solely for middle-range theory but also by

> an acceptance – or even a celebration – of the fact that one cannot combine these into a general theory (at least not in a fully harmonious way). The theories cannot be combined because each defines some factors in a particular way – including factors that are at the core of other 'middle range theories'. They appropriate material from each other. You choose to structure a study *around* one of these 'places' and its accompanying theory, and then you try to explain as much as possible of 'foreign policy'. (Wæver, 1990b, p. 153)

In contrast, he suggests, there seems to be emerging a Scandinavian approach to foreign policy analysis which, while theoretically more ambitious, does not follow mainstream American comparative foreign policy analysis (or, one should perhaps add, what is left of it) by trying to achieve 'large' explanations built on 'strong' theory. The aim, rather, is to propose 'weak' theory, but theory which covers larger chunks of reality than middle-range approaches focusing exclusively on the role, for instance, of bureaucracy, belief systems or decision-making in foreign policy. It is, in short, theoretically more encompassing and integrative in scope than the type of analysis characterized above as British; but this does not mean that the logic underlying its theoretical aims is that of wanting to explain *all* cases by a simple model and with the aid of a limited number of factors (characteristic, in Wæver's view, of the American – or neo-positivistic – approach).

If we accept that this is – at least in some sense – an apposite classification of some current schools in foreign policy analysis, then it seems to me that whereas the divide between, on the one hand, either the British or the Scandinavian and, on the other, the American approaches is fundamental and perhaps even insuperable, this is certainly not the case with respect to the differences between the first two. If this creative tension-cum-affinity characterizes European scholars of foreign policy more generally as well (which seems indeed to be the case if the three meetings preceding the publication of this volume are anything to go by), it most certainly invites a continuation and expansion of the kind of collaboration initiated by this group.

Note

1 However, see Ole Wæver's discussion (Chapter 13), which *inter alia* contains a plea for precisely this type of approach. I did not have the opportunity to read it before completing my own chapter.

2 See also Wæver's discussion (Chapter 13) especially pp. 249–52.

Bibliography

Alker, H. (1992). The Humanistic Moment in International Studies: Reflections on Machiavelli and las Casas. *International Studies Quarterly*, 36(4), 347–71.

Allison, G. (1971). *Essence of Decision*. Boston: Little Brown.

Amstrup, N. (1976). The Perennial Problem of Small States: A Survey of Research Efforts. *Cooperation and Conflict*, 11, 163–82.

Andrén, N. (1991). On the Meaning and Uses of Neutrality. *Cooperation and Conflict*, 26(2), 67–83.

Archer, M. (1985). Structuration versus Morphogenesis. In S. N. Eisenstadt and H. J. Helle (eds), *Macro-Sociological Theory: Perspectives on Sociological Theory, Vol. 1*. Newbury Park, CA: Sage.

Arendt, H. (1958). *The Human Condition*. Chicago: University of Chicago Press.

Aron, R. (1964). *Peace and War: A Theory of International Relations*. London: Weidenfeld and Nicholson.

Ashley, R. K. (1987). The Geopolitics of Geopolitical Space: Towards a Critical Social Theory of International Politics. *Alternatives*, 12(4), 403–34.

Ashley, R. K. (1989a). Imposing International Purpose: Notes on a Problematique of Governance. In E.-O. Czempiel and J. N. Rosenau (eds), *Global Changes and Theoretical Challenges*. Lexington: Lexington Books.

Ashley, R. K. (1989b). Living on Border Lines: Man, Poststructuralism and War. In J. Der Derian and M. J. Shapiro (eds), *International/Intertextual Relations*. Lexington: Lexington Books.

Bacchi, C. L. (1990). *Same Difference*. London: Unwin Hyman.

Baehr, P. (1975). Small States: A Tool for Analysis? *World Politics*, 27, 457–65.

Baker Fox, A. (1959). *The Power of Small States. Diplomacy in World War II*. Chicago: University of Chicago Press.

Banks, M. (1984). The Evolution of International Relations Theory. In M. Banks (ed.), *Conflict in World Society*. Brighton: Wheatsheaf Books.

Barany, Z. D., and Reisch, A. (1990). Hungary: Withdrawal of all Soviet Troops by End of 1990 Demanded. *Report on Eastern Europe*, 1(6), 22–5.

Bassnett, S. (1992). Crossing Cultural Boundaries: Or How I Became an Expert on East European Women Overnight. *Women's Studies International Forum*, 15(1), 11–16.

Benedick, R. E. (1991). *Ozone Diplomacy. New Directions in Safeguarding the Planet*. Cambridge, MA: Harvard University Press.

Bertramsen, R., Thomsen, J. P., and Torfing, J. (1991). *State, Economy and Society*. London: Unwin Hyman.

Beyer, M. (1992). The Situation of East German Women in Postunification Germany. *Women's Studies International Forum*, 15(1), 111–14.

Bhaskar, R. (1979). *The Possibility of Naturalism: A Philosophical Critique of the Contemporary Human Sciences*. Brighton: Harvester.

Blair, B., and Gottfried, K. (eds) (1988). *Crisis Stability and Nuclear War*. New York: Oxford University Press.

Bourdieu, P. (1977). *Outline of a Theory of Practice*. Cambridge: Cambridge University Press.

Brewer, A. (1990). *Marxist Theories of Imperialism* (2nd edn). London: Routledge.

Bull, H. (1977). *The Anarchical Society: A Study of Order in World Politics*. London: Macmillan.

Bull, H. (1979). The State's Positive Role in World Affairs. *Daedalus*, 108(4), 111–23.

Buteux, P. (1983). *The Politics of Nuclear Consultation in NATO: 1965–1980*. Cambridge: Cambridge University Press.

Buzan, B. (1991). *People, States and Fear: An Agenda for International Security Studies in the Post-Cold-War Era* (2nd rev. edn). Hemel Hempstead: Harvester Wheatsheaf.

Buzan, B. (1994). The Level of Analysis Problem in International Relations Reconsidered. In K. Booth and S. Smith (eds), *International Political Theory Today*. London: Polity Press.

Buzan, B., and Wæver, O. (1992). Framing Nordic Security: Scenarios for European Security in the 1990s and Beyond. In J. Øberg (ed.). *Nordic Security in the 1990s: Options in the Changing Europe*. London: Pinter.

Buzan, B., Little, R., and Jones, C. (1993). *The Logic of Anarchy: Neorealism to Structural Realism*. New York: Columbia University Press.

Buzan, B., Kelstrup, M., Lemaitre, P., Tromer, E., and Wæver, O. (1990). *The European Security Order Recast: Scenarios for the Post-Cold-War Era*. London: Pinter.

Buzan, B., and Rizvi, G., et al. (1986). *South Asian Insecurity and the Great Powers*. London: Macmillan.

Cadava, E., Connor, P., and Nancy, J.-L. (eds) (1991). *Who Comes after the Subject?* New York: Routledge.

Calleo, D. P. (1987). *Beyond American Hegemony: The Future of the Western Alliance*. Brighton: Wheatsheaf.

Campbell, D. (1992). *Writing Security: United States Foreign Policy and the Politics of Identity*. Manchester: Manchester University Press.

Carlsnaes, W. (1987). *Ideology and Foreign Policy: Problems of Comparative Conceptualization*. Oxford: Basil Blackwell.

Carlsnaes, W. (1992). The Agency–Structure Problem in Foreign Policy Analysis. *International Studies Quarterly*, 36(3), 245–70.

Carlsnaes, W. (1993a). On Analysing the Dynamics of Foreign Policy Change: A Critique and Reconceptualisation. *Cooperation and Conflict*, 28(1), 5–30.

Carlsnaes, W. (1993b). Sweden Facing the New Europe: Whither Neutrality? *European Security*, 2(1), 71–89.

Chernoff, F. (1992). Cooperation in the Western Alliance – Why States Work Together. Unpublished manuscript, Colgate University.

Christensen, T., and Snyder, J. (1990). Chain Gangs and Passed Bucks: Predicting Alliance Patterns in Multipolarity. *International Organization*, 44(2), 137–68.

Christmas-Møller, W. (1983). Some Thoughts on the Scientific Applicability of the Small State Concept: A Research History and a Discussion. In O. Höll (ed.), *Small States in Europe and Dependence*. Vienna: Braumüller.

Clark, C., and Welch, S. (1972). Western European Trade as a Measure of Integration: Untangling the Interpretations. *Journal of Conflict Resolution*, 16, 363–82.

Clark, M., and Serfaty, S. (eds) (1991). *New Thinking and Old Realities: America, Europe, and Russia.* Washington, DC: Seven Locks Press.

Clarke, D. L. (1990a). Soviet Experts Again Propose Strengthening Warsaw Pact's Political Role. *Report on Eastern Europe*, 1(20), 39–42.

Clarke, D. L. (1990b). Warsaw Pact: The Transformation Begins. *Report on Eastern Europe*, 1(25), 34–7.

Clarke, D. L. (1990c). Soviets Resume Troop Withdrawal from East Germany. *Report on Eastern Europe*, 1(36), 33–6.

Clarke, M., and White, B. (eds) (1989). *Understanding Foreign Policy: An Introduction to Foreign Policy Analysis.* Aldershot: Edward Elgar/Gower.

Cohen, B. C., and Harris, S. A. (1975). Foreign Policy. In F. I. Greenstein and N. Polsby (eds), *Handbook of Political Science*, vol. 6. Reading, MA: Addison-Wesley.

Cohen, S. D. (1981). *The Making of United States International Economic Policy.* New York: Praeger.

Cook, D. (1989). *Forging the Atlantic Alliance: NATO 1945–1950.* New York: Arbor House/William Morrow.

Corrin, C. (ed.) (1992). *Superwoman and the Double Burden.* London: Scarlet Press.

Cox, R. W. (1981). Social Forces, States and World Order: Beyond International Relations Theory. *Millennium*, 10(2), 126–55.

Cox, R. W. (1983). Gramsci, Hegemony and International Relations: An Essay in Method. *Millennium*, 12(2), 162–75.

Cox, R. W. (1986). States, Social Forces and World Order: Beyond International Relations Theory. In R. Keohane (ed.), *Neorealism and its Critics.* New York: Columbia University Press.

Cox, R. W. (1987). *Production, Power and World Order.* New York: Columbia University Press.

Cox, R. W. (1989). Production, the State and Change in World Order. In E.-O. Czempiel and J. N. Rosenau (eds), *Global Changes and Theoretical Challenges.* Lexington, MA: Lexington Books.

Cox, R. W. (1992). Multilateralism and World Order. *Review of International Studies*, 18(2), 161–80.

Czempiel, E.-O. (1984). Friedenspolitik im europäischen Ost–West Konflikt. In F. Böckle and G. Krell (eds), *Politik und Ethik der Abschreckung.* Mainz-München: Grünewald-Kaiser.

Czempiel, E.-O. (1986). *Friedensstrategien.* Paderborn: Schöningh.

Daalder, I. (1991). *The Nature and Practice of Flexible Response. NATO Strategy and Theatre Nuclear Forces since 1967.* New York: Columbia University Press.

Dekker, W. (1984). Europe 1990. Speech given at the Centre for European Policy Studies in Brussels, 13 November 1984.

Delors, J. (1991). European Integration and Security. *Survival*, XXXIII(2), 99–109.

DePorte, A. (1986). *Europe between the Superpowers* (2nd edn). New Haven: Yale University Press.

Der Derian, J. (1987). *On Diplomacy: A Genealogy of Western Estrangement.* Oxford: Basil Blackwell.

Der Derian, J., and Shapiro, M. (eds) (1989). *International/Intertextual Relations.* Lexington: Lexington Books.

Derrida, J. (1991). Interview by Jean-Luc Ferry: 'Eating Well', or the Calculation of the Subject. In E. Cadava, P. Connor, and J.-L. Nancy (eds), *Who Comes after the Subject?* New York: Routledge.

Dessler, D. (1989). What's at Stake in the Agency–Structure Debate? *International Organization*, 43(3), 441–73.

Destler, I. M. (1980). *Making Foreign Economic Policy*. Washington, DC: Brookings.

Destler, I. M., and Odell, J. S. (1987). *Anti-Protection: Changing Forces in U.S. Trade Politics*. Washington, DC: Institute for International Economics.

Deudney, D., and Ikenberry, G. J. (1991a). The International Sources of Soviet Change. *International Security*, 16(3), 74–118.

Deudney, D., and Ikenberry, G. J. (1991b). Soviet Reform and the End of the Cold War: Explaining Large-Scale Historical Change. *Review of International Studies*, 17(3), 225–51.

Deutsch, K. W. (1976). *Die Schweiz als ein paradigmatischer Fall politischer Integration*. Bern: Paul Haupt.

Deutsch, K. W., and Singer, J. D. (1964). Multipolar Power Systems and International Stability. *World Politics*, 16, 390–406.

Deutsch, K. W., et al. (1957). *Political Community and the North Atlantic Area. International Organization in the Light of Historical Experience*. Princeton: Princeton University Press.

Dicken, P. (1992). *Global Shift: The Internationalisation of Economic Activity* (2nd edn). London: Paul Chapman.

Doty, R. (1993). 'Race' in International Relations: Is It Relevant and Can We Study It? Paper presented at the International Studies Association Conference in Acapulco, March 1993.

Dougherty, J. N., and Pfaltzgraff, Robert L. Jr (1981). *Contending Theories of International Relations: A Comprehensive Survey* (2nd edn). New York: Harper and Row.

Downs, G. W., and Rocke, D. M. (1987). Tacit Bargaining and Arms Control. *World Politics*, 39(3), 297–325.

Downs, G. W., et al. (1986). Arms Races and Cooperation. In K. Oye (ed.), *Cooperation Under Anarchy*. Princeton: Princeton University Press.

Doyle, M. (1986). Liberalism and World Politics. *American Political Science Review*. 80(4), 1151–69.

Duchen, C. (1992). Understanding the European Community: A Glossary of Terms. *Women's Studies International Forum*, 15(1), 17–20.

Dunn, J. (ed.) (1990). *The Economic Limits to Modern Politics*. Cambridge: Cambridge University Press.

Dunning, J. H., and Robson, P. (1988). Multinational Corporate Integration and Regional Economic Integration. In J. H. Dunning and P. Robson (eds), *Multinationals and the European Community*. Oxford: Basil Blackwell.

East, M. A. (1969). *Stratification and International Politics: An Empirical Study Employing the International Systems Approach*. PhD dissertation, Princeton University.

East, M. A. (1973). Foreign Policy Making in Small States. *Policy Sciences*, 4, 491–508.

East, M. A. (1978). National Attributes and Foreign Policy. In M. A. East et al. (eds), *Why Nations Act*. Beverly Hills: Sage.

East, M. A. (1981). The Organizational Impact of Interdependence on Foreign Policy-Making: The Case of Norway. In P. McGowan (ed.), *Sage International Yearbook of Foreign Policy Studies*. Beverly Hills: Sage.

Economist (1990). Survey of International Financial Markets. *The Economist*, 21 July, p. 7.

Economist (1992). Survey of the World Economy: Fear of Finance. *The Economist*, 19 September.

Einhorn, B. (1991). Where Have All the Women Gone? Women and the Women's Movement in East Central Europe. *Feminist Review*, 39, 16–36.

Einhorn, B. (1993a). Polish Backlash. *Everywoman*, April 1993, p. 20.

Einhorn, B. (1993b). *Cinderella Goes to Market: Citizenship, Gender and Women's Movements in East Central Europe*. London: Verso.

Enloe, C. (1989). *Bananas, Beaches and Bases*. London: Pandora.

Enloe, C. (1993). *The Morning After: Sexual Politics at the End of the Cold War*. California: University of California Press.

Evans, P. B., Rueschemeyer, D., and Skocpol, T. (eds) (1985). *Bringing the State Back In*. Cambridge: Cambridge University Press.

Foucault, M. (1972). *The Archeology of Knowledge* (1969). New York: Pantheon Books.

Foucault, M. (1987). *The Use of Pleasure: The History of Sexuality, Vol. 2*. London: Penguin.

Foucault, M. (1988). *The Care of the Self: The History of Sexuality, Vol. 3*. New York: Vintage.

Gaddis, J. L. (1987). *The Long Peace*. New York: Oxford University Press.

Gaddis, J. L. (1991). Toward the Post-Cold-War World. *Foreign Affairs*, 70 (spring), 102–22.

Galtung, J. (1969). *Theory and Methods of Social Research* (2nd rev. edn). Oslo: Universitetsforlaget.

Gambles, I. (1991). *European Security Integration in the 1990s*. Chaillot Papers 3. Institute for Security Studies, Western European Union.

Garthoff, R. (1985). *Détente and Confrontation*. Washington, DC: Brookings.

George, A. (1980). Domestic Constraints on Regime Change in United States Foreign Policy: The Need for Policy Legitimacy. In O. Holsti, R. Siverson, and A. George (eds), *Change in the International System*. Boulder: Westview Press.

George, S. (1992). Managing the Global House: Redefining Economics. In C. Hartman and P. Vilanova (eds), *Paradigm Lost – The Post Cold War Era*. London: Pluto Press.

Giddens, A. (1984). *The Constitution of Society: Outline of the Theory of Structuration*. Cambridge: Polity Press.

Gilpin, R. (1975). *U.S. Power and the Multinational Corporations. The Political Economy of Foreign Direct Investment*. London: Macmillan.

Gilpin, R. (1981). *War and Change in World Politics*. Cambridge: Cambridge University Press.

Gilpin, R. (1987). *The Political Economy of International Relations*. Princeton: Princeton University Press.

Ginsberg, R. H. (1990). European Trade Policy at Mid-Decade: Coping with the Internal Menace and the External Challenge. In R. Rummel (ed.), *The Evolution of an International Actor: Western Europe's New Assertiveness*. Boulder: Westview.

Goldmann, K. (1982). Change and Stability in Foreign Policy. *World Politics*, 34, 230–66.

Goldmann, K. (1988). *Change and Stability in Foreign Policy: The Problems and Possibilities of Detente*. Princeton: Princeton University Press.

Goldmann, K. (1989). The Line in the Water: International and Domestic Politics. *Cooperation and Conflict*, 24(3–4), 103–16.

Goldstein, J. (1988). Ideas, Institutions and American Trade Policy. *International Organization*, 42(1), 179–218.

Goldstein, J. (1989). The Impact of Ideas on Trade Policy: The Origins of U.S. Agricultural and Manufacturing Policies. *International Organization*, 43(1), 31–72.

Gourevitch, P. (1986). *Politics in Hard Times: Comparative Responses to International Economic Crises*. Ithaca: Cornell University Press.

Grant, R., and Newland, K. (eds) (1991). *Gender and International Relations*. Milton Keynes: Open University Press.

Gray, C. (1979). Nuclear Strategy: A Case for a Theory of Victory. *International Security*, 4(summer), 54–87.

Grieco, J. (1988). Anarchy and the Limits of Cooperation. *International Organization*, 42, 485–507.

Groom, A. J. R., and Taylor, P. (eds) (1975). *Theory and Practice in International Relations: Functionalism*. New York: Crane Rusak.

Grunberg, I. (1990). Exploring the 'Myth' of Hegemonic Stability. *International Organization*, 44(4), 431–77.

Grunberg, I., and Risse-Kappen, T. (1992). A Time of Reckoning? Theories of International Relations and the End of the Cold War. In P. Allan and K. Goldmann (eds), *The End of the Cold War. Evaluating Theories of International Relations*. Dordrecht: Martinus Nijhoff.

Guzzini, S. (1988). *T.S. Kuhn and International Relations: International Policy Economy and the Inter-Paradigm Debate*. MSc thesis, London School of Economics.

Haas, E. B. (1958). *The Uniting of Europe: Political, Social, and Economic Forces*. Stanford: Stanford University Press.

Haas, E. B. (1964). *Beyond the Nation-State: Functionalism and International Organization*. Stanford: Stanford University Press.

Haas, E. B. (1967). The 'Uniting of Europe' and the Uniting of Latin America. *Journal of Common Market Studies*, 5, 315–43.

Haas, E. B. (1970). The Study of Regional Integration: Reflections on the Joy and Anguish of Pre-Theorizing. *International Organization*, 24, 607–46.

Haas, E. B. (1976). Turbulent Fields and the Theory of Regional Integration. *International Organization*, 30, 173–212.

Haas, E. B. (1990). *When Knowledge is Power*. Berkeley: University of California Press.

Hagan, J. D. (1987). Regimes, Political Oppositions, and the Comparative Analysis of Foreign Policy. In C. F. Hermann, C. W. Kegley, and J. N. Rosenau (eds), *New Directions in the Study of Foreign Policy*. Boston: Allen and Unwin.

Hagedoorn, J. (1990). Organizational Modes of Inter-Firm Cooperation and Technology Transfer. *Technovation*, 10(1), 17–28.

Hakovirta, H. (1988). *East–West Conflict and European Neutrality*. Oxford: Clarendon Press.

Hall, S. (1984). The State in Question. In G. McLennan, D. Held, and S. Hall (eds), *The Idea of the Modern State*. Milton Keynes: Open University Press.

Hallenberg, J. (1984). *Foreign Policy Change: United States Foreign Policy toward the Soviet Union and the People's Republic of China 1961–80*. PhD dissertation, Stockholm University.

Halliday, F. (1987). State and Society in International Relations: A Second Agenda. *Millennium*, 16(2), 215–30.

Hamilton, A., Jay, J., and Madison, J. (1911). *The Federalist or the New Constitution* (1787–9). Everyman's Library no. 519. London: Dent.

Handel, M. (1981). *Weak States in the International System*. London: Frank Cass.

Hanrieder, W. (1978). Dissolving International Politics: Reflections on the Nation-State. *American Political Science Review*, 72(4), 1276–87.

Harding, S. (1986). *The Science Question in Feminism*. Milton Keynes: Open University Press.

Harding, S. (1992). *Whose Science? Whose Knowledge?* Milton Keynes: Open University Press.

Hartsock, N. (1985). *Money, Sex and Power*. Boston: Northeastern University Press.

Henderson, N. (1982). *The Birth of NATO*. London: Weidenfeld and Nicholson.

Hermann, C. F. (1990). Changing Course: When Governments Choose to Redirect Foreign Policy. *International Studies Quarterly*, 34(1), 3–21.

Hermann, C. F., Kegley, C. W., and Rosenau, J. N. (eds) (1987). *New Directions in the Study of Foreign Policy*. Boston: Allen and Unwin.

Hermann, C. F., and Peacock, G. (1987). The Evolution and Future of Theoretical Research in the Comparative Study of Foreign Policy. In C. F. Hermann, C. W. Kegley, and J. N. Rosenau (eds), *New Directions in the Study of Foreign Policy*. Boston: Allen and Unwin.

Herz, J. (1951). *Political Realism and Political Idealism*. Chicago: University of Chicago Press.

Herz, J. (1976). *The Nation-State and the Crisis of World Politics*. New York: McKay.

Hill, C. (1990). European Foreign Policy: Power Bloc, Civilian Model – or Flop? In R. Rummel (ed.), *The Evolution of an International Actor: Western Europe's New Assertiveness*. Boulder: Westview.

Hill, C. (1991). The European Community: Towards a Common Foreign and Security Policy. *The World Today*, 47, 189–93.

Hine, R. C. (1985). *The Political Economy of European Trade: An Introduction to the Trade Policies of the EEC*. Brighton: Wheatsheaf Books.

Hoffman, M. (1987). Critical Theory and the Inter-Paradigm Debate. *Millennium*, 16(2), 231–50.

Hoffmann, S. (1966). The Fate of the Nation-State. *Daedelus*, 95, 862–915.

Hoffmann, S. (1968). *Gulliver's Troubles, or the Setting of American Foreign Policy*. New York: McGraw-Hill.

Hoffmann, S. (1989). The European Community and 1992. *Foreign Affairs*, 68, 27–47.

Hoffmann, S. (1992). Balance, Concert, Anarchy, or None of the Above. In G. Treverton (ed.), *The Shape of the New Europe*. New York: Council on Foreign Relations Press.

Hoffmann, S., and Keohane, R. (eds) (1991). *The New European Community. Decisionmaking and Institutional Change*. Boulder: Westview.

Hollis, M., and Smith, S. (1990). *Explaining and Understanding International Relations*. Oxford: Clarendon Press.

Hollis, M., and Smith, S. (1991). Beware of Gurus: Structure and Action in International Relations. *Review of International Studies*, 17(4), 393–410.

Hollis, M., and Smith, S. (1992). Structure and Action: Further Comment. *Review of International Studies*, 18(2), 187–8.

Holm, C., and Hansen, K. B. (1992). *Nationalstatens placering i international politik: en metodisk og teoretisk analyze af stabilitet og forandring i den europæiske nationalstats udenrigspolitik.* Student paper, University of Copenhagen.

Holm, U. (1993). *Det franske Europa.* Aarhus: Aarhus Universitetsforlag.

Holm, U., Clemmesen, M., Olsen, L., and Wæver, O. (1993). *Paris–Bonn–København: Rapport om Europas udvikling efter den 18. maj 1993.* Copenhagen: European Movement in Denmark.

Holsti, K. (ed.) (1982). *Why Nations Realign.* London: Allen and Unwin.

Hopf, T. (1991). Polarity, the Offence–Defense Balance, and War. *American Political Science Review*, 85(2), 475–93.

Hoskyns, C. (1985). Women's Equality and the European Community. *Feminist Review*, 20, 71–88.

Hoskyns, C. (1986). Women, European Law and Transnational Politics. *International Journal of the Sociology of Law*, 14, 299–315.

Hoskyns, C. (1992). The European Community's Policy on Women in the Context of 1992. *Women's Studies International Forum*, 15(1), 21–8.

House of Lords (1984). *Sessions 1984–85, 8th Report, Select Committee on the European Communities, Minutes of Evidence.*

Ifestos, P. (1987). *European Political Cooperation: Towards a Framework of Supranational Diplomacy.* Aldershot: Avebury.

Ikenberry, G. J. (1986). The State and Strategies of International Adjustment. *World Politics*, 39(1), 53–77.

Ikenberry, G. J. (1988). Conclusion: An Institutional Approach to American Foreign Economic Policy. *International Organization*, 42(1), 219–43.

Ikenberry, G. J., Lake, D. A., and Mastanduno, M. (1988a). *The State and American Foreign Economic Policy.* Special issue of *International Organization*, 42(1).

Ikenberry, G. J., Lake, D. A., and Mastanduno, M. (1988b). Introduction: Approaches to Explaining American Foreign Economic Policy. *International Organization*, 42(1), 1–14.

Janis, I., and Mann, L. (1977). *Decision Making: A Psychological Analysis of Conflict, Choice and Commitment.* New York: Free Press.

Jarvis, A. (1989). Societies, States and Geopolitics: Challenges from Historical Sociology. *Review of International Studies*, 15(3), 281–92.

Jervis, R. (1976). *Perception and Misperception in International Politics.* Princeton: Princeton University Press.

Jervis, R. (1978). Cooperation under the Security Dilemma. *World Politics*, 30(2), 167–214.

Jervis, R. (1989). *The Meaning of the Nuclear Revolution.* Ithaca: Cornell University Press.

Joffe, J. (1984). Europe's American Pacifier. *Foreign Policy*, 14, 64–82.

Jonson, L. (1991). The Role of Russia in Nordic Regional Cooperation. *Cooperation and Conflict*, 26(3), 129–44.

Journal of Conflict Resolution (1991). Democracy and Foreign Policy: Community and Constraint. Special issue, 35(2).

Kaiser, K. (1969). Transnationale Politik. In E.-O. Czempiel (ed.), *Die anachronistische Souveränität.* Opladen: Westdeutscher Verlag.

Kaiser, K. (1970). Transnational Relations as a Threat to the Democratic Process. In R. O. Keohane and J. S. Nye (eds), *Transnational Relations and World Politics.* Cambridge, MA: Harvard University Press.

Kaiser, K. (1972). Toward the Copernican Phase of Regional Integration Theory. *Journal of Common Market Studies*, 10, 207–32.

Kant, I. (1795). Perpetual Peace. A Philosophical Sketch. In H. Reiss (ed.), *Kant. Political Writings*. Cambridge: Cambridge University Press.

Kaplan, M. (1957). *System and Process in International Politics*. New York: Wiley.

Karvonen, L. (1981). Semi-Domestic Politics: Policy Diffusion from Sweden to Finland. *Cooperation and Conflict*, 16(2), 91–107.

Karvonen, L., and Sundelius, B. (1990). Neutrality Freeze: Explaining Policy Rigidity Amidst International Change. Paper presented at the American Political Science Association Annual Conference, San Francisco.

Karvonen, L., and Sundelius, B. (1991). Surviving the New Europe: Nordic Neutrality between International Change and Domestic Institutionalisation. Paper presented to a meeting of the US-European Comparative Foreign Policy Group, Helsinki.

Katzenstein, P. (1984). *Corporatism and Change*. Ithaca: Cornell University Press.

Katzenstein, P. (1985). *Small States in World Markets*. Ithaca: Cornell University Press.

Keck, O. (1991). Der neue Institutionalismus in der Theorie der Internationalen Politik. *Politische Vierteljahresschrift*, 32, 635–53.

Kegley, C. W. (1987). Decision Regimes and the Comparative Study of Foreign Policy. In C. F. Hermann, C. W. Kegley, and J. N. Rosenau (eds), *New Directions in the Study of Foreign Policy*. Boston: Allen and Unwin.

Kennedy, P. (1987). *The Rise and Fall of Great Powers*. New York: Random House.

Keohane, R. O. (1983). The Demand for International Regimes. In S. Krasner (ed.), *International Regimes*. Ithaca: Cornell University Press.

Keohane, R. O. (1984). *After Hegemony*. Princeton: Princeton University Press.

Keohane, R. O. (ed.) (1986). *Neorealism and Its Critics*. New York: Columbia University Press.

Keohane, R. O. (1988). *International Institutions and State Power*. Boulder: Westview Press.

Keohane, R. O. (1989). International Institutions: Two Approaches. In R. Keohane (ed.), *International Institutions and State Power*. Boulder: Westview.

Keohane, R. O. (1990a). International Liberalism Reconsidered. In J. Dunn (ed.), *The Economic Limits to Modern Politics*. Cambridge: Cambridge University Press.

Keohane, R. O. (1990b). Multilateralism: An Agenda for Research. *International Journal*, 45, 731–64.

Keohane, R. O., and Hoffmann, S. (1991). Institutional Change in Europe in the 1980s. In R. Keohane and S. Hoffmann (eds), *The New European Community: Decision Making and Institutional Change*. Boulder: Westview.

Keohane, R. O., and Nye, J. S. (eds) (1972). *Transnational Relations and World Politics*. Cambridge, MA: Harvard University Press.

Keohane, R. O., and Nye, J. S. (1974). Transgovernmental Relations and International Organizations. *World Politics*, 27, 39–62.

Keohane, R. O., and Nye, J. S. (1977). *Power and Interdependence*. Boston: Little, Brown.

Keohane, R. O., and Nye, J. S. (1987). Power and Interdependence Revisited. *International Organization*, 41(4), 725–53.

Keohane, R. O., and Nye, J. S. (1993). The End of the Cold War: An Introduction. In R. O. Keohane, J. S. Nye, and S. Hoffmann (eds), *After the Cold War:*

International Institutions and State Strategies in Europe, 1989–1991. Harvard: Harvard University Press.

Kindleberger, C. (1973). *The World in Depression, 1929–1939*. Berkeley: University of California Press.

Kiss, Y. (1991). The Second 'No': Women in Hungary. *Feminist Review*, 39, 49–57.

Kissinger, H. A. (1957). *A World Restored: Castlereagh, Metternich and the Restoration of Peace, 1812–1822*. Boston: Houghton Mifflin.

Knudsen, O. F. (1991). Small States' Reactions to Sudden Power Shifts. Paper presented to the US-European Comparative Foreign Policy Group, Helsinki.

Knudsen, O. F. (1992). *Diagnostic Statements as Indicators of a Power Shift*. NUPI Notat 479. Oslo: Norwegian Institute of International Affairs.

Kofman, E., and Sales, R. (1992). Towards Fortress Europe? *Women's Studies International Forum*, 15(1), 29–40.

Koslowski, R., and Kratochwil, F. (1994). Understanding Change in International Politics: The Soviet Empire's Demise and International Politics. *International Organization*, (spring).

Krasner, S. D. (ed.) (1983). *International Regimes*. Ithaca: Cornell University Press.

Kratochwil, F. (1989). *Rules, Norms, and Decisions*. Cambridge: Cambridge University Press.

Kull, S. (1988). *Minds at War: Nuclear Reality and the Inner Conflict of Defense Policymakers*. New York: Basic Books.

Kupchan, C., and Kupchan, C. (1991). Concerts, Collective Security, and the Future of Europe. *International Security*, 16(1), 114–61.

Labs, E. (1992). Do Weak States Bandwagon? *Security Studies*, 1(3), 383–416.

Laclau, E. (1990). *New Reflections on the Revolution of Our Time*. London: Verso.

Laclau, E., and Mouffe, C. (1985). *Hegemony and Socialist Strategy: Towards a Radical Democracy*. London: Verso.

Lamborn, A. C. (1991). *The Price of Power: Risk and Foreign Policy in Britain, France and Germany*. Boston: Unwin Hyman.

Lapid, Y, (1989). The Third Debate: On the Prospects of International Theory in a Post-Positivist Era. *International Studies Quarterly*, 33(3), 235–54.

Lebow, R. N. (1981). *Between Peace and War: The Nature of International Crisis*. Baltimore: Johns Hopkins University Press.

Lebow, R. N. (1987). *Nuclear Crisis Management. A Dangerous Illusion*. Ithaca: Cornell University Press.

Lebow, R. N. (1994). Stability and Change in International Relations: A Critique of Realism. *International Organization*, (spring).

Lebow, R. N., and Stein, J. G. (1994). *We All Lost the Cold War*. Princeton: Princeton University Press.

Lehmbruch, G. (1969). Konkordanzdemokratien im internationalen System. In E.-O. Czempiel (ed.), *Die anachronistische Souveränität – Sonderheft der Politischen Vierteljahresschrift 1*.

Lemaitre, P., and Goybet, C. (1984). *Les Entreprises multinationales dans la Communité Européenne*. Les Dossiers de l'Institut de Recherche et d'Information sur les Multinationales, nos 1 and 2, Genève.

Levy, J. (1985). The Polarity of the System and International Stability: An Empirical Analysis. In A. N. Sabrosky (ed.), *Polarity and War: The Changing Structure of International Conflict*. Boulder: Westview.

Lijphart, A. (1974). International Relations Theory: Great Debates and Lesser Debates. *International Social Science Journal*, 26(1), 11–21.

Lindberg, L. N. (1963). *The Political Dynamics of European Economic Integration*. Stanford: Stanford University Press.

Lindberg, L. N., and Scheingold, S. A. (1970). *Europe's Would-Be Polity: Patterns of Change in the European Community*. Englewood Cliffs: Prentice-Hall.

Lindell, U., and Persson, S. (1984). The Paradox of Weak State Power. *Cooperation and Conflict*, 21, 79–97.

Link, W. (1988). *Der Ost–West Konflikt* (2nd edn). Stuttgart: Kohlhammer.

Linklater, A. (1990). *Beyond Realism and Marxism*. London: Macmillan.

Little, R., and Smith, M. (eds) (1991). *Perspectives on World Politics*. London: Routledge.

Little, R., and Smith, S. (eds) (1988). *Belief Systems and International Relations*. Oxford: Basil Blackwell.

Lorange, P., and Roos, J. (1992). *Strategic Alliances. Formation, Implementation and Evolution*. Oxford: Basil Blackwell.

Luke, T. (forthcoming). Space, Society and the State: The Impact of Informalization on Security. In B. Crawford and R. Lipschutz (eds), *Security and the Nation State*.

MacKinnon, C. (1989). *Toward a Feminist Theory of the State*. London: Harvard University Press.

Maclean, J. (1988). Marxism and International Relations: A Strange Case of Mutual Neglect. *Millennium*, 17(summer), 295–320.

Mäki, U. (1991). Practical Syllogism, Entrepreneurship, and the Invisible Hand. In D. Lavoie (ed.), *Economics and Hermeneutics*. London: Routledge and Kegan Paul.

Mandel, E. (1968). *Amerika und Europa. Widersprüche des Imperialismus*. Frankfurt: Europäische Verlagsanstalt.

Mann, M. (1986). *The Sources of Social Power: A History of Power from the Beginning to A.D. 1760*. Cambridge: Cambridge University Press.

Manning, C. A. W. (1957). Varieties of Worldly Wisdom. *World Politics*, IX(2), 149–65.

Manning, C. A. W. (1962). *The Nature of International Society*. London: London School of Economics.

Mansbach, R., Ferguson, Y., and Lampert, D. (1976). *The Web of World Politics*. Englewood Cliffs: Prentice-Hall.

Maoz, Z., and Russett, B. (1991). Alliances, Contiguity, Wealth, and Political Stability: Is the Lack of Conflict Among Democracies a Statistical Artifact? *International Interactions*, 17, 245–67.

Mastanduno, M., Lake, A., and Ikenberry, J. (1989). Toward a Realist Theory of State Action. *International Studies Quarterly*, 33(4), 457–74.

McGrew, A., and Lewis, P. (eds) (1992). *Global Politics*. Cambridge: Polity Press.

Mearsheimer, J. (1990). Back to the Future: Instability in Europe after the Cold War. *International Security*, 15(1), 5–56.

Michalet, C.-A. (1982). From International Trade to World Economy: A New Paradigm. In H. Makler, A. Martinelli, and N. Smelser (eds), *The New International Economy*. London: Sage.

Miller, J. D. B. (1981). *The World of States*. London: Croom Helm.

Milner, H. V. (1988). *Resisting Protectionism: Global Industries and the Politics of International Trade*. Princeton: Princeton University Press.

Moravcsik, A. (1991). Negotiating the Single European Act: National Interests and Conventional Statecraft in the European Community. *International Organization*, 45(1), 651–88.

Moravcsik, A. (1992). *Liberalism and International Relations Theory*. Working Paper no. 92–6, Center for International Affairs, Harvard University.

Morgenthau, H. J. (1946). *Scientific Man vs. Power Politics*. Chicago: University of Chicago Press.

Morgenthau, H. J. (1951). *In Defense of the National Interest*. New York: Alfred A. Knopf.

Morgenthau, H. J. (1952). Another Great Debate: The National Interest of the United States. *American Political Science Review*, 46, 961–88.

Morgenthau, H. J. (1973). *Politics Among Nations: The Struggle for Power and Peace* (5th edn). New York: Alfred A. Knopf.

Morse, E. (1976). *Modernization and the Transformation of International Relations*. New York: Free Press.

Mouritzen, H. (1988). *Finlandization. Towards a General Theory of Adaptive Politics*. Aldershot: Gower.

Mouritzen, H. (1991). Tension Between the Strong and the Strategies of the Weak. *Journal of Peace Research*, 28(2), 217–30.

Mouritzen, H. (1993). The Two Musterknaben and the Naughty Boy: Sweden, Finland, and Denmark in the Process of European Integration. *Cooperation and Conflict*, 28(4), 373–402.

Mouritzen, H. (1994). The 'Nordic' Model: Its Usefulness and its Downfall as a Foreign Policy Instrument. Reflections on a Silent Revolution. *Journal of Peace Research*, 31(4).

Müller, H. (1993). The Internalization of Principles, Norms, and Rules by Governments: The Case of Security Regimes. In Volker Rittberger (ed.), *The Study of Regimes in International Relations*. New York: Oxford University Press.

Murphy, C. N., and Tooze, R. (eds) (1991). *The New International Political Economy*. Boulder: Lynne Rienner.

Murray, R. (1971). The Internationalization of Capital and the Nation State. *New Left Review*, 67 (May–June), 84–109.

Mytelka, L. K. (1991). *Strategic Partnerships. States, Firms and International Competition*. London: Pinter.

Mytelka, L. K., and Delapierre, M. (1988). The Alliance Strategies of European Firms in the Information Technology Industry and the Role of ESPRIT. In J. H. Dunning and P. Robson (eds), *Multinationals and the European Community*. Oxford: Blackwell.

Nancy, J.-L. (1991). Introduction. In E. Cadava, P. Connor, and J.-L. Nancy (eds), *Who Comes After the Subject?* New York: Routledge.

Nielsson, G. (1990). The Parallel National Action Process. In P. Taylor and A. J. R. Groom (eds), *Frameworks for International Cooperation*. London: Pinter.

Northedge, F. S. (1978). *The International Political System*. London: Faber.

Nugent, N. (1988). *The Government and Politics of the European Community*. London: Macmillan.

Nycander, S. (1991). Neutralitet i Sovjetkrisen. *Dagens Nyheter*, 22 August.

Nye, J. S. (1971). *Peace in Parts: Integration and Conflict in Regional Organization*. Boston: Little, Brown.

Nye, J. S. (1987). Nuclear Learning and U.S.–Soviet Security Regimes. *International Organization*, 41(3), 371–402.

Nye, J. S. (1988). Neorealism and Neoliberalism. *World Politics*, 40, 235–52.

Nye, J. S. (1990). *Bound to Lead*, New York: Basic Books.

Obrman, J. (1990). Czechoslovakia. Foreign Policy: Sources, Concepts, Problems. *Report on Eastern Europe*, 1(37), 6–26.

Odell, J. S. (1982). *U.S. International Monetary Policy*. Princeton: Princeton University Press.

Odell, J. S. (1990). Understanding International Trade Policies: An Emerging Synthesis. *World Politics*, 43(1), 139–67.

Ohmae, K. (1985). *Triad Power. The Coming Shape of Global Competition*. London: Macmillan.

Onuf, N. G. (1989). *World of Our Making: Rules and Rule in Social Theory and International Relations*. Columbia, SC: University of South Carolina Press.

Oye, K. (ed.) (1986). *Cooperation under Anarchy*. Princeton: Princeton University Press.

Palme Commission (1982). *Common Security. Report by the Independent Commission for Disarmament and Security*. London: Pan.

Patomäki, H. (1992). *Critical Realism and World Politics: An Explication of a Critical Theoretical and Possibilistic Methodology for the Study of World Politics*. Studies on Political Science no. 12, Turku: Department of Political Science.

Pelkmans, J. (1992). An Economic Perspective on Federalism. Paper presented to a conference on 'Federalism and the Nation State', Toronto.

Penttilä, R. (1991). *Finland's Search for Security Through Defence 1944–89*. London: St Martin's Press.

Peterson, V. S. (ed.) (1992a). *Gendered States: Feminist (Re)Visions of International Relations Theory*. Boulder: Lynne Rienner.

Peterson, V. S. (1992b). Transgressing Boundaries: Theories of Knowledge, Gender and International Relations. *Millennium*, 21(2), 183–206.

Pettman, J. (1992). *Living in the Margins: Racism, Sexism and Feminism in Australia*. North Sydney: Allen and Unwin.

Pfetsch, F. R. (1988). *West Germany: Internal Structures and External Relations*. New York: Praeger.

Phillips, A. (ed.) (1987). *Feminism and Equality*. Oxford: Basil Blackwell.

Pijpers, A. (1990). *The Vicissitudes of European Political Cooperation: Towards a Realist Interpretation of the EC's Collective Diplomacy*. Leiden: Leiden University Press.

Pijpers, A. (ed.) (1992). *The European Community at the Crossroads*. Dordrecht: Martinus Nijhoff.

Pijpers, A., et al. (eds) (1988). *European Political Cooperation in the 1980s: A Common Foreign Policy for Western Europe?* Dordrecht: Martinus Nijhoff.

Platias, A. (1986). *High Politics in Small Countries*. PhD dissertation, Cornell University.

Polanyi, K. (1944). *The Great Transformation*. Boston: Beacon Press.

Praet, P. (1987). Economic Objectives in European Foreign Policy Making. In J. K. De Vree et al. (eds), *Towards a European Foreign Policy. Legal, Economic and Political Dimensions*. Dordrecht: Martinus Nijhoff.

Puchala, D. J. (1981). Of Blind Men, Elephants and International Integration. In M. Smith, R. Little, and M. Shackleton (eds), *Perspectives on World Politics*. London: Croom Helm.

Putnam, R. (1988). Diplomacy and Domestic Politics: The Logic of Two Level Games. *International Organization*, 42(3), 427–60.

Rapoport, C. (1992). Getting Tough with the Japanese. *Fortune*, 4 May, 26–33.

Regelsberger, E. (1988). EPC in the 1980s: Reaching Another Plateau? In A. Pijpers, E. Regelsberger, and M. Wessels (eds), *European Political Cooperation in the 1980s: A Common Foreign Policy for Western Europe?* Dordrecht: Martinus Nijhoff.

Reisch, A. (1990a). The Hungarian Dilemma: After the Warsaw Pact, Neutrality or NATO? *Report on Eastern Europe*, 1(15), 17–22.

Reisch, A. (1990b). Hungary: Government Wants Negotiated Withdrawal from the Warsaw Pact. *Report on Eastern Europe*, 1(23), 24–34.

Reisch, A. (1990c). Hungary: Interview with Foreign Minister Geza Jeszenszky. *Report on Eastern Europe*, 1(30), 16–32.

Richardson, N. R. (1987). Dyadic Case Studies in the Comparative Study of Foreign Policy. In C. F. Hermann, C. W. Kegley, and J. N. Rosenau (eds), *New Directions in the Study of Foreign Policy*. Boston: Allen and Unwin.

Risse-Kappen, T. (1988). *The Zero Option. INF, West Germany, and Arms Control*. Boulder: Westview.

Risse-Kappen, T. (1991). From Mutual Containment to Common Security: Europe During and After the Cold War. In M. Klare and D. Thomas (eds), *World Security*. New York: St Martin's Press.

Risse-Kappen, T. (1994a). Cooperation among Democracies. Norms, Transnational Relations, and the European Influence on U.S. Foreign Policy. Princeton: Princeton University Press.

Risse-Kappen, T. (1994b). Ideas do not Float Freely: Transnational Relations, Domestic Structures, and the End of the Cold War. *International Organization*, (spring).

Riste, O. (ed.) (1985). *Western Security: The Formative Years: European and Atlantic Defense, 1947–1953*. Oslo: Norwegian University Press.

Rittberger, V. (ed.) (1990). *International Regimes in East–West Politics*. London: Frances Pinter.

Rittberger, V., and Zürn, M. (1991). Transformation der Konflikte in den Ost–West-Beziehungen. *Politische Vierteljahresschrift*, 32(3), 399–424.

Ritzer, G. (1990). Micro–Macro Linkage in Sociological Theory: Applying a Metatheoretical Tool. In G. Ritzer (ed.), *Frontiers of Social Theory: The New Syntheses*. New York: Columbia University Press.

Ritzer, G. (1993). Agency–Structure and Micro–Macro Linkage: Crossroads in Contemporary Theorising. In B. Wittrock (ed.), *Social Theory and Human Agency*. London: Sage.

Robinson, J. (1986). *EEC Business Strategies to 1990: Threats and Opportunities*. Brussels: European Research Associates.

Roodbeen, H. (1992). *Trading the Jewel of Great Value. The Participation of The Netherlands, Belgium, Switzerland and Austria in the Western Strategic Embargo*. Dissertation, Leiden.

Rosecrance, R. N. (1966). Bipolarity, Multipolarity and the Future. *Journal of Conflict Resolution*, 10, 314–27.

Rosecrance, R. N. (1991). Regionalism and the Post-Cold-War Era. *International Journal*, XLVI(3), 373–93.

Rosenau, J. N. (1980) Pre-Theories and Theories of Foreign Policy. In J. S. Rosenau (ed.), *The Scientific Study of Foreign Policy* (rev. and enlarged edn). London: Pinter.

Rosenau, J. N. (1981). *The Study of Political Adaptation*. London: Pinter.

Rosenau, J. N. (1988). CFP and IPE: The Anomaly of Mutual Boredom. *International Interactions*, 14(1), 17–26.

Rosenau, J. N. (1990). *Turbulence in World Politics: A Theory of Change and Continuity*. Princeton: Princeton University Press.

Ross, J. (1991). Sweden, the European Community, and the Politics of Economic Realism. *Cooperation and Conflict*, 26(3), 117–28.

Rothstein, R. (1968). *Alliances and Small Powers*. New York: Columbia University Press.

Ruggie, J. G. (1986). Continuity and Transformation in the World Polity: Towards a Neorealist Synthesis. In R. O. Keohane (ed.), *Neorealism and Its Critics*. New York: Columbia University Press.

Ruggie, J. G. (1993). Territoriality and Beyond: Problematizing Modernity in International Relations. *International Organization*, 47(1), 139–74.

Ruigrok, W. (1991). Paradigm Crisis in International Trade Theory. *Journal of World Trade*, 1, 77–89.

Russett, B. (1985). The Mysterious Case of Vanishing Hegemony; Is Mark Twain Really Dead? *International Organization*, 39, 207–31.

Russett, B. (1990). *Controlling the Sword, the Democratic Governance of Nuclear Weapons*. Cambridge, MA: Harvard University Press.

Russett, B. (1993). *Grasping the Democratic Peace*. Princeton: Princeton University Press.

Sadykiewicz, M., and Clarke, D. L. (1990). The New Polish Defense Doctrine: A Further Step Towards Sovereignty. *Report on Eastern Europe*, 1(18), 20–3.

Sandholtz, W. (1992). *High-Tech Europe. The Politics of International Cooperation*. Berkeley: University of California Press.

Sandholtz, W., and Zysman, J. (1989). 1992: Recasting the European Bargain. *World Politics*, 42, 95–128.

Scharpf, F. W. (1990). Decision Rules, Decision Styles, and Policy Choices. In R. L. Kahn and M. N. Zald (eds), *Organizations and Nation States: New Perspectives on Conflict and Cooperation*. San Francisco: Jossey Bass.

Scharrer, H.-E. (1984). Abgestufte Integration. In E. Grabitz (ed.), *Abgestufte Integration – eine Alternative zum herkömmlichen Integrationskonzept?* Kehl: Engel.

Schlesinger, Arthur (1967). Origins of the Cold War. *Foreign Affairs*, October.

Schmitter, P. C. (1969). Three Neo-Functionalist Hypotheses about International Integration. *International Organization*, 23, 161–6.

Schmitter, P. C. (1991). *The European Community as an Emergent and Novel Form of Political Domination*. Working Paper 1991/26, Center for Advanced Study in the Social Sciences of the Juan March Institute, Madrid.

Schrodt, P. A. (1991). Review of *The World in their Minds* by Y.Y.I. Vertzberger. *American Political Science Review*, 85(4), 1502–3.

Schwartz, D. (1983). *NATO's Nuclear Dilemmas*. Washington, DC: Brookings.

Senghaas, D. (1966). Kybernetik und Politikwissenschaft. *Politische Vierteljahreschrift*, 2, 252–76.

Senghaas, D. (1990). *Europa 2000. Ein Friedensplan*. Frankfurt: Suhrkamp.

Servan-Schrieber, J.-J. (1967). *Le défi américain*. Paris: Denoël.

Shapiro, I., and Wendt, A. (1992). The Difference that Realism Makes: Social Science and the Politics of Consent. *Politics and Society*, 20(2), 197–223.

Sherwood, E. (1990). *Allies in Crisis*. New Haven: Yale University Press.

Sjöstedt, G. (1977). *The External Role of the European Community*. Westmead: Saxon House.

Skak, M. (1992). The Changing Soviet–East European Relationship. In R. E. Kanet, D. N. Miner, and T. J. Resler (eds), *Soviet Foreign Policy in Transition.* Cambridge: Cambridge University Press.

Smith, M. (1981). Significant Change and the Foreign Policy Response: Some Analytical and Operational Implications. In B. Buzan and R. J. B. Jones (eds), *Change and the Study of International Relations: The Evaded Dimension.* London: Pinter.

Smith, M. (1991). The European Community and a Changing European Order: A Framework of Analysis. Paper presented to the European Community Studies Association Conference, Washington, DC.

Smith, M. (1992). Modernisation, Globalisation and the Nation-State. In A. McGrew, P. Lewis et al. (eds), *Global Politics.* Cambridge: Polity Press.

Smith, M., and Woolcock, S. (1993). *The United States and the European Community in a Transformed World.* London: Pinter for the Royal Institute of International Affairs.

Smith, M., et al. (eds) (1988). *British Foreign Policy.* London: Unwin Hyman.

Smith, S. (1983). Foreign Policy Analysis: British and American Orientations and Methodologies. *Political Studies,* 31(4), 556–65.

Smith, S. (1986). Theories of Foreign Policy: An Historical Overview. *Review of International Studies,* 12(1), 13–29.

Snidal, D. (1985). The Limits of Hegemonic Stability Theory. *International Organization,* 39(4), 579–614.

Snyder, G. H. (1984). The Security Dilemma in Alliance Politics. *World Politics,* 36, 461–95.

Snyder, J. (1990). Avoiding Anarchy in the New Europe. *International Security,* 14(4), 5–41.

Stefanowski, R. (1990). Soviet Troops in Poland. *Report on Eastern Europe,* 1(9), 15–17.

Stein, A. (1983). Coordination and Collaboration: Regimes in an Anarchic World. In S. Krasner (ed.), *International Regimes.* Ithaca: Cornell University Press.

Stein, A. (1990). *Why Nations Cooperate.* Ithaca: Cornell University Press.

Stein, J. G. (1988). Building Politics into Psychology: The Misperception of Threat. *Political Psychology,* 9(2), 245–71.

Stenelo, L.-G. (1980). *Foreign Policy Predictions.* Lund: Studentlitteratur.

Stopford, J., and Strange, S. (1991). *Rival States, Rival Firms.* Cambridge: Cambridge University Press.

Strange, S. (1986). The Bondage of Liberal Economics. *SAIS Review.*

Strange, S. (1988). *States and Markets: An Introduction to International Political Economy.* London: Pinter.

Stromseth, J. (1988). *The Origins of Flexible Response: NATO's Debate over Strategy in the 1960s.* London: Macmillan.

Stuart, D., and Tow, W. (1990). *The Limits of Alliance. NATO Out-of-Area Problems Since 1949.* Baltimore: Johns Hopkins University Press.

Sullivan, M. P. (1990). *Power in Contemporary International Politics.* Columbia, SC: University of South Carolina Press.

Sundelius, B. (1990). Neutralitet och konfliktfylld interdependens. In U. Nordlöf-Lagerkranz (ed.), *Svensk neutralitet, Europa och EG.* Stockholm: Swedish Institute of International Affairs.

Sylvester, C. (forthcoming). *Feminist Theory and International Relations Theory in a Postmodern Era.* Cambridge: Cambridge University Press.

Taylor, P. (1989). The New Dynamics of EC Integration in the 1980s. In J. Lodge (ed.), *The European Community and the Challenge of the Future*. London: Pinter.

Thornton, M. (1986). Sex Equality Is Not Enough for Feminism. In C. Pateman and E. Gross (eds), *Feminist Challenges*. London: Unwin Hyman.

Tickner, J. A. (1992). *Gender in International Relations*. New York: Columbia University Press.

Tooze, R. (1988). Economic Belief Systems and Understanding International Relations. In R. Little and S. Smith (eds), *Belief Systems and International Relations*. Oxford: Basil Blackwell.

Treverton, G. (ed.) (1992). *The Shape of the New Europe*. New York: Council on Foreign Relations Press.

Tsoukalis, L. (1991). *The New European Economy: The Politics and Economics of Integration*. Oxford: Oxford University Press.

Twitchett, K. (ed.) (1976). *Europe and the World*. London: Europa Publications.

UNCTC (1991). *World Investment Report 1991, The Triad in Foreign Direct Investment*. New York: United Nations.

Van Evera, S. (1990/91). Primed for Peace: Europe After the Cold War. *International Security*, 15(3), 7–57.

Van Tulder, R., and Junne, G. (1988). *European Multinationals in Core Technologies*. Chichester: Wiley.

Vasquez, J. A. (1983). *The Power of Power Politics: A Critique*. London: Frances Pinter.

Väyrynen, R. (1983). Small States in Different Theoretical Traditions of International Relations Research. In O. Höll (ed.), *Small States in Europe and Dependence*. Vienna: Braumuller.

Väyrynen, R. (1987). Adaptation of a Small Power to International Tensions: The Case of Finland. In B. Sundelius (ed.), *The Neutral Democracies and the New Cold War*. Boulder: Westview Press.

Vincent, A. (1987). *Theories of the State*. Oxford: Basil Blackwell.

Viotti, P., and Kauppi, M. (eds) (1987). *International Relations Theory*. New York: Macmillan.

Wæver, O. (1990a). The Language of Foreign Policy. A Review Essay on Walter Carlsnaes, *Ideology and Foreign Policy: Problems of Comparative Conceptualisation*. *Journal of Peace Research*, 27(3), 335–43.

Wæver, O. (1990b). Thinking and Rethinking in Foreign Policy (Kjell Goldmann: *Change and Stability in Foreign Policy*). *Cooperation and Conflict*, 25(3), 153–70.

Wæver, O. (1990c). Three Competing Europes: German, French, Russian. *International Affairs*, 66(3), 153–70.

Wæver, O. (1991). Territory, Authority and Identity: The Late 20th Century Emergence of Neo-Medieval Political Structures in Europe. Paper presented at the European Peace Research Association Conference, Florence.

Wæver, O. (1992). *Introduktion til studiet af International Politik*. Copenhagen: Politiske Studier.

Wæver, O. (1993a). The Neo–Neo Synthesis of Realism and Liberalism: An International Relations Conception of Our Waning Modern System. Unpublished manuscript.

Wæver, O. (1993b). Security and Integration: Europe According to IR Theory. Unpublished manuscript.

Wæver, O. (1994). Tradition and Transgression in International Relations: A Post-Ashleyan Position. In N. Rengger and M. Hoffman (eds), *Beyond the Inter-Paradigm Debate*. Hemel Hempstead: Harvester Wheatsheaf.

Wæver, O., Buzan, B., Kelstrup, M., and Lemaitre, P. (eds) (1993). *Identity, Migration and the New Security Agenda in Europe*. London: Pinter.

Wæver, O., Holm, U., and Larsen, H. (forthcoming). *The Struggle for 'Europe': French and German Concepts of State, Nation and European Union*.

Walker, R. B. J. (1987). Realism, Change and International Political Theory. *International Studies Quarterly*. 31(1), 65–86.

Walker, R. B. J. (1988). World Order and the Reconstitution of Political Life. Unpublished manuscript.

Walker, R. B. J. (1989). History and Structure in the Theory of International Relations. *Millennium*, 18(2), 163–83.

Walker, R. B. J. (1990). Security, Sovereignty, and the Challenge of World Politics. *Alternatives*, 15(1), 3–28.

Walker, R. B. J. (1993). *Inside/Outside: International Relations as Political Theory*. Cambridge: Cambridge University Press.

Wallace, H., Wallace, W., and Webb, C. (eds) (1983). *Policy Making in the European Community* (2nd edn). Chichester: Wiley.

Wallace, H., et al. (eds) (1977). *Policy-Making in the European Communities*. London: Wiley.

Wallace, W. (ed.) (1990). *The Dynamics of European Integration*. London: Pinter.

Wallerstein, I. (1974). The Rise and Future Demise of the World Capitalist System: Concepts for Comparative Analysis. *Comparative Studies in History and Society*, 16 (September), 387–415.

Wallerstein, I. (1991). The Rise and Future Demise of the World Capitalist System: Concepts for Comparative Analysis. In R. Little and M. Smith (eds), *Perspectives on World Politics*. London: Routledge.

Walt, S. (1987). *The Origins of Alliances*. Ithaca: Cornell University Press.

Waltz, K. N. (1959). *Man, the State and War*. New York: Columbia University Press.

Waltz, K. N. (1964). The Stability of a Bipolar World. *Daedalus*, 93 (summer).

Waltz, K. N. (1979). *Theory of International Politics*. Reading, MA: Addison-Wesley.

Waltz, K. N. (1986). Reflections on Theories of International Politics: A Response to My Critics. In R. O. Keohane (ed.), *Neorealism and Its Critics*. New York: Columbia University Press.

Waltz, K. N. (1993). The Emerging Structure of International Politics. *International Security*, 18(2), 44–79.

Warner, H. (1984). EC Social Policy in Practice: Community Action on Behalf of Women and its Impact in the Member States. *Journal of Common Market Studies*, XXIII(2), 141–67.

Watson, A. (1992). *The Evolution of International Society*. London: Routledge.

Watson, P. (1993). The Rise of Masculinism in Eastern Europe. *New Left Review*, 198, 71–82.

Wellenstein, E. (1992). Unity, Community, Union – What's in a Name? *Common Market Law Review*, 16, 363–82.

Wendt, A. (1987). The Agent–Structure Problem in International Relations Theory. *International Organization*, 41(3), 335–70.

Wendt, A. (1991). Bridging the Theory/Metatheory Gap in International Relations. *Review of International Studies*, 17(4), 385–92.

Wendt, A. (1992a). Anarchy Is What States Make of It. *International Organization*, 46(2), 391–425.

Wendt, A. (1992b). Levels of Analysis vs. Agents and Structures: Part III. *Review of International Studies*, 18(2), 181–5.

Wendt, A., and Duvall, R. (1989). Institutions and International Order. In E.-O. Czempiel and J. N. Rosenau (eds), *Global Changes and Theoretical Challenges: Approaches to World Politics for the 1990s*. Lexington: Lexington Books.

White, B. (1989). Analysing Foreign Policy: Problems and Approaches. In M. Clarke and B. White (eds), *Understanding Foreign Policy: The Foreign Policy System Approach*. Aldershot: Edward Elgar/Gower.

Wight, M. (1977). *Systems of State*. Leicester: Leicester University Press.

Wohlstetter, A. (1985). Between an Unfree World and None. *Foreign Affairs*, 63, 962–94.

Young, O. (1968). Political Discontinuities in the International System. *World Politics*, 20, 369–92.

Young, O. (1989). *International Cooperation*. Ithaca: Cornell University Press.

Zacher, M. W. (1992). The Decaying Pillars of the Westphalian Temple: Implications for International Order and Governance. In J. N. Rosenau and E.-O. Czempiel (eds), *Governance Without Government: Order and Change in World Politics*. Cambridge: Cambridge University Press.

Zalewski, M. (1992). Feminist Theory and International Relations. In R. Brown and M. Bowker (eds), *From Cold War to Collapse: World Politics in the 1980s*. Cambridge: Cambridge University Press.

Zalewski, M. (1993). Feminist Standpoint Theory Meets International Relations Theory: A Feminist Version of David and Goliath? *Fletcher Forum of World Affairs*, 17(2), 13–32.

Zellentin, G. (ed.) (1976). *Annäherung, Abgrenzung und friedlicher Wandel in Europa*. Boppard: Boldt.

Žižek, S. (1990). Beyond Discourse-Analysis. Reprinted as appendix to Ernesto Laclau, *Reflections on the Revolution of our Times*. London: Verso.

Zürn, M. (1987). *Gerechte internationale Regime. Bedingungen und Restriktionen der Entstehung nicht-hegemonialer Regime*. Frankfurt: Haag and Herchen.

Index